China's Policy towards the South China Sea

This book provides an explanation of Chinese policy towards the South China Sea, and argues that this has been sculpted by the changing dynamics of the law of the sea in conjunction with regional geopolitical flux.

The past few decades have witnessed a bifurcated trend in China's management of territorial disputes. Over the years, while China gradually calmed and settled most land-border disputes with its neighbors, disputes on the ocean frontier continued to simmer in a seething cauldron. *China's Policy towards the South China Sea* attributes the distinctive path of China's approach to maritime disputes to a unique factor – the law of the sea (LOS) as the "rules of the road" in the ocean. By deconstructing the concept of "sovereignty" and treating the LOS as an evolving regime, the book examines how the changing dynamics of the LOS regime have complicated and reshaped the nature and content of sovereign disputes in the ocean regime as well as the options of settlement. Applying the findings to the South China Sea case, the author traces the learning curve on which China has embarked to comprehend the complexity of the dispute accordingly and finds that it is the dynamic interaction of the law of the sea regime and the geopolitical conditions that has driven the evolution of China's South China Sea policy.

This book will be of great interest to students of Chinese and Asian politics, international law, international relations and security studies.

Lingqun Li is a research fellow at the China Center for Collaborative Studies of the South China Sea, Nanjing University, China. She holds a PhD in Political Science and International Relations from the University of Delaware, USA. Her research interests include Great Power relations in the South China Sea, maritime security in East and Southeast Asia, regional maritime cooperation in the South China Sea and other enclosed and semi-enclosed sea areas, and China's marine governance system.

Contemporary Issues in the South China Sea

Series Editors: Shicun Wu, National Institute for South China Sea Studies, China; Keyuan Zou, University of Central Lancashire, UK

The South China Sea involves a wide array of complex issues covering sovereignty over islands and reefs, maritime delimitation, maritime security, cooperation against piracy and terrorism, resource development and environmental protection, all of which require extensive research. The area's importance largely results from one-third of the world's shipping transiting through its waters and that it is believed to hold huge oil and gas reserves beneath its seabed. Several countries have made competing territorial claims over the South China Sea with such disputes being regarded as Asia's most potentially dangerous source of conflict. This series seeks to provide thoughtful consideration of these issues from a variety of interdisciplinary perspectives. It provides an opportunity for early career researchers as well as established scholars to publish theoretically informed monographs and edited volumes that engage with key issues in this region.

Also in the series

UN Convention on the Law of the Sea and the South China Sea
Edited by Shicun Wu, Mark Valencia and Nong Hong

Non-Traditional Security Issues and the South China Sea
Shaping a New Framework for Cooperation
Edited by Shicun Wu and Keyuan Zou

Major Law and Policy Issues in the South China Sea
European and American Perspectives
Edited by Yann-huei Song and Keyuan Zou

Assessing Maritime Disputes in East Asia
Political and Legal Perspectives
Edited by Barthélémy Courmont, Frédéric Lasserre and Éric Mottet

China's Policy towards the South China Sea
When Geopolitics Meets the Law of the Sea
Lingqun Li

China's Policy towards the South China Sea

When Geopolitics Meets the Law of the Sea

Lingqun Li

Routledge
Taylor & Francis Group
LONDON AND NEW YORK

First published 2018 by Routledge

2 Park Square, Milton Park, Abingdon, Oxfordshire OX14 4RN
52 Vanderbilt Avenue, New York, NY 10017

Routledge is an imprint of the Taylor & Francis Group, an informa business

First issued in paperback 2019

British Library Cataloguing in Publication Data
A catalogue record for this book is available from the British Library

Library of Congress Cataloging in Publication Data
A catalog record for this book has been requested

ISBN: 978-1-138-06736-3 (hbk)
ISBN: 978-0-367-88898-5 (pbk)

Typeset in Times New Roman
by Taylor & Francis Books

This book is dedicated to my entire family.

Contents

Illustrations

Figures

Tables

Acknowledgments

The book is based on my PhD dissertation. Along the long journey of writing the dissertation and turning it into a book, I feel very fortunate to have the company of numerous incredible individuals whose support, guidance, and patience have helped me reach my destination.

I am deeply grateful to my supervisor, Dr. Alice Ba, for her intellectual guidance, encouragement and inspiration. She has closely watched over me throughout my graduate study and kept a perfect balance between providing abundant guidance and encouraging my independent thinking. I am also very grateful to Dr. Jeremy Firestone for serving as my external committee member and providing information, materials, and advice on the subject of the Law of the Sea throughout the writing of the dissertation.

I would also like to express my thanks to Dr. Daniel M. Green, Dr. David Wilson, Dr. Marian L. Palley, Dr. Ann Towns, Dr. Stuart Kaufman, and Dr. Julio Carrion. The instruction I received from these professors broadened my academic horizon and their mental support strengthened me during my time in graduate school.

I am deeply indebted to Dr. Wu Shicun, a leading Chinese historian on the South China Sea, who inspired the original idea of this research and generously granted me access to the archival resources of the National Institute for South China Sea Studies for dissertational research. I am very fortunate to be able to continue to receive his guidance and kind support.

I owe my sincere appreciation to Dr. Zou Keyuan and Dr. Hong Nong. Without their guidance and encouragement, this book would not have been possible. Dr. Zou's pioneering scholarship laid a solid foundation upon which this research was built. His crucial guidance and warm words infused me with the courage to complete this book project. Dr. Hong's valuable advice and encouragement lightened my days of book writing.

Special thanks go to Dr. Zhu Feng and my other colleagues at the China Center for Collaborative Studies of the South China Sea. I could not be more appreciative of Dr. Zhu, whose intellectual aspirations and working ethics have been a tower of strength to me. He is always generous in providing valuable advice and timely guidance. My other colleagues at the China Center for Collaborative Studies of the South China Sea are a precious source of inspiration for my academic pursuits.

My gratitude also extends to Andrew Humphrys and Hannah Ferguson at Routledge, for their patience and kind help. Their timely reminders have been indispensable in keeping my writing at a good pace and smoothing the preparation of all the materials.

Last but not the least, I owe my deepest gratitude to my family. Their love and care have given me the courage to pursue my dream.

Abbreviations

ADMM	ASEAN Defense Ministers' Meeting
ADMM-Plus	ASEAN Defense Minister's Meeting-Plus
AMM	ASEAN Ministerial Meeting
APEC	Asia Pacific Economic Cooperation
APFIC	Asia-Pacific Fishery Commission
APT	ASEAN Plus Three
ARF	ASEAN Regional Forum
ASEAN	Association of Southeast Asian Nations
ASEAN-China SOC	ASEAN-China Senior Official Consultations
BCM	Bilateral Consultation Mechanism
CAFTA	China-ASEAN Free Trade Agreement
CBMs	confidence-building measures
CCOP	Committee for Coordination of Joint Prospecting for Mineral Resources in Asian Offshore Areas
CCS	Convention on the Continental Shelf
CFCLR	Convention on Fishing and Conservation of the Living Resources of the High Seas
CHM	common heritage of mankind
CHS	Convention on the High Seas
CITES	Convention on International Trade in Endangered Species of Wild Fauna and Flora
CLCS	Commission on the Limits of the Continental Shelf
CMC	Central Military Committee
CNOOC	Chinese National Offshore Oil Corporation
COBSEA	Coordinating Body of the Seas of East Asia
COC	Code of Conduct
CS	Continental Shelf
CTS	Convention on the Territorial Sea and the Contiguous Zone
CZ	Contiguous Zones
DFID	Department for International Cooperation
DOC	Declaration on Conduct of Parties in the South China Sea

DRV	Democratic Republic of Vietnam
EAS	East Asian Seas
EEZ	Exclusive Economic Zone
EIA	Environmental Impact Assessment
FAO	Food and Agriculture Organization of the United Nations
FON	Freedom of Navigation
FONOPs	Freedom of Navigation Operations
GDP	Gross Domestic Product
GEF	Global Environment Facility
GLOSS	Global Sea Level Observing System
IACJ	Inter-American Council of Jurists
ICCAT	International Commission for the Conservation of Atlantic Tunas
ICJ	International Court of Justice
ICM	integrated coastal management
IL	International Law
ILC	International Law Commission
IMCO	Inter-governmental Maritime Consultative Organization
IMO	International Maritime Organization
IMR	International Maritime Regime
IO	inter-governmental organization
IOTC	Indian Ocean Tuna Commission
IR	International Relations
ISA	International Seabed Authority
ISG	Inter-sessional Support Group
ITLOS	International Tribunal on the Law of the Sea
IWC	International Whaling Commission
JMSU	Joint Marine Seismic Undertaking
JWG	Joint Working Group
LOS	Law of the Sea
LOSC	1982 UN Convention on the Law of the Sea
MARPOL	International Convention for the Prevention of Pollution from Ships
MEPL	Marine Environmental Protection Law
MFA	Ministry of Foreign Affairs
MOA	Ministry of Agriculture
MPP-EAS	Marine Pollution Prevention in the East Asian Seas
NACA	Network of Aquaculture Centers in Asia and the Pacific
NAM	Non-Aligned Movement
nm	nautical mile
NPAFC	North Pacific Anadromous Fish Commission

OPSD	Optional Protocol of Signature concerning the Compulsory Settlement of Disputes
PCA	Permanent Court of Arbitration
PD	preventive diplomacy
PEMSEA	Partnerships in Environmental Management for the Seas of East Asia
PLAN	People's Liberation Army and Navy
PMC	Post-Ministerial Conference
PNOC	Philippine National Oil Company
PRC	People's Republic of China
RCEP	Regional Comprehensive Economic Partnership
RVN	Republic of Vietnam
SAR	Search and Rescue
SCS	South China Sea
SEPA	State Environment Protection Agency
SLOCs	Sea Lanes of Communication
SOA	State Oceanic Administration
SOC	Senior Official Consultations
SOM on DOC	Senior Officials' Meeting on the implementation of the DOC
SPLOS	States Parties to the 1982 United Nations Convention on the Law of the Sea
SRV	Socialist Republic of Vietnam
SUA Convention	Convention on the Suppression of Unlawful Acts against the Safety of Maritime Navigation
TAC	Treaty of Amity and Cooperation
TPP	Trans-Pacific Partnership
TWGs	technical working groups
UN	United Nations
UNCED	United Nations Conference on Environment and Development
UNCLOS	United Nations Convention on the Law of the Sea
UNCTED	United Nations Conference on Trade and Development
UNDP	United Nations Development Programme
UNEP	United Nations Environmental Programme
UNESCO	United Nations Educational, Scientific and Cultural Organization
WCED	World Commission on Environment and Development
WCPFC	The Western and Central Pacific Fisheries Commission

Introduction

Over the past few decades, maritime disputes in the South China Sea have proven a perennial sore point in Asia, straining intra-regional relations. To date, due to its long-running nature and the significant number of different claimants involved, the South China Sea issue has developed into one of the most complicated inter-state disputes in Asia. Over the years, one after another, altogether seven parties (China, Vietnam, Malaysia, the Philippines, Brunei, Indonesia, and Taiwan) have asserted overlapping claims to maritime space in the South China Sea.[1]

The South China Sea (SCS) contains one of the world's busiest international sea lanes and is home to many of the world's busiest shipping ports, and its position connecting the Pacific and Indian Oceans is of paramount importance to major naval powers. Given the tremendous value of the SCS in both the regional geostrategic environment and international trade, the countries of the Association of Southeast Asian Nations (ASEAN) display a marked wariness over China's intentions and ambitions in the South China Sea.[2] For the same reason, many extra-regional countries, including the United States, Japan, India, and Australia, have also kept a cautious eye on the moving direction of China's policy towards territorial and jurisdictional disputes in the South China Sea.[3]

This sort of uneasiness is not ill-founded. A good deal of scholarship suggests that territorial issues tend to have a greater probability of ending in war than other sources of conflict.[4] John A. Vasquez, for example, shows that issues related to territory account for an overwhelming majority of the instances of war between 1648 and 1989 and account for 79 percent of wars from 1945 to 1989.[5] In the short history of the People's Republic of China, territorial disputes have been at the center of several major military confrontations, including the Sino-Indian War in 1962, the Sino-Russian skirmish in 1969, and the Sino-Vietnamese conflicts of 1978, to name but a few.

More importantly, concerns about China's SCS policy are situated in a larger context: the debate over the "rise of China." China's integration into the outside world began in 1978 with the policy of Reform and Opening. Today, China has emerged as an influential player both in Asia and on the global stage. The past three decades have witnessed the rapid ascendance of

China on both the economic and military fronts. In 2010, with a gross domestic product (GDP) of $5.88 trillion, China surpassed Japan (at $5.47 trillion) to become the world's second-largest economy, "capping the nation's three-decade rise from Communist isolation to emerging superpower."[6] Sustained economic growth sped up the pace of China's military development, enabling robust investment in modern hardware and technology. According to Chinese official budget figures, the average annual increase in defense expenditure has been in the double digits for the past two decades. From 1998 to 2007, the average annual increase of defense expenditure was 15.9 percent, while that of GDP was 12.5 percent.[7] In 2016, China's defense expenditure budget was 954.4 billion RMB (about US$141.9 billion).[8] Backed by strong financial support, the PLA Navy (PLAN) has rapidly transformed from a large fleet of low-capability, single-mission platforms, to a leaner force equipped with more modern, multi-mission platforms.

Since the early 1990s, both regional and extra-regional countries have been debating the implications of this growth in capability and influence unprecedented in China's modern history, a debate that continues unabated today. The central question is: what does China's ascendance mean? More specifically, what does a more powerful China mean to regional security, to the existing international order, and to the global superpower, the United States?

The debate over China rising and the South China Sea case

Discussions among international relations (IR) theorists and China watchers on the trajectory of China's rise and its impact on the international order have followed two lines of exploration.

Status quo or revisionism?[9]

This line of exploration focuses on whether China is a status quo power or a revisionist power.[10] A status quo power, broadly put, is a power satisfied with the existing system, while a revisionist power is dissatisfied with the existing power structure and seeks to alter it. In the case of China, if a rising China is satisfied with existing international order at the apex of which sits the United States, it is a status quo power and its ascendance is conducive to maintaining the existing order. If China is a revisionist power, viewing the existing system as disadvantaging its national interests, then its growing capability will enable it to alter the current system.

Despite the popularity of these two terms in international relations theorizing and in policy discourse, the criteria for differentiating status quo states and revisionist states have remained underdeveloped.[11] It is beyond the scope of this book to explore these criteria, but suffice it to say that the most uncontroversial criterion is the frequency and intensity of direct military confrontations, since a revisionist power is often inclined to use force to achieve its goals. In the modern history of China, most direct military confrontations took place long before China's Reform and Opening. In the three decades since, China has gradually settled most of its land border disputes with its neighbors through peaceful bilateral negotiations and only in one case did it use force (that is, the Spratly clash against Vietnam in 1988).

System maintainer or a system reformer?

The other line of exploration examines China's participation in regional and international institutions and regimes for indications of the impact of China's rising on the existing world order. The reasoning here is, if China is a status quo power satisfied with the existing structure of international system, it would be performing the role of a system maintainer. In this case, a considerable degree of conformity should be observed between China's behavior and the rules of those transnational institutions as well as the performance of other member states; otherwise, we should be expecting an aggressive China acting as a system reformer, determined to reform or rewrite the rules and structure of institutions that it perceives unfair or disadvantaging.

In international regimes, is China a system reformer or system maintainer? To date, the broad conclusion of existing studies is that for the most part, China's behavior is in accordance with the role of a system maintainer.[12] In the meantime, China has demonstrated ultrasensitivity to any perceived impingement on its sovereignty and dignity. In other words, while China has shown considerable acceptance of a variety of international norms, insistence on unconditional sovereignty has remained relatively stable.[13]

In light of these narratives surrounding "China's ascendance," how China deals with the South China Sea issue will be critically examined as an example of how a rising China defines and achieves its national interests and its vision of the appropriate regional and world order. Will a more powerful China be more inclined to rely on its newly acquired muscle to solve disputes with its neighbors? What kind of security order does China prefer – a rule-based one or a power-based one? The South China Sea case serves as a perfect testing ground for these questions.

China's South China Sea policy involves both indicators important to debates over discerning China's intentions regarding its position in the global hierarchy: direct military confrontations and participation in international regimes.

In territorial disputes, a revisionist power seldom makes concessions and is often willing to use force to back up its claims to sovereignty. Therefore, China's flexibility in making concessions or pragmatic adjustments and whether it is inclined to use force to resolve the South China Sea dispute are indicative of whether it is a status quo power or a revisionist power. If China is a status quo power, its participation in the Law of the Sea (LOS) regime[14] should follow the pattern of learning and abiding by prevalent maritime laws, norms, and principles. In this case, China would apply those maritime rules, norms, and laws to the South China Sea and adjust its own position and policy accordingly. If China is a revisionist power, China would not apply these laws and rules, since such action often entails impairing its maritime interests.

The unique course of China's evolving policy towards the South China Sea

China's policy towards the South China Sea has taken on a unique course different from that of China's policy towards land disputes. Over the years, while China gradually calmed and settled most of its land-border disputes with its neighbors (see Table 0.1), disputes on the ocean frontier continue to simmer in a seething cauldron (see Table 0.2).[15]

What sets the development of China's maritime disputes and continental disputes on such a bifurcated course? What makes the difference in the way China deals with these two types of territorial disputes? This is an empirical

Table 0.1 Summary of China's land border disputes, 1949–2005[16]

	Continental frontier	
Disputed area	*Year of final settlement*	*Uses of force*
1. Afghanistan border	1965	
2. Bhutan border	1998*	
3. Burma border	1961	
4. India border	2005**	1956–61: expansion 1962: offense 1967: clashes 1986: occupation
5. Kazakhstan border	2002	
6. Kyrgyzstan border	2004	
7. Laos border	1993	
8. Mongolia border	1964	
9. Nepal border	1963	
10. North Korea border	1964	
11. Pakistan border	1965	
12. Russia border	2004	1969: ambush
13. Tajikistan border	2002	
14. Vietnam border	1999	1980: assault 1981: assault 1984: assault

** 2005 Agreement on the Political Parameters and Guiding Principles for the Settlement of the Boundary Question, setting principles for final settlement.

Table 0.2 Summary of China's maritime disputes, 1949–2017

	Ocean frontier	
Disputed area	*Year of final settlement*	*Confrontations*
Gulf of Tonkin (including White Dragon Tail island)	2000	– –
Paracel Islands	–	1974: military clash
Macclesfield Bank	–	2012: Standoff over Scarborough Shoal
Spratly Islands	–	1988: military clash 1995: escalation over Mischief Reef 2013: friction over the Second Thomas Shoal
Senkaku Islands	–	– –

puzzle often overlooked in the existing literature and which this book attempts to address.

This book is devoted to providing an accurate and comprehensive understanding of China's evolving policy towards the South China Sea.[17] It attributes the distinctive path of China's approach to maritime disputes, in particular, the South China Sea disputes, to a unique factor – the law of the sea as the "rules of the road" in the ocean. By deconstructing the concept of "sovereignty" and treating the Law of the Sea as an evolving international regime, this research examines how the changing dynamics of the Law of the Sea regime (hereafter the LOS regime) have complicated and reconstructed the SCS disputes and, consequently, options of dispute management and settlement. I argue that Chinese SCS policy is shaped by two sets of factors. One is the evolving legal normative and institutional dynamics of the LOS regime at both the international and regional levels, and the other is the shifting geostrategic environment in the SCS region. Developments in the LOS regime have exerted an incremental and sustained influence on China's conceptualization of the territorial dispute in the SCS and enhanced its leaders' knowledge of modern maritime governance. These normative and institutional dynamics in the LOS regime interact with concurrent geopolitical flux, such as crises or changing landscape of power and alliance, offering a blend of incentives and pressure that shapes the calculus of the Chinese leadership.

Tracing the influence of the LOS regime and the correlated changes in China's SCS policy is analytically challenging. In existing studies, China's policy towards the SCS disputes and to territorial disputes in general is often classified into two or three mutually exclusive categories – the policy of unyielding/the policy of compromise, or cooperation/delaying/escalation.[18] Such bipartite or tripartite categorization underestimates the complexity of the SCS policy and is analytically weak, if not flawed, in tracing policy changes and nuanced modifications. On the one hand, this categorization takes a state's sovereign claims as resistant to change. As a result, those bipartite or tripartite categories are only suitable for defining changes in a state's approach to realizing unchanging claims of sovereignty, but are incapable of capturing changes in the state's claims and understanding of the nature of sovereign disputes. On the other hand, the bipartite or tripartite categorization dictates an exclusiveness of each category that is both unnecessary and impractical. As detailed analyses in subsequent chapters reveal, China's policy in a given period is often mixed. For instance, Taylor Fravel defined China's policy orientation in the early 1990s as escalation, but a close look at Beijing's SCS policy in this period shows that it did not neatly fit into a clear-cut escalation strategy. Rather, it was a mixture of confrontation, cooperation, and compromise.

In light of the weaknesses identified in the conventional conception of "policy" as highlighted above, an analytically powerful conception of "policy" is critically important in understanding China's evolving policy towards the SCS. To this end, I borrow Allen Carlson's conceptualization of sovereign boundaries as institutions constituted by the ongoing enactment of a broad set of social practices between states rather than singular sites of confrontation.[19] This conceptualization directs attention to the broader diplomatic and representational practices that construct sovereign boundaries, and underscores the dynamic and constitutive nature of a state's territorial and jurisdictional sovereignty. Viewed through this conceptual lens, China's understanding of sovereignty and its claims in the SCS should not be treated *a priori* as fixed in their original status. Rather, they are constantly expressed and reconstructed through dynamic diplomatic and representational practices, and changes can only be identified by examining these practices.

This conception is of particular pertinence to the unique nature of maritime disputes in the SCS. Shifting dynamics within the international maritime regime transform the issue of territorial dispute in the SCS beyond a simple question of who owns a given piece of territory by adding at least three dimensions: (1) which territory can be claimed; (2) who has the right to claim it; and (3) how sovereignty can be exercised or what sort of sovereign and jurisdictional rights can be generated by ownership over a given piece of territory. Therefore, examining the broader diplomatic and representational practices constructing sovereign boundaries helps to trace changes in these dimensions of China's SCS policy more precisely and systematically.

More specifically, this research breaks down China's SCS policy into four components for close examination.

1 *Legal position.* This is the most important aspect of China's SCS policy. It involves China's legal claims in the SCS; the legal justification for its claims to sovereignty; official views on the applicability of relevant laws, norms, and principles to the SCS disputes; and relevant domestic legislation.

2 *Political engagement with other disputant parties and user states.* The main approaches in this category are confrontation, unilateralism, bilateralism, and multilateralism.
3 *Practices of maritime governance in the SCS.* This category is comprised of China's concrete policy practices in terms of exercising sovereign rights and practicing maritime governance with regard to a variety of issue areas, including maritime transportation and security, fisheries, marine environmental protection, and resource exploration in the SCS. Maritime legislation, marine policy, and law enforcement activities form an essential part of China's sovereign practices in the SCS. Since sovereignty is expressed through actual sovereign practices, China's practices of marine governance are important indicators reflecting its understanding and position of its sovereignty in the SCS. Moreover, pending the final resolution of the SCS disputes, what the claimant states actually do in terms of exercising and practicing marine governance has great implication in shaping the content of maritime sovereign rights and obligations as well as the final shape of resolution of the SCS disputes.[20]
4 *Managing the SCS situation and best solutions.* This includes China's position towards and practices of possible solutions for the disputes.

Finally, focusing on the SCS disputes, this study also intends to shed light on the ongoing research on the interaction of international law and international politics. By calibrating on the theoretical conception of "sovereignty," which is a political concept and also a concept of international law, this research project finds an innovative way to demonstrate that international law plays an independent and influential role in shaping international politics.

Structure of the book

This book consists of eight chapters. Chapter 1 addresses two theoretical issues critical for understanding China's SCS policy. Using regime theory developed in the International Relations scholarship, the chapter first delineates the LOS regime and the roles it could play in shaping and reshaping China's policy towards the South China Sea disputes. The second theoretical issue explored in this chapter is the concept of "sovereignty." From the perspective of constructivism, the conception of "sovereignty" is deconstructed and the theoretical possibility is explored of how the shifting dynamics of the law of the sea as an evolving regime may reshape the nature and content of sovereignty in the ocean.

Chapters 2–7, arranged in chronological order, examine the PRC's evolving policy towards the SCS over the past six decades. Chapter 2 investigates the PRC's original claims to the South China Sea disputes as well as the competing claims of Vietnam and the Philippines, which provides a useful starting point from which we can track the transformation of the South China Sea disputes and the evolution of China's policy towards the South China Sea. China's initial attitude towards international law and regimes is also examined as it set the initial tone of the PRC's negotiating position in the third UN Conference on the Law of the Sea.

Chapter 3 examines how China's participation in the third LOS conference and other maritime organizations affected the leadership's perception of the South China Sea disputes, changed its calculation of maritime interests, and expanded its knowledge of ocean governance. These perceptional changes resulted in a series of policy adjustment in this period.

The conclusion of the UN Convention on the Law of the Sea in 1982 generated profound and far-reaching influence on the world oceans' order.[21] The emerging concepts underpinning the legal regime of the new maritime order, particularly the concepts of the Exclusive Economic Zone and the Continental Shelf, transformed the SCS disputes from a typical bilateral territorial dispute into a complex, multilateral and multi-issue web of disputes with no ready-to-use solutions. Chapter 4 situates the SCS issue in the wider legal institutional environment of this new maritime order, at the center of which sits the new LOS Convention, and analyzes changes to the SCS issue and, consequently, China's policy practices resulting from the legal and institutional developments in the LOS regime.

Chapter 5 continues to trace the learning and adapting process through which Chinese decision-makers gradually comprehended the new face of the SCS disputes. Increased knowledge of the dispute resulted in the legalization of China's SCS policy through a series of national legislation and other legal practices. In the meantime, the end of the Cold War unveiled a new geopolitical environment and redefined intra-regional relations, particularly between China and the ASEAN. The chapter shows that these geostrategic dynamics and growing awareness of a variety of policy options combined led to the formalization of China's SCS policy and a multilateral turn in China's political engagement concerning the disputes in this period.

Focusing on the 2002–2012 period, Chapter 6 provides an illustrating example in terms of how geopolitics and the evolving LOS regime are blended together to intensify SCS disputes and propel China's SCS policy adjustment. The 2009 deadline to submit information regarding the continental shelf to the Commission on the Limits of Continental Shelf, the US strategic rebalancing towards Asia, increasing interference of extra-regional countries, etc. – these events all created a series of crises forcing China to respond and systemize its management of the disputes and, more importantly, helped to untangle some of the messy legal issues surrounding the disputes.

Chapter 7 assesses the most recent changes in China's policy towards the SCS since 2013. This post-2013 period started with the Philippines' initiation of an arbitration case against China concerning the South China Sea disputes. The case has important bearings on China's legal position and elicited nuanced changes in China's legal deliberation of its SCS claims. In light of the tribunal's ruling, this chapter tracks China's legal adjustments and other policy reactions in response to the gradual unfolding of the arbitration case.

The chapter also provides a timely investigation of the ongoing domestic discourse and related policy repercussions generated by this case and the development of geopolitical dynamics in this period.

This book concludes with a review of the major findings of this research, in particular, the patterns through which the interaction of the LOS regime and shifting geostrategic environment has shaped and continues to influence China's policy towards the SCS disputes. Based on the findings of this research and current legal and geopolitical developments in the South China Sea region, this chapter puts forward some policy recommendations based on the findings of this research.

Notes

1 An explanation of the South China Sea disputes will be given in Chapter 2. For a comprehensive review of the disputes in the South China Sea in the existing scholarship, see Greg Austin, *China's Ocean Frontier* (Canberra, Australia: Allen & Unwin University Printery, 1998). Also see Shicun Wu, *Origin and Development of the South China Sea Disputes* (Beijing: China Economic Publishing House, 2010), in Chinese.
2 Allen S. Whiting, "ASEAN Eyes China," *Asian Survey* 37, no. 4 (1997): 299–301.
3 The concerns and policies of extra-regional countries pertinent to the SCS disputes will be introduced in Chapter 4.
4 For exemplary works, see Michael Brecher, *Crises in World Politics: Theory and Reality* (Oxford: Pergamon, 1993), Paul K. Huth, *Standing Your Ground* (Ann Arbor, MI.: University of Michigan Press, 1996), John A. Vasquez, "Why Do Neighbors Fight? Proximity, Interaction, or Territoriality," *Journal of Peace Research* 32, no. 3 (1995): 277–293, Paul F. Diehl, *A Road Map to War: Territorial Dimensions of International Conflict* (Nashville, TN.: Vanderbilt University Press, 1999), Stuart A. Bremer, "Dangerous Dyads: Conditions Affecting the Likelihood of Interstate War, 1816–1965," *Journal of Conflict Resolution* 36, no. 2 (1992): 309–341, and Paul F. Diehl and Gary Goertz, *War and Peace in International Rivalry* (Ann Arbor, MI: University of Michigan Press, 2000).
5 Vasquez, "Why Do Neighbors Fight?" 284.
6 "China Overtakes Japan as World's Second-Biggest Economy," *Bloomberg*, August 16, 2010, available at: www.bloomberg.com/news/2010-08-16/china-economy-passes-japan-s-in-second-quarter-capping-three-decade-rise.html (accessed March 1, 2014).
7 Chinese Ministry of National Defense, "Defense Expenditure," available at: http://eng.mod.gov.cn/Database/Expenditure/index.htm (accessed February 20, 2014).
8 Chinese Ministry of Finance, "2016 Central Government Annual General Public Budget – Expenditure Budget," available at: http://yss.mof.gov.cn/2016czys/201603/t20160325_1924496.html (accessed July 1, 2017).
9 The debate over whether China is a status quo power or a revisionist power is summarized in Alastair I. Johnston, "Is China a Status Quo Power?" *International Security* 27, no. 4 (2003): 5–11.
10 Given their theoretical interest in power, realists are particularly interested in the impact that China's rising brings into the international system. The realist camp tends to have a pessimistic forecast, that is, a rising China is going to change the status quo power structure of the international system and such a challenge might involve force. Such forecast, to a large extent, is rooted in realist theoretical propositions. Classical realists articulate that states are presumably power maximizers.

Hans J. Morgenthau argues that uncertainty about other states' intentions forces states to adopt a "worst case" scenario. As a result, each state in the system tries to seek superiority and prepares for challenges that are aimed at "reversal of the power relations among two or more nations, reducing, for instance, A from a first rate to a second rate power and raising B to the eminent position A formerly held," see Hans J. Morgenthau, *Politics among Nations: The Struggle for Power and Peace* (New York: Alfred A. Knopf, 1978), 42–43. Similarly, John Mearsheimer postulates that the international system creates powerful incentives for aggression, see John J. Mearsheimer, "Back to the Future: Instability in Europe after the Cold War," *International Security* 15, no. 1 (1990): 12.

11 For an overview of the conceptualization of status quo and revisionism in the major IR schools, see Lingqun Li, "China Marching into Africa: Status Quo or Revisionism?," paper presented to the annual conference of the International Studies Association-Northeast, Baltimore, MD, October 2009.

12 The theme "system maintainer versus system reformer" is thoroughly discussed in Alastair I. Johnston and Robert S. Ross, eds., *New Directions in the Study of China's Foreign Policy* (Stanford, CA: Stanford University Press, 2006).

13 See Margaret M. Pearson, "China in Geneva: Lessons from China's Early Years in the World Trade Organization," and Allen Carlson, "More Than Just Saying No," in Johnston and Ross, *New Directions in the Study of China's Foreign Policy*, 217–242.

14 In this book, I use the Law of the Sea regime, international maritime regime, the maritime regime and the ocean regime interchangeably.

15 Existing studies on China's policy towards territorial disputes treat indiscriminately disputes on the continental border and those on the ocean frontier and fail to either recognize or explain the bifurcating pattern identified in China's approach towards territorial disputes. While China has settled most of its land border disputes over the years, disputes over offshore islands in the South China Sea remain hotly contested to date, adding a major source of serious friction to the nation's outward interactions. Since the 1970s, China has used force three times to solve territorial disputes, two of which focused exclusively on maritime boundaries in the South China Sea – one was related to the Paracel Islands dispute with Vietnam in 1974 and the other in 1988 over the Spratly Islands. The third one, which took place in 1979, was indirectly related to Vietnam's challenge to China's maritime sovereign claims in the SCS. According to Allen Carlson's calculation of the frequency of territorial claims appearing in *Beijing Review*, an influential official mouthpiece in China, during the period from 1989 to 2000, continental claims were completely mute, in contrast with maritime claims which totaled 73 times, see Allen Carlson, *Unifying China, Integrating with the World: Securing Chinese Sovereignty in the Reform Era* (Stanford, CA: Stanford University Press, 2005), 47.

16 Table 0.1 and Table 0.2 are based on Table 1 in M. Taylor Fravel's article "Power Shifts and Escalation," *International Security* 32, no. 3 (2007/08): 54–55.

17 Most studies of China's SCS policy limit the focus to a specific period of time, see, for example, John W. Garver, "China's Push through the South China Sea: The Interaction of Bureaucratic and National Interests," *The China Quarterly* 132 (1992): 999–1028, Chi-kin Lo, *China's Policy towards Territorial Disputes: The Case of the South China Sea Islands* (New York: Routledge, 1989), Eric Hyer, "The South China Sea Disputes: Implications of China's Earlier Territorial Settlements," *Pacific Affairs* 68, no. 1 (1995): 34–55, Bob Catley and Makmur Keliat, *Spratlys: The Dispute in the South China Sea* (Brookfield, VA: Aldershot, 1997), and M. Taylor Fravel, "China's Strategy in the South China Sea," *Contemporary Southeast Asia* 33, no. 3 (2011): 297. While the explanation may be valid in the designated time period, it is unclear whether such explanation can account for a longer period time. For example, John Garver's study on the military clashes between China and Vietnam in March 1988 illustrates how bureaucratic politics contributed to

China's decision to insert a physical presence in the Spratly area. However, Garver's study loses sight of the broader scope of China's SCS policy. As a result, it remains unexplained why the Chinese leaders had thought about advancing to the Spratlys in the first place and why the Vietnamese and Filipinos already did so in the late 1970s and early 1980s. It is also unclear whether domestic politics can account for all the major changes in China's SCS policy.

18 For example, Eric Hyer uses a two-track "hard/soft" approach to characterize Chinese policy toward the South China Sea disputes. He argues that Beijing stridently asserted an unwillingness to negotiate (the hard approach), but as strategic considerations changed, quickly sought a compromise settlement (the soft approach), see Eric Hyer, "The South China Sea Disputes," 35. Fravel classified China's SCS policy into three categories – cooperation, delaying and escalation, see M. Taylor Fravel, "China's Strategy in the South China Sea," 297.

19 Allen Carlson, "Constructing the Dragon's Scales: China's Approach to Territorial Sovereignty and Border Relations in the 1980s and 1990s,"*Journal of Contemporary China* 12, no. 37 (2003): 680.

20 This point will be elaborated in Chapter 4.

21 In this book, I also use the terms "the UNCLOS," "the new LOS," "the LOS Convention," and "the LOSC" to refer to the 1982 UN Convention on the Law of the Sea.

Bibliography

Acharya, A. 2004. "How Ideas Spread: Whose Norms Matter? Norm Localization and Institutional Change in Asian Regionalism," *International Organization*, vol. 58, no. 2, pp. 239–275.

Anand, R.P. 1983. *Origin and Development of the Law of the Sea: History of International Law Revisited*, Martinus Nijhoff, Boston.

Austin, G. 1998. *China's Ocean Frontier*, Allen and Unwin University Printery, Canberra, Australia.

Ba, A.D. 2005. "On Norms, Rule-Breaking and Security Communities: A Constructivist Response," *International Relations of the Asia-Pacific*, vol. 5, no. 2, pp. 255–266.

Ba, A.D. 2006. "Who's Socializing Whom? Complex Engagement in Sino-ASEAN Relations," *The Pacific Review*, vol. 19, no. 2, pp. 157–179.

Barrett, J. and Barnes, R. 2016. *Law of the Sea: UNCLOS as a Living Treaty*, British Institute of International and Comparative Law, London.

Benson, L. and Svanberg, I. 1998. *China's Last Nomads: The History and Culture of China's Kazaks*, ME Sharpe, Armonk, New York.

Brecher, M. 1993. *Crises in World Politics: Theory and Reality*, Pergamon, Oxford.

Bremer, S.A. 1992. "Dangerous Dyads: Conditions Affecting the Likelihood of Interstate War, 1816–1965," *Journal of Conflict Resolution*, vol. 36, no. 2, pp. 309–341.

Carlson, A. 2003. "Constructing the Dragon's Scales: China's Approach to Territorial Sovereignty and Border Relations in the 1980s and 1990s," *Journal of Contemporary China*, vol. 12, no. 37, pp. 677–698.

Carlson, A. 2005. *Unifying China, Integrating with the World: Securing Chinese Sovereignty in the Reform Era*, Stanford University Press, Stanford, CA.

Catley, B. and Keliat, M. 1997. *Spratlys: The Dispute in the South China Sea*, Dartmouth Publications, Aldershot.

Chang, L.T. 1982. *China's Boundary Treaties and Frontier Disputes: A Manuscript*, Oceana Publications, London.

Chang, P.M. 1986. *The Sino-Vietnamese Territorial Dispute*, Praeger, New York.
Christensen, T.J. 1996. "Chinese Realpolitik," *Foreign Affairs*, vol. 75, no. 5, pp. 37–52.
Diehl, P.F. 1999. *A Road Map to War: Territorial Dimensions of International Conflict*, Vanderbilt University Press, Nashville, TN.
Diehl, P.F. and Goertz, G. 2000. *War and Peace in International Rivalry*, University of Michigan Press, Ann Arbor, MI.
Fravel, M.T. 2005. "Regime Insecurity and International Cooperation: Explaining China's Compromises in Territorial Disputes," *International Security*, vol. 30, no. 2, pp. 46–83.
Fravel, M.T. 2007. "Power Shifts and Escalation," *International Security*, vol. 32, no. 3, pp. 44–83.
Fravel, M.T. 2008. *Strong Borders, Secure Nation: Cooperation and Conflict in China's Territorial Disputes*, Princeton University Press, Princeton, NJ.
Fravel, M.T. 2011. "China's Strategy in the South China Sea," *Contemporary Southeast Asia*, vol. 33, no. 3, pp. 292–319.
Garver, J.W. 1992. "China's Push through the South China Sea: The Interaction of Bureaucratic and National Interests," *The China Quarterly*, vol. 132, pp. 999–1028.
Gill, B. 2007. *Rising Star: China's New Security Diplomacy*, Brookings Institution Press, Washington, DC.
Ginsberg, G. and Pinkle, C.F. 1978. *The Sino-Soviet Territorial Dispute, 1949–1964*, Praeger, New York.
Hong, N. 2012. *UNCLOS and Ocean Dispute Settlement: Law and Politics in the South China Sea*, Routledge, New York.
Huth, P.K. 1996. *Standing Your Ground*, University of Michigan Press, Ann Arbor, MI.
Hyer, E. 1995. "The South China Sea Disputes: Implications of China's Earlier Territorial Settlements," *Pacific Affairs*, vol. 68, no. 1, pp. 34–55.
Jacobson, H.K. 1990. *China's Participation in the IMF, the World Bank, and GATT: Toward a Global Economic Order*, University of Michigan Press, Ann Arbor, MI.
Johnston, A.I. 2003. "Is China a Status Quo Power?" *International Security*, vol. 27, no. 4, pp. 5–56.
Johnston, A.I. 2008. *Social States: China in International Institutions, 1980–2000*, Princeton University Press, Princeton, NJ.
Johnston, A.I. and Ross, R.S. (eds.) 2006. *New Directions in the Study of China's Foreign Policy*, Stanford University Press, Stanford, CA.
Kaup, K.P. 2000. *Creating the Zhuang: Ethnic Politics in China*, Lynne Rienner Publishers, Boulder, CO.
Kent, A.E. 2007. *Beyond Compliance*, Stanford University Press, Stanford, CA.
Kim, S.S. 1979. *China, the United Nations, and World Order*, Princeton University Press, Princeton, NJ.
Kim, S.S. 1989. *China and the World: New Directions in Chinese Foreign Relations*, Westview Press, Boulder, CO.
Lampton, D.M. (ed.) 2001. *The Making of Chinese Foreign and Security Policy in the Era of Reform, 1978–2000*, Stanford University Press, Stanford, CA.
Lanteigne, M. 2005. *China and International Institutions: Alternate Paths to Global Power*, Routledge, New York.
Lee, S.K. and Gullett, W. 2016. *Asia-Pacific and the Implementation of the Law of the Sea*, Brill, Leiden.
Lipman, J.N. 1998. *Familiar Strangers: A History of Muslims in Northwest China*, Seattle: University of Washington Press, Seattle.

Litzinger, R.A. 2000. *Other Chinas: The Yao and the Politics of National Belonging*, Duke University Press, Durham, NC.
Lo, C.K. 1989. *China's Policy towards Territorial Disputes: The Case of the South China Sea Islands*, Routledge, New York.
Lu, C.H. 1986. *The Sino-Indian Border Dispute: A Legal Study*, Greenwood Press, New York.
Mearsheimer, J.J. 1990. "Back to the Future: Instability in Europe after the Cold War," *International Security*, vol. 15, no. 1, pp. 5–56.
Morgenthau, H.J. 1978. *Politics among Nations: the Struggle for Power and Peace*, Alfred A. Knopf, New York.
Paasi, A. 1996. *Territories, Boundaries, and Consciousness: The Changing Geographies of the Finnish-Russian Boundary*, John Wiley & Sons, Inc., New York.
Pearson, M.M. 2006. "China in Geneva: Lessons from China's Early Years in the World Trade Organization," in A.I. Johnston and R.S. Ross, eds. *New Directions in the Study of China's Foreign Policy*, Stanford University Press, Stanford, CA.
Prescott, J.R.V. 1998. *The South China Sea: Limits of National Claims*, Maritime Institute of Malaysia, Kuala Lumpur, Malaysia.
Rothwell, D.R., Oude, A.G., Scott, K.N. and Stephens, T. (eds.) 2015. *Oxford Handbook of the Law of the Sea*, Oxford University Press, Oxford.
Samuels, M.S. 1982. *Contest for the South China Sea*, Methuen, New York.
Tai, S.A. 1973. *The Sino-Soviet Territorial Dispute*, Westminster Press, Philadelphia, PA.
Tsui, T.H. 1983. *The Sino-Soviet Border Dispute in the 1970s*, Mosaic Press, Ontario, Canada.
Tzou, B.N. 1990. *China and International Law: The Boundary Disputes*, Praeger, New York.
Valencia, M.J. 1988. "The Spratly Islands: Dangerous Ground in the South China Sea," *The Pacific Review*, vol. 1, no. 4, pp. 438–443.
Valencia, M.J. 1995. *China and the South China Sea Disputes: Conflicting Claims and Potential Solutions in the South China Sea*, Oxford University Press, Oxford.
Vasquez, J.A. 1995. "Why Do Neighbors Fight? Proximity, Interaction, or Territoriality," *Journal of Peace Research*, vol. 32, no. 3, pp. 277–293.
Waltz, K.N. 1979. *Theory of International Relations*, Addison-Wesley, Reading, MA.
Whiting, A.S. 1975. *The Chinese Calculus of Deterrence: India and Indochina*, University of Michigan Press, Ann Arbor, MI.
Whiting, A.S. 1997. "ASEAN Eyes China," *Asian Survey*, vol. 37, no. 4, pp. 299–322.
Wu, S.C. 1999. *The Origin and Development of the Nansha Disputes*, Ocean Press, Beijing (in Chinese).
Wu, S.C. 2001. *Collection of Documents Relating to South China Sea Issues*, Hainan Publishing House, Haikou, China (in Chinese),
Wu, S.C. 2005. *A Study on the South China Sea Disputes*, Hainan Publishing House, Haikou, China (in Chinese).
Wu, S.C. 2010. *Origin and Development of the South China Sea Disputes*, China Economic Publishing House, Beijing (in Chinese).
Wu, S.C., Valencia, M. and Hong, N. (eds.) 2015. *UN Convention on the Law of the Sea and the South China Sea*, Routledge, New York.
Xue, G.F. 2008. *International Fisheries Law and China's Practice*, China Ocean University Press, Qingdao, China (in Chinese),

Yu, S.K.T. 1989. "Who Owns the Paracels and Spratlys? An Evaluation of the Nature and Legal Basis of the Conflicting Territorial Claims," *Chinese Yearbook of International Law and Affairs*, vol. 9, pp. 1–28.

Zou, K.Y. 2005. *Law of the Sea in East Asia: Issues and Prospects*, Routledge, New York.

Zou, K.Y. 2016. "China's Approach to UNCLOS and its Application to Disputed Issues in the South China Sea," in J. Barrett and R. Barnes (eds.), *Law of the Sea: UNCLOS as a Living Treaty*, British Institute of International and Comparative Law, London, pp. 363–382.

1 The Law of the Sea regime and the transformation of sovereign disputes in the South China Sea

The main argument of this book is that the evolving contours of China's South China Sea policy are sculpted by two major factors: (1) the changing dynamics of the Law of the Sea regime; and (2) shifting geopolitics in the region. While the question of how geopolitics influences China's policy towards the South China Sea and Chinese foreign policy in general has been extensively addressed in the literature, little has been said about the profound impact of the dynamics in the LOS regime in shaping China's South China Sea policy.

In this book, I attribute the distinctive path of China's approach to the South China Sea dispute to a unique factor – the law of the sea as "rules of the road" in the ocean. More specifically, I argue that in the post-World War II era, a series of legal breakthroughs in the LOS regime set forth a movement of "enclosure of the ocean" which greatly intensified and complicated conflicts of maritime interests in many areas across the world, especially in semi-enclosed seas like the South China Sea. In the South China Sea case, this movement, galvanized by the establishment of the United Nations Convention on the Law of the Sea, transformed the South China Sea dispute from a zero-sum game with clearly defined boundaries into a multi-issue, multi-dimensional, non-zero-sum game with a new parameter of policy options that goes beyond conventional wisdom of managing territorial disputes – confrontation, delay and compromise. It is within this context that significant changes have gradually unfolded in China's policy towards the South China Sea over the course of time.

Examining the influence of the international maritime regime on China's evolving policy towards the South China Sea touches upon several important theoretical questions. What is a regime? What does the LOS regime look like? Why does it matter? How is the LOS regime restructuring the South China Sea dispute possible in theory? What roles can the LOS regime play in shaping and reshaping China's policy towards the South China Sea dispute? This chapter will clarify these questions by building upon constructivist work on the conceptualization of "international regimes" and "sovereignty".

The evolving Law of the Sea (LOS) regime

The concept of regime in International Relations (IR)

Regime is quite an amorphous entity. The concept of regime emerged in the common parlance of International Relations (IR) in the 1970s. John Ruggie was one of the first IR scholars to advocate the concept of regime. He defines regime as "a set of mutual expectations, rules and regulations, plans, organizational energies and financial commitments, which have been accepted by a group of States."[1] Robert Keohane and Joseph Nye define regime as "sets of governing arrangements" that include "networks of rules, norms, and procedures that regularize behavior and control its effects."[2] Ernst Haas argues that a regime encompasses a mutually coherent set of procedures, rules, and norms.[3] The definition formulated by Stephen Krasner remains the standard formulation: "Regimes can be defined as sets of implicit or explicit principles, norms, rules, and decision-making procedures around which actors' expectations converge in a given area of international relations."[4]

Nearly four decades have passed since students of International Relations began to ask questions about "international regimes." Earlier debates focused on the theoretical usefulness and analytical importance of the concept of "regime," with the more substantive questions that define the regime-analytical research agenda continuing to expand and count among the major foci of IR scholarship.[5] The central question to be answered in this regard is why and how regimes or institutions matter.[6] What accounts for the emergence of instances of rule-based cooperation in the international system? How do international regimes and institutions affect the behavior of state and non-state actors in the issue areas for which they have been created?[7]

Neoliberalism and constructivism are two major schools of thought in IR that take regime seriously. Analyses of neoliberal theories suggest that regimes or institutions may have a significant impact in a highly complex world in which ad hoc, individualistic calculations of interest could not possibly provide the necessary level of coordination.[8] These theories start from a conventionally rationalist perspective, a world of sovereign states seeking to maximize their interest and power, and they argue that international politics is not always a zero-sum game; rather, states in many situations have mutual interests and regimes assume an influential role in helping states to coordinate their behavior so that they may realize common interests, avoid collectively suboptimal outcomes and achieve desired outcomes in particular issue areas.[9] In addition, states are shown to have an interest in maintaining existing regimes even when the factors that brought them into being are no longer extant.[10]

The constructivist approaches represent a sociological turn in the research paradigm of IR scholarship. IR constructivists have developed a more robust and complex understanding of international regimes. Constructivists are critical of the rationalist assumptions prevalent in mainstream theories of international politics, whether of neoliberal or realist provenance. These scholars problematize states' identities and interests which are treated as exogenously given by rationalist theorists. They point out that by black-boxing the processes which produce the self-understandings of particular states (i.e., their identities) as well as the objectives which they pursue in their foreign policy (i.e., what they perceive to be in their interests), a significant source of variation in international behavior and outcomes is ignored and *ipso facto* trivialized.

Consequently, constructivist work features attempts to unlock the black box that is the formation process of states' interests and preferences. Constructivist theory argues that actors' perception and interpretation of international problems and their preferences and interests are, in part, produced by their causal and normative beliefs which, in turn, are considered partially independent of actors' material environment (e.g., the distribution of power and wealth).[11] To constructivists, it is misleading to regard actors' preferences as something that is simply "given"; rather, preferences are to be seen and *to be treated analytically* as contingent upon how actors understand the natural and social world.[12] Therefore, constructivists treat international regimes as inter-subjective socially constructed environments in which states interact and constantly (re)shape their perception of interests, preferences and identities, thus stressing the analytical power of knowledge, ideas and norms as explanatory variables.

Constructivists argue that the power of norms and ideas as pillars of international regimes runs much deeper than might appear at first glance. Norms and ideas not only inform states of cause-effect relationships which derive authority from the shared consensus of recognized elites, but provide "compelling ethical or moral motivations for action,"[13] or what some constructivists call the "logic of appropriateness."[14] It is the normative structure and corresponding practices that provide "a condition of the possibility" of individual choice. In this sense, constructivists emphasize not only regulative but also the constitutive and ontological nature of international regimes or institutions, making regular reference to such fundamental regimes or institutions of international society as sovereignty, diplomacy, and international law.[15] "These institutions constitute state actors as subjects of international life in the sense that they make meaningful interaction by the latter possible."[16] For instance, the norms and rules that make up the regime of sovereignty define inter-subjectively the responsibilities and rights of each member of the international system.[17]

Moreover, constructivists emphasize that in the dynamic, socially constructed environment of each individual international regime, static actors are conscious role-players who through dense interactions reach and renew an inter-subjective consensus of shared identity and convergent expectations concerning the right forms of conduct as well as inappropriate behavior in circumscribed situations. Together these regimes weave a "web of meaning" in the daily operation of international relations.[18] In other words, norms and rules emerging out of international regimes are not objectively influencing the behavior of member states by affecting their calculations of interests; rather they achieve this goal through influence at a more fundamental and inter-subjective level: they define the self-understanding of states ("who am I?") and prescribe rules of the game ("what is appropriate/legitimate for me to do?").[19]

The aforementioned theories advanced by neoliberals and constructivists provide the theoretical foundation for conceptualizing the LOS regime and the roles the regime can play in shaping and reshaping China's perception and behavior in the South China Sea dispute. As we will see below, the ocean regime, as a social normative environment in which both states and non-states actors engage and interact, is governed by laws, norms and principles that define appropriate, legitimate and meaningful state behavior.

Defining the Law of the Sea regime

The LOS regime is an evolving entity that has existed throughout the history of the use of the ocean by human beings. For centuries it remained in a pristine state and governed the vast oceans, based on a very limited number of norms, the predominant norm being what Haas called "maximum open access": outside the territorial sea (a narrow strip, usually 3 nautical miles along a nation's coast), any state could do anything.[20] This situation was fundamentally changed by the convening of three UN conferences on the Law of the Sea, thanks to a host of developments concurrently sweeping economic, political and technological arenas in the wake of the end of the World War II. In Chapter 3, the history of the LOS regime will be briefly reviewed so as to provide a background and a starting point for analysis. Suffice it to say that the three UN conferences on the LOS rewrote a new order for the world's oceans, which is crystallized in the form of the United Nations Convention of the Law of the Sea, approved in 1982.

Since the PRC officially joined the LOS regime during the preparatory stage of the third United Nations Conference on the Law of the Sea (UNCLOS III) in 1971, discussion of the LOS regime in this book is mainly focused on the period after China's entry, drawing on the pre-entry period when necessary. What does the LOS regime look like in the post-China-entry period? Drawing on the neoliberal and constructivist theories of international regimes reviewed earlier, this book defines the LOS regime as an evolving entity consisting of three basic elements. Figure 1.1 is an illustration of the LOS regime.

The normative component: law, norms, principles, procedures and practices

In the category of implicit or explicit principles, norms, rules, regulations, rights, duties and decision-making procedures, the LOS Convention is considered the "Constitution for the Oceans," replacing the old law of the sea loosely bound by a few simple rules such as the freedom of the high seas.[21] As the core component of the LOS regime, it brings legal breakthroughs to many fronts in the maritime domain, and provides a comprehensive, internally

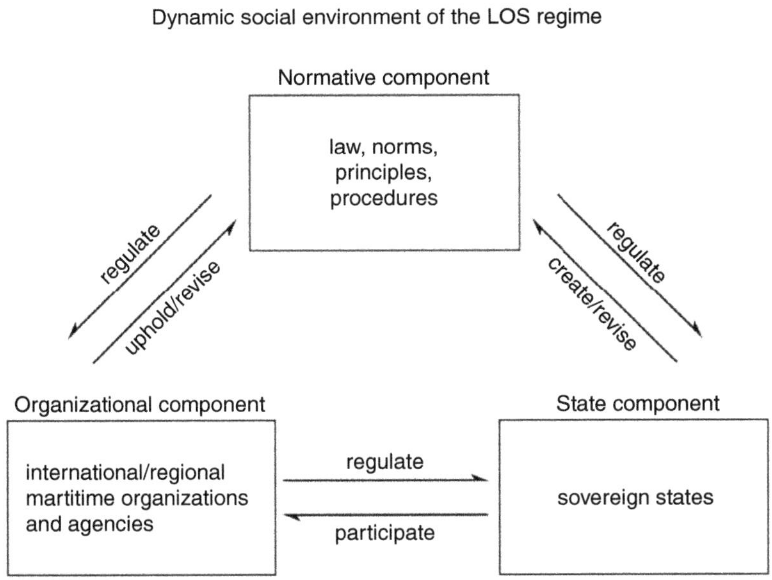

Figure 1.1 Composition of the evolving LOS regime

cohesive, legal framework for ocean governance. The Convention establishes five major zones for the world seas, each governed by a very specific set of rules and regulations: (1) the Territorial Seas and Contiguous Zones; (2) the Exclusive Economic Zone (EEZ); (3) the Continental Shelf (CS); (4) the High Seas; and (5) the Area (see Figure 1.2). The Convention develops new legal concepts, principles, and obligations that are now in everyday use and revised the content of many old concepts including, *inter alia*, common heritage of mankind (CHM), freedom of navigation (FON), provisional arrangement and Dispute Settlement. In particular, the concepts of EEZ and CS have been influential in reshaping China's legal position on its sovereignty in the South China Sea.

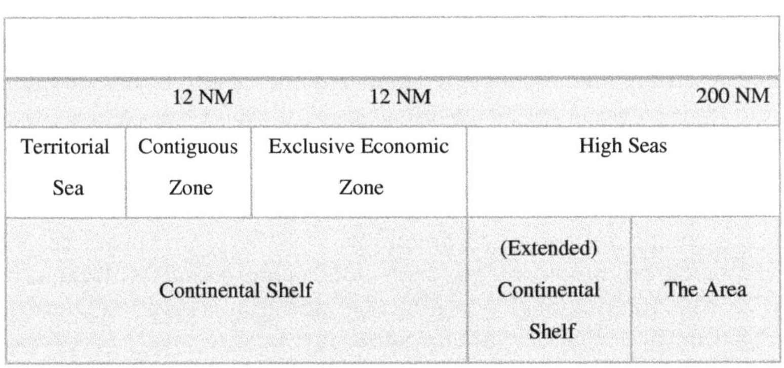

Figure 1.2 Zoning system of the world's oceans

In addition to the LOS Convention and general principles of international law, there exist a number of maritime treaties, agreements, and other legal undertakings that also have a bearing on ocean governance. Examples include the 1973 Convention on the Prevention of Pollution from Ships, bilateral or multilateral maritime boundary agreements, and those dealing with matters such as access to ports, fishing rights, and so on.[22]

Also falling into this category is customary international law expressed in general state practices and enhanced through judicial decisions and the writings of publicists in relation to joint development, straight baseline method, historic rights and equidistance measurement, domestic marine legislation, and relevant institution building.

The organizational component: organizational entities

This category includes organizations and specialized agencies either created by, under the auspices of, or in certain issue areas closely related to, maritime governance. The LOS Convention directly created new institutions to regulate a number of LOS concepts: the International Seabed Authority (ISA), the Commission on the Limits of the Continental Shelf (CLCS), and International Tribunal on the Law of the Sea (ITLOS), to act as an important new part of the LOS family of institutions. Some of these bodies have significant judicial power in the dispute settlement system that the new LOS established and continue to expand their judicial scope.[23] Some have become the venue through which states publicize, exchange, and negotiate official positions regarding a specific maritime matter. For example, the CLCS provided a forum for disputants to publicize and legitimize their claims to sovereignty in the South China Sea, and its activities in 2009 stirred up a new round of tension among the claimants in the SCS region, resulting in China's submission to the UN of the Dotted Line map in support of its SCS claims.

Moreover, as mentioned earlier, the interface between the LOS Convention and the wider legal environment also operates at the institutional level. Some major international institutions, many from the UN family, are also of enormous influence in guiding and shaping states' maritime practices. For instance, the International Court of Justice (ICJ) assumes an eminent and authoritative position in settling interstate territorial disputes. It is also designated as one of the four major means for the settlement of disputes concerning the interpretation or application of the LOS Convention.[24] The judicial opinions it offers have far-reaching influence in terms of interpreting the Law of the Sea as well as the law applicable to the delimitation of maritime boundaries. Given the conflicting legal interpretations of SCS sovereignty, the ICJ will continue to be an important player in influencing countries' legal claims in the SCS. The International Maritime Organization (IMO) is another UN specialized agency. Tasked with responsibility for the safety and security of shipping and the prevention of marine pollution by ships, the IMO probably has had the most substantial direct effect upon the development of LOS.[25] It plays a leading role in introducing international measures for cooperation among governments in the field of governmental regulation and practices relating to international shipping and administrative and legal matters related to seaborne transportation. The Global Environment Facility and the World Bank also take active part in assisting developing countries more systematically to manage and capture the benefits the LOS regime has to offer.[26]

In addition, the functioning of the LOS regime is complemented by specialized agencies and diplomatic frameworks operating at the regional level. In response to the requirement to implement the highly legal technical and systematic maritime governance envisaged by the LOS Convention, a range of multilateral arrangements were either established or widened by regional states to deal with transboundary and unique regional oceanic affairs. In the South China Sea region, coastal countries in the SCS established a variety of regional multilateral arrangements and frameworks to manage different aspects of maritime governance, including navigation, environmental preservation, fisheries, maritime security, and others. For instance, regional multilateral frameworks such as the ASEAN Regional Forum (ARF) and the Asia Pacific Economic Cooperation (APEC) widened their scope in the 1990s to deal with traditional and non-traditional maritime security issues. The Coordinating Body of the Seas of East Asia (COBSEA) under the United Nations Environment Programme (UNEP) was created for marine environmental protection and fisheries in the South China Sea. The emergence of these regional cooperative agencies and arrangements represents a regional response to the changing nature of the South China Sea dispute.

The state component: member states

Theoretically speaking, all states are entitled to membership in the LOS regime. With regards to the membership to the LOS Convention, as of the time of this writing, 168 countries have ratified it. In the case of the South China Sea dispute, major state actors include those directly involved in the dispute (the claimants) and those with political and economic interests heavily invested in this region (mainly user states such as the United States, Japan, India, and Australia).

Roles the LOS regime plays in shaping China's SCS policy

Drawing on the neoliberal and constructivist theories of international regimes reviewed earlier, we can specify six roles that the LOS regime plays in shaping China's SCS policy:

1 *(Re)defining the nature of the game.* The maritime regime plays a unique and largely independent role in constructing the first aspect of China's SCS policy, which is Beijing's legal position in the SCS. The legal and normative developments of the regime constantly (re)shape the international maritime order. They have transformed the nature of the SCS dispute and redefined the applicable rules. Interaction with the regime informs China

of these developments and affects conceptions of the dispute and claims to sovereignty in the SCS, although this process may unfold in an incremental and nuanced manner. Other countries bordering the SCS are equally affected by these normative dynamics and make adaptations accordingly. Their adaptations create additional pressure for Beijing to undergo similar processes.

2 *Provider of the playground.* Many issues pertinent to maritime governance require the cooperation, negotiation, and collective action on the part of a large number of state actors. The maritime regime and its institutional branches at all levels provide venues, coordinating mechanisms, information, and monitoring facilities for disputant parties to negotiate issues, manage inter-state interactions, facilitate long-term cooperation, and avoid collective suboptimal outcomes. The regime also contains a number of influential inter-governmental organizations (IOs), especially those in the UN family, which have potential "soft" power as authoritative institutions with a worldwide audience, including the potential power of legitimization. By participating in these IOs, countries can take advantage of these influential and authoritative fora to assert and publicize their territorial claims, which helps them to potentially legitimize their claims in front of an international audience and obtain additional credentials for their position. Non-participation might incur the potential cost of de-legitimizing its claims and damage its reputation as a responsive power. All these features make the maritime regime intrinsically attractive to states. Actively participating in the maritime regime and complying with its norms and rules build important reputational assets for China.

3 *A medium for flexible and effective political engagements.* The regime provides the medium through which other state actors exert pressure on China. This pressure forms an essential component of the (dis)incentives of the regime. In traditional state-to-state engagement, one state directly pressures another state. Sometimes such pressure may be too weak to elicit desired changes or backfires if the pressure is too great. Utilizing the state-regime-state setting, states can form alliances or coordinate their positions to present a united voice when pressuring China, thus making their pressure more effective in eliciting corresponding changes.

4 *Deadlines and critical dates.* This is similar to external pressure but more direct in its effect. There are a number of deadlines set by the regime that require unequivocal responses from states. For instance, under Article 4 of Annex II to UNCLOS, a coastal state with a shelf area beyond 200 nautical miles intending to establish the outer limits of its continental shelf beyond 200 nautical miles is obligated to submit information of such limits to the Commission on the Limits of the Continental Shelf (CLCS) along with supporting scientific and technical data within 10 years of the entry into force of the Convention for that state. The deadline for submission to the CLCS is a barometer testing China's compliance with the LOSC. It also forces China to clarify its own stance on the application of the

continental shelf regime in the SCS and respond to the submissions to the CLCS of other disputants. These critical dates might exacerbate the already tense situation in the SCS, creating some type of crisis, which is often a tipping point for change. By pressuring SCS states to be more explicit about their claims, such deadlines are crucially helpful in bringing states to a common ground for future negotiation.

5 *Teaching policy-related knowledge.* Participation in the regime creates tremendous opportunities for China to gain policy-related knowledge. Sometimes this learning results from direct teaching by officials from international organizations or experts from epistemic communities. Other times, learning is a natural product of long-term participation. Before entering into the preparatory stage of the UNCLOS III, China had extremely limited knowledge of maritime governance. Day-to-day involvement in the intensive negotiation processes in the UNCLOS III helped China become familiar with legal matters and the technicalities necessary for modern maritime governance and gain the technical expertise involved in the exploration of oceanic resources made possible with new technologies. Continuous interaction with the regime also informs China of useful policy options, the latest innovations, and other popular practices. In particular, the Chinese government has learned from international practices of joint development to devise its own policy proposals for managing the SCS dispute. All the information, knowledge, and policy options learned by China promote the pluralization of China's SCS policy and shape its policy parameters. It also helps to define what a state can do in the SCS, an important element constituting maritime sovereignty in the SCS.

6 *Lock-in effect.* Regimes have resilient effect. That is, once a state enters, it is not easy to opt out. Continuous participation inevitably leads to institutionalized and habitualized interaction which helps maintain a certain level of compliance, even in the absence of original incentives. The lock-in effect may also cultivate in a state the awareness of the logic of appropriateness. That is, a locked-in state's behavior is guided by norms and identities suggesting the *appropriate* action in a given situation.

Some of these roles have a direct influence while others are indirect and incremental. In particular, role 3 is where geopolitical factors and regime dynamics interact. The maritime regime provides the medium through which other state actors exert pressure on China, and in this process the dynamics of the regime blend with geopolitical factors. Previous studies have amply demonstrated that geopolitical and normative dynamics often work in conjunction to provide an integrated set of motives for China's policy-making. There are generally two types of effects when these factors blend together: (1) a reinforcement which multiplies the final effect when they work in the same direction; and (2) an offset which partially neutralizes the final effect when they work in the opposite direction. This shows that geopolitics alone does not determine the final shape of China's SCS policy because of its potential to work in opposite directions.

The concept of sovereignty revisited

Most students of International Relations trace the root of sovereignty back to the 1648 Westphalian system which is often viewed as the prototype of contemporary international system. In the eyes of the founding figures of International Relations, such as Hans Morgenthau, one of the defining features of the Westphalian system is anarchy, and sovereignty, which entails internal hierarchy and external equality, is the fundamental organizing principle based on which states interact with each other in an anarchic international system. In other words, it is sovereignty that makes possible international relations under anarchy. Sovereignty as the anchoring principle governing modern international relations was enshrined in the Charter of the United Nations in the wake of World War II. Article 2 of the UN Charter clearly stipulates that "the Organization is based on the principle of the sovereign equality of all its Members."

The rising tide of economic interdependence, political integration, and globalization in the 1970s started to cast doubts on the conceptual simplicity of sovereignty which had too easily been treated as the synonymy of autonomy and pushed the field of International Relations to undertake a new research agenda to gauge the impact of these new phenomena on inter-state interactions and state behavior. It was argued that students of IR often conflated sovereignty with autonomy or independence, and thereby underestimated, if not completely ignored the complexity of sovereignty in the daily functioning of international relations in the contemporary world. Thus, in the face of such increasingly complicated and dense nature of contemporary international system, the central question confronting students of IR is: as the fundamental organizing principle of international system, what is it about sovereignty that is actually organizing or being organized?

To answer this question, one must clarify the conceptual haze surrounding it. Stephen Krasner is an early influential theorist in this regard. Zooming in on the concept of sovereignty, Krasner catalogs four facets of the term: (1) internal public authority of a state (internal hierarchy); (2) the Westphalian model (external equality or autonomy); (3) control over transborder flows; and (4) international legal sovereignty. Krasner finds that sovereignty has always been subject to incursions, although some facets of sovereignty are more vulnerable to incursions than the others.[27] Krasner's reconceptualization of sovereignty gives rise to the theoretical possibility of sovereignty being changed or challenged by the ongoing dynamics of international relations and potentially unlocks the black box within which such changes in state behavior can take place.

Developing along this line, a number of scholars deconstruct sovereignty as a game comprising constitutive rules and regulative or functional rules. Janice Thomson defines the constitutive aspect of sovereignty as residing in the privileged position of the state within the sovereign system, whereas the functional aspect relates to a range of specific activities or practices over which states can legitimately exercise their authority in the system.[28] Georg Sorenson argues that while the constitutional independence of states as the foundational feature of modern international system remains quite static, the regulative or functional rules of sovereignty have changed substantially over time to absorb or adapt to new challenges mainly stimulated by changes in substantial statehood.[29]

To sum up, breaking the term of sovereignty down to two facets – one is constitutive rules and the other regulative or functional rules – loosens this otherwise quite static concept and enables us to pinpoint what and where exactly the changes in state behavior take place (Table 1.1). We can find that sovereignty, in particular, the regulative or functional dimension which defines the parameter of a state's legitimate practices and activities, is much more fluid and frequently updated than was conventionally acknowledged in the field of International Relations. State behavior as practices or functioning of sovereignty in contemporary international system is defined and redefined, shaped and reshaped by laws, norms, and regulative rules, and procedures that are in themselves constantly evolving in the environment in which states live and interact.

Building upon the theoretical developments highlighted above, I argue that it is mainly the regulative or functional dimension of sovereignty into which the ongoing dynamics of the LOS regime penetrate in order to exert its influence. On the one hand, at the center of the LOS regime is a sophisticated set of laws, norms, and procedures regulating the uses of the world's oceans and thereby defining the precise range of activities and practices over which states can legitimately exercise authority in the international maritime domain. On the other hand, the LOS regime provides a social environment in which a host of organizations and institutions help to implement the maritime legal order and coordinate inter-state interactions. As we will see in

Table 1.1 The concept of sovereignty deconstructed

Sovereignty	
Constitutive aspect, relatively stable	*Regulative/functional aspect, more fluid and constantly updating*
1. Fundamental organizing principle of modern international system 2. Sovereign states as basic unit and major players of international relations 3. Sovereign equality and authority of internal affairs	1. The precise range of activities and practices over which state can legitimately exercise their authority in contemporary international system 2. Evolving laws, norms, regulations and procedures setting the parameter of appropriate activities in each specific issue-regime (e.g., the international trade regime, the maritime regime, the nuclear and non-proliferation regime)

subsequent chapters, the fluid and malleable nature of the regulative facet of sovereignty makes possible the transformation of the South China Sea dispute from a typical zero-sum game of territorial dispute into a multi-layered complex network of disputes with open-ended solutions.

It is also from this constructivist perspective of understanding sovereignty that this book conceptualizes sovereign boundaries as institutions constituted by the ongoing enactment of a broad set of social practices between states. The book takes a broad yet focused scope to examine Beijing's practices constructing sovereign boundaries: broad in that all relevant practices (including those often overlooked in conventional security studies) are included; focused in that these practices are selected solely based on the criteria that they either embody pertinent efforts to (re)interpret and (re)construct its sovereignty or reflect official policy and position. There are five major sources of diplomatic and representational practices:[30]

1 *Official boundary claims and boundary enforcement*. This category mainly includes specific statements on the location of given segments of the boundary, explanations and legal justifications, national legislation, pronouncements on general principles for handling maritime disputes, and official responses to perceived infringements upon a state's sovereignty. Unilateral actions directed at contested territory also belong to this category. These may include the occupation of contested territory, removal of landmarks erected by other disputant parties on the contested territory, and administrative consolidation of occupied territory.
2 *Bilateral and multilateral political negotiations* on managing and resolving the dispute.
3 *China's participation in regional and international cooperative initiatives and mechanisms regarding maritime issues.* These cooperative efforts may include international measures to preserve the SCS marine environment and biodiversity, bilateral or multilateral fishery arrangements, multilateral dialogues on maritime security, and other regional frameworks that include maritime issues in their scope. It is worth noting that China's participation in these maritime cooperation arrangements yields considerable detail about which activities are allowed in sensitive waters, which issues are negotiable, and who are judged to be qualified players involved in disputed waters. In other words, these details speak to Beijing's understanding of its sovereignty in the SCS in relation to the three dimensions of sovereignty dispute mentioned earlier.
4 *Signing, enactment, and observation of maritime treaties and other legal instruments, either binding or non-binding*. Previous studies often ignore this type of practice as not directly related to border relations. However, in the maritime world, the Convention and other relevant legal developments are influential in constructing the order of the ocean and form an indispensable part of both the legal and practical basis of states' sovereign activities in the SCS region. Hence, examining China's attitude towards

these multilateral agreements helps identify possible changes in China's sovereign practices in the SCS.

5 *Analyses by Chinese foreign policy elites.* While this type of practice does not carry the weight of official territorial claims, it is also less restrained by the protocols of diplomatic discourse. These analyses include elites' personal memoirs, press releases, editorials and commentaries published in media outlets, and domestic academic discourses. Before the 1990s, academic discourses on the SCS issue were constrained to either supporting or reflecting the official position and could be treated indiscriminately as part of the analyses of foreign policy elites. After the 1990s, as official control over academic discourse loosened, researchers were relatively free to express their independent views. Therefore, the materials chosen are limited to those authored by senior scholars with government backgrounds or whose voices are regularly heard by the central government.

Conclusion

The world is constantly changing, so is state policy. States change their policy to realize and maximize their national interests, but as constructivists have convincingly demonstrated, this explanation is oversimplified. Theoretical advancement in the field of International Relations has yielded a more nuanced and accurate explanation for policy changes. States change their policy when their perception of what constitutes national interests and how to achieve their goals changes. This chapter demonstrates that it is on the perception level that the normative structure of the ocean regime operates. By treating the LOS regime as a dynamic social environment undergirded by a normative structure within which China and other states interact, and revealing the rather fluid and malleable nature of "sovereignty," this chapter explores from the theoretical perspective how the evolving LOS regime could redefine the South China Sea game and consequently shape China's understanding of the game

Notes

1 John G. Ruggie, "International Responses to Technology: Concepts and Trends," *International Organization* 29, no. 3 (1975): 570.
2 Robert O. Keohane and Joseph S. Nye, *Power and Interdependence* (Boston: Little, Brown, 1977), 19.
3 Ernst B. Hass, "Technological Self-Reliance for Latin America: The OAS Contribution," *International Organization* 34, no. 4 (1980): 553.
4 Stephen D. Krasner, ed., *International Regimes* (Ithaca, NY: Cornell University Press, 1983), 2.
5 Earlier debates were mostly engaged by neorealists and neoliberals. The main arguments of their discussions have well been documented in Krasner, ibid. More recent rounds of the attacks and counter-attacks engaged by scholars from these two schools on the analytical importance and benefits of the regime concept can be found in David A. Baldwin, *Neorealism and Neoliberalism: The Contemporary*

Debate (New York: Columbia University Press, 1993) and Andreas Hasenclever, Peter Mayer, and Volker Rittberger, *Theories of International Regimes* (New York: Cambridge University Press, 1997), 1. Also see John J. Mearsheimer, "A Realist Reply," *International Security* 20, no. 1 (1995): 82–93, Robert O. Keohane and Lisa L. Martin, "The Promise of Institutionalist Theory," *International Security* 20, no. 1 (1995): 39–51, and Charles A. Kupchan and Clifford A. Kupchan, "The Promise of Collective Security," *International Security* 20, no. 1 (1995): 52–61.

6 Regimes and institutions are often used interchangeably as both refer to international arrangements for cooperation and interaction among states and between states and non-state actors. These arrangements are sometimes in the form of a large overarching institution or manifested as a group of interrelated institutions.

7 Hasenclever, *et al. Theories of International Regimes*, 1.

8 Krasner, *International Regimes*, 7–8.

9 For example, Keohane and Stein posit that regimes can have an impact when Pareto-optimal outcomes could not be achieved through uncoordinated individual calculations of self-interest. They may have an autonomous effect on outcomes when purely autonomous behavior could lead to disastrous results for both parties, see Robert O. Keohane, "The Demand for International Regimes," and Arthur A. Stein, "Coordination and Collaboration: Regimes in an Anarchic World," in Krasner, *International Regimes*.

10 Robert Powell, "Anarchy in International Relations Theory: The Neorealist-Neoliberal Debate," *International Organization* 48, no. 2 (1994): 340–341.

11 Classical works in this regard include: Peter M. Haas, ed., *Knowledge, Power, and International Policy Coordination* (Columbia, SC: University of South Carolina Press, 1997), Peter M. Haas, "Do Regimes Matter? Epistemic Community and Mediterranean Pollution Control," *International Organization* 43, no. 3 (1989): 377–403, Judith Goldstein and Robert O. Keohane, eds., *Ideas and Foreign Policy: Beliefs, Institutions, and Political Change* (Ithaca, NY: Cornell University Press, 1993); Martha Finnemore, "International Organizations as Teachers of Norms: The UNESCO and Science Policy," *International Organization* 47, no. 4 (1993): 565–597, Friedrich Kratochwil, *Rules, Norms, and Decisions: On the Conditions of Practical and Legal Reasoning in International Relations and Domestic Affairs* (New York: Cambridge University Press, 1989), John G. Ruggie, "The False Promise of Realism," *International Security* 20, no. 1 (1995): 62–70, Alexander Wendt, "Constructing International Politics," *International Security* 20, no. 1 (1995): 71–81, Alexander Wendt, "Anarchy Is What States Make of It: The Social Construction of Power Politics," *International Organization* 46, no. 2 (1992): 391–425, Peter J. Katzenstein, ed., *The Culture of National Security: Norms and Identity in World Politics* (New York: Columbia University Press, 1996).

12 Hasenclever *et al., Theories of International Regimes*, 140.

13 Goldstein and Keohane, *Ideas and Foreign Policy*, 9–10.

14 The "logic of appropriateness" stipulates that behaviors are guided by norms and identities suggesting *appropriate* action in a given situation, whereas the "logic of consequence" suggests that choice is made from rational calculation by actors to maximize preferences. For the distinction between the "logic of appropriateness" and the "logic of consequence," see James G. March and Johan P. Olsen, *Rediscovering Institutions: The Organizational Basis of Politics* (New York: Free Press, 1989), 21–26, 160–162.

15 For a classical elaboration of the ontological nature and constitutive dimension of international institutions, see Wendt, "Anarchy Is What States Make of It," and "The Agent-Structure Problem in International Relations Theory," *International Organization* 41, no. 3 (1987): 335–370, and "Levels of Analysis vs. Agent and Structures: Part III," *Review of International Studies* 18, no. 2 (1992): 181–185.

16 Alexander Wendt and Raymond Duvall, "Institutions and International Order," in *Global Changes and Theoretical Challenges: Approaches to the World Politics for the 1990s*, ed. Ernst-Otto Czempiel and James N. Rosenau (Lexington, MA: Lexington Books, 1989), 53.
17 Hasenclever *et al., Theories of International Regimes,* 158–159.
18 Mark Neufeld, "Interpretation and the 'Science' of International Relations," *Review of International Studies* 19, no. 1 (1993): 43.
19 The power of identity in shaping states' behavior in international institutions is particularly emphasized by Alexander Wendt in his works cited in previous notes.
20 Ernst B. Hass, "Words Can Hurt You; or, Who Said What to Whom about Regimes," *International Organization* 36, no. 2, (1982): 208.
21 See the famous closing statement of the Third United Nations Conference on the Law of the Sea (the UNCLOS III) by President Tommy Koh, reproduced in *The Law of the Sea: Official Text of the UN Convention on the Law of the Sea* (New York: UN Publications, 1983), xxxiv, cited in David Freestone, "Editorial: Twenty-Five Years of the Law of the Sea Convention, 1982–2007," *The International Journal of Marine and Coastal Law* 22, no. 1 (2007), footnote 3.
22 Robin R. Churchill and A. V. Lowe, *The Law of the Sea*, 3rd edn. (Manchester: Manchester University Press, 1999), 6–7.
23 For example, legal scholars observe that in recent years the ITLOS has expanded its juridical scope to cover issues such as territorial disputes and marine protection. See Irina Buga, "Territorial Sovereignty Issues in Maritime Disputes: A Jurisdictional Dilemma for Law of the Sea Tribunals," *International Journal of Marine and Coastal Law* 27, no. 1 (2012): 59–95, and Donald R. Rothwell, "The International Tribunal for the Law of the Sea and Marine Environmental Protection: Expanding the Horizons of International Oceans Governance," *Ocean Yearbook Online* 17, no. 1 (2003): 26–52.
24 In addition to the ITLOS and ICJ, the LOS Convention also provides two other types of arbitral tribunals: the arbitral tribunal constituted in accordance with Annex VII and the special arbitral tribunal constituted in accordance with Annex VIII. The Conclusion will discuss the Philippines' recent invocation of special arbitral tribunal procedure for its dispute with China over the Scarborough Shoal and the potential implication of this action on the SCS dispute.
25 Churchill and Lowe, *The Law of the Sea*, 23.
26 Freestone, "Editorial," 4.
27 Stephen D. Krasner, *Sovereignty: Organized Hypocrisy* (Princeton, NJ: Princeton University Press, 1999), 9.
28 Janice E. Thomson, "State Sovereignty in International Relations: Bridging the Gap Between Theory and Empirical Research," *International Studies Quarterly* 39, no. 2 (June 1995): 224.
29 Georg Sorenson, "Sovereignty: Change and Continuity in a Fundamental Institution," *Political Studies* 47, no.3 (1999): 604.
30 Some of these types of practice were originally identified in Carlson's discussion on China's practice of the norm of sovereignty. See Allen Carlson, "Constructing the Dragon's Scales: China's Approach to Territorial Sovereignty and Border Relations in the 1980s and 1990s,"*Journal of Contemporary China* 12, no. 37 (2003): 680–681.

Bibliography

Acharya, A. 2004. "How Ideas Spread: Whose Norms Matter? Norm Localization and Institutional Change in Asian Regionalism," *International Organization*, vol. 58, no. 2, pp. 239–275.

Ba, A.D. 2005. "On Norms, Rule-Breaking and Security Communities: A Constructivist Response," *International Relations of the Asia-Pacific*, vol. 5, no. 2, pp. 255–266.

Ba, A.D. 2006. "Who's Socializing Whom? Complex Engagement in Sino-ASEAN Relations," *The Pacific Review*, vol. 19, no. 2, pp. 157–179.

Baldwin, D.A. 1993. *Neorealism and Neoliberalism: The Contemporary Debate*, Columbia University Press, New York.

Barrett, J. and Barnes, R. 2016. *Law of the Sea: UNCLOS as a Living Treaty*, British Institute of International and Comparative Law, London.

Buga, I. 2012. "Territorial Sovereignty Issues in Maritime Disputes: A Jurisdictional Dilemma for Law of the Sea Tribunals," *International Journal of Marine and Coastal Law*, vol. 27, no. 1, pp. 59–95.

Carlson, A. 2003. "Constructing the Dragon's Scales: China's Approach to Territorial Sovereignty and Border Relations in the 1980s and 1990s," *Journal of Contemporary China*, vol. 12, no. 37, pp. 677–698.

Carlson, A. 2005. *Unifying China, Integrating with the World: Securing Chinese Sovereignty in the Reform Era*, Stanford University Press, Stanford, CA.

Churchill, R.R. and Lowe, A.V. 1999. *The Law of the Sea*, 3rd edn, Manchester University Press, Manchester.

Czempiel, E.O. and Rosenau, J.N. (eds.) 1989. *Global Changes and Theoretical Challenges: Approaches to the World Politics for the 1990s*, Lexington Books, Lexington, MA.

Finnemore, M. 1993. "International Organizations as Teachers of Norms: The UNESCO and Science Policy," *International Organization*, vol. 47, no. 4, pp. 565–597.

Finnemore, M. 1996. *National Interests in International Society*, Cornell University Press, Ithaca, NY.

Freestone, D. 2007. "Editorial: Twenty-Five Years of the Law of the Sea Convention, 1982–2007," *The International Journal of Marine and Coastal Law*, vol. 22, no. 1, pp. 1–5.

Goldstein, J. and Keohane, R.O. (eds.) 1993. *Ideas and Foreign Policy: Beliefs, Institutions, and Political Change*, Cornell University Press, Ithaca, NY.

Haas, P.M. 1989. "Do Regimes Matter? Epistemic Community and Mediterranean Pollution Control," *International Organization*, vol. 43, no. 3, pp. 377–403.

Haas, P.M. (ed.) 1997. *Knowledge, Power, and International Policy Coordination*, University of South Carolina Press, Columbia, SC.

Hasenclever, A., Mayer, P., and Rittberger, V. 1997. *Theories of International Regimes*, Cambridge University Press, New York.

Hass, E.B. 1980. "Technological Self-Reliance for Latin America: The OAS Contribution," *International Organization*, vol. 34, no. 4, pp. 541–570.

Hass, E.B. 1982. "Words Can Hurt You: Or, Who Said What to Whom about Regimes," *International Organization*, vol. 36, no. 2, pp. 207–243.

Hong, N. 2012. *UNCLOS and Ocean Dispute Settlement: Law and Politics in the South China Sea*, Routledge, New York.

Jacobson, H.K. 1990. *China's Participation in the IMF, the World Bank, and GATT: Toward a Global Economic Order*, University of Michigan Press, Ann Arbor, MI.

Johnston, A.I. 2008. *Social States: China in International Institutions, 1980–2000*, Princeton University Press, Princeton, NJ.

Johnston, A.I. and Ross, R.S. (eds.) 2006. *New Directions in the Study of China's Foreign Policy*, Stanford University Press, Stanford, CA.

Katzenstein, P.J. (ed.) 1996. *The Culture of National Security: Norms and Identity in World Politics*, Columbia University Press, New York.
Kent, A.E. 2007. *Beyond Compliance*, Stanford University Press, Stanford, CA.
Keohane, R.O. 1983. "The Demand for International Regimes," in S.D. Krasner (ed.) *International Regimes*, Cornell University Press, Ithaca, NY.
Keohane, R.O. 1984. *After Hegemony*, Princeton University Press, Princeton, NJ.
Keohane, R.O. 1989. *International Institutions and State Power: Essays in International Relations Theory*, Westview Press, Boulder, CO.
Keohane, R.O. and Martin, L.L. 1995. "The Promise of Institutionalist Theory," *International Security*, vol. 20, no. 1, pp. 39–51.
Keohane, R.O. and Nye, J.S. 1977. *Power and Interdependence: World Politics in Transition*, Little, Brown & Company, Boston.
Kim, S.S. 1979. *China, the United Nations, and World Order*, Princeton University Press, Princeton, NJ.
Krasner, S.D. (ed.) 1983. *International Regimes*, Cornell University Press, Ithaca, NY.
Krasner, S.D. 1988. "Sovereignty – An Institutional Perspective," *Comparative Political Studies*, vol. 21, no. 1, pp. 66–94.
Krasner, S.D. 1999. *Sovereignty: Organized Hypocrisy*, Princeton University Press, Princeton, NJ.
Krasner, S.D. 2001a. *Problematic Sovereignty*, Columbia University Press, New York.
Krasner, S.D. 2001b. "Abiding Sovereignty," *International Political Science Review*, vol. 22, no. 3, pp. 229–251.
Kratochwil, F. 1989. *Rules, Norms, and Decisions: On the Conditions of Practical and Legal Reasoning in International Relations and Domestic Affairs*, Cambridge University Press, New York.
Kupchan, C.A. and Kupchan, C.A. 1995. "The Promise of Collective Security," *International Security*, vol. 20, no. 1, pp. 52–61.
Lake, D.A. 2003. "The New Sovereignty in International Relations 1," *International Studies Review*, vol. 5, no. 3, pp. 303–323.
Lampton, D.M. (ed.) 2001. *The Making of Chinese Foreign and Security Policy in the Era of Reform, 1978–2000*, Stanford University Press, Stanford, CA.
Lanteigne, M. 2005. *China and International Institutions: Alternate Paths to Global Power*, Routledge, New York.
March, J.G. and Olsen, J.P. 1989. *Rediscovering Institutions: The Organizational Basis of Politics*, Free Press, New York.
Martin, L.L. and Simmons, B.A. 1998. "Theories and Empirical Studies of International Institutions," *International Organization*, vol. 52, no. 4, pp. 729–757.
Mearsheimer, J.J. 1995. "A Realist Reply," *International Security*, vol. 20, no. 1, pp. 82–93.
Neufeld, M. 1993. "Interpretation and the 'Science' of International Relations," *Review of International Studies*, vol. 19, no. 1, pp. 39–61.
Powell, R. 1994. "Anarchy in International Relations Theory: The Neorealist-Neoliberal Debate," *International Organization*, vol. 48, no. 2, pp. 313–344.
Rittberger, V. and Mayer, P. (eds.) 1995. *Regime Theory and International Relations*, Clarendon Press, Oxford.
Rothwell, D.R. 2003. "The International Tribunal for the Law of the Sea and Marine Environmental Protection: Expanding the Horizons of International Oceans Governance," *Ocean Yearbook Online*, vol. 17, no. 1, pp. 26–52.
Ruggie, J.G. 1975. "International Responses to Technology: Concepts and Trends," *International Organization*, vol. 29, no. 3, pp. 557–583.

Ruggie, J.G. 1995. "The False Promise of Realism," *International Security*, vol. 20, no. 1, pp. 62–70.
Sorensen, G. 1999. "Sovereignty: Change and Continuity in a Fundamental Institution," *Political Studies*, vol. 47, no. 3, pp. 590–604.
Stein, A.A. 1983. "Coordination and Collaboration: Regimes in an Anarchic World," in S.D. Krasner (ed.) *International Regimes*, Cornell University Press, Ithaca, NY.
Thomson, J.E. 1995. "State Sovereignty in International Relations: Bridging the Gap Between Theory and Empirical Research," *International Studies Quarterly*, vol. 39, no. 2, pp. 213–233.
United Nations 1983. *The Law of the Sea: Official Text of the UN Convention on the Law of the Sea*, UN Publications, New York.
Waltz, K.N. 1979. *Theory of International Relations*, Addison-Wesley, Reading, MA.
Wendt, A. 1987. "The Agent-Structure Problem in International Relations Theory," *International Organization*, vol. 41, no. 3, pp. 335–370.
Wendt, A. 1992a. "Anarchy is What States Make of It: The Social Construction of Power Politics," *International Organization*, vol. 46, no. 2, pp. 391–425.
Wendt, A. 1992b. "Levels of Analysis vs. Agent and Structures: Part III," *Review of International Studies*, vol. 18, no. 2, pp. 181–185.
Wendt, A. 1995. "Constructing International Politics," *International Security*, vol. 20, no. 1, pp. 71–81.
Wendt, A. and Duvall, R. 1989. "Institutions and International Order," in E-O. Czempiel and J.N. Rosenau (eds.) *Global Changes and Theoretical Challenges: Approaches to the World Politics for the 1990s*, Lexington Books, Lexington, MA.
Xue, G.F. 2008. *International Fisheries Law and China's Practice*, China Ocean University Press, Qingdao, China (in Chinese).

2 The pre-1971 period

The PRC's initial claims in the SCS and its view of international regimes

This chapter explores the origin of the South China Sea dispute in five sections. The first section provides a brief introduction of the South China Sea. Certainly, the South China Sea is an area that has a geographically defined location and boundary, but it is also an area falling nicely in the category of semi-enclosed sea as specified in the United Nations Convention on the Law of the Sea (UNCLOS) in the eyes of international legal scholars, an area enjoying the world's richest biodiversity in the eyes of ecologists, an area supporting a vital artery of global trade in the eyes of economists, and an area that can potentially choke naval mobility between the Indian Ocean and the Pacific during wartime in the eyes of strategists. These key features of the South China Sea are simultaneously contentious issues intrinsically linked to the South China Sea dispute. Tackling these issues requires sophisticated knowledge of international maritime rules and governance, something that takes Chinese policy-makers years to gradually learn and internalize in their management of the dispute.

The second section offers an overview of the PRC's original position on the South China Sea, which is basically a straightforward sovereign claim to the land features (and related territorial seas added in 1958) in the South China Sea. Compared to the claims deliberated in response to the verdict on the South China Sea Arbitration case in July 2016, Beijing's original claim was relatively primitive and therefore serves as a useful starting point from which we can track the evolution of China's policy towards the South China Sea. Examined in the third section are competing claims made by Vietnam as well as the diplomatic exchanges between China and the Philippines in this period, concerning some of the features in the South Chins Sea (SCS). In the pre-1971 period, Vietnam and the Philippines, like China, justified their positions on the grounds of international law on territory acquisition but later, as we will see in Chapter 3, modified the legal reasoning on the basis of the newly established UNCLOS. The fourth section reviews the new communist regime's attitude to international law and international regimes, which set the initial tone for the PRC's negotiating position in the third UN conference on the law of the sea in 1971. The final section summarizes the major findings in this chapter.

The South China Sea

The South China Sea is usually defined as encompassing a portion of the Pacific Ocean extending from the Strait of Malacca in the southwest to the Taiwan Strait in the northeast (see Figure 2.1). This area includes more than 200 small islands, rocks, and reefs used to bolster claims to the surrounding sea and its resources.[1] Over 500 million people in China, Taiwan, the Philippines, Malaysia, Brunei, Indonesia, Singapore, Cambodia, Thailand, and Vietnam live within 100 miles of the coastline.

The SCS is an integrated ecosystem with remarkable biological diversity, including over 30 percent of the world's coral reefs. It is one of the richest seas in the world in terms of marine flora and fauna, coral reefs, mangroves, sea grass beds, and fish.[2] In addition to marine living resources, the SCS is thought to contain abundant oil and natural gas reserves, a prospect of vital

Figure 2.1 The South China Sea
The U.S. Energy Information Administration, available at: www.eia.gov/countries/analysisbriefs/South_China_Sea/south_china_sea.pdf (accessed March 1, 2014).

interest to energy-importing countries around the region. Because of this, the SCS is sometimes called the "second Persian Gulf."

The fact that the South China Sea contains one of the world's busiest international sea lanes and is home to many of the world's busiest shipping ports further increases its strategic importance. One-third of the world's oil tankers sail through its waters every year, constituting about two-thirds of South Korean energy supplies and almost 60 percent of Japanese and Taiwanese energy supplies (see Figure 2.2). Over half of the world's merchant fleet (by tonnage) passes annually through the Straits of Malacca, Sunda, and Lombok, with the majority continuing into the SCS.[3] It is a strategic maritime link between the Pacific Ocean and the Indian Ocean, and therefore of paramount importance to major naval powers.

Moreover, increasing human activities in this marine space have given rise to non-traditional security challenges such as piracy, poaching, resource depletion, pollution, drug trafficking, illegal migration, and terrorist threats. These issues are threatening the livelihood of millions of people in the SCS region which can only be effectively tackled by close and institutionalized cooperation at both the regional and international levels.

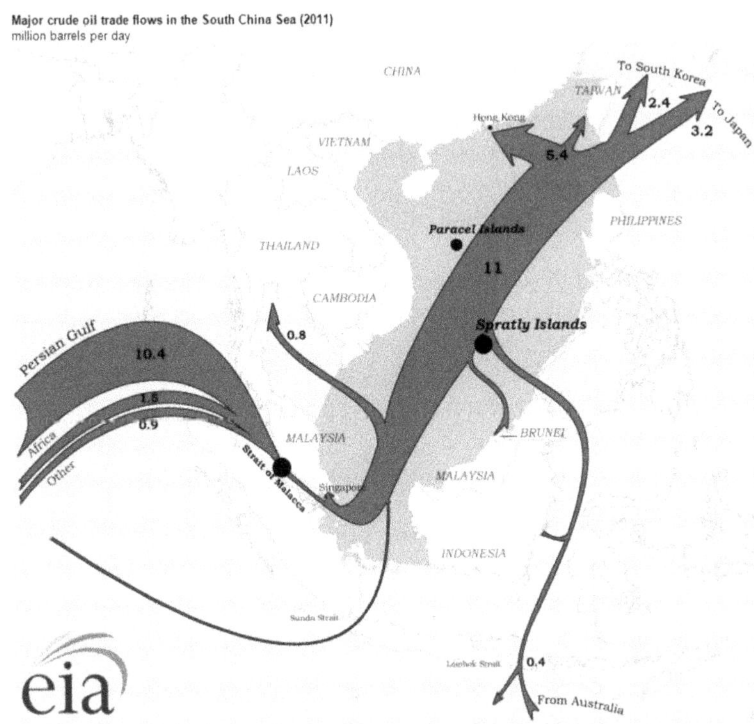

Figure 2.2 Major crude oil trade flows in the SCS
The U.S. Energy Information Administration, available at: www.eia.gov/countries/analysisbriefs/South_China_Sea/south_china_sea.pdf (accessed March 1, 2014).

It should be noted that many of these features of the SCS were either absent or not built into the Chinese policy elites' conception of the SCS when the issue was first raised in the diplomatic arena in the early 1950s. Rather, as will be demonstrated in this book, they were gradually incorporated into Beijing's evolving understanding of the SCS dispute.

The PRC's original claims to the South China Sea

China's original claims of sovereignty in the South China Sea mainly focused on the land features in the South China Sea. The official position of the People's Republic of China (PRC) on sovereignty in the South China Sea was first revealed in a lengthy statement issued before the opening of the 1951 San Francisco Peace Conference. Speaking in Beijing, Zhou Enlai, as China's Foreign Minister, stated that:

> The Draft Treaty stipulated that Japan should renounce all rights to Nan Wei (Spratly) Island and Xi Sha Islands (Paracels), but again deliberately makes no mention of the problem of restoring sovereignty over them. As a matter of fact, just like all the Nan Sha Islands (Spratlys), ZhongSha Islands (Macclesfield Bank) and Dong Sha Islands (Pratas), Xi Sha Islands and Nan Wei Island have always been China's territory.[4]

At the San Francisco Conference, the Vietnamese delegation asserted its claims to sovereignty over the Paracel and Spratly Islands. Since Beijing was not invited to attend the San Francisco Conference, the Soviet delegation conveyed China's position on its behalf, stating that:

> Japan recognizes the full sovereignty of the Chinese People's Republic over Manchuria, the Island of Taiwan with all islands adjacent to it, the Penghu Islands, the Dong Sha Islands, as well as over the islands of Xi Sha and ZhongSha, and Nan Sha Islands including the Spratly, and renounces all right, title and claim to the territories named herein.[5]

Another authoritative document expressing China's claims to the SCS is the *Declaration on Territorial Sea* (hereinafter the *1958 Declaration*). Issued on September 4, 1958, it marks a milestone of domestic legal development regarding the Law of the Sea prior to the PRC's entry into UNCLOS III. In this legislation, the Chinese government laid sovereign claim to the four island groups in the South China Sea as well as a 12 nautical miles belt of territorial sea surrounding them, using the straight baseline method for measuring territorial seas. Article 1 of the *1958 Declaration* reads:

> The breadth of the territorial sea of the People's Republic of China shall be twelve nautical miles. This provision applies to all territories of the People's Republic of China, including the Chinese mainland and its

> coastal islands, as well as Taiwan and its surrounding islands, the Penghu islands, the Dong Sha Islands, the Xi Sha Islands, the Zhong Sha Islands, the Nan Sha Islands and all other islands belonging to China ...[6]

Moreover, the Chinese government tried to bolster its claims by displaying historical evidence. In 1951, a *People's China* commentary claimed that records in Chinese history regarding the Paracel and Spratly Islands "dated back to the Sung Dynasty." In 1956, a professor of history at Beijing University, Shao Xunzheng, put forward a systemic historical argument supporting China's claim of sovereignty over islands in the South China Sea, also published in *People's China*.[7]

It is worth noting that in the pre-1971 period, the legal developments of the maritime regime had already started to influence China's legal position regarding its maritime sovereignty.[8] The PRC's claim of a 12 nautical miles territorial belt as reflected in the *1958 Declaration* was informed by an emerging trend in the international maritime sphere calling for wider territorial waters beyond the traditional 3 nautical miles limit.[9]

In most maps produced in the 1950s, including those used in schoolbooks for the following decades, claims to the South China Sea were drawn in the form of a U-shape line, also called the Dashed Line or the Dotted Line. It was this map that ignited heated debate in 2009 when China submitted it to the Commission on the Limits of the Continental Shelf (CLCS). A thorough discussion of this map and China's understanding of its legal implications, altered under the influence of the legal dynamics of the LOS regime, will be provided in subsequent chapters. Suffice it to say that the Dashed Line, formalized in 1947, was the line used by the Nationalist government to delineate China's maritime boundary.[10] From the analysis above, it can be concluded that at least in the 1950s and the 1960s, the map was not a salient issue. the Dashed Line was circulated with little public elaboration of its legal implications, either from the government or the academia, partially because the central government in Beijing never invoked the map to make or support its claims. In this period, the government did not pay much attention or carefully contemplate, in legal terms, what the vast area of waters enclosed in the Dashed Line meant to its SCS claim.

As a matter of fact, Beijing's actual practice in the pre-1971 period appears to contradict the claim put forward by some commentators that China regarded the waters enclosed in the boundary line as "internal waters." For instance, Article 1 of the *1958 Declaration* cited earlier, states that "the Dong Sha Islands, the Xi Sha Islands, the Zhong Sha Islands, the Nan Sha Islands ... are *separated from the mainland and its coastal islands by the high seas*" (emphasis added) The existence of high seas negates the possibility that the waters enclosed by the maritime boundary line on the map were given the status of "internal waters." From May 1959 to December 1971, China issued more than 200 warnings to the United States for violating the territorial airspace and waters of the Paracel islands.[11] These warnings did not mention any violation of internal waters. Instead, they were issued only when US jets and vessels intruded into sea areas within the 12 nautical miles limit of the Paracel islands.

Claims and counter-claims between China and other disputants

In the pre-1971 period, the SCS was the subject of a dispute mainly between two governments: the government of the People's Republic of China and the government of the Republic of Vietnam (RVN).[12]

China versus Vietnam

The claims and counter-claims between the governments of the PRC and the RVN overlapped two groups of land features commonly called the Paracel Island group and the Spratly Island group. Both governments based their claims on historical argument. That is, both claimed discovery and historical uses of these land features.

Vietnam's claim to these SCS islands was first made internationally as early as 1951. During the San Francisco Conference, the Vietnamese delegation delivered its claim to the Paracel and Spratly Islands, which was protested by the Soviet delegation on behalf of the PRC. The Paracels consist of two separate island groups, the Crescent (Yongle) Group in the southwest and the Amphitrite (Xuande) Group in the northeast (see Figure 2.3). Traditionally, Chinese fishermen from Hainan operated in the Paracels' surrounding waters, using many of the islands in the Crescent Group as shelters. Despite the Vietnamese declaration, this situation remained unchallenged in the years following the San Francisco Conference.

The RVN began to alter the status quo in early 1959.[13] In February 1959, the RVN's naval forces arrested 82 Chinese fishermen on Duncan Island (Chenghang Dao), which sparked a sharp response from China. The Ministry of Foreign Affairs in Beijing protested that "the South Vietnam Navy illegally violated China's sovereignty and territorial integrity" and reaffirmed that the "Xi Sha (Paracel) Islands are part of China's territory."[14] After the successful eviction of the Chinese fishermen, Saigon consolidated its hold of the Crescent Group, leaving the Paracels divided.

China protested Vietnam's provocation in the Spratlys, too. In the summer of 1956, the RVN government sent naval units to some of the Spratly Islands, planting flags and setting up landmarks to symbolize its occupation. China strongly protested, claiming that the Spratlys were a part of Chinese territory to be used as a baseline from which to draw the 12 nautical miles territorial sea boundary.[15]

China versus the Philippines

The Philippine government did not make any official claims to the SCS in the pre-1971 period. The first official move to assert sovereignty over some islands

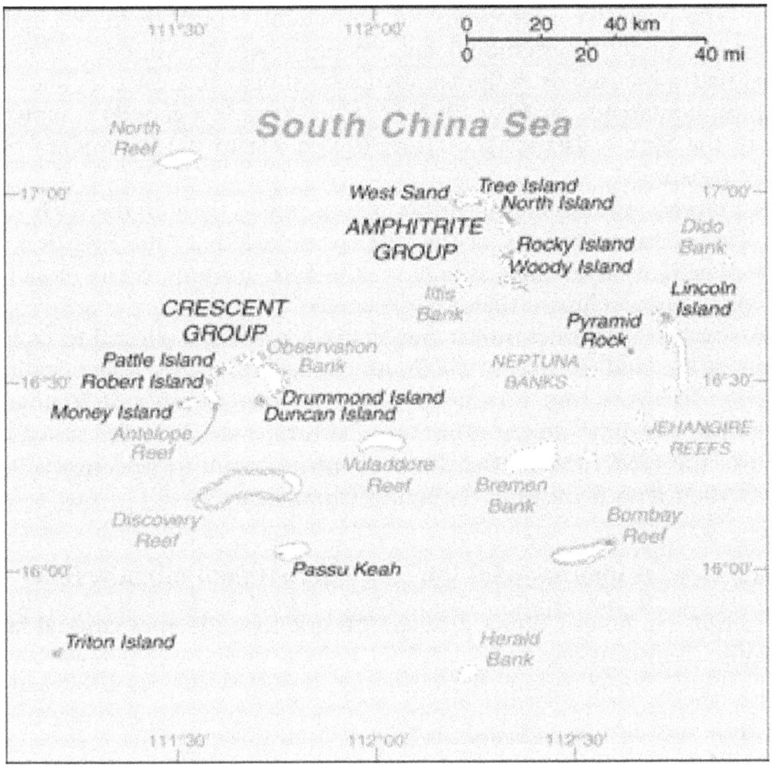

Figure 2.3 The Paracel Islands
Central Intelligence Agency, "World Factbook," available at: www.cia.gov/library/publications/the-world-factbook/geos/pf.html (accessed January 1, 2014).

in the Spratly group was made on July 10, 1971. In the pre-1971 period, most exploration in the South China Sea was conducted by private adventurers, to which the Filipino government issued a number of expressions of interest in non-specific terms. The most famous one was Kalayaan. On May 11, 1956, Tomas A. Cloma, a Filipino lawyer and businessman, explored the Spratly area and asserted ownership by discovery and occupation of 33 islands, reefs, sand bars, and cays. He established a new state named Freedomland (Kalayyan), which encompassed most islands in the Spratly group.[16]

The Filipino government remained restrained in its endorsement of Cloma's claim. In the meantime, it attempted to take advantage of this opportunity to make legal preparations for possible future claims. Vice President Carlos Garcia of the Philippines replied to Cloma's letter saying that the Department of Foreign Affairs regarded all the islands, islets, cays, and shoals within the boundaries of Freedomland, "with the exclusion of the seven-island group known internationally as the Spratlys," as *res nullius.* Then, with respect to the territories he described as unowned, Garcia said that Filipino nationals had as much right to exploit them commercially as any other national "so long as the exclusive sovereignty of any country over them has not been established" under international law. In other words, Manila attempted to suggest that some islands in the Spratly group should be treated as unoccupied. At a press conference on May 19, 1956, Garcia made a general comment that some of the Spratly Islands should rightly belong to the Philippines because of their proximity.

The Filipino government's position was protested by both the RVN and the PRC. The Foreign Ministry of the PRC protested that "the PRC has undisputed sovereignty over these islands ... the PRC government is intolerant of any type of encroachment under any excuses."[17]

This suggests two conclusions: one, that while Manila alluded to its interest in some of the land features in the South China Sea, the legal justification was based on discovery and proximity. Two, just like China and Vietnam, the Philippines was only interested in land features. Indeed, it was not until the advent of the UNCLOS III that these countries began to be concerned about areas beyond land features in the South China Sea.

China's view of international law and international organizations

This section examines China's original attitude towards international law and international institutions.

A socialist view of international law

Many pioneering scholars of Chinese foreign policy have pointed out that during the early years of the Cold War, socialist states in general tended to perceive traditional norms of international law as originating from capitalist states in order to meet the needs of a capitalist world order. Marxist-Leninist theology, to which the Chinese Communist party adheres, inserted class ideology into the PRC's view of the international law of the early days. Arthur Steiner observes that "Communist China is motivated by a revolutionary ethic thoroughly incompatible with the existing structure of international law and relations."[18] In the "great debate" (a symposium organized by the Shanghai Law Association and the East China Institute of Political Science and Law in 1958), participants reached the agreement that "the law which at present adjusts the different relations between states with different types of social systems is a kind of general international law."[19] However, they argued that it was also necessary to distinguish between a bourgeois science of international law, fabricated to serve the foreign policy of capitalism, and a proletariat science of international law. This distinction based on ruling class was reflected in a critique by the eminent Chinese international lawyer, Hua Xiang:

> Principles and rules of international law since Hugo Grotius' time reflected the interests and demands of the bourgeoisie, the colonialists and in particular, of the imperialists. The big and strong powers have long been

> bullying the small and weak nations, sometimes even resorting to armed aggression. International law has often been used by the imperialists and hegemonists as a means to carry out aggression, oppression and exploitation and to further their reactionary foreign policies.[20]

Although not completely rejecting international law, China viewed international law as heavily tainted by European imperialism and capitalism. Therefore, it determined to strive for "peace and democracy" in the international law regime in order to defend the proletariat and all the laboring populations in the world and to guarantee international equality among states, especially laboring countries and the Third World.

China's changing view of international organizations and its Third World identity

Before entering the United Nations, the PRC had extremely limited interaction with major international regimes, including the maritime regime. This is mainly due to the fact that most Western countries only recognized the Nationalist regime in Taiwan, rather than the Communist regime in mainland China, as the legitimate representative of the Chinese people in the UN and its subordinate organizations. The Communist government in Beijing had established diplomatic relationships with only a handful of countries, mostly in the Socialist Bloc.[21] Constant rejection of its attempts at membership of the UN frustrated China, leading to a dismissive view of the UN among the political elites in Beijing.[22]

Concurrently, an important trend was unfolding in the international arena in this period. Thanks to the two world wars, which had significantly weakened the colonial European powers, a wave of decolonization gained momentum and yielded a series of newly independent countries. India and Pakistan became independent in 1947; Burma and Ceylon (Sri Lanka) in 1948; Laos and Indonesia in 1949; Libya in 1951; Cambodia in 1953; Egypt in 1954 after the Suez Crisis; Tunisia, Morocco, and Sudan in 1956; Iraq in 1958; Nigeria and Benin in 1960; and Uganda, Rwanda, and Algeria in 1962, to name but a few. Consequently, enthusiastic internationalist leaders from those newly independent countries coordinated themselves in an effort to push for a new world order and assert their place on the international stage.[23]

China sympathized with the efforts made by these newly independent countries in pushing for a fair international world order. In the two decades preceding its entry into the UN, Beijing set as one of its major foreign policy goals cultivating a fraternal bond with these Third World countries. The 1955 Bandung Conference was a milestone in Beijing's early effort in this regard. As one commentator wrote, the "Bandung conference marked the initiation of a policy of Chinese Communist cooperation with the states of Afro-Asia."[24] It was from deliberations in the Bandung Conference that Beijing came to realize that a united force was gradually emerging in the Third World, capable of challenging the dominant role of Western powers in the arena of international politics, a view further strengthened by the development of the Non-Aligned Movement (NAM)[25] and the Group of 77.[26] Through its interaction with these Third World countries, Beijing cultivated for itself a Third World identity.

These efforts eventually amounted to a harvest of reciprocal support from the Third World regarding the proposal for the PRC's entry into the United Nations in 1971.[27] Countries belonging to the Third World rallied their voting power around the Albanian Resolution regarding the PRC's entry into the UN and the expulsion of the Republic of China, support which was strong enough to finally overcome the obstacles set out by the United States and its allies.[28]

As a result, Beijing's view of international organizations also changed accordingly. While its dismissive perception of the major international organizations as tools of Western powers was not so easily dispelled, Beijing began to see hopeful opportunities for these organizations to transform into something more balanced and fair as the influence of the united Third World grew. This revised view directed Beijing to consciously align itself with the Third World countries when it began to participate in the third UN conference on drafting a new Law of the Sea Convention.

In conclusion, before 1971, geopolitical reality commanded that the PRC craved an international order based on equality and fairness and gradually perceived itself as part of the Third World camp, a fact that set the initial tone for China's engagement with the international maritime regime beginning in 1971. Given the geopolitical realities, the Chinese leaders definitely wanted to see changes in the maritime regime to alter the traditional maritime order dominated by Western powers. To this end, they initially chose to align with the Third World in an attempt to balance Western domination in the UNCLOS III and adopted a combative posture against the United States consistent with domestic propaganda on anti-imperialism. However, as we will see in Chapter 3, geopolitics did not determine the policy consequences or the outcome for China on its own. Due to a lack of necessary knowledge and expertise, in the first few years of its participation in the UNCLOS III, the Chinese leadership was supportive of almost all policy proposals from developing countries, being unaware of the possibility that many of the policy proposals they supported, once realized, might actually work against China's maritime interests. It was through years of negotiation and interaction with experts and delegations from other countries that the Chinese delegation gradually accumulated knowledge on modern maritime governance, learned the implications of different policy proposals, and became more cautious and conscious in making choices and formulating its policy position to safeguard its own maritime interests.

Conclusion

This chapter makes two observations regarding the impact of the evolving Law of the Sea regime on the PRC's claims to the South China Sea. First, although the Beijing government was excluded from the first two conferences negotiating a new overarching maritime order for the world's oceans, it was not completely unaware of the legal developments within the Law of the Sea regime. Rather, the Chinese leadership was quite sensitive to the changing dynamics in the maritime realm, as demonstrated in the 1958 *Declaration on Territorial Sea*. By adding territorial seas of 12 nautical miles to its South China Sea claims, the PRC made its first attempt to adjust its South China Sea policy in accordance with the evolving international maritime law.

The second observation concerns the legal basis of the SCS disputes before the UNCLOS III officially started. As the analysis above shows, China and Vietnam, two major competing parties in the SCS, used very similar, if not identical, legal reasoning to justify their claims. Both governments claimed sovereignty over the Paracels and the Spratlys on the ground of general principles in international law concerning territory acquisition and documented historical records and evidence to support their respective claims. The Philippines did not make official claims to the South China Sea, but the government supported private expeditions of its citizens in a bid to establish title to the Spratlys, which is a common practice of territory acquisition – discovery and occupation – recognized in general international law.[29]

The convening of the UNCLOS III, as the following chapters show, certainly changed this situation. The legal basis on which these three countries asserted their respective claims began to change, so did the composition of claimants as new disputing parties such as Malaysia and Brunei joined in the dispute.

Notes

1 United States Energy Information Administration, "The SCS Region," available at: www.eia.gov/todayinenergy/detail.cfm?id=10671 (accessed March 1, 2014).
2 See Daniel Y. Coulter, "SCS Fisheries: Countdown to Calamity," *Contemporary Southeast Asia* 17, no. 4 (1996): 371–388.
3 South China Sea, "Introduction of the SCS," available at: www.southchinasea.org/introduction/ (accessed March 1, 2014).
4 *Supplement to People's China*, September 1, 1951, 1–6, cited in Lo Chi-Kin, *China's Policy toward Territorial Disputes: The Case of the SCS Islands* (New York: Routledge, 1998), 50, endnote 4.
5 San Francisco Conference for the Conclusion and Signature of Treaty of Peace with Japan (1951), Records 94305–6010 (Stanford, CA: Hoover Institution Archives), 119.
6 See Appendix A for the English version of the 1958 Declaration.
7 Xunzheng Shao, "Chinese Islands in the South China Sea," *People's China* 1956 (7): 25–27, in Chinese.
8 Zerong Liu, "A Major Step to Protect China's Sovereign Rights," *Peking Review* 29 (September 16, 1958): 12, in Chinese.
9 The legal development of the territorial sea regime will be reviewed in Chapter 3.
10 The history of the Dashed Line is expounded in the White Paper of Chinese Foreign Ministry on *China Adheres to the Position of Settling Through Negotiation the Relevant Disputes Between China and the Philippines in the South China Sea*, July

13, 2016, available at: www.fmprc.gov.cn/nanhai/eng/sn hwtlcwj_1/t1380615.htm (accessed July 31, 2017).

11 "Xi Sha and Nan Sha Have Been Chinese Territory since Ancient Times," *People's Daily*, April 7, 1980.

12 In this period, there were two Chinese governments: one was the communist regime in Beijing and the other was the Nationalist government in Taipei, and each claimed to be the legitimate government of China. Since the focus of this research is on the PRC and the two governments made identical claims to the SCS, I only count the government of the PRC. With regard to the RVN, it faced domestic challenges from the Viet Minh, which in the 1970s successfully toppled the RVN regime and became the only legitimate government of Vietnam.

13 M. Taylor Fravel, *Strong Borders, Secure Nation: Cooperation and Conflict in China's Territorial Disputes* (Princeton, NJ: Princeton University Press, 2008), 274.

14 Shicun Wu, *Collection of Documents on the South China Sea Issue* (Haikou: Hainan Press, 2000), 54–55, in Chinese.

15 Min Gyo Koo, *Island Disputes and Maritime Regime Building in East Asia: Between a Rock and a Hard Place* (New York: Springer, 2009), 140.

16 A good summary account of Cloma and other adventurers' activities can be found in Marwyn S. Samuels, *Contest for the South China Sea* (New York: Methuen, 1982), 81–86.

17 Chinese Foreign Ministry, *Papers of Outward Relations of People's Republic of China*, vol. 4 (Beijing: Shijie Zhishi Press, 1958), 61–62, in Chinese.

18 H. Arthur Steiner, "The Mainsprings of Chinese Communist Foreign Policy," *The American Journal of International Law* 44, no. 1 (1950): 89.

19 Byron N. Tzou, *China and International Law: The Boundary Disputes* (New York: Praeger, 1990), 9.

20 Hua Xiang, cited in Ann E. Kent, *Beyond Compliance* (Stanford, CA: Stanford University Press, 2007), 40.

21 Jerome A. Cohen and Hungdah Chiu, eds., *People's China and International Law* (Princeton, NJ: Princeton University Press, 1974), 1400–1401.

22 Kent, *Beyond Compliance*, 47.

23 "Bandung Conference of 1955 and the resurgence of Asia and Africa," *Daily News*, April 21, 2005, available at: www.dailynews.lk/2005/04/21/fea01.htm (accessed May 1, 2012).

24 Tareq Y. Ismael, "The People's Republic of China and Africa," *The Journal of Modern African Studies* 9, no. 4 (1971): 507.

25 The NAM played a crucial role in rallying support for the PRC's entry into the UN from its member countries. The issue of the PRC's legitimate seat in the UN was on the agendas of the first three NAM conferences, even though China was not a member of the NAM.

26 Another important development in the global arena during the demise of colonialism was the formation of the Group of 77. The Group of 77 (G-77) was established on June 15, 1964 by 77 developing countries signatories of the "Joint Declaration of the Seventy-Seven Countries" issued at the end of the first session of the United Nations Conference on Trade and Development (UNCTAD) in Geneva. It represented a unified force of the Third World countries in international negotiations in "creating a new and just economic order." See Group of 77, "Joint Declaration of the Seventy-Seven Developing Countries Made at the Conclusion of the UN Conference on Trade and Development," available at: www.g77.org/doc/Joint%20Declaration.html (accessed May 1, 2012).

27 United Nations, "Restoration of the Lawful Rights of the People's Republic of China in the United Nations," UN document A/RES/2758(XXVI), Resolution 2758, available at: www.un.org/en/ga/search/view_doc.asp?symbol=A/RES/2758%28XXVI%29&Lang=E&Area=RESOLUTION (accessed March 1, 2014).

28 A brief description of the process of the formation and final voting of Resolution 2758 (XXVI) is available on the website of the repertory of practice of UN organs at: http://legal.un.org/repertory/art3/english/rep_supp5_vol1-art3_e.pdf (accessed March 1, 2014).

29 In contemporary international law, methods of acquisition of a clear title to territory include effective administration (often called occupation), cession through treaty, or prescription. International law recognizes acquisition of title to territory belonging to no-one (*terra nullius*) through first discovery, which establishes an inchoate title. This title can be converted to a more complete title through effective administration. See R. Y. Jennings, *The Acquisition of Territory in International Law* (Manchester: Manchester University Press, 1962), 6–7, 16–27.

Bibliography

Chinese Foreign Ministry. 1958. *Papers of Outward Relations of People's Republic of China*, vol. 4, Shijie Zhishi Press, Beijing (in Chinese).

Chinese Foreign Ministry. 2016. *China Adheres to the Position of Settling Through Negotiation the Relevant Disputes Between China and the Philippines in the South China Sea*, July 13, available at: www.fmprc.gov.cn/nanhai/eng/snhwtlcwj_1/t1380615.htm (accessed July 31, 2017).

Cohen, J.A. and Chiu, H.D. (eds.) 1974. *People's China and International Law*, Princeton University Press, Princeton, NJ.

Coulter, D.Y. 1996. "SCS Fisheries: Countdown to Calamity," *Contemporary Southeast Asia*, vol. 17, no. 4, pp. 371–388.

Fravel, M.T. 2008. *Strong Borders, Secure Nation: Cooperation and Conflict in China's Territorial Disputes*, Princeton University Press, Princeton, NJ.

Group of 77. 1964. "Joint Declaration of the Seventy-Seven Developing Countries Made at the Conclusion of the UN Conference on Trade and Development," available at: www.g77.org/doc/Joint%20Declaration.html (accessed May 1, 2012).

Ismael, T.Y. 1971. "The People's Republic of China and Africa," *The Journal of Modern African Studies*, vol. 9, no. 4, pp. 507–529.

Jennings, R.Y. 1962. *The Acquisition of Territory in International Law*, Manchester University Press, Manchester.

Kent, A.E. 2007. *Beyond Compliance*, Stanford University Press, Stanford, CA.

Koo, M.G. 2009. *Island Disputes and Maritime Regime Building in East Asia: Between a Rock and a Hard Place*, Springer, New York.

Liu, Z. 1958. "A Major Step to Protect China's Sovereign Rights," *Peking Review*, vol. 29, September 16, p. 12 (in Chinese).

Lo, C.K. 1989. *China's Policy toward Territorial Disputes: The Case of the South China Sea Islands*, Routledge, New York.

Samuels, M.S. 1982. *Contest for the South China Sea*, Methuen, New York.

Shao, X. 1956. "Chinese Islands in the South China Sea," *People's China*, vol. 7, pp. 25–27 (in Chinese).

Stanford University. *San Francisco Conference for the Conclusion and Signature of Treaty of Peace with Japan 1951, Records 94305–96010*, Hoover Institution Archives, Stanford, CA.

Steiner, H.A. 1950. "The Mainsprings of Chinese Communist Foreign Policy," *The American Journal of International Law*, vol. 44, no. 1, pp. 69–99.

Tzou, B.N. 1990. *China and International Law: The Boundary Disputes*, Praeger, New York.

United Nations. n.d. "Restoration of the Lawful Rights of the People's Republic of China in the United Nations," UN document A/RES/2758(XXVI), Resolution 2758, available at: www.un.org/en/ga/search/view_doc.asp?symbol=A/RES/2758%28XXVI%29&Lang=E&Area=RESOLUTION (accessed March 1, 2014).

United States Energy Information Administration. n.d. "The SCS Region," www.eia.gov/todayinenergy/detail.cfm?id=10671 (accessed March 1, 2014).

Wu, S.C. 2001. *Collection of Documents Relating to South China Sea Issues*, Hainan Publishing House, Haikou, China (in Chinese).

Wu, S.C. and Zou, K.Y. (eds.) 2013. *Securing the Safety of Navigation in East Asia: Legal and Political Dimensions*, Chandos Publishing, Oxford.

Yu, S.K.T. 1989. "Who Owns the Paracels and Spratlys? An Evaluation of the Nature and Legal Basis of the Conflicting Territorial Claims," *Chinese Yearbook of International Law and Affairs*, vol. 9, pp. 1–28.

Zou, K.Y. 2010. "International Law in the Chinese Domestic Context," *Valparaiso University Law Review*, vol. 44, no. 3, pp. 935–956.

Zou, K.Y. 2012. "China's U-Shaped Line in the South China Sea Revisited," *Ocean Development and International Law*, vol. 43, no. 1, pp. 18–34.

Zou, K.Y. 2015. "Managing Biodiversity Conservation in the Disputed Maritime Areas: The Case of the South China Sea," *Journal of International Wildlife Law and Policy*, vol. 18, no. 2, pp. 97–109.

Zou, K.Y. 2017. "Navigation in the South China Sea: Why Still an Issue?," *International Journal of Marine and Coastal Law*, vol. 32, no. 2, pp. 243–267.

3 China in the UNCLOS III era

Where changes began

Chapter 1 and Chapter 2 introduced the theoretical and historical background to the South China Sea disputes and China's policy towards the South China Sea. This chapter and subsequent chapters seek to trace in chronological order changes and adjustments in China's policy towards the South China Sea. This chapter consists of four parts. The first section provides a short overview of the history of the Law of the Sea with an emphasis on a series of international attempts to codify the LOS in the twentieth century. The second part explores the question of how participation in the negotiation process of the third UN Conference on the Law of the Sea (UNCLOS III) and the maritime regime in general affected China's conceptual and practical positions in respect to the SCS dispute. The third section looks at the military confrontation between China and Vietnam that occurred in this period and identifies the factors shaping the decision-making of central leaders in Beijing. The final section analyses the concrete ways through which the maritime regime exerted its influence in the UNCLOS III period, independently and jointly with geopolitical flux.

A historical overview of the LOS regime

Mare Clausum *versus* Mare Liberum

Though it is beyond the scope of this book to discuss in detail the historical evolution of the Law of the Sea, it is still worth devoting a few lines to the basic principles of the Law of the Sea and the controversies which in a great part propelled the changing course of the modern LOS. "The bulk and essence of maritime law during the last more than two centuries can be summed up in the simple phrase, "Freedom of the Seas" (*Mare Liberum*)."[1] *Mare Liberum* is a concept propounded by the seventeenth-century Dutch jurist, Hugo Grotius. He used the idea of freedom of the seas to defend his country's right to navigate in the Indian Ocean and Eastern seas and to trade with India and the East Indies (Southeast Asian Islands), over which Spain and Portugal asserted a commercial monopoly as well as political dominion. As competition over maritime trade continued among European powers, especially between the Dutch and the English, the British came to realize that *Mare Liberum* no longer benefited their expansive maritime interests as they had the power to assert control over the seas. John Selden, a British scholar and statesman, argued that the sea was in practice as capable of appropriation as terrestrial territory. Backed by the powerful British navy, *Mare Clausum* as maritime law dominated Europe for the next 200 years.

The advent of the Industrial Revolution in the late eighteenth century altered the fate of *Mare Clausum* and revived the principle of *Mare Liberum*. As maritime European powers benefited from commercial prosperity, free trade, and overseas colonies, they were no longer satisfied with pretensions to sovereignty which obstructed their access to the vast unexplored areas of the world.[2] They finally reached consensus on a formula that combined *Mare Clausum* and *Mare Liberum* in the late nineteenth century, concluding that the vast seas were demarcated into "territorial waters" where sovereignty claims covered a 3-mile strip extending seawards from one country's land, within which cannon range could effectively protect it, and *res communis*, or high seas, where freedom of navigation was granted.[3]

At this point in time, the law governing the sea was composed of a very primitive commitment to a vague freedom of the seas, which said nothing about other aspects of rule over the sea. European powers constantly challenged each other over a number of marine issues. Freedom of fisheries, for instance, was one of the major causes of three wars between England and Holland and continued to be a subject of serious dispute among Europeans. In 1909, Russia's unilateral decision to extend its jurisdiction from the traditional 3-mile limit to 12 nautical miles provoked strong protests from other maritime powers. Another issue derived from the primitive nature of the Law of the Sea gained salience in the late nineteenth and early twentieth centuries pertaining to lack of regulation on activities in the high seas. "Beyond a limited maritime belt, the vast areas of the ocean – more than 70 per cent of the globe – remained a *legal vacuum*, an area of no law beyond what are referred to as a few rules of the road."[4] The consequence of this legal vacuum is elaborated by R.P. Anand:

> Freedom of the seas meant essentially non-regulation and *laissez faire* which was in the interests of the big maritime powers. This law, or rather lack of law under the freedom of the seas doctrine, was often used in the nineteenth century by European powers to threaten small states, to get concessions from them, or simply to subjugate them.[5]

Three international attempts at redrafting the LOS in the twentieth century

The 1930 League of Nations Codification Conference

Disagreements among traditional maritime powers and between traditional maritime powers and smaller coastal states led to the first major inter-governmental attempt to codify the law under the auspices of the League of Nations in 1930.[6] This conference was held in The Hague from March 13 to April 12, 1930.[7] Due to differences in position between traditional maritime powers which insisted on the maximization of open seas and smaller states deeply concerned about their coastal interests, the conference failed to reach agreement.[8] However, it served as a forum for open debate of maritime jurisdiction to which members for first time were not limited to traditional maritime powers (42 countries participated), marking the beginning of a series of attempts at the international level to redraft the traditional maritime order.[9] Table 3.1 presents a summary of the four international LOS conferences in the twentieth century.

1958–1960: The first and second UN conferences on the Law of the Sea[10]

The years following 1930 witnessed two important trends that cast doubt on the validity of the old LOS. First, smaller coastal countries' requests to extend their jurisdiction beyond the 3-mile limit gathered momentum. As of 1960, 36 countries made unilateral claims of a national jurisdiction wider than 3 miles. For example, countries like Greece, Italy, Spain, Yugoslavia, India, and Thailand claimed a 6-mile strip. Countries with 12-mile limit claims included Bulgaria, the PRC, the Soviet Union, Libya, Iraq, Sudan, Indonesia, and Ethiopia. El Salvador made the most extreme claim: 200 miles.

Table 3.1 Summary of four international LOS conferences in the twentieth century

Conference name	*Date*	*Participants*	*Results*
League of Nations Codification Conference	1930	47 states	No formal written agreement
UNCLOS I	1958	86 states	1. The Convention on the Territorial Sea and the Contiguous Zone 2. The Convention on the Continental Shelf 3. The Convention on the High Seas 4. The Convention on Fishing and Conservation of the Living Resources of the High Seas 5. Optional Protocol of Signature Concerning the Compulsory Settlement of Disputes
UNCLOS II	1960	88 states	Final Act of the Second United Nations Conference on the Law of the Sea
UNCLOS III	1973–1982	160 states	The United Nations Convention on the Law of the Sea

The technology boom in the wake of World War II accounted for a second development in the international political realm: a new agenda for the international maritime regime. "From oil to tin, diamonds to gravel, metals to fish, the resources of the sea are enormous. The reality of their exploitation grows day by day as technology opens new ways to tap those resources."[11] The emergence of new technology directed international attention to a historically untouched area: the seabed and sea soil. Truman's "Proclamation on U.S. Policy Concerning Natural Resources of Seabed and Fisheries on High Seas" introduced the concept of "continental shelf" in 1945. In this proclamation, President Truman claimed that

> having concern for the urgency of conserving and prudently utilizing its natural resources, the Government of the United States regards the natural resources of the subsoil and sea bed of the continental shelf beneath the high seas but contiguous to the coasts of the United States as appertaining to the United States, subject to its jurisdiction and control.

Latin American countries took Truman's proclamation one step further to support their extension of territorial waters.[12] They began to coordinate and unite their efforts in pushing for a new LOS on a regional level through the Inter-American Council of Jurists (IACJ). The pioneering efforts of these Latin American countries permitted them to play a leading role in the three LOS conferences.

The first and second UN conferences (UNCLOS I and II) had more than 80 participant countries.[13] The two conferences resulted in the 1958 Geneva Conventions on the Law of the Sea, comprising four conventions and an optional protocol: the Convention on the Territorial Sea and the Contiguous Zone (CTS); the Convention on the High Seas (CHS); the Convention on Fishing and Conservation of the Living Resources of the High Seas (CFCLR); the Convention on the Continental Shelf (CCS); and the Optional Protocol of Signature concerning the Compulsory Settlement of Disputes (OPSD).[14] The Geneva Conventions reflected a strong attempt to timely incorporate the changes wrought by the technology boom into the Law of the Sea, especially the inclusion of many new maritime concepts such as natural prolongation, contiguous zone, straight baseline, and explorability. However, the divergent interests of traditional maritime powers and developing coastal countries were too diverse to reach a compromise. Many participants were not satisfied with the outcome and the conventions were not unanimously ratified. According to Barry Buzan's observation, the bargaining power of the Third World in these two conferences was relatively weaker than the traditional maritime powers, and the latter's position dominated the final outcome of the conferences.[15]

The third UN Conference on the Law of the Sea (UNCLOS III)

Informal negotiations continued in the years leading up to the convening of the third LOS conference. It was realized that another conference was needed to take on the urgent challenge of establishing a holistic and systemic LOS to govern the increasingly sophisticated uses of the oceans in a peaceful and fair manner and alleviate growing inter-state contentions over a host of maritime issues left unsettled in UNCLOS I and II. The Sea Bed Committee was established in 1967 by the United Nations General Assembly following a proposal by Dr. Arvid Pardo, the Maltese ambassador. Through debate over the internationalization of the use of the seabed and other maritime matters, states came to the recognition that various parts of the LOS were inextricably linked and that a review of the whole LOS was needed. It was agreed in 1970 in General Assembly Resolution 2570 to convene UNCLOS III with the task of producing a comprehensive LOS Convention. The conference was convened in New York in 1973.

> It ended nine years later with the adoption in 1982 of a constitution for the seas – the United Nations Convention on the Law of the Sea. During those nine years, shuttling back and forth between New York and Geneva, representatives of more than 160 sovereign States sat down and discussed the issues, bargained and traded national rights and obligations in the course of the marathon negotiations that produced the Convention.[16]

The UN Convention on the Law of the Sea was approved with 130 in favor, 4 against, and 17 abstentions on 10 December 1982. The 1982 UNCLOS came into force in 1994, twelve months after Guyana became the 60th state to ratify the treaty. As of June 23, 2016, 168 states and the European Union had ratified the UNCLOS.[17]

China's interaction with the LOS regime

China's participation in the UNCLOS III: initial performance in the conference

China joined the UNCLOS III immediately after its entry into the UN. Its maiden speech was made on March 3, 1972, only four months after its UN debut. Representatives submitted a total of three working papers: (1) Working Paper on Sea Area within the Limits of National Jurisdiction on July 16, 1973; (2) Working Paper on Marine Scientific Research on July 19, 1973; and (3) Working Paper on General Principles for the International Sea Area on August 6, 1973.

The first Working Paper comprised three sections: (1) the territorial sea; (2) Exclusive Economic Zones (EEZ); and (3) the Continental Shelf (CS).[18] In general, China did not support the idea of a universal breadth of territorial seas. While China believed it was a state's sovereign right to lay its own claim regarding national jurisdiction over the sea, it supported a regional unified breadth for coastal states in the same sea area through equal consultation in accordance with principles of mutual respect for sovereignty and territorial integrity, equality, and reciprocity. For EEZ and CS, China suggested that EEZ should be jointly decided by the adjacent or opposite coastal states based on consultation. China also addressed the issue of innocent passage in this paper, claiming that only non-military ships enjoy innocent passage through territorial seas.

The second Working Paper dealt with marine scientific research, in which China elucidated its requirements for prior consent for marine scientific research conducted within its national jurisdiction.[19]

The last Working Paper focused on the concept of the "high seas."[20] In this paper, China attempted to extend the concept of a common heritage of mankind originally applied to the ocean floor to cover the whole ocean space, including water volumes beyond the limits of national jurisdiction. According to China's proposal, the traditional "high seas" became "international sea areas" and would be governed by some regional and international authority established to regulate fisheries and other living resources.

China was also careful in crafting its image as a Third World country. Two of the Working Papers were co-submitted with countries from the developing world. The second Working Paper was submitted as a draft proposal to subcommittee III by China and 14 other countries, including Algeria, Brazil, Egypt, and the Philippines.[21] The third Working Paper was submitted by China in conjunction with Iraq, Kenya, Yugoslavia, and some Latin American countries as a draft decision.[22] In these Working Papers, China reaffirmed general principles such as the principle of mutual respect for sovereignty and territorial integrity as a kind of support for a wide range of unilateral claims made by developing countries on those technical legal issues.

This pattern prevailed in the numerous statements and speeches made by the Chinese delegation to the conference in the first few years of membership in the UNCLOS III. As illustrated in an excerpt from China's statement at the 25th plenary meeting on July 2, 1974, these statements were excessively lengthy and dominated by two themes: (1) showing unconditional support for proposals and statements submitted by Third World and developing countries; and (2) criticizing the superpowers for hegemonic behavior and obstructing the emergence of a new ocean order:

> *The Third World* countries had now become the main force combating colonialism, *imperialism and hegemony* … the two *super-powers* were now struggling for control of the seas by building up naval forces, establishing military bases, and plundering other countries' off-shore fishery and sea-bed resources … It was to safeguard their national security and coastal resources against such policies of aggression and expansion that a number of *Latin American countries* had declared their sovereignty and national jurisdiction over a zone extending for 200 nautical miles … The *Organization of African Unity* and the Summit Conference of *Non-Aligned Countries* had proclaimed that coastal States had the right to establish such zones … Several just and reasonable proposals relating to the law of

> the sea had been made by developing countries at recent sessions of the United Nations sea-bed Committee ... The legal regime of the sea affected the interests of all countries and should therefore be worked out jointly by all countries on an equal footing. *This delegation supported* those proposals and suggested that they should be the basis for consideration by the Conference. *This delegation supported* the resolution adopted at Algiers in 1973 by the Conference of Heads of State or Government of Non-Aligned Countries stating that the new rules of the law of the sea should eliminate threats to the security of States and ensure respect for their *sovereignty and territorial integrity* ...
>
> (emphasis added)[23]

Changes in China's behavior in the UNCLOS III negotiation

Changes began to take place in both the style and content of China's participation in the UNCLOS III, reflecting the accumulation of policy-related knowledge and experience. In the initial years of its interaction with the conference, as illustrated above, the Chinese delegation often used the debate floor for political purposes, condemning maritime hegemony and proclaiming China an integral part of the Third World.

More importantly, China's pre-1978 statements and the Working Papers were characterized by a lack of specificity. As pointed out by Lo Chi-kin, China's statements were mostly expositions of general principles and short of clear and specific provisions concerning its own claim.[24] Jeanette Greenfield also observed that China was often unaware of legal terminology and legal technicalities. For instance, while the Chinese delegation objected to the passage of foreign military vessels in international straits, they did not make any distinction "between such straits within territorial waters which link two parts of high seas, or territorial sea and high seas." Hence they failed to point out specifically to what they were objecting, as these two types of straits were suitable for different rules and practices.[25]

Starting in 1978, China dropped its relentless attacks on the "two superpowers" and assumed a more professional role at the negotiation table. Throughout the seventh session in 1978, the terms "super-powers," "hegemony," and "imperialism" were mentioned only once, all appearing in one speech delivered in the 98th plenary meeting. In the 109th plenary meeting, the term "super-powers" was replaced by "great powers," which appeared only twice. From the eighth session onward, the Chinese delegation made no reference to any of these terms.

Meanwhile, from 1978 onwards, statements issued by the Chinese delegation became more succinct and focused on specific issues. The language of ideology turned into a language of diplomacy, legal technicality, and specificity, demonstrating a considerable degree of familiarity with maritime legal technicalities. An excerpt from China's statement on the 100th plenary meeting on Wednesday, May 17, 1978 is quoted as an illustration:

> This delegation stressed that the relevant provisions in *articles 212, 221 and 231* should not unduly restrict the right of coastal States to exercise their sovereignty and jurisdiction within their territorial sea and exclusive economic zones in order to *prevent pollution from vessels* ... This delegation believed that the *proposal in document MP/16* not only extended the *scope of applicability* of the relevant safeguard clauses but also introduced substantive changes which restricted the legitimate rights of the coastal State. During the discussion in the Third Committee, this delegation had made it clear that that proposal was unacceptable to it, and its position remained unchanged. As to the question of marine scientific research, this delegation had consistently supported the position of the Group of 77, which was that such research conducted by a foreign country within the exclusive economic zone and along the continental shelf of a coastal State should receive the explicit consent of that State and should comply with the relevant rules and regulations. This delegation therefore *proposed the deletion in articles 248 and 253* of any negative elements which restricted the jurisdiction of the coastal State over the conduct of marine scientific research.

The Chinese delegation was also showing greater prudence on controversial issues. For example, China stood firm in its objection to a compulsory disputes mechanism, stressing that "any compulsory and binding third-party settlement of a dispute concerning sea boundary delimitations must have the consent of all parties to the dispute." At the same time, however, it also left room for further negotiation by suggesting "further consultations on the matter were necessary,"[26] and showed considerable caution by indicating that "the question of the settlement of disputes was very complex and this delegation would like to study the Chairman's report in greater detail before expressing a view."[27]

Moreover, China used to grant unconditional moral support in a vague manner to a wide range of proposals submitted by the Group of 77, the Latin American group, and other regional groups in the Third World camp, but in the years leading up to the conclusion of the LOSC it assumed a more reserved and pragmatic position concerning proposals from the Third World, and only co-submitted one proposal. On April 13, 1982, China joined Algeria, Bahrain, Benin, Cape Verde, the Congo, the Democratic People's Republic of Korea, Democratic Yemen, Djibouti, Egypt, Guinea-Bissau, Iran, Libyan Arab Jamahiriya, Malta, Morocco, Oman, Pakistan, Papua New Guinea, the Philippines, Romania, São Tome and Principe, Sierra Leone, Somalia, Sudan, Suriname, Syria, Uruguay, and Yemen in the amendment to Article 21 of the draft convention, proposing in paragraph 1 to add "security" after "immigration." The fact that China became more selective in choosing to co-sponsor proposals which shared its interests further indicates the familiarity with the rules and principles of the ocean regime as the delegation accumulated experience in the course of participation.

Prior to entry into the UNCLOS III, the PRC had limited interaction with the international maritime regime. It did not participate in the first two international conferences on LOS codification and its knowledge about maritime governance was limited. All the changes identified above were produced by China's direct participation in the LOS conference. As Ling Qing, head of the Chinese delegation to UNCLOS III, recollected in his memoir, knowledge of many legal, technical and practical issues was acquired through informal and off-the-table conversations with delegations from other countries. For instance, a delegation member from a Northern European country once gave Ling Qing a chart calculating the potential costs and benefits to China's maritime interests implied by China's position on EEZ and CS. This chart prompted the Chinese delegation to reconsider their position. It was the first time that the Chinese delegation realized that their long-held position might not serve China's best interests.[28] This type of knowledge was necessary for understanding and practicing maritime sovereignty in light of the new LOS and paved the way for formulating more sophisticated policy in subsequent periods.

Changes in China's SCS policy

Changes also began to unfold outside the LOS conference. First, beginning in 1974, small modifications emerged in the first aspect of China's SCS policy: China's legal position on its sovereignty in the SCS. Lo Chi-kin was among the first to allude to this trend. By comparing China's statement on the Philippines' claim over some of the Spratly Islands in 1971 and its statements from 1974 onwards, he found that by 1971, China was not yet fully aware of the implications of the dispute over the islands in the SCS. However, "its participation in the United Nations Seabed Committee during 1972–1973 certainly changed that," as "from 1974 onwards, claims to maritime space in the South China Sea have always been included in China's statements on the disputes over the Paracel and Spratly Islands."[29]

In July 1971, Huang Yongsheng, then General Chief of Staff, told a visiting North Korean delegation in response to the Filipino government's first official claim to sovereignty over some of the Spratly Islands that:

> The Nansha Islands and the Xisha Islands have always been China's territory. The People's Republic of China has indisputable legitimate sovereignty over these islands and absolutely allows no country to encroach upon this sovereignty right under whatever pretext and in whatever form.[30]

In this speech, there was no mention of maritime rights associated with these islands. From 1974 on, terms like "adjacent sea areas," "surrounding sea areas," or "nearby waters" of the islands, and "the resources thereof," were frequently inserted in China's official claims. On January 11, 1974, China issued a statement responding to the South Vietnamese government's decision in September 1973 to incorporate the Spratly Islands into Phuoc Tuy

Province, marking the first time that China linked territorial claims to offshore islands with maritime space and rights.[31] It stated:

> The government of the People's Republic of China hereby reiterates that the Nansha, Xisha, Zhongsha, and Dongsha Islands are all part of China's territory. The PRC has indisputable sovereignty over these islands. The *natural resources in the sea areas around them* also belong to China.
>
> (emphasis added)[32]

One month later, China claimed in another statement that it enjoyed indisputable sovereignty over both the South China Sea islands *and their adjacent seas.*[33] By these terms Beijing started to expand its sovereign claims to ocean space beyond the 12 nautical miles strip of territorial seas to which it had previously claimed itself entitled, although what exactly these sea areas referred to remained unclear, which was indeed one of the main targets of the UNCLOS III negotiation process.

The second aspect of China's SCS policy is its approach of political engagement with other states involved in the SCS. While China mainly adopted a bilateral approach, as Vietnam was the only other state involved in the SCS dispute, a nuanced change occurred when the Chinese delegation and their Vietnamese counterparts brought the SCS issue to the floor of the third UN Conference. Both sides of the dispute took advantage of this international stage to legitimize their claims. This signals that the maritime legal regime began to gain a foothold as the medium through which China interacted with other disputant parties with regard to the SCS issue and China's intention to take advantage of this medium to publicize and legitimize its sovereign claims. During the 22nd plenary meeting on Friday, June 28, 1974, Vuong Van Bag, representative of the Republic of Vietnam, raised the SCS dispute:

> Nor would South Viet-Nam accept any attempt to violate its territorial integrity on land or at sea. He reiterated that, as the Secretary-General of the United Nations and the Security Council had already been informed, the Hoang-Sa (Paracel) and Truong-Sa (Spratly) Archipelagos were part of the national territory of the Republic of Viet-Nam. At the beginning of 1974, a neighboring Power had gone so far as to use force to take illegal possession of some of the islands.

Four days later, at the 25th meeting on Tuesday, July 2, 1974, Chinese representative Chai Shufan responded to RVN's accusation:

> He could not accept what the representative of the Saigon authorities had said in his statement concerning the Xisha and Nansha islands which, as the Government of the People's Republic of China had on more than one

occasion solemnly declared, had always been an inalienable part of Chinese territory.

China's interaction with other parts of the maritime regime also brought changes to the third policy dimension – concrete practices of maritime governance. Apart from the LOS conference, China also started participating in the Inter-governmental Maritime Consultative Organization (IMCO) and the UN Stockholm Environment Conference, and acceded to a number of transnational maritime treaties and frameworks. In March 1973, it ratified the IMCO Convention and acceded to the 1969 International Convention on Civil Liability for Oil Pollution Damage. Subsequently, it acceded to a number of IMCO agreements, such as the 1973 International Convention for the Prevention of Pollution by Ships of the London conference and the 1966 International Load Line Convention with reservation of Article 49 and 50 of Appendix II. In 1975, Beijing signed the International Convention for the Safety of Life at Sea. During 1979 and 1980, China acceded to ten additional international maritime treaties. Between 1972 and 1983, China signed and observed a total of 15 multi-national treaties.[34] As we will see in the following chapters, China's continuous participation in these two organizations has important policy bearings on its practices of maritime governance in the SCS.

Along with the proliferation of transnational multilateral maritime treaties came the proliferation of domestic maritime legislation. Before 1970, China's domestic legislation was slowly developing and limited to administrative regulations: the 1958 Declaration on Territorial Sea; the 1957 General Regulations Governing Foreign Vessels, Entry and Departure, PRC Ports; the 1959 Regulations Governing the Investigation of Maritime Accidents and Losses; and the 1964 Rules Governing Passage, Qiongzhou Strait. The years of China's membership in the third LOS conference witnessed a proliferation of legislation germane to maritime regulations: Regulation on Investigation and Disposal of Marine Casualties in 1972, Regulations on Port Pilotage in 1976, Regulations, Supervision and Control of Foreign Vessels in 1979, Regulations of the People's Republic of China on Exploitation of Offshore Petroleum Resources in Cooperation with Foreign Enterprises in 1982, and Law on the Protection of Marine Environment in 1982, to name but a few. In total, there were 16 regulations and laws promulgated from 1972 to 1983. Some of the new legislation reflects upgrades from previous versions to better govern maritime issues, such as the Regulations, Supervision and Control of Foreign Vessels. Others are part of the effort to institutionalize at the domestic level those multilateral treaties to which China had recently acceded, such as the Law on the Protection of Marine Environment and the Regulation on Investigation and Disposal of Marine Casualties.[35]

Legalization at both the domestic and transnational levels brought China's maritime practices to meet the standards of modern ocean governance. This legislation also informed China's everyday practice in the South China Sea by defining what China can and should do to the ocean and how to do it. They also added new content to the third dimension of maritime sovereignty: how sovereignty could be exercised.

The 1974 Paracel clash

Another major event in the UNCLOS III period was the 1974 Paracel confrontation, which occurred in the early stage of China's participation in the UNCLOS III. Many studies have demonstrated that the timing of the Paracel Incident was mainly motivated by geostrategic considerations.[36] Still, the ongoing development of the maritime regime also played an important role in raising the value of the islands in states' calculations. In other words, it was the combination of the geostrategic environment and the dynamics of the maritime regime that factored into the escalation and showdown of Sino-RNV confrontation.

Before 1975, the only rival China faced in the SCS dispute was the South Vietnamese government (RVN) in Saigon, which was challenged domestically by the opposing regime, the North Vietnam (Viet Minh) in Hanoi.[37] As mentioned in Chapter 2, at the 1950 San Francisco Conference, it was the South Vietnamese delegation which issued claims to those islands groups in the SCS. Saigon was also the only legitimate representative of Vietnam in the third LOS conference. Therefore, the Paracel clash in 1974 was really between China and the RVN in Saigon. It is worth noting that, before toppling the Southern regime to form the Socialist Republic of Vietnam (SRV) in 1975, the North Vietnamese in Hanoi had raised no opposition to China's claims in the SCS.

A combination of two developments in the maritime regime in the early 1970s influenced the SCS region and contributed to the contention between China and the RVN. First, in 1969, the Committee for Coordination of Joint Prospecting for Mineral Resources in Asian Offshore Areas (CCOP) conducted a scientific survey regarding the hydrocarbon potential of the area and predicted potentially large hydrocarbon deposits in the Asian seas.[38] Second, in the UNCLOS III was emerging a trend of legalization of entitling islands to large areas of water and the seabed. The promising estimates of natural resources, together with the emerging legal trend of expanding state jurisdiction to larger areas of the ocean, greatly raised the value of islands in states' perceptions and motivated states to create *de facto* control of those potential maritime entitlements. The RVN took advantage of the domestic turmoil in China during the Cultural Revolution to quickly expand resource exploration activities in the Paracels, initiating a program in 1971 offering oil concessions to foreign companies for exploration blocks in the SCS. In July 1973, South Vietnam conducted seismic surveys around Triton (Zhongjian) and Duncan Islands in the Crescent Group of the Paracels.[39] These unilateral moves escalated tensions between Saigon and Beijing.

The geostrategic environment at that time was favorable for China to take action. For one thing, North Vietnam acquiesced to its socialist ally's sovereignty claims over the SCS. For another, as the Vietnam War approached its final stage, U.S. President Nixon indicated a willingness to pull back American military forces in his 1969 Guam Speech as well as in the 1973 Paris Peace Accords. Moreover, the Paracels were already in a state of divided control prior to the confrontation. Saigon controlled the Crescent (Yongle) Group in the southwest, and the Amphitrite (Xuande) Group in the northeast was in the hands of PLA Navy. All Beijing needed was to advance a little southwest onto the Crescent (Yongle) Group, which lay comfortably in the (albeit limited) range of the PLAN's power projection.

In late 1973, China prepared to adopt an assertive posture to defend its claim to the Paracels. The first move was to expand its physical presence into the unoccupied western group of the Paracel Islands. In mid-December, crews from two Chinese fishing boats established a camp on Duncan Island. One month later, they moved to Robert Island, close to the RVN position on Pattle Island, and planted flags on Money Island.[40] It was reported that although China adopted a more aggressive posture, it was not prepared to escalate the situation. Rather, it hoped to wait for Saigon to abandon its position or to occupy Saigon's position after its fall, as the victory of North Vietnam loomed in the ongoing civil war.[41] The Saigon government responded quickly. On January 15, it announced the incorporation of the Paracels into Danang and dispatched a destroyer escort ship to the islands. On January 17, a second RVN ship arrived, deploying troops on Robert and Money Islands and thereby securing control of the western part of the Crescent Group. After several confrontations between the RVN cutter and Chinese fishing boats and calls for reinforcements on both sides, the tactical situation greatly escalated. On the morning of January 19, the first armed clash occurred. RVN ships approached China's position on Duncan, Drummond, and Palm islands from two sides, squaring off against the four PLA Navy boats. The two sides clashed on Palm before the RVN force suffered three casualties and withdrew. In response, RVN ships were ordered to attack. When the smoke cleared, one Chinese minesweeper was badly damaged and beached on Duncan. The RVN cutters sustained light damage. An RVN minesweeper was sunk by Chinese sub chasers as it withdrew. When the fighting was over, RVN ships were ordered to retreat and the PLAN took control over all contested features in the Paracels.

Analysis

This chapter has identified a number of changes in regard to China's interaction with the international maritime regime and its SCS policy. As explained in Chapter 2, Chinese leaders were dissatisfied with Western domination in the maritime regime and joined the Third World to alter the traditional maritime order favoring Western powers. While geopolitics created new opportunities to rewrite the old maritime order and made China more open to changes, this alone does not account for all the identified changes in China's maritime policies. The normative and institutional dynamics of the maritime regime were an indispensable part of shaping China's maritime policies, mainly through three mechanisms.[42]

First, through the mechanism of teaching policy-related knowledge (role 5 in Chapter 1), the maritime regime transformed the style and content of China's participation in the LOS conference. Initially the Chinese delegation was supportive of almost all policy proposals, so long as they were submitted by developing countries. Due to a lack of the necessary knowledge and expertise, the Chinese leadership was unaware of the possibility that many of the policy proposals they supported might have been working against China's interests. Participation in the actual negotiation processes and frequent interaction with experts and delegations from other countries exposed China to a great deal of technical, legal, and other policy-related information and knowledge previously unavailable, and turned China into a more professional and pragmatic negotiator in the LOS conference. The political posturing previously ubiquitous in statements and speeches issued by the Chinese delegation was replaced with a sound understanding of technical details and a clear and specific expression of views. In addition, the Chinese delegation came to realize that there were some unexpected and unintended disadvantages associated with their position. One of the major disadvantages was the potential intensification of conflict in the SCS, which will be explained in Chapter 4. Another important consequence was that some of the major legal innovations China had originally thought would most benefit developing countries turned out to move major maritime powers to top positions on the list of leading beneficiaries (see Table 3.2).

These negative policy ramifications associated with Beijing's position evoked fervent debate in the 1990s when ratification of the LOSC was put on the national agenda, which will be addressed in detail in Chapter 5.

Table 3.2 Leading EEZ beneficiaries[43]

Rank	*Country*	*Area of 200-mile zone (square nautical miles)*
1	USA	2,831,400
2	France	2,083,400
3	Indonesia	1,577,300
4	New Zealand	1,409,500
5	Australia	1,310,900
6	Russia	1,309,500
7	Japan	1,126,000
8	Brazil	924,000
9	Canada	857,000
10	Mexico	831,500

Second, the maritime regime induced China's participation and compliance through offering instrumental incentives (role 2 in Chapter 1). The Chinese leadership was well aware of China's primitive maritime industry and was eager to fill the large gap between its own legal, institutional, and economic capabilities and the standards of modern maritime governance. For instance, the shipping and transportation standards embodied in the IMO served as the motivation behind Beijing's active participation in the IMO. Consequently, China acceded to various multilateral treaties of the IMO and institutionalized them at the domestic level so as to bring its own maritime practices to meet the international standards of modern ocean governance. These legislations provided both the legal and practical basis for China's concrete sovereign practices in the South China Sea.

The third role the maritime regime played was reconstructing China's conception of its sovereignty in the SCS (role 1 in Chapter 1). The revolutionary developments of the ocean regime in the 1970s nurtured new legal grounds for SCS-bordering countries to lay claims over the SCS which focused not only on land features but also the vast ocean space. This represents the unique power of the maritime regime functioning independently from geopolitics. The emerging trend of associating large oceanic areas with islands encouraged China to expand its original sovereign claims over islands to enclose additional sea areas. The same trend also encouraged other littoral countries in the SCS region to undergo a similar reconceptualization of sovereignty, resulting in several new disputant parties – mainly the Philippines, Malaysia, and Brunei.[44] Details of the claims of these new disputant parties will be discussed in Chapter 4. Table 3.3 summarizes claims in the SCS and their

Table 3.3 Summary of SCS territorial claims in the UNCLOS III period

Country	*Year*	*South China Sea*	*Spratly Islands*	*Paracel Islands*	*New claims: water volume and CS*
China	1950	Traditional international law of acquisition	All	All	Yes
Vietnam	1950	Traditional international law of acquisition	All	All	Yes
The Philippines	1971	Proximity and security, traditional international law of acquisition, UNCLOS	Significant portions	No	Yes
Malaysia	1979	UNCLOS	Significant portions	No	Yes
Brunei*	1981, 1984	UNCLOS	Louisa Reef	No	Yes

*In 1981, Brunei protested against Malaysia's 1979 map as including part of its CS. After it acquired independence in 1984, Brunei published a map that claimed sovereignty of the Louisa Reef (Chinese: Nantong Jiao).

respective legal bases in the UNCLOS III period. As will be explained in the following chapters, the participation of these new disputant parties, supported by the new legal and normative developments in the LOS regime, gave China additional impetus and pressure to reconceptualize the SCS dispute and modify its own sovereignty claims accordingly.

Notes

1 R. P. Anand, "Law of the Sea in Historical Perspective," Lecture = 4 * ROMANIV delivered at the Xiamen Academy of International Law, Xiamen, China, September 2006, available at: www.publicinternationallaw.in/sites/default/files/articles/LectureIV-slides.pdf (accessed April 1, 2014), 126.
2 Geoffrey G. Butler and Simon Maccoby, *The Development of International Law* (Union, NJ: The Lawbook Exchange, Ltd., 2003), 53–56.
3 Scandinavian countries traditionally had a 4-mile limit, including Norway, Sweden, Iceland, and Finland, and a 6-mile limit was claimed by Portugal in 1885.
4 Anand, "Law of the Sea in Historical Perspective," 136. Also see United Nations Documents on the Development and Codification of International Law, *Supplement to American Journal of International Law*, 41, no. 4, October 1947, available at: http://untreaty.un.org/ilc/documentation/english/ASIL_1947_study.pdf (accessed March 1, 2014).
5 Anand, "Law of the Sea in Historical Perspective," 136.
6 For a good review of the four major inter-governmental attempts to codify the peacetime rules of the LOS, see Robin R. Churchill and A. V. Lowe, *The Law of the Sea*, 3rd edn. (Manchester: Manchester University Press, 1999).
7 This conference endeavored to thoroughly address and formulate accepted rules in international law in three areas: (1) conflicting nationality laws; (2) territorial waters; (3) and international responsibility of states for damage done in their territory to the person or property of foreigners, and only achieved consensus on the first issue. See United Settlement, "First report submitted to the Council by the Preparatory Committee for the Codification Conference," available at: www.uniset.ca/naty/maternity/24AmJIntLSpSup1.pdf (accessed March 1, 2014).
8 See Jesse S. Reeves, "The codification of the law of territorial waters," *American Journal of International Law* 24 (1930): 493. Also see Rosenne Shabtai, "Codification Revisited after 50 Years," *Max Planck Yearbook of United Nations Law Online* 2, no. 1 (1998): xvii–22.
9 Fuxing Shi, trans., *Seabed Politics* (Shanghai, China: Sanlian Publisher, 1981), 13, in Chinese.
10 The first and second conferences could be treated as one conference because the agenda, organization, and participants of the two conferences were almost the same and the second conference, convened two years later than the first, made no identifiable progress.
11 See United Nations, "UNCLOS: A Historical Perspective," available at: www.un.org/depts/los/convention_agreements/convention_historical_perspective.htm#Historical%20Perspective (accessed March 1, 2014).
12 Josef L. Kunz, "Continental Shelf and International Law: Confusion and Abuse," *The American Journal of International Law* 50, no. 4 (1956): 843.
13 Some 86 countries participated in the first conference, and 88 countries in the second.
14 United Nations, "Geneva Conventions on the Law of the Sea," available at: http://untreaty.un.org/cod/avl/ha/gclos/gclos.html (accessed March 1, 2014).
15 Shi, *Seabed Politics,* 62–63.

16 "UNCLOS: A Historical Perspective."
17 United Nations, "Chronological list of UNCLOS," available at: www.un.org/Depts/los/reference_files/chronological_lists_of_ratifications.htm (accessed March 1, 2017).
18 Documents of the United Nations, A/AC.138/SC.II/L.34, 16 July 1973.
19 Documents of the United Nations, A/AC.138/SC.III/L.42, 19 July 1973.
20 Documents of the United Nations, A/AC.138/SC.II/L.45, 6 August 1973.
21 Documents of the United Nations, A/AC.138/SC.III/L.55, 1973.
22 Documents of the United Nations, A/AC.138/L II/Rev. I, 17 August 1972.
23 Shufan Chai, the 25th plenary meeting, Tuesday, July 2, 1974. All of the Chinese delegation's statements on the UNCLOS III are compiled in *The File Set of Chinese Delegation to the UN Conferences (1972–1984)* (Beijing: People's Publishing House), vols. 1–24. These statements are also available at United Nations, http://legal.un.org/diplomaticconferences/lawofthesea-1982/lawofthesea- 1982.html.
24 Chi-kin Lo, *China's Policy towards Territorial Disputes: The Case of the South China Sea Islands* (New York: Routledge, 1989), 40.
25 Jeanette Greenfield, *China's Practice in the Law of the Sea* (Oxford: Clarendon Press, 1992), 51.
26 Tieya Wang, 112th plenary meeting, April 26, 1979.
27 Guangjian Xu, 58th meeting, April 24, 1979.
28 Qing Ling, *From Yan'an to the United Nations* (Fujian, China: Fujian Renmin Press, 2008), 166–169.
29 Lo, *China's Policy toward Territorial Disputes*, 40.
30 Xinhua News Agency, August 22, 1951, cited in Lo, *China's Policy toward Territorial Disputes*, 51, note 28.
31 M. Taylor Fravel, *Strong Borders, Secure Nation: Cooperation and Conflict in China's Territorial Disputes* (Princeton, NJ: Princeton University Press, 2008), 280.
32 *Beijing Review*, January 18, 1974, 3.
33 Zhenhua Han, ed., *Collection of Historical Materials on Our Country's South China Sea Islands* (Beijing: Dongfang Publishing House, 1988), 451–452, in Chinese.
34 The data are based on a list compiled by Jianjun Gao. See "Listing of Multilateral LOS Treaties to Which China Acceded (1920–2003)," in *China and the Law of the Sea* (Beijing: Ocean Press, 2004), 176–179.
35 Ibid.
36 See in particular Lo, *China's Policy toward Territorial Disputes*, Fravel, *Strong Borders, Secure Nation* and John W. Garver, "China's Push through the South China Sea: The Interaction of Bureaucratic and National Interests," *The China Quarterly* 132 (1992): 999–1028.
37 The Viet Minh with support from the PRC fought with French Colonialists and finally struck a peace accord with France at the Geneva Conference in Geneva, Switzerland, in 1954, according to which Vietnam was divided into North Vietnam (Viet Minh) and South Vietnam (RVN) at the 17th Parallel. The North Vietnamese finally toppled the RVN regime in Saigon on April 30, 1975. South Vietnam was briefly ruled by a provisional government while under military occupation by North Vietnam. On July 2, 1976, North and South Vietnam were merged to form the Socialist Republic of Vietnam (SRV).
38 Phiphat Tangsubkul, *ASEAN and the Law of the Sea* (Singapore: Institute of Southeast Asian Studies, 1982), 82–83.
39 Fravel, *Strong Borders, Secure Nation*, 277.
40 Ge Xu, *Steel Anchors Consolidating Maritime Frontiers: Record of the Republic's Naval Battles* (Beijing: Haichao Publisher, 1999), 289–90, in Chinese.
41 Fravel, *Strong Borders, Secure Nation*, 281.

42 In this book, the mechanisms through which the maritime regime influences China's SCS policy are tantamount to the roles the maritime regime plays in shaping Chinese policy.

43 Churchill and Lowe, *The Law of the Sea*, 148.

44 In addition, part of the EEZ of Indonesia's Natuna Islands is located within China's U-shaped line, which may be a potential area of dispute. Indonesia raised its concern with China in the early 1990s and was assured that China did not have any dispute with Indonesia concerning the overlapping part of the EEZ of the Natuna Islands.

Bibliography

Anand, R.P. 1983. *Origin and Development of the Law of the Sea: History of International Law Revisited*, Martinus Nijhoff, Boston.

Anand, R.P. 2006. "Law of the Sea in Historical Perspective," Lecture IV delivered at the Xiamen Academy of International Law, Xiamen, China. Available at: www.publicinternationallaw.in/sites/default/files/articles/LectureIV-slides.pdf (accessed Jan. 4, 2014).

Anon. n.d.a. "First Report Submitted to the Council by the Preparatory Committee for the Codification Conference," United Settlement. Available at: www.uniset.ca/naty/maternity/24AmJIntLSpSup1.pdf (accessed Jan. 3, 2014).

Anon. n.d.b. *The File Set of Chinese Delegation to the UN Conferences (1972–1984)*, vols. 1–24, People's Publishing House, Beijing.

Butler, G.G. and Maccoby, S. 2003. *The Development of International Law*, The Lawbook Exchange, Ltd., Union, NJ.

Buzan, B. 1981. *Seabed Politics*, trans. F.X. Shi, Sanlian Publisher, Shanghai, China.

Churchill, R.R. and Lowe, A.V. 1999. *The Law of the Sea*, 3rd edn, Manchester University Press, Manchester.

Fravel, M.T. 2008. *Strong Borders, Secure Nation: Cooperation and Conflict in China's Territorial Disputes*, Princeton University Press, Princeton, NJ.

Gao, J.J. 2004. *China and the Law of the Sea*, Ocean Press, Beijing, China (in Chinese).

Garver, J.W. 1992. "China's Push through the South China Sea: The Interaction of Bureaucratic and National Interests," *The China Quarterly*, vol. 132, pp. 999–1028.

Greenfield, J. 1992. *China's Practice in the Law of the Sea*, Clarendon Press, Oxford.

Han, Z.H. (ed.) 1988. *Collection of Historical Materials on Our Country's South China Sea Islands*, Dongfang Publishing House, Beijing. (in Chinese).

Kunz, J.L. 1956. "Continental Shelf and International Law: Confusion and Abuse," *The American Journal of International Law*, vol. 50, no. 4, pp. 828–853.

Ling, Q. 2008. *From Yan'an to the United Nations*, Fujian Renmin Press, Fujian, China.

Lo, C.K. 1989. *China's Policy toward Territorial Disputes: The Case of the South China Sea Islands*, Routledge, New York.

Reeves, J.S. 1930. "The Codification of the Law of Territorial Waters," *American Journal of International Law*, vol. 24, pp. 486–495.

Shabtai, R. 1998. "Codification Revisited after 50 Years," *Max Planck Yearbook of United Nations Law Online*, vol. 2, no. 1, pp. xvii–22.

Tangsubkul, P. 1982. *ASEAN and the Law of the Sea*, Institute of Southeast Asian Studies, Singapore.

United Nations. 1947. "United Nations Documents on the Development and Codification of International Law," *Supplement to American Journal of International Law*, vol. 41, no. 4. Available at: http://untreaty.un.org/ilc/documentation/english/ASIL_1947_study.pdf (accessed January 3, 2014).

United Nation. 1958. *Geneva Conventions on the Law of the Sea*. Available at: http://untreaty.un.org/cod/avl/ha/gclos/gclos.html (accessed January 3, 2014).

United Nations. 1972. *Documents of the United Nations*, A/AC.138/L II/Rev. I, 17 August 1972. United Nations, New York.

United Nations. 1973a. *Documents of the United Nations*, A/AC.138/SC. II/L.34, 16 July 1973. United Nations, New York.

United Nations. 1973b. *Documents of the United Nations*, A/AC.138/SC.III/L.42, 19 July 1973. United Nations, New York.

United Nations. 1973c. *Documents of the United Nations*, A/AC.138/SC.II/L.45, 6 August 1973. United Nations, New York.

United Nations. 1973d. *Documents of the United Nations*, A/AC.138/SC.III/L.55, 1973. United Nations, New York.

4 The 1980s

Shaping a new game in the SCS

This chapter consists of three sections. The first section analyzes changes in the SCS issue resulting from developments in the wider legal institutional environment of the maritime regime, at the center of which sits the new LOS Convention. The emerging concepts underpinning the legal regime of the new maritime order, particularly the concepts of the Exclusive Economic Zone (EEZ) and the Continental Shelf (CS), distinguished maritime sovereignty from continental sovereignty and interplayed with the historic regime in transforming the SCS dispute from a traditional bilateral territorial dispute into a complex, multilateral and multi-issue web of disputes with no ready-to-use solutions. The second part looks at China's policy practices in the 1980s, exploring linkages between the influence of the maritime regime, the geopolitical environment, and China's policy outcomes. The final section summarizes the influence of the maritime regime and explains the role that geopolitical factors played in this period.

Transforming the SCS dispute

Restructuring the legal basis of the sovereign dispute

By deconstructing the concept of "sovereignty," it was revealed in Chapter 1 that "sovereignty" has a rather fluid and malleable nature, particularly with regard to the regulative facet of the concept. It is this fluid and malleable nature that makes possible and creates room for the transformation of the South China Sea dispute from a typical zero-sum game of territorial dispute into a multi-layered complex network of disputes with open-ended solutions.

The SCS disputes first emerged in the 1950s as a typical territorial dispute involving two disputants: China and Vietnam. The two countries disagreed solely over the ownership of two compounds of land features dispersed in the waters of the SCS, the Paracels and the Spratly Islands. Both countries based their claims on first discovery and effective occupation, which are general principles of international law on territorial acquisition.[1] The emergence of the Law of the Sea Convention (LOSC) framework in the 1970s began to change the legal basis of the SCS dispute. The United Nations Convention of the Law of the Sea (UNCLOS) and its related legal deliberations amount to a different source of law for appropriation of, or establishing jurisdiction over, maritime features, thus blurring the boundaries of the territory being claimed in the South China Sea.

In the South China Sea are widely dispersed hundreds of maritime features; many islands, especially in the Spratly area, are barren and submerged by waters at high tide. In the 1950s, the PRC and Vietnam started to claim sovereignty over these features, basing their legal justification on conventional international law of territory acquisition. The establishment of the regimes of the Exclusive Economic Zone and the Continental Shelf, however, potentially offered a different legal basis on which states could assert claims of sovereignty or exclusive jurisdiction. In the case of the South China Sea dispute, it gave rise to the possibility that some features in the South China Sea, in particular low-tide elevations, might be claimed as forming part of a state's Continental Shelf or being located in its EEZ, thereby creating a legal loophole subject to conflicting interpretations or applications of international law. The countries bordering the SCS, aside from China and Vietnam, came to realize that the newly formulated provisions of the LOSC could help them extend their sovereignty and jurisdiction to areas of the SCS not previously available to them. Consequently, as indicated at the end of Chapter 3, the Philippines, Malaysia, and Brunei, one after another, embroiled themselves in the sovereignty row in the SCS.

With regard to the Philippines, on July 10, 1971, President Ferdinand Marcos issued a statement which for the first time articulated an official claim by the Philippines to Freedomland (also called Kalayaan), which encompassed part of the Spratly Islands.[2] Manila gave two main arguments to support its claims. The first was based on proximity. Because of the proximity of Itu Aba (called Ligaw by the Filipino government) to the Philippines, military occupation thereof constituted a "serious threat" to the Philippines' national security. Second, Manila asserted that the islands composing "Freedomland" were *terra nullius* when discovered by a Filipino citizen, Tomas Cloma. Neither one of these arguments was based on the new LOS Convention.

The Philippines renewed its claims in 1976 when Manila sanctioned the exploration activities of a Swedish-Filipino oil consortium in the Reed Bank Area. This time, the Filipino government justified oil drilling with a new argument: its rights to the continental shelf.[3] The consolidation of the CS regime in the third LOS conference inspired the Filipino government to shift its emphasis to the evolving CS concept as the legal foundation of its claims. On June 11, 1978, Manila issued Presidential Decree no. 1596, formalizing its claims to the Kalayaan island group. The first reason in the decree was "whereas, much of the above area is part of the continental margin of the Philippine archipelago."[4] In this decree, administration of the Kalayaan island group was expanded from the islands and islets to the sea-bed, subsoil, and the continental margin.[5] This reflects Manila's prompt realization of the extensive ocean space made possible by the development of the third LOS conference.[6] Indeed, the same day when Presidential Decree no. 1596 was issued another piece of legislation was also promulgated: Presidential Decree no. 1599. In this decree, the Filipino government established an EEZ extending to "a distance of 200 nautical miles beyond and from the baseline from which the territorial sea is measured."[7] The most recent attempt by the Philippines to assert and expand its territorial and jurisdictional rights in the SCS was the 2013 South China Sea Arbitration case in which the Philippines sought to exploit the legal loophole concerning low-tide elevations to deprive of the right of appropriation as territory a number of maritime features in the Spratlys, such as Mischief Reef and Second Thomas Shoal.[8]

The Malaysian government further enlarged the number of contestants in the SCS row using the CS regime as the basis of its legal justification. Malaysia's claim to the SCS did not surface until December 1979, when Kuala Lumpur published an official map of Malaysia's continental shelf. On that map, a number of islands and reefs of the Spratly group were marked as Malaysian territory, including Amboyna Cay (in Chinese: Anbo Shazhou), Commodore Reef (in Chinese: Siling Jiao), and Swallow Reef (in Chinese: Danwan Jiao). On May 19, 1983, Malaysia's Deputy Minister in charge of legal matters was reported to have said that Malaysia's rights to Amboyna Cay were a matter of geography. Another senior official said that Malaysia had conducted as survey of the location of Amboyna Cay and had found it to be in Malaysian waters.[9] These statements suggested that Malaysia claimed some of the islands of the Spratly group because they formed part of its continental shelf.[10]

Brunei was the third new disputant laying claims to some part of the SCS. Not long after its formal independence in 1984, Brunei promulgated national legislation establishing an EEZ in accordance to relevant provisions in UNCLOS, and published a map that claimed sovereignty of the Louisa Reef (in Chinese: Nantong Jiao).[11]

Vietnam's position also witnessed a significant change in relation to the historic concept developed in the maritime regime. Vietnam's case was complicated by a regime transition in the mid-1970s. Prior to 1974, Vietnam was divided into two regimes: South Vietnam represented by the RVN government in Saigon, and North Vietnam represented by the DRV regime in Hanoi. Prior to the collapse of South Vietnam, the RVN government was the one making claims for Vietnam in the SCS. In contrast, the communist regime in the North had no dispute over, and for the most part acquiesced to, China's claims to sovereignty in the SCS. With the DRV's victory in the Vietnamese civil war at hand in 1974, Communist leaders began to signal to Beijing that their position towards the SCS dispute was about to change.

As it turned out, the DRV inherited the RVN's position on the Paracels and the Spratlys.[12] North Vietnam first in a tactical manner used unofficial venues to voice its departure from China's position on the issue of ownership over islands in the SCS. In 1974, Tran Binh, Chargé d'Affaires of the National

Liberation Front in Beijing (the Communist ally of North Vietnam in the South), told a press conference:

> The question of sovereignty over their territories is a sacred issue for every people. As to the problem of conflict over territories bequeathed by history, these are complex questions which need careful examination. The problem, the Paracels incident, must be solved by peaceful negotiations on the basis of equality, mutual respect and friendship.

During Le Duan's visit to China in September 1975, the Vietnamese Communists officially raised the issue of sovereignty over the Paracel and Spratly Islands for the first time and proposed holding bilateral talks.

Vietnam's position in the Gulf of Tonkin was influenced by the development of the concept of historic title in the maritime regime. Apart from the claims to the Paracels and Spratlys, Hanoi added the Gulf of Tonkin to its SCS claims, catching Chinese leaders by surprise. In 1974, the government in Hanoi proposed to China launching bilateral negotiations on the maritime boundary of the Gulf.[13] It proposed treating the median line specified in the 1887 Sino-French Boundary Convention as the "historic demarcation line" for the Gulf of Tonkin.[14] On November 12, 1982, Hanoi formally declared the Gulf of Tonkin as historic waters in the Declaration on Baseline of Territorial Waters.[15] Article 3 stated:

> The Bac Bo Gulf is a gulf situated between the Socialist Republic of Vietnam and the People's Republic of China. The maritime frontier drawn in the Gulf between Vietnam and China is defined in Article 2 of the Convention on the Delimitation of the Frontier between Vietnam and China signed on June 27, 1887, between France and the Qing Dynasty. The waters in the part of the gulf belonging to Vietnam constitute the historic waters pertaining to the juridical regime of the internal waters of the Socialist Republic of Vietnam. The baseline from Con Co Island to the opening of the gulf will be defined following the settlement of the question of the opening line of the gulf.

Historic title or historic regime refers to claims to certain portion of sea areas asserted by states based on historical grounds.[16] Historic assertions or claims encompass three forms: historic bays, historic waters, and historic rights. Historic bays were the most frequently invoked historic claims in the 1950s and 1960s. Later on, the more inclusive term "historic waters" was gradually emerging to embody, if not to replace, the term "historic bays."[17] Although historic assertions were practiced by a number of states, due their controversial and complex nature, the international legal community failed to reach consensus on a general formula of historic title acceptable to all.[18] The UNCLOS I in 1958 agreed in recognizing "the importance of the juridical status" of "historic waters including historic bays" and adopted a resolution requesting the General Assembly of the United Nations "to arrange for the study of the juridical regime of historic waters, including historic bays, and for the communication of the results of such study to all states Members of the United Nations."[19] In 1962, the UN Secretariat, at the request of the ILC, produced a juridical study on the concept of historic regime. The study looked at the elements of title to historic waters, the issue of the burden of proof, the legal status of waters regarded as historic waters, and dispute settlements. However, due to theoretical controversy, no conclusive definition of historic title was offered, nor criteria or standards by which this concept could be applied.[20] For similar reasons, the UNCLOS III deliberately avoided a clear elaboration of the grounds for historic title, leaving few references in the 1982 United Nations Convention on the Law of the Sea (the LOS Convention).[21]

Because of the absence of a specific definition in the LOSC, the legality of historic claims became a subject of debate among legalists.[22] However, scant provisions in the LOSC on the historic regime did not necessarily lead to a complete negation of the legality of any historic claims, which remain an often-invoked legal concept in judicial cases and numerous state practices.[23] In the South China Sea, for example, Vietnam made historic claims to the Gulf of Tonkin and reached a boundary agreement with Cambodia on historic waters on July 7, 1982.[24] For this reason, the drafters of the LOSC have given due respect to this concept, since all references to historic title appear in provisions that could potentially affect or cause conflict to claims based on historic title. For instance, Article 15 of the LOSC does not allow the median line to apply to special circumstances such as "by reason of historic title" for the delimitation of the territorial seas of the two states. Another example is found in the dispute settlement regime, which provides historic claims with specific opt-out options in the application of dispute settlement mechanisms.[25] In the section on the EEZ, Article 62 (3) stipulates that giving other states' fishermen access to its own EEZ for fishery surpluses:

> The coastal State shall take into account all relevant factors, including *inter alia*, the significance of the living resources of the area to the economy of the coastal State concerned ..., the need to minimize economic dislocation in States *whose nationals have habitually fished in the zone* ...
> (emphasis added)

By doing so, the LOS Convention leaves the historic regime to be governed by customary international law as reaffirmed in its preamble.[26] In subsequent chapters, I will discuss China's shifting standpoint regarding the historic regime, which underscores the effect of the LOS regime's legal dynamics on China's conception of its sovereignty in the SCS.

These legally transitioning claims gave rise to another thorny feature of the new SCS dispute: the substantial indeterminacy associated with the boundary of maritime sovereignty in the SCS. The EEZ and CS regimes set out in the LOSC entitle land features in the SCS to multiple strips of ocean space with varying sovereign and jurisdictional rights and responsibilities. Yet, states continue to hold different views in terms of exact boundary limits and detailed rights and duties of these maritime entitlements, due to different interpretations of the legal regimes in question. Vagueness and ambiguity in the wording of pertinent provisions in the LOSC have rendered it difficult for SCS states to arrive at unequivocal interpretations.[27]

A case in point is the island regime: according to the UNCLOS, an island automatically generates territorial sea, regardless of its geological or geographical characteristics. Article 3 of the UNCLOS stipulates that "every State has the right to establish the breadth of its territorial sea up to a limit not exceeding 12 nautical miles, measured from baselines." However, whether an island is entitled to more extensive zones such as the EEZ and the CS remains less certain. The Regime of Islands provides the definition of an island and rules for the generation of maritime zones of islands in Article 121:

> **Article 121**
> Regime of Islands
>
> 1 An island is a naturally formed area of land, surrounded by water, which is above water at high tide.
> 2 Except as provided for in paragraph 3, the territorial sea, the contiguous zone, the exclusive economic zone and the continental shelf of an island are determined in accordance with the provisions of this Convention applicable to other land territory.
> 3 Rocks, which cannot sustain human habitation or economic life of their own, shall have no exclusive economic zone or continental shelf.

Paragraph 3 of Article 121 places an important restriction on the capacity of islands to claim an EEZ and continental shelf. It distinguishes a clustering of rocks not eligible for an EEZ and CS claims because they are not capable of sustaining human habitation. But the terms "human habitation" and "economic life" used in this paragraph are not otherwise defined in the convention, leaving the definition open to interpretation and making the criteria subject to state practices.[28] Consequently, the regime of islands in the South China Sea region has introduced conflicting interpretations as to what kind of maritime zones can be generated by which land features.[29] It is based on the conflicting interpretations of the island regime that the Philippines formulated Submissions No. 3 and 7 in the South China Sea Arbitration case requesting the tribunal to adjudicate that Scarborough Shoal, Johnston Reef, Cuarteron Reef, and Fiery Cross Reef have no exclusive economic zone or continental shelf.[30]

Indeed, a large number of the land features dispersed in South China Sea, especially in the Spratly area, is barren and submerged by waters at high tide. The ability of these land features to generate a maritime zone beyond the territorial seas might be limited under the regime of island, which means there possibly exist high seas, or international areas, in the middle of the vast South China Sea surrounded by EEZs and territorial seas of coastal countries.[31] The usage and potential exploration activities of natural resources of these possible high seas in the middle of the SCS would then become another issue in the agenda of negotiation between user states and coastal states, perplexing the already complicated situation.[32]

Moreover, the existence of historic regime claims gives rise to additional uncertainty of the exact limit of the sovereign boundary each disputant is claiming in the SCS. As discussed earlier, this regime is of a different origin than other parallel regimes such as the EEZ and the CS, and claims based on the historic concept often overlap claims of other legal regimes. These maritime regimes bestow upon the maritime dispute in the SCS a kind of distinctiveness in contrast to the conventional type of territorial dispute, which will be further elaborated later.

From bilateral to multilateral engagement

The second aspect affected by the changing nature of the SCS dispute is the approach to political engagement among the disputant parties. In light of the new maritime order, countries in the SCS came to realize that traditional bilateral state-to-state engagement was no longer sufficient in dealing with the SCS issue. It became difficult if not impossible to negotiate solutions in a traditional bilateral manner, because any unilateral or bilateral move would inevitably have a potential impact on the whole SCS region, as well as on other parties involved. As a result, countries in the SCS region were in urgent need of normative, technical, and institutional innovations to promote effective political engagement involving multiple states. As will be shown in Chapter 5, it was against this backdrop that the idea of multilateral engagement emerged in the early 1990s to help facilitate effective and constructive political engagement and create new venues for geopolitical factors to exert influence in ways unavailable in traditional bilateral state-to-state diplomacy.

This does not mean that multilateral engagement would naturally be acceptable to China. Rather, as shown in Chapter 5, it was an incremental process for Chinese leaders to adapt to the new face of the SCS dispute and adjust to multilateralism. The resulting acceptance of multilateralism becomes important proof of Beijing's reconceptualization of the SCS issue in line with the new LOS.

Practices of maritime governance

Practices of maritime governance in the SCS were changed considerably by the new rules of the road emerging in the regime of ocean governance. State practices in turn add new dynamics to the customary and formal rules of modern maritime governance, which are constantly developing. For instance, the universal establishment of 200-mile EEZs submits about 36 percent of the total area of the sea to state sovereign jurisdiction. As a result, "virtually all the major shipping routes of the world pass through the EEZs of States other than those in which the ports of departure and destination are situated."[33] This "divide and rule" imposed on shipping routes gives rise to tensions between coastal states and user states. State practices in terms of governing EEZs and reconciling different usages have significant impact in shaping the content of sovereign rights and obligations in the EEZs.

In the SCS, as explained earlier, the legal ambiguities of the new maritime law give rise to controversy surrounding the sovereign boundaries of SCS states and varying interpretations of maritime entitlements. These legal controversies and competing interpretations are not easily solvable. Their resolution not only depends on legalists' deliberation but also relies on states' practices of maritime governance in the SCS. Through practice of maritime governance in areas such as fisheries, environment protection, and resource exploration, claimant states interact with (or sometimes confront) each other and engage with user states, which gradually help them form consensus on the interpretation of relevant provisions, nurture common ground for negotiation, and explore innovative solutions and arrangements for resolving the dispute.

Non-state actors like regional and international institutions also take part in maritime governance in the SCS. For example, as we will see in the following chapters, starting in the 1990s, the United Nations Environmental Programme (UNEP) and the Global Environment Facility (GEF) cooperated with China and other SCS countries to tackle the problem of marine environment degradation.

Informing policy options of the best solutions

The new LOS has set up a movement of "enclosure of ocean" which has intensified conflicts of maritime interests in many areas around the world, especially in semi-enclosed seas like the SCS.[34] In the meantime, the world has also witnessed persistent efforts to explore possible solutions to these maritime disputes, some of which are directly offered in the LOS Convention. For example, the LOSC provides direct dispute settlement mechanisms with binding decisions.[35] Compared to many other bodies of international law, the Convention provides states with a comprehensive system for dispute settlement and establishes an elaborate set of guidelines for its operation. Proceeding from the broader UN-wide stipulation that states must resolve their disputes peacefully, the drafters of the Convention ensured that Parts XI and XV would cover any conceivable conflict that might arise.[36] A plethora of legal works and state practices also contribute to the pool of possible options for resolving maritime disputes.[37] These factors influenced China's attitude toward the SCS issue and provided the leaders in China with various options from which to choose. In particular, the concept of joint development has played an influential part in China's practice of proposing workable regional solutions to manage the SCS issue since the 1980s, which will be addressed later in this chapter. In other words, the installation of the new maritime order has transformed the SCS dispute from a simple bilateral territorial dispute into a complex, multi-issue web of disputes with indeterminate boundaries. It has no ready-to-use solutions and its management and final resolution require China and other disputants to embark on a journey of legal and practical innovations. In this sense, the maritime regime provides an ideal resource pool for countries bordering the SCS to find inspiration and useful practices.

Conventional territorial disputes and the dispute in the SCS

The issues elaborated above bestow upon the maritime dispute in the SCS distinctiveness in contrast to conventional disputes over sovereignty on the continent. Conventional territorial disputes are over a clear-cut issue: who owns the territory? It is a zero-sum game usually between two disputants, either "you have it, I lose it," or "I have it, you lose it." The boundary of the territory in question is definite. A State that owns a specific piece of territory usually has sovereign rights over all the relevant elements residing within its boundaries: mainly soil, airspace, population, and resources (Figure 4.1) (solid lines are used to highlight the definitive nature of conventional dispute of sovereignty). It is based on this understanding of conventional territorial disputes that many IR scholars, in particular, security scholars, view a disputing state's sovereign claims as change-resistant and classify its relevant policy into three categories: escalation, delay, and cooperation.

In contrast, shifting dynamics in the maritime regime problematize the maritime dispute in the SCS in three ways: (1) what territory can be claimed; (2) who has the right to make claims and based on what principles; and (3) how sovereignty should be exercised or what kind of sovereign rights can be generated by ownership of a given piece of territory. First, new developments in the maritime regime blur the boundary of territory being claimed in the SCS. As mentioned earlier, while land features and their territorial seas have boundaries which are relatively certain, their additional entitlements are associated with substantial indeterminacy and conflicting legal reasoning. Second, the movement of the "enclosure of ocean" creates new maritime

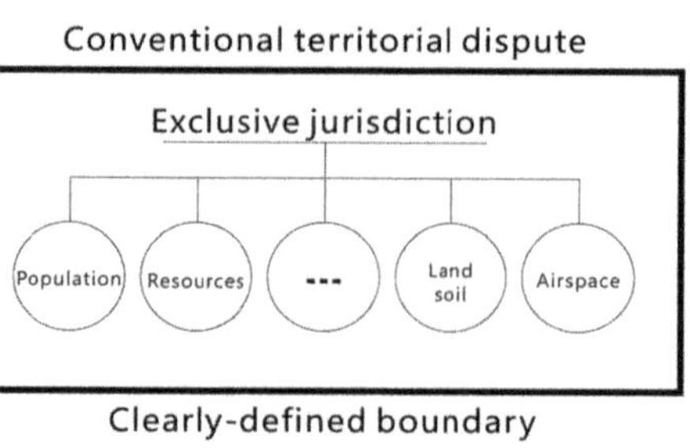

Figure 4.1 Illustration of continental territorial disputes

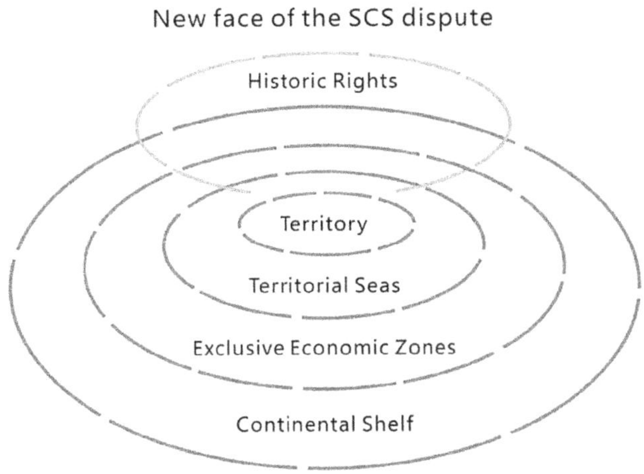

Figure 4.2 Illustration of the transformed SCS disputes

disputants in the SCS, and user states also get involved in shaping the new maritime rules governing the usage of the SCS. Third, apart from islands and their territorial seas, which enjoy full sovereignty, sea areas beyond them are attached with varying degrees and kinds of sovereign and jurisdictional rights and responsibility. Since the LOSC framework does not provide an exhaustive list of these rights and duties, and leaves many areas to be continuously defined by customary law and practices, these legal regimes cause conflict and interaction both among claimant states and between coastal states and user states, the results of which determine the content of maritime sovereignty in these extensive maritime zones.

The maritime dispute in the SCS is illustrated in Figure 4.2 (dashed lines are used to emphasize the indeterminate nature of those maritime zones).

In light of the new maritime order, territorial disputes in the SCS take place in a complicated and highly contested system involving multiple issues. These issues fall into four main independent categories: (1) the issue of ownership of land features; (2) the issue of ownership and exact boundaries of EEZs and CSs; (3) the issue of concrete sovereign and jurisdictional rights; and (4) the issue of historic rights. The resolution of one category does not automatically lead to the final solution in other categories. For this reason, some legal scholars argue that "the South China Sea disputes will only be settled when the bordering countries change their mindsets from one of sovereignty, sole ownership of resources and seeking 'fences in the sea' to one of functional cooperation and cooperative management."[38]

The wider legal institutional environment

There is no doubt that the LOSC as the "Constitution of the Oceans" provides a comprehensive legal system with well-devised provisions guiding the usage of the oceans. In addition, there are other systems and rules operating in conjunction with the LOSC in the maritime regime. Appreciating the influence of the maritime regime thus requires an understanding of the wider legal institutional context within which it resides. The LOSC was not developed in isolation from existing structures of international law. Rather, the LOS is fundamentally a part of international law, and its development is integrated within the broader system. Accordingly, it is bound by the same rules and procedures that shape international law and international governance more generally.[39] These may include general principles of international law, relevant international conventions, customary maritime laws, judicial decisions, and publicists' opinions.[40] For instance, the presence of general principles of international law in Article 38 of the International Court's Statute permits the Court to fill in gaps in treaty and customary law by applying principles of law which are common to the major legal systems of the world and are suitable for transposition into the international legal system.[41] Another example is the principle of peaceful or voluntary settlement of dispute. The UNCLOS urges that prior to resorting to the compulsory procedures entailing binding decisions, parties should seek to settle disputes between them concerning the interpretation or application of the Convention by peaceful means in accordance with Article 2, paragraph 3 of the Charter of the United Nations. The "peaceful means" articulated in the UN Charter include negotiation, enquiry, mediation, conciliation, arbitration, judicial settlement, resort to regional agencies or arrangements, or other peaceful means of their own choice.[42]

The interface between the LOSC and the wider legal environment also operates at the institutional level. When formatting the Convention, the drafters meant to provide a standard against which any cooperative arrangement regarding the disputed islands as well as sea areas should be measured.[43] While the UNCLOS constitutes a reference point for the validity of subsequent rules on ocean matters, the actual responsibility of developing and maintaining rules is transferred to a diverse body of specialized international institutions.[44] The LOS Convention directly created new institutions to regulate a number of LOS concepts: the International Seabed Authority (ISA), the Commission on the Limits of the Continental Shelf (CLCS), and International Tribunal on the Law of the Sea (ITLOS), to act as an important new part of the LOS family of institutions. Some of these bodies have significant judicial power in the dispute settlement system that the new LOS established and have taken an expansive view on their jurisdiction.[45] Some have become the venue through which states publicize, exchange, and negotiate official positions regarding a specific maritime matter. For example, as shown in Chapter 6, the CLCS provided a forum for disputants to publicize and legitimize their claims to sovereignty in the SCS and its activities in 2009 stirred up a new round of tensions among the claimants in the SCS region, resulting in China's clarification of its legal position in the SCS.

Apart from these newly established institutions, some major international institutions, many from the UN family, are also of enormous influence in guiding and shaping states' maritime practices. For instance, the International Court of Justice (ICJ) assumed an eminent and authoritative position in settling interstate territorial disputes. It is also designated as one of the four major means for the settlement of disputes concerning the interpretation or application of the LOS Convention.[46] The judicial opinions it offers have far-reaching influence in terms of interpreting the law applicable to the delimitation of maritime boundaries. Given the conflicting legal interpretations of SCS sovereignty, the ICJ may be an important player in influencing countries' legal claims in the SCS.[47] The International Maritime Organization (IMO) is another UN specialized agency tasked with responsibility for the safety and security of shipping and the prevention of marine pollution by ships. It plays a leading role in introducing international measures for cooperation among governments in the field of governmental regulation and practices relating to international shipping and administrative and legal matters related to sea-borne transportation.[48] The UNEP has several programs implemented by its regional agency, the Coordinating Body of the Seas of East Asia (COBSEA), for marine environmental protection and fisheries in the SCS. At the regional level, as discussed further in Chapter 5, coastal countries in the SCS established a variety of regional multilateral arrangements and frameworks to manage different aspects of maritime governance, including navigation, environmental preservation, fisheries, maritime security, and others. The emergence of regional cooperative agencies and arrangements represents a regional response to the changing nature of the SCS dispute.

China's practice in the 1980s

The 1980s did not witness any major changes to China's legal position regarding its sovereignty in the SCS. China's SCS policy in large part was to respond to physical expansions of other disputants in the SCS.

China's reactive approach toward other disputants: scramble in the SCS

In the face of significant changes brought into force by the emerging new maritime order, littoral states in the SCS reacted not only with words but also with deeds. The 1970s witnessed a trend of increasing activities of physical occupation and control of uninhabited islands. The Philippines was the first country in the region to initiate the trend of using military occupation and control to back its claims. These activities stirred up regional tensions in the SCS which peaked in the 1980s and led to a deadly confrontation between China and Vietnam in 1988. Figure 4.3 is a map showing each disputant's expansive claims in the SCS and their overlap.

By 1974, the Filipino government had announced that it was in effective occupation and control of five islands, including Thitu Island (in Chinese: Zhongye Dao), Nanshan Island (in Chinese: Mahuan Dao), and Flat Island (in Chinese: Feixin Dao).[49] In 1978, Manila advanced its foothold to a

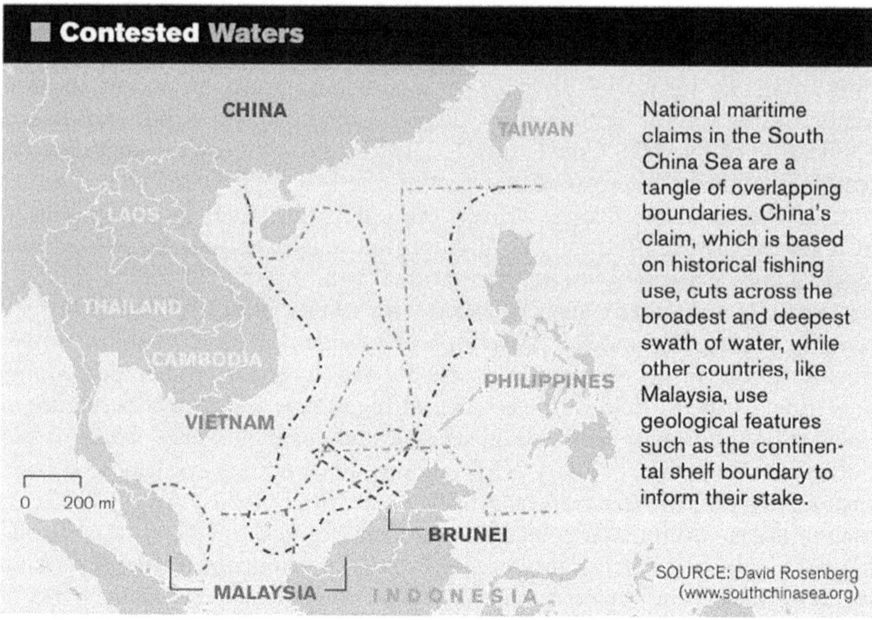

Figure 4.3 Overlapping claims in the South China Sea
The South China Sea website, www.southchinasea.org/files/2011/08/southChinaSea_claims-RyanMorris1.jpg (accessed July 31, 2017). The image is reproduced with the kind permission of David Rosenburg.

seventh island, the Panata island (in Chinese: Shuanghuang Shazhou).[50] In 1980, just a few months after Malaysia published an official map of the Malaysian continental shelf, the Philippines occupied the Commodore Reef (in Chinese: Siling Jiao) (marked on that map as Malaysian territory), bringing the total number of islands under Filipino control to nine. Vietnam was swift in following the Philippines' footsteps. In April 1975, on the eve of liberating Saigon, North Vietnam took over six islands of the Spratly group, which had hitherto been under the control of the RVN, including Southwest Cay (in Chinese: Nanzi Dao), Sin Cowe Island (in Chinese: Jinghong Dao), and Amboyne Cay (in Chinese: Anbo Shazhou).[51] Between 1975 and 1976, another seven islands and islets fell under Vietnam's control. Before the naval skirmish in the Spratlys in March 1988, Vietnam occupied a total of 18 islands. Malaysia made its first move onto SCS islands in the summer of 1983 when it occupied Swallow Reef (in Chinese: Danwan Jiao). Three years later, Malaysia sent troops to another two uninhabited land features, the Mariveles Reef (in Chinese: Nanhai Jiao) and Dallas Reef (in Chinese: Guangxingzai Jiao).[52]

China had been keeping a close eye on these developments in the SCS, but no countermeasures were taken in earnest until 1988, when the Chinese Navy and the Vietnamese Navy clashed in the Spratlys. The Chinese Navy was gradually building up its capacity in the 1980s. The first PLA patrol in the

Spratly area was on November 8, 1980, carried out by two Hong-6 bombers. By 1983, there were repeated PLA Navy air patrols in the Spratlys with the aim of conducting geographic and geological surveys. In the meantime, the Oceanographic Bureau undertook operations to investigate depths, layers, currents, weather, and marine environment in a wide expanse of the ocean north of the Spratlys, from near the Vietnamese coast eastward to just off the Philippines' coast.[53] Another research program was conducted in May 1983, and it included 85 naval vessel commanders, professionals and chief navigators; 15 school and college instructors; 40 naval and fleet operations and navigation systems cadres; 13 scientific research cadres; and 235 sailors. The research took 30 days and reportedly surveyed James Shoal, the southernmost outpost of China's territory.[54]

As of 1987, despite the hot race in the Spratly Islands between Vietnam, the Philippines, and Malaysia, China had zero presence in the region. The convening of the 14th annual inter-governmental United Nations Educational, Scientific and Cultural Organization (UNESCO) conference in March 1987 in Paris provided a convenient opportunity for China to station a permanent presence in the Spratlys. As part of setting up a Global Sea Level Observing System (GLOSS), UNESCO requested that China establish five oceanic observation stations: three along the coast, one in the Paracels (station code 76), and one in the Spratlys (station code 74). In April and May of 1987, the Chinese Academy of Sciences and the State Oceanic Bureau dispatched a research expedition to investigate possible oceanic observation station sites on several uninhabited islands and shoals. Fiery Cross Shoal (in Chinese: Yongshu Jiao) was chosen as the best place for such a station. It is 26 kilometers long, 7.5 kilometers wide, submerged under one-half to 1 meter of water at high tide, but with a large proportion of land above water at low tide.[55] In August, a formal site proposal was submitted to the State Council and the Central Military Committee (CMC) and approved in November.[56] Construction started in January of 1988. In the meantime, China increased patrols and research operations in the area around the Fiery Cross Shoal. Vietnam was acutely concerned with the increased Chinese activities in the Spratly Islands. It was reported that aside from lodging diplomatic protests, Hanoi increased its own patrols, carried out by airplanes and warships in the vicinity of islands where China's survey and construction activities were taking place.[57]

A showdown finally took place in the form of an armed clash at Johnson Reef (in Chinese: Chigua Jiao) on March 14, 1988. According to the Chinese account, two Vietnamese Navy freighters and an amphibious landing ship disembarked 43 armed men on Johnson Reef. When Chinese personnel already on the reef shouted to the Vietnamese to withdraw, the Vietnamese opened fire, wounding one Chinese. The Chinese ships then exchanged fire with the Vietnamese vessels, sinking one freighter and damaging the other two. Hanoi reported that three Vietnamese were killed in the clash and 74 were missing.[58] After this skirmish, China controlled six features, and Vietnam went on to occupy three vacant rocks in the vicinity of the Chinese-controlled islands.

China's maritime practices: continued participation and domestic legislation

In the 1980s, China continued its participation in relevant marine governance institutions, most notably the IMO.[59] It acceded to a number of international maritime treaties and protocols, many of which were IMO conventions.[60] These include the International Convention for the Prevention of Pollution from Ships modified by the Protocol of 1978 in 1983; the Convention on the Prevention of Marine Pollution by Dumping of Wastes and Other Matter in 1985; the International Convention on Civil Liability for Oil Pollution Damage in 1986; and the International Convention on Salvage in 1989.[61] China also signed the Convention for the Suppression of Unlawful Acts against the Safety of Maritime Navigation (the 1988 SUA) in 1988 and ratified it on August 20, 1991.[62] These treaties contain comprehensive provisions prescribing the ways in which the Sea Lanes of Communication (SLOCs) in the SCS can be used.

With regard to the issue of environmental protection, following the trend in the 1970s of an emerging international awareness of the threat of environmental deterioration epitomized by the Stockholm Conference, the 1980s witnessed continuing efforts on the global stage to find solutions to balance environmental protection and economic development. In December 1983, Gro Harlem Brundtland, the Prime Minister of Norway, chaired a special independent commission established by the UN, the World Commission on Environment and Development (WCED), also known as the Brundtland Commission. China became a member state of WCED. The mission of WCED was to re-examine critical environmental and development problems around the world and formulate realistic proposals to address them.[63] In 1987, the Commission released the official report, *Our Common Future*, elaborating the concept of "sustainable development."[64] This report and the concept of "sustainable development" strongly influenced the Earth Summit in Rio de Janeiro, Brazil, in 1992. As elaborated here and in the remaining chapters, China's engagement with the environmental regime infused the concept of sustainable development into China's maritime practices in the areas of marine environment protection and fisheries.

China undertook a series of measures to implement these international standards of maritime governance through domestic legislation (see Table 4.1). From 1982 to 1990, the Chinese government promulgated 15 maritime laws and regulations in an attempt to establish a comprehensive maritime institution in line with modern international standards. These legislations covered several specialized areas of marine governance, including marine maritime traffic safety, environmental protection, pollution from ships and ship dismantling, dumping of wastes at sea, fisheries, submarine cables and pipelines, and exploitation of offshore petroleum resources.

China's practice of best solutions for the South China Sea: embracing joint development

The influence of the maritime regime was also manifested in China's embrace of the concept of joint development. In the 1980s, Chinese leaders began to

Table 4.1 Domestic maritime legislation in the 1980s

	Regulation	*Date*	*Entry into force*
1.	Regulations on Exploitation of Offshore Petroleum Resources in Cooperation with Foreign Enterprises	January 30, 1982	Entry into force on the same day. Revised on September 23, 2001.
2.	Marine Environment Protection Law	August 23, 1982	Entry into force on March 1, 1983. Revised on December 25, 1999.
3.	Maritime Transport Safety Law	September 2, 1983	Entry into force on January 1, 1984
4.	Regulations on the Prevention and Control of Marine Pollution from Vessels	December 29, 1983	Entry into force on the same day
5.	Regulations Concerning Environmental Protection in Offshore Oil Exploration and Exploitation	29 December 29, 1983	Entry into force on the same day
6.	Regulations Concerning the Dumping of Wastes at Sea	March 6, 1985	Entry into force on April 1, 1985
7.	Fisheries Law	January 20, 1986	Entry into force on July 1, 1986. Revised on October 31, 2000.
8.	Implementation Guidelines for the Fisheries Law	October 19, 1987	Entry into force on the same day
9.	Regulations Concerning Environmental Pollution Caused by Ship Dismantling	May 18, 1988	Entry into force on June 1, 1988
10.	Regulations on the Laying of Submarine Cables and Pipelines	February 11, 1989	Entry into force on March 1, 1989
11.	Regulations Concerning Protecting Underwater Historic Objects	October 20, 1989	Entry into force on the same day
12.	Regulations on Inspecting and Handling Maritime Traffic Accidents	January 11, 1990	Entry into force on the same day
13.	Regulations on the Prevention and Control of Pollution from Coastal Construction	May 25, 1990	Entry into force on August 1, 1990
14.	Regulations on the Prevention and Control of Marine Pollution from Land-based Sources	May 25, 1990	Entry into force on August 1, 1990
15.	Implementation Measures for Regulations on the Dumping of Wastes at Sea	September 25, 1990	Entry into force on the same day

Compiled by the author. Based on Office of Policy, Law, and Regulation of State Oceanic Administration of China, ed. *Collection of the Sea Laws and Regulations of the People's Republic of China* (Beijing: Ocean Press, 1998).

borrow this popular state practice and employed it as a promising future solution for managing the SCS issue.

The view of joint development as an alternative approach to solving maritime disputes is in line with the spirit of the UNCLOS and general international law. The 1982 UNCLOS provides a legal basis for joint development as an interim arrangement. Articles 74 (3) and 83 (3) provide that, pending agreement on the delimitation of the EEZ and continental shelf, "the States concerned, in a spirit of understanding and cooperation, shall make every effort to enter into provisional arrangements of a practical nature and, during this transitional period, not to jeopardize or hamper the reaching of the final agreement."[65] Previously, there existed several precedents for joint development arrangements in international practice. The 1969 *North Sea Case* of the International Court of Justice is generally seen as a milestone in the application of joint development as an approach to solving maritime disputes. It was also a popular practice in Asia in the 1980s. For example, the Malaysian and Thai governments agreed to a joint development area of 7250 km^2 in the Gulf of Thailand as an interim measure to solve their overlapping claims over continental shelf areas. The two governments signed a memorandum of understanding on February 21, 1979. On May 30, 1990, an agreement to constitute the joint development authority was signed in Kuala Lumpur, Malaysia.[66] Similarly, Indonesia and Vietnam discussed arrangements for the Natuna Sea area.[67] A more complex joint development scheme, called a "zone of cooperation," was established between Australia and Indonesia in the East Timor continental shelf area in 1989, and entered into force in 1991.[68]

The 1980s witnessed Beijing's growing interest in the idea of joint development, which formed one of the core principles guiding China's handling of maritime disputes. At this time, the proposal of joint development was mainly discussed on a bilateral level. It was not until the 1990s that the Chinese leaders promulgated the idea of joint development across the whole SCS region.

The concept of joint development first appeared in February 1984 when the late Chinese leader Deng Xiaoping attended a meeting with delegations from the Center for Strategic and International Studies of Georgetown University. During this meeting, he said: "I have also considered the possibility of resolving certain disputes by having the countries concerned jointly develop the disputed areas before discussing the question of sovereignty. New approaches should be sought to solve such problems according to realities."

Subsequently, the joint development model as a means to address territorial disputes was extended to the SCS. In April 1988, during a state visit by Filipino president Aquino, Deng Xiaoping expounded on his thoughts on joint development. Regarding the disputes in the SCS, he said, "For the sake of a cordial relationship between the two countries, we could shelve the disputes and adopt a joint development approach instead."[69]

Analysis

With the conclusion of the LOS Convention, the maritime regime gradually situated the SCS dispute in a wider legal institutional context. This context influenced the SCS dispute in three ways. First, it reconstructed the legal basis of the SCS dispute (role 1 in Chapter 1), an immediate result of which was the intensification of the dispute in the 1980s. As we will see in Chapter 5, this reconstruction also led to important changes in China's legal position regarding its claims to sovereignty in the SCS. Second, engagement with this legal institutional context of the maritime regime helped the Chinese government to improve its domestic maritime governance system (roles 2 and 5 in Chapter 1).[70] Third, the Chinese government learned to borrow the concept of joint development for solving the SCS dispute (role 5 in Chapter 1).

With regard to the military skirmish between China and Vietnam in 1988, power distribution combined with developments of the maritime regime in factoring into the escalation and showdown of the Sino-Vietnam confrontation. Many security scholars were correct in pointing out power factor, mainly China's naval capability, influenced the escalation. They argue that in the first half of the 1980s, in the face of other countries' aggressive moves to occupy disputed islands, Chinese leaders were constrained by the nascent naval power incapable of either deterring these occupations or projecting its own power into the southern part of the SCS.[71] It was only after several years of hydro-geological exploration and military preparation that China finally asserted its presence in the SCS.

While the timing of the military confrontation has to do with the distribution of military power among the countries bordering the SCS, the scramble and the consequent escalation were co-determined by two other factors related to the maritime regime. First, the legal revolution in the maritime sphere intensified the SCS dispute in the early 1980s and was the motivation for relevant littoral states to expand in the SCS in the first place. The second factor is institutional weakness. In this period, the new maritime law was just concluded and the maritime regime was slow to develop pertinent norms and coordinating mechanisms at both international and regional levels to cope with the negative consequences associated with the shifts of maritime order. It also took some time for relevant countries to either establish or join institutional arrangements to manage the dispute in a more peaceful manner. When an effective multilateral institutional architecture was gradually put in place in the 1990s, continued occupation and consolidation of land features in the SCS did not result in deadly military confrontations. This multilateral institutional turn in the SCS region played an influential part in shaping the contour of China's SCS policy in the 1990s, which will be elaborated in Chapter 5.

Notes

1 In contemporary international law, methods of acquisition of a clear title to territory include effective administration (often called occupation), cession through treaty, or prescription. International law recognizes acquisition of title to territory

belonging to no-one (*terra nullius*) through first discovery, which establishes an inchoate title. This title can be converted to a more complete title through effective administration. See R. Y. Jennings, *The Acquisition of Territory in International Law* (Manchester: Manchester University Press, 1962), 6–7, 16–27.

2 Chi-kin Lo, *China's Policy towards Territorial Disputes: The Case of the South China Sea Islands* (New York: Routledge, 1989), 143–144.

3 Ibid.

4 Chanrobles, *Presidential Decree no. 1596*, available at: www.chanrobles.com/presidentialdecrees/presidentialdecreeno1596.html#.Ugj7kW12n5w (accessed February 26, 2014).

5 The text reads: "including the sea-bed, sub-soil, continental margin and space shall belong and be subject to the sovereignty of the Philippines."

6 It is worth noting that the Philippines' claim of continental shelf was not inspired by the 1958 Geneva Convention on Continental Shelf, for two reasons. First, the Philippines neither signed nor ratified the 1958 Geneva Convention on Continental Shelf. Second, this claim was made in 1976 in the middle of the UNCLOS III.

7 United Nations, *Presidential Decree no. 1599*, available at: www.un.org/depts/los/LEGISLATIONANDTREATIES/PDFFILES/PHL_1978_Decree.pdf (accessed February 26, 2014).

8 The Philippines claimed in its submission No. 5 to the arbitral tribunal of the South China Sea Arbitration case that "Mischief Reef and Second Thomas Shoal are part of the exclusive economic zone and continental shelf of the Philippines". See Award on the South China Sea Arbitration, para. 385. The whole text of the Award on the South China Sea Arbitration is available at Permanent Court of Arbitration, https://pcacases.com/web/sendAttach/2086 (accessed July 31, 2017).

9 Victor Prescott, *The South China Sea: Limits of National Claims* (Kuala Lumpur: Maritime Institute of Malaysia, 1998), 222.

10 Lo, *China's Policy towards Territorial Disputes*, 154–155.

11 Shicun Wu, *Origin and Development of the South China Sea Disputes* (Beijing: China Economic Publishing House, 2010), 150, in Chinese.

12 There is an important legal implication associated with SRV's changing position. After the founding of SRV by the Communist government in 1975, Vietnam's claims had to face the problem of estoppel given previous North Vietnam's attitudes towards China's SCS claims. Since this implication is beyond the scope of this text, readers can find a good discussion of how DRV estopped SRV's SCS claims in Greg Austin, *China's Ocean Frontier: International Law, Military Force and National Development* (St. Leonards, Australia: Allen and Unwin,1998), 126–130.

13 The Gulf of Tonkin negotiation will be further elaborated in Chapter 6.

14 E. C. Farrell, *The Socialist Republic of Vietnam and the Law of the Sea: An Analysis of Vietnamese Behavior within the Emerging International Oceans Regime* (The Hague: Martinus Nijhoff, 1998), 70. For an overview of the controversy surrounding the meridian line of the 1887 Sino-French Treaty, see Keyuan Zou, "Maritime Boundary Delimitation in the Gulf of Tonkin," *Ocean Development and International Law* 30, no. 3 (1999): 235–254.

15 See US Department of State Bureau of Intelligence and Research, "Straight Baseline: Vietnam," *Limits in the Sea*, no. 99, available at: www.state.gov/documents/organization/58573.pd (accessed December 21, 2013).

16 I use historic regime and historic title interchangeably and under them I place historic bays, historic rights, historic waters, which are the terms used by China (including Taiwan) when invoking the legal concept of historic regime. It is unnecessary for this book and difficult to define each term individually because these terms have been used interchangeably in the LOS parlance and the Chinese government has not clarified the specific meaning of its own historic claims.

17 Keyuan Zou, "Historic Rights in International Law and in China's Practice," *Ocean Development and International Law* 32, no. 2 (2001): 150.

18 For a succinct review of the origins and development of historic assertions and the difficulties of achieving a general formula of historic title, see Myres S. McDougal and William T. Burke, *The Public Order of the Oceans* (New Haven, CT: Yale University Press, 1962), 357–368. Also see D. P. O'Connell, *The International Law of the Sea*, vol. 1, ed. I. A. Shearer (Oxford: Clarendon Press, 1982), 417–438.

19 R. P. Anand, *Origin and Development of the Law of the Sea: History of International Law Revisited* (Boston: Martinus Nijhoff, 1983), 185, and McDougal and Burke, *The Public Order of Oceans*, 367.

20 UN Doc. A/CN.4/143, "Juridical Regime of Historic Waters, Including Historic Bays," *Yearbook of the International Law Commission*, vol. 2, (March 9, 1962), 6.

21 Zou, "Historic Rights," 151.

22 For example, some legalists have argued that the historic regime, while still relevant in the new LOS, had been significantly weakened relative to other legal regimes such as the EEZ and CS in terms of its independent legality in generating maritime jurisdiction, and that under the new maritime regime, many traditional claims were believed to have either lapsed *ipso jure*, replaced by a juridical claim, or to have been absorbed into the 1982 UNCLOS's TS, EEZ, or CS regimes. See Clive R. Symmons, *Historic Waters in the Law of the Sea: A Modern Re-appraisal* (Leiden: Martinus Nijhoff, 2008), 271–283, Yann-Huei Song and Peter Kien-Hong Yu, "China's 'Historic Waters' in the South China Sea: An Analysis from Taiwan, R.O.C.," *The American Asian Review* 12, no. 4 (1994): 91, and Nong Hong, "Law and Politics in the South China Sea: Assessing the Role of UNCLOS in Ocean Dispute Settlement" (PhD diss., University of Alberta, 2010), 100–101.

23 There are three well-known judicial cases invoking historic claims. One is in the *Fisheries Case* in 1951 and the other is the *Gulf of Fonseca Case*. See ICJ reports on *Fisheries Case 1951 (U.K. v. Norway)* and on *Land, Island and Maritime Frontier Dispute 1992 (El Salvador/Honduras)*, respectively.

24 For the full text of the Agreement in English, see "Appendix 2," in Kriangsak Kittichaisaree, *The Law of the Sea and Maritime Boundary Delimitation in South-East Asia* (Singapore: Oxford University Press, 1987), 180–181.

25 For instance, Article 298 permits contracting states to exclude the compulsory procedure provided for in the LOS Convention from applying to the disputes "involving historic bays or titles."

26 The preamble of the LOS Convention affirms that "matters not regulated by this Convention continue to be governed by the rules and principles of general international law."

27 Furtado has an informative review of this problem in applying the UNCLOS to the SCS case. See Xavier Furtado, "International Law and the Dispute over the Spratly Islands: Whither UNCLOS?" *Contemporary Southeast Asia* 21, no. 3 (1999): 386–404.

28 Robin R. Churchill and A. V. Lowe, *The Law of the Sea*, 3rd edn (Manchester: Manchester University Press, 1999), 163.

29 For a legal discussion on the application of the regime of islands in the SCS, see Marius Gjetnes, "The Spratlys: Are They Rocks or Islands?" *Ocean Development and International Law* 32, no. 2 (2001): 191–204.

30 The Philippines claimed in its submissions No. 3 and 7 to the arbitral tribunal of the South China Sea Arbitration case that "Scarborough Shoal generates no entitlement to an exclusive economic zone or continental shelf" and that "Johnson Reef, Cuarteron Reef and Fiery Cross Reef generate no entitlement to an exclusive economic zone or continental shelf." See Award on the South China Sea Arbitration, para. 385.

31 I would like to thank Professor Jeremy M. Firestone for suggesting this point. Also see Clive Schofield, "What's at Stake in the South China Sea? Geographical and

Geopolitical Considerations," in Robert C. Beckman *et al.* (eds.) *Beyond Territorial Disputes in the South China Sea: Legal Frameworks for the Joint Development of Hydrocarbon Resources* (Northampton, MA: Edward Elgar, 2013), 25.

32 Currently, the issue of a potential international area has not raised serious concerns in the SCS. This is in a large part due to the fact that exploration activities of oil and gas fields in the waters are still in the nascent stage and located mostly near the disputed land features.

33 Churchill and Lowe, *The Law of the Sea*, 162.

34 Semi-enclosed seas are defined in Section 122 of UNCLOS.

35 See Robin R. Churchill, "Dispute Settlement under the UN Convention on the Law of the Sea: Survey for 2004," *International Journal of Marine and Coastal Law* 21, no. 1 (2006): 1–14, A. O. Adede, *The System for Settlement of Disputes Under the United Nations Convention on the Law of the Sea: A Drafting History and a Commentary* (Boston: Martinus Nijhoff, 1987) and Natalie Klein, *Dispute Settlement in the UN Convention on the Law of the Sea* (Cambridge: Cambridge University Press, 2005).

36 Part XV also provides opting-out options for states to choose to exclude certain categories of disputes.

37 Hasjim Djalal, "Indonesia and the South China Sea Initiative," *Ocean Development and International Law* 32, no. 2 (2001): 97–103; Timo Kivimaeki, ed. *War or Peace in the South China Sea* (Copenhagen: NIAS Press, 2002), 131–165; Mark J. Valencia and Jon M. Van Dyke, "Comprehensive Solutions to the South China Sea Disputes: Some Options," in Gerald Blake *et al.* (eds.) *Boundaries and Energy: Problems and Prospects*, (London: Kluwer Law International, 1998), 85–117.

38 Sam Bateman, "Managing the South China Sea: Sovereignty Is Not the Issue," *RSIS Commentaries*, no. 136 (2011).

39 David Freestone, Richard Barnes and David M. Ong, eds. *The Law of the Sea: Progress and Prospects* (Oxford: Oxford University Press, 2006), 7.

40 Churchill and Lowe, *The Law of the Sea*, 5–27.

41 Ibid., 12.

42 United Nations Charter, *The UN Chapter* VI, Article 33 (1), available at: www.un.org/en/documents/charter/chapter6.shtml (accessed March 1, 2014).

43 Furtado, "Whither UNCLOS?," 387.

44 Freestone *et al., LOS: Progress and Prospects*, 5–6.

45 For example, legal scholars observe that in recent years the ITLOS has expanded its juridical scope to cover issues such as territorial disputes and marine protection. See Irina Buga, "Territorial Sovereignty Issues in Maritime Disputes: A Jurisdictional Dilemma for Law of the Sea Tribunals," *International Journal of Marine and Coastal Law* 27, no. 1 (2012): 59–95, and Donald R. Rothwell, "The International Tribunal for the Law of the Sea and Marine Environmental Protection: Expanding the Horizons of International Oceans Governance," *Ocean Yearbook Online* 17, no. 1 (2003): 26–52.

46 In addition to the ITLOS and ICJ, the LOS Convention also provides two other types of arbitral tribunals: the arbitral tribunal constituted in accordance with Annex VII and special arbitral tribunal constituted in accordance with Annex VIII. The Conclusion will discuss the Philippines' recent invocation of special arbitral tribunal procedure for its dispute with China over the Scarborough Shoal and the potential implication of this action on the SCS dispute.

47 The ITLOS plays a similar role in this regard and is designated more authority under the UNCLOS compared to the ICJ in settling maritime disputes.

48 International Maritime Organization, "A Brief History of IMO," available at: www.imo.org/About/Pages/Default.aspx (accessed March 1, 2014).

49 Lo, *China's Policy towards Territorial Disputes*, 144.

50 Wu, *Origin and Development of the South China Sea Disputes,* 127.

51 Ibid., 94.
52 Ibid., 146.
53 *Oceanographic Almanac* (1986): 404–405, cited in John W. Garver, "China's Push through the South China Sea: The Interaction of Bureaucratic and National Interests," *The China Quarterly* 132 (1992): 1008.
54 Garver, "China's Push," 1008.
55 Ibid., 1010.
56 Liqun Deng *et al.* eds., *Modern Chinese Navy* (Beijing: Chinese Social Science Publisher, 1987), 324–325.
57 *Da gong Bao*, May 8, 1988, cited in Garver, "China's Push," 1012.
58 Garver, "China's Push," 1013.
59 China also participated in other areas of the LOS regime. I do not discuss them here since they are not of particular relevance in the SCS dispute. For instance, while the LOS conference was concluded in 1982, China participated in the Preparatory Commission for the establishment of the International Seabed Authority, see International Seabed Authority, available at: www.isa.org.jm/en/scientific/exploration/contractors; also see http://politics.people.com.cn/GB/8198/236802/16626758.html (accessed January 1, 2014).
60 The data are based on "Listing of Multilateral LOS Treaties to Which China Acceded (1920–2003)," in Jianjun Gao, *China and the Law of the Sea* (Beijing: Ocean Press, 2004), 176–179, in Chinese.
61 International Maritime Organization, "Status of Conventions," available at: www.imo.org/About/Conventions/StatusOfConventions/Pages/Default.aspx (accessed January 1, 2014).
62 Gao, *China and the Law of the Sea*, 178. For the full text of the SUA 1988, see United Nations, http://treaties.un.org/doc/db/Terrorism/Conv8-english.pdf (accessed January 1, 2014).
63 United States Environmental Protection Agency, "History of Sustainability," available at: http://yosemite.epa.gov/r10/oi.nsf/8bb15fe43a5fb81788256b58005ff079/398761d6c3c7184988256fc40078499b!OpenDocument (accessed February 12, 2014).
64 World Commission on Environment and Development, *Our Common Future* (New York: Oxford University Press, 1987), 43–66.
65 UNCLOS, Article 74 (3).
66 David M. Ong, "The 1979 and 1990 Malaysia-Thailand Joint Development Agreements: A Model for International Legal Co-operation in Common Offshore Petroleum Deposits?" *International Journal of Marine and Coastal Law* 14, no. 2 (1999): 207–246.
67 Mark J. Valencia, "Taming Troubled Waters: Joint Development of Oil and Mineral Resources in Overlapping Claim Areas," *San Diego Law Review* 23 (1986): 661–684.
68 Stuart Kaye, "The Timor Gap Treaty," *Natural Resources and Environment* 14, no. 2 (1999): 92–144.
69 Chinese Foreign Ministry, "Shelving Disputes, Joint Developing," *Review of the History of New China's Diplomacy,* based on Office of Policy, Law, and Regulation of State Oceanic Administration of China, ed. *Collection of the Sea Laws and Regulations of the People's Republic of China* (Beijing: Ocean Press, 1998). www.fmprc.gov.cn/chn/pds/ziliao/wjs/2159/t8958.htm (accessed March 1, 2014). It is worth noting that at this point in time, the Chinese leaders had a very basic understanding of the concept of joint development, and the concept was proposed on a bilateral basis. Following the official embrace of joint development, scholarly deliberation began to develop and more concrete and practical models were proposed, which will be discussed in Chapter 5 and Chapter 6.

70 The maritime regime draws China into the playground to interact with other states and international organizations, and provides material benefits and policy-related knowledge.

71 See, for example, Garver, "China's Push," 1020–1025.

Bibliography

Adede, A.O. 1987. *The System for Settlement of Disputes Under the United Nations Convention on the Law of the Sea: A Drafting History and a Commentary*, Martinus Nijhoff, Boston.

Anand, R.P. 1983. *Origin and Development of the Law of the Sea: History of International Law Revisited*, Martinus Nijhoff, Boston.

Austin, G. 1998. *China's Ocean Frontier*, Allen and Unwin University Printery, Canberra, Australia.

Barrett, J. and Barnes, R. 2016. *Law of the Sea: UNCLOS as a Living Treaty*, British Institute of International and Comparative Law, London.

Bateman, S. 2011. "Managing the South China Sea: Sovereignty Is Not the Issue," *RSIS Commentaries*, no. 136.

Beckman, R.C., Townsend-Gault, I., Schofield, C.H., Davenport, T., and Bernard, L. (eds.) 2013. *Beyond Territorial Disputes in the South China Sea: Legal Frameworks for the Joint Development of Hydrocarbon Resources*, Edward Elgar Publishing Limited, Northampton, MA.

Blake, G., Pratt, M., Schofield, C.H., and Brown, J.A. (eds.) 1998. *Boundaries and Energy: Problems and Prospects*, Kluwer Law International, London, pp. 85–117.

Buga, I. 2012. "Territorial Sovereignty Issues in Maritime Disputes: A Jurisdictional Dilemma for Law of the Sea Tribunals," *International Journal of Marine and Coastal Law*, vol. 27, no. 1, pp. 59–95.

Chanrobles. *Presidential Decree no. 1596*, available at: www.chanrobles.com/presidentialdecrees/presidentialdecreeno1596.html#.Ugj7kW12n5w. (accessed Feb. 26, 2014).

Chinese Foreign Ministry. n.d. "Shelving Ddisputes, Joint Developing," *Review of the History of New China's Diplomacy*, available at: www.fmprc.gov.cn/chn/pds/ziliao/wjs/2159/t8958.htm (accessed Jan. 3, 2014).

Churchill, R.R. 2006. "Dispute Settlement under the UN Convention on the Law of the Sea: Survey for 2004," *International Journal of Marine and Coastal Law*, vol. 21, no. 1, pp. 1–14.

Churchill, R.R. and Lowe, A.V. 1999. *The Law of the Sea*, 3rd edn, Manchester University Press, Manchester.

Deng, L.Q. (ed.) 1987. *Modern Chinese Navy*, Chinese Social Science Publisher, Beijing (in Chinese).

Djalal, H. 2001. "Indonesia and the South China Sea Initiative," *Ocean Development and International Law*, vol. 32, no. 2, pp. 97–103.

Farrell, E.C. 1999. *The Socialist Republic of Vietnam and the Law of the Sea: An Analysis of Vietnamese Behavior within the Emerging International Oceans Regime*, Martinus Nijhoff, The Hague.

Freestone, D., Barnes, R., and Ong, D.M. (eds.) 2006. *The Law of the Sea: Progress and Prospects*, Oxford University Press, Oxford.

Furtado, X. 1999. "International Law and the Dispute over the Spratly Islands: Whither UNCLOS?," *Contemporary Southeast Asia*, vol. 21 no. 3, pp. 386–404.

Gao, J.J. 2004. *China and the Law of the Sea*, Ocean Press, Beijing (in Chinese).
Garver, J.W. 1992. "China's Push through the South China Sea: The Interaction of Bureaucratic and National Interests," *The China Quarterly*, vol. 132, pp. 999–1028.
Gjetnes, M. 2001. "The Spratlys: Are They Rocks or Islands?," *Ocean Development and International Law*, vol. 32, no. 2, pp. 191–204.
Hong, N. 2010. "Law and Politics in the South China Sea: Assessing the Role of UNCLOS in Ocean Dispute Settlement," PhD diss., University of Alberta.
ICJ. 1951. *I.C.J. Reports: Fisheries Case (U.K. v. Norway)*. ICJ, Brussels.
ICJ. 1992. *I.C.J. Reports: Land, Island and Maritime Frontier Dispute (El Salvador/ Honduras)*, ICJ, Brussels.
Jennings, R.Y. 1962. *The Acquisition of Territory in International Law*, Manchester University Press, Manchester.
Jensen, Ø. 2014. *The Commission on the Limits of the Continental Shelf-Law and Legitimacy*, Brill, Leiden.
Kaye, S. 1999. "The Timor Gap Treaty," *Natural Resources and Environment*, vol. 14, no. 2, pp. 92–144.
Kittichaisaree, K. 1987. *The Law of the Sea and Maritime Boundary Delimitation in South-East Asia*, Oxford University Press, Singapore.
Kivimaeki, T. (ed.) 2002. *War or Peace in the South China Sea*, NIAS Press, Copenhagen.
Klein, N. 2005. *Dispute Settlement in the UN Convention on the Law of the Sea*, Cambridge University Press, Cambridge.
Lee, S.K. and Gullett, W. 2016. *Asia-Pacific and the Implementation of the Law of the Sea*, Brill, Leiden.
Lo, C.K. 1989. *China's Policy towards Territorial Disputes: The Case of the South China Sea Islands*, Routledge, New York.
McDougal, M.S. and Burke, W.T. 1962. *The Public Order of the Oceans*, Yale University Press, New Haven, CT.
O'Connell, D.P. 1982. *The International Law of the Sea*, Clarendon Press, Oxford.
Ong, D.M. 1999. "The 1979 and 1990 Malaysia-Thailand Joint Development Agreements: A Model for International Legal Co-operation in Common Offshore Petroleum Deposits?," *International Journal of Marine and Coastal Law*, vol. 14, no. 2, pp. 207–246.
Permanent Court of Arbitration. 2016. "Award on the South China Sea Arbitration," available at: https://pcacases.com/web/sendAttach/2086 (accessed July 31, 2017).
Prescott, J.R.V. 1998. *The South China Sea: Limits of National Claims*, Maritime Institute of Malaysia, Kuala Lumpur, Malaysia.
Rothwell, D.R. 2003. "The International Tribunal for the Law of the Sea and Marine Environmental Protection: Expanding the Horizons of International Oceans Governance," *Ocean Yearbook Online*, vol. 17, no. 1, pp. 26–52.
Rothwell, R., Elferink, A.O., Scott, K., and Stephens, T. (eds) 2015. *Oxford Handbook of the Law of the Sea*, Oxford University Press, Oxford.
Schofield, C.H. and Wang, D.K. 2012. "The Regime of Islands under the United Nations Convention on the Law of the Sea: Implications for the South China Sea," *NBR Special Report*, no. 37, pp. 61–77.
State Oceanic Administration of China, Office of Policy, Law, and Regulation. 1998. *Collection of the Sea Laws and Regulations of the People's Republic of China*, Ocean Press, Beijing.
Symmons, C.R. 2008. *Historic Waters in the Law of the Sea: A Modern Re-appraisal*, Martinus Nijhoff, Boston.

Song, Y.H. and Yu, P.K.H. 1994. "China's 'Historic Waters' in the South China Sea: An Analysis from Taiwan, R.O.C.," *The American Asian Review*, vol. 12, no. 4. 94–99.
Song, Y.H. and Zou, K.Y. (eds.) 2014. *Major Law and Policy Issues in the South China Sea: European and American Perspectives*, Routledge, New York.
United Nations. n.d.a. *Presidential Decree no. 1599*, available at: www.un.org/depts/los/LEGISLATIONANDTREATIES/PDFFILES/PHL_1978_Decree.pdf (accessed Feb. 26, 2014).
United Nation. n.d.b. *United Nations Charter*, available at: www.un.org/en/documents/charter/chapter6.shtml (accessed January 3, 2014).
United Nations. 1962. "Juridical Regime of Historic Waters, Including Historic Bays," Doc. A/CN.4/143, *Yearbook of the International Law Commission*, vol. 2.
United States Department of State Bureau of Intelligence and Research. "Straight Baseline: Vietnam," *Limits in the Sea*, no. 99, available at: www.state.gov/documents/organization/58573.pdf (accessed December 21 2013).
Valencia, M.J. 1986. 'Taming Troubled Waters: Joint Development of Oil and Mineral Resources in Overlapping Claim Areas," *San Diego Law Review*, vol. 23, pp. 661–684.
World Commission on Environment and Development. 1987. *Our Common Future*, Oxford University Press, New York.
Wu, S.C. 2010. *Origin and Development of the South China Sea Disputes*, China Economic Publishing House, Beijing (in Chinese).
Wu, S.C. 2013. *Solving Disputes for Regional Cooperation and Development in the South China Sea: A Chinese Perspective*, Chandos Publishing, Oxford.
Wu, S.C., Valencia, M., and Hong, N. (eds.) 2015. *UN Convention on the Law of the Sea and the South China Sea*, Routledge, New York.
Wu, S.C. and Zou, K.Y. (eds.) 2013. *Securing the Safety of Navigation in East Asia: Legal and Political Dimensions*, Chandos Publishing, Oxford.
Wu, S.C. and Zou, K.Y. (eds.) 2014. *Non-Traditional Security Issues and the South China Sea: Shaping a New Framework for Cooperation*, Routledge, New York.
Zou, K.Y. 1999. "Maritime Boundary Delimitation in the Gulf of Tonkin," *Ocean Development and International Law*, vol. 30, no. 3, pp. 235–254.
Zou, K.Y. 2001. "Historic Rights in International Law and in China's Practice," *Ocean Development and International Law*, vol. 32, no. 2, pp. 149–168.
Zou, K.Y. 2008. 'Law of the Sea Issues between the United States and East Asian States," *Ocean Development and International Law*, vol. 39, no. 1, pp. 69–93.
Zou, K.Y. 2012. "How Coastal States Claim Maritime Geographic Features: Legal Clarity or Conundrum?," *Chinese Journal of International Law*, vol. 11, no. 4, pp. 749–765.

5 A multilateral turn in the SCS

1990–2002

This chapter looks at the evolution of China's South China Sea (SCS) policy in the 1990s. The first section identifies important changes taking place in the legal arena of China's SCS policy by examining three important pieces of national legislation. These changes resulted from China's internalization of the normative impact of the maritime regime outlined in Chapter 4 on its legal claims in the SCS. The second section concentrates on China's approach to other countries regarding the negotiations on the SCS issue. Entering the 1990s, multilateralism appeared as a normative innovation proposed by some Southeast Asian countries as a method to cope with the new nature of the SCS issue as a multi-state, multi-issue dispute. Concurrently, a complex institutional architecture emerged to uphold multilateralism as the new norm. A combination of geostrategic pressure and normative institutional incentives elicited China's involvement in this institutional architecture, which in turn led to a multilateral turn in its approach of political engagement with other concerned countries from the 1990s onwards. Engagement with the maritime regime at both regional and international levels also informed Beijing of new policy orientations and options with respect to the usage of SCS waters, which is the focus of the third section. The fourth section is devoted to China's attitude and policy practices regarding possible solutions to the SCS issue. In the final section are summarized the policy changes resulting from China's interaction with the maritime regime and how the geostrategic environment and the normative institutional dynamics of the maritime regime blended into an integrative set of forces shaping the contours of China's SCS policy.

China's legal position on the SCS

This section focuses on three pieces of national maritime legislation: (1) China's ratification of the 1982 UNCLOS; (2) the Law of the People's Republic of China on the Territorial Sea and the Contiguous Zone; and (3) the Law on the Exclusive Economic Zone and the Continental Shelf. They represent the official position of China in the 1990s regarding its sovereignty in the SCS and reflect a number of changes to China's previous claims in the SCS. These changes are very important for an accurate reading of China's SCS policy, but so far they have been overlooked by security scholars, as they do not fit into either the category of cooperative policy or the category of delay policy.

Ratification of the LOSC

On May 15, 1996, the Standing Committee of the Eighth National People's Congress issued a declaration on the ratification of the 1982 LOS Convention during the nineteenth session. Although China had signed the LOS Convention on December 10, 1982, the first day the Convention opened for signature, a total of 14 years passed before China finally acceded to the Convention. There are mainly two reasons accounting for this delay.

First, the Chinese delegation was not completely satisfied with the final text of the Convention. During the concluding period of the third LOS conference, the Chinese delegates raised their concerns with a number of provisions in the final draft, mainly regarding innocent passage in territorial seas, the definition of the continental shelf, and the delimitation of maritime jurisdictional space.[1]

Second, critical voices emerged in the domestic discourse of the 1990s, questioning China's previous position on the LOS Convention and calling for a reassessment of the impact of the UNCLOS on China's maritime interests and practice.[2] These voices argued that the Convention might affect China adversely, and that it was vital to first study the costs and benefits before entering into the process of ratification.[3] Since the seas surrounding China were mostly semi-closed in nature, it might even have been a better strategy during the negotiating rounds of the UNCLOS III to place China in the group of geographically disadvantaged countries.[4] Ling Qing, head of the Chinese delegation to the UNCLOS III, echoed this rethinking of China's position in his memoirs, published in 2008.[5] He noted that during the 1976 conference, discussion began to emerge within the Chinese delegation that touched upon the potential negative impact on China's maritime interests, especially regarding the concept of the Exclusive Economic Zone (EEZ), which might reduce the share of marine resources to which China could otherwise be entitled. When the text of the LOSC was eventually finalized and submitted in the concluding session of the UNCLOS III, Ling raised the concern over the concept of EEZ in front of the leadership circle and suggested China make certain reservations. However, in the end, the central leadership decided that China would continue its original position of unconditionally supporting the Third World.[6]

Notwithstanding these concerns, China still held a positive view of the 1982 UNCLOS, perceiving it as a dominant force shaping global ocean governance.[7] After the Agreement Relating to the Implementation of Part XI was successfully negotiated in 1994, China saw the wide-ranging acceptance of the UNCLOS governing the world ocean regime as an international trend it should follow.[8] The snowballing ratification of the UNCLOS worldwide was seen as a good opportunity for China to consolidate its image-building process. Li Zhaoxing, Vice Minister of Foreign Affairs, when explaining the benefits of ratifying UNCLOS before the Standing Committee of the Eighth National People's

Congress, argued that acceding to the Convention was conducive to building a good image of the People's Republic of China (PRC) in the international community, as well as enhancing its participation in those institutions established under the UNCLOS, bringing its role in global maritime affairs into full play.[9] In other words, despite the potential negative impact on China's interests in the SCS associated with ratifying the LOSC, the Chinese government felt considerable normative pressure imposed by the maritime regime and perceived the ratification as an appropriate and responsible action China should take as a member of the international maritime community.

It is worth noting that Li specifically raised the SCS issue during this presentation. He stated that its provisions concerning historic waters could be used to strengthen PRC rights and interests in the waters adjacent to the Spratly Islands in the SCS.[10] The important implications of this mentioning of the concept of historic waters will be further elaborated later.

The Laws on the Territorial Sea, and the Law on the EEZ and the CS

The Law of the People's Republic of China on the Territorial Sea and the Contiguous Zone (hereafter referred to as the Law on Territorial Sea) was promulgated in 1992 and the Law on the Exclusive Economic Zone and the Continental Shelf (hereafter referred to as the Law on EEZ and CS) in 1998. These two pieces of legislation reflect the impact of the new LOS on China's legal claims in the SCS.

The Law on Territorial Sea used the same wording as the 1958 Declaration in asserting sovereignty over the four island groups in the SCS.[11] Changes to China's legal claims were mainly expressed in the Law on EEZ and CS. First, this legislation embraced the regimes of the EEZ and the CS and brought China's legal claims in line with the new LOS. According to Article 2, the exclusive economic zone is an area beyond and adjacent to the territorial sea extending 200 nautical miles from the baselines from which the breadth of the territorial sea is measured.[12] This definition is very similar to Article 57 of UNCLOS in measuring the breadth of the exclusive economic zone.[13] The provision on CS adopted the same wording of Article 76 (1) of the UNCLOS on the definition of the continental shelf.[14]

The second change was found in the clause on historic claims. Article 14 declared that "the provisions of this Law shall not affect the historic rights enjoyed by the People's Republic of China." This clause signaled the growing emphasis Beijing placed on historic claims, to which we will turn next, as part of its incremental modifications of Chinese legal position in the SCS.

China's historic claims in the South China Sea[15]

Prior to the 1990s, the Chinese government had expressed its position on the historic regime only twice, both related to "historic bays."[16] The first instance took place when the former Soviet Union claimed the Peter the Great Bay as a "historic bay." This claim was fiercely opposed by Western countries, including the United States, but China publicly supported the Soviet Union. An editorial in the *People's Daily* on September 23, 1957 claimed:

> Peter the Great Bay has always been Russia's *historic bay* ... The Communique of the government of the Soviet Union regarding the *internal water* boundary of the Peter the Great Bay was just a restatement of a fact that stands the test for history.
>
> (emphasis added)[17]

The second case was related to the Bohai Bay in the Yellow Sea. The central government in Beijing used the term "internal waters." The 1958 Declaration reads "the water areas inside the baseline, including Bohai Bay and the Qiongzhou Straits, are Chinese internal waters." Since the editorial piece cited above used "internal water" and "historic bay" interchangeably, the Bohai Bay could be seen as the second case where historic claims were invoked by China.[18]

Moreover, there is no record showing that the Chinese government ever invoked the historic regime for its claims to sovereignty in the SCS before the 1990s. In the 1970s and 1980s, when Vietnam proposed to China that the Gulf of Tonkin be shared by the two sides as historic waters, China rejected this standpoint as the basis for delimitating the Gulf.[19] This is probably because during this period, China placed an almost exclusive focus on the ownership of land features, and paid little attention to the possibility of historic claims in the SCS. In the time between the two naval skirmishes between the Chinese Navy and the Vietnamese Navy (in 1974 and in 1988), the two sides engaged an intermittent legal battle. Both sides worked arduously to publicize available historical evidence to prove the superiority of the claim over that of their opponent. In May 1979, Hanoi disseminated a classified compilation of historical evidence to demonstrate Vietnamese first discovery and occupation of those land features scattered in the SCS. In response, China's Ministry of Foreign Affairs circulated a dossier of legal documents discrediting the legitimacy of Vietnam's evidence and condemning Hanoi for violating the principle of *estoppel*. The documents included Vietnam's previous official letters and statements indicating recognition of China's sovereignty over the disputed islands. In January 1980, China's Ministry of Foreign Affairs came up with an exhaustive and comprehensive compilation of historical archives and records. This document was entitled "China's Indisputable Sovereignty over Xisha and Nansha Islands," indicating that historic evidence and archives from past dynasties mentioned in this document were solely used to support China's claims of sovereignty to the islands.

In the 1990s, however, historic claims began to gain an important foothold in China's official attitude towards its sovereignty over waters in the SCS. In 1996, Li Zhaoxing, when presenting the ratification proposal, proclaimed that the UNCLOS provisions concerning historic waters could be used to strengthen national rights and interests in the waters adjacent to the Spratly

Islands in the SCS. This was the first time the issue of historic claims had been officially linked to the SCS disputes. Two years later, in 1998, as mentioned earlier, the claim of historic rights was inserted into the Law on EEZ and CS, which stated "the provisions of this Law shall not affect the historic rights enjoyed by the People's Republic of China." In doing so, Beijing indicated a growing interest in the potential application of the historic regime concerning its SCS policy stances, although the concrete meaning of its historic claims were left unexplained.

The historic claims explained above suggest a departure from Beijing's previous understanding of the legal basis of the SCS disputes. Previously, claims to sovereignty in the SCS rested on the traditional international law on territory acquisition. China was confident in the legal superiority of its claims to sovereignty over land features in the SCS when challenged by Vietnam. Yet, in the 1990s, the Chinese leadership faced a legal dilemma presented by the LOSC. On the one hand, the Chinese leaders felt the snowballing normative pressure to ratify and internalize the LOSC. On the other, they were clearly aware of the fact that the legal framework of the LOSC restructured the legal basis for the SCS dispute, potentially weakening China's position and adversely impacting its maritime interests, while simultaneously empowering its Southeast Asian counterparts. For instance, according to the regime of islands of the LOSC, the scattered land features in the SCS might not be entitled to waters other than territorial seas. It is possible that eventually these islands would be enclosed by the maritime jurisdictional zones of claimants other than China, even if the title of these islands belonged to China. In the face of such a legal dilemma, China undertook a two-step response. First, by ratifying the LOSC and internalizing it through a series of domestic legislations, China demonstrated its willingness to abide by the law and accept the LOSC as the legal basis for claims of sovereignty in the SCS. Second, to mitigate the negative impact on its legal position, China came up with a legal solution – adding a new claim of historic rights – to strengthen its position. It is worth noting that China was not claiming internal waters by historic rights. Rather, as will be discussed in subsequent chapters, China left room for future negotiation as to what type of rights could be accepted.

Beijing's official explanation concerning Chinese construction on the Mischief Reef might help illuminate the type of rights China envisioned in this period.[20]

In 1995, a dispute over the Mischief Reef (Meiji Jiao) erupted in Sino-Filipino relations. Mischief Reef is a barely submerged coral reef in the Spratlys claimed by both China and the Philippines. In February 1995, Philippine fishermen reported that China had erected structures on the reef, where Chinese boats were anchored. The Philippines accused Beijing of sovereignty intrusion and violation of the 1992 ASEAN Declaration on the South China Sea. Chen Jian, the Spokesperson of the Chinese Ministry of Foreign Affairs, explained China's construction works on the Mischief Reef as "a production-related installation protecting life security of fishermen operating in the SCS areas."[21]

This seems to signal that China was envisaging fishery rights in the SCS. As we will see in Chapter 6, following the revelation of the official stance on historic rights, Chinese scholars worked on elaborating the meaning of this concept and exploring policy options in relation to its application to the SCS.

The adjustments to China's legal position outlined above serve as the evidence of the normative impact of the maritime regime on the Chinese leadership's mindset towards the SCS dispute. These adjustments have two important implications in terms of the long-term development of the SCS dispute. The first implication is related to China's changing attitude towards the concept of historic rights. As will be addressed in Chapter 6, the embrace of historic rights continued to have significant bearings on China's SCS policy. Second, the changes made to the legal position conveyed the Chinese view that the LOSC as the legal bedrock for claims to sovereignty not only applied to China but also to other SCS-bordering countries, including its opponents. By acceding to the LOSC and transferring it into domestic legislation, the Chinese government situated the SCS dispute in the legal framework of the LOSC, signaling its willingness to be bound by the new LOS and comply with the rule of the law. As discussed in the Conclusion, the deciphering of this legalist layer of China's SCS policy will help formulate effective policy tools to push for resolving the SCS dispute in peaceful manner through legal means.

These legal adjustments were made in a prompt manner, as they appeared around the same time the LOSC entered into force, and were inevitably associated with negative consequences. The acceptance of the LOSC clearly enhanced the legitimacy of the claims of its opponents, and it was not entirely promising that China's solution in the form of historic claims would work out. Geopolitics did not play a noticeable role in this process, nor could it explain these changes. The USA was stronger than China and had significant interests in the SCS, but it did not force China to take the steps above to modify its legal position. Other claimants in the SCS were relatively weaker compared to China. They did not and could not force China to do so either. Had it not been for the normative pressure of the maritime regime, China could have adopted a delaying strategy even though it might not be able to resist the international trend eventually. In other words, had it not been for the normative pressure of the maritime regime, China could have postponed these efforts to a future time after it acquires the ability to enforce its own claims instead of ratifying the LOSC in 1996 right after its entry into force and thus modified its legal position in a prompt manner.

A multilateral turn in political engagement in the 1990s

China's approach to political engagement in the SCS region took a multilateral turn in the 1990s. Undoubtedly, geopolitics played an influential role in this process. But geopolitics did not accomplish this multilateral turn on its own and the incremental process through which it worked was shaped by the normative and institutional dynamics of the maritime regime. As demonstrated below, geopolitics worked through the medium provided by the regional multilateral architecture and combined with the normative and institutional dynamics of the regime in inducing China's adaptation to multilateralism.

The workshop on managing potential conflicts in the South China Sea

The norm of multilateralism first emerged during the workshop on Managing Potential Conflicts in the South China Sea (the SCS workshop) held in Bali in 1990. This workshop was attended only by participants of the Association of Southeast Asian Nations (ASEAN). During this workshop, leaders of the ASEAN countries came to realize that in face of the entangled network of multi-issue multi-party disputes that the SCS dispute had become, the traditional bilateral state-to-state engagement was no longer sufficient for constructive political engagement. They also feared that bilateral solutions, especially between China and Vietnam, could have a negative impact on other claimants or on the region as a whole.[22]

After lengthy discussion, multilateralism was adopted by the workshop, as "it was considered necessary to follow an all-inclusive approach that excludes no one who has interests and presence in the South China Sea region."[23] Topics were outlined and the involvement of non-ASEAN participants was agreed upon. In view of the sensitive issues on the workshop agenda, an informal approach was deployed concerning territorial and jurisdictional disputes. The SCS workshop was considered a Track 2 institutional network, since participants, some of whom were government officials, attended the meetings in their private capacities.[24] After this workshop, the ASEAN began to assume a major role in the maritime regime at the regional level, engaging China and developing new norms and mechanisms for managing and resolving the SCS issue.

Based on the consensus reached in the first workshop, the second workshop invited non-ASEAN countries (China, Chinese Taipei and Vietnam, which was not yet a member of ASEAN) to attend. This was the first time that all the disputant parties sat at the same table discussing issues related to the SCS. The meeting laid down six principles as the basis for cooperation:

1. Without prejudice to territorial and jurisdictional claims, to explore areas of cooperation in the South China Sea.
2. Such areas of cooperation may include cooperation: (a) to promote safety of navigation and communication; (b) to combat piracy and armed robbery; (c) to promote the rational utilization of living resources; (d) to protect and preserve the marine environment; (e) to conduct marine scientific research; and (f) to eliminate illicit traffic in drugs in the South China Sea.
3. In areas where conflicting territorial claims exist, the relevant states may consider the possibility of undertaking cooperation for mutual benefit, including exchange of information and joint development.

4 Any territorial and jurisdictional dispute in the South China Sea should be resolved by peaceful means through dialogue and negotiation.
5 Force should not be used to settle territorial and jurisdictional disputes.
6 The parties involved in such disputes are urged to exercise self-restraint in order to avoid complicating the situation.[25]

These principles, also called the Bandung Principles, later became elements of various declarations on the Code of Conduct in the South China Sea, including the 1992 ASEAN Declaration and the 2002 Declaration on the Code of Conduct in the South China Sea.[26]

At the third workshop in Yogjakarta in July 1992, various aspects of maritime affairs were discussed in detail, resulting in a number of technical working groups (TWGs) set in motion to carry out related works. "Coordinator countries" were assigned to lead studies on specific issues. Another major achievement was the development of confidence-building measures (CBMs), in particular, those on restraint and the transparency of military activities in disputed areas. The CBMs were designed to facilitate subsequent negotiation and cooperation among countries during hostilities. As part of the multilateral approach, it was also agreed that the participation of non-South China Sea states or organizations would be welcome in implementing any agreed-upon project proposals.[27]

China's attendance at the SCS workshop did not lead to an immediate embrace of multilateralism. At first, the Chinese government resisted any discussion or collective action on the SCS issue on a multilateral basis. On July 22, 1992, the ASEAN foreign ministers signed the ASEAN Declaration on the South China Sea in Manila. The Manila Declaration represented the first ASEAN-wide common position on the South China Sea. Following the framework of the SCS workshop, the Declaration urges countries to "resolve all sovereignty and jurisdictional issues pertaining to the South China Sea by peaceful means, without resort to force."[28] Envisioning a dim possibility of a final resolution in the near future, the Declaration commended "all parties concerned to apply the principles contained in the Treaty of Amity and Cooperation in Southeast Asia as the basis for establishing a code of international conduct over the South China Sea."[29]

The ASEAN ministers sought China's endorsement for the declaration. The Chinese Foreign Minister, Qian Qichen, together with his Russian counterpart, was in Manila as guest of the ASEAN chair. Qian rejected the request on the grounds that China had not been involved in the declaration's drafting. He added that while subscribing to the declaration's "principles,"[30] Beijing repeated its preference for bilateral rather than multilateral discussions on the South China Sea.[31]

Nevertheless, participation in the SCS workshop led to several policy-related outcomes for China. First, it prepared China to becoming familiar with multilateralism as both a norm and a practical approach in interacting with other claimant states. Second, it helped facilitate China's initial engagement with the ASEAN, and to build institutional bonds. Following the workshop, China began to participate in other multilateral institutional networks and dialogue mechanisms, responding positively to the establishment of the ASEAN-China framework. The SCS workshop also influenced China's policy-making regarding maritime governance. It increased China's policy-related knowledge and involved China in cooperative projects with international organizations. The influence of the SCS workshop in maritime governance will be further elaborated in the third section.

The ASEAN Regional Forum

Due to institutional weaknesses, the SCS workshop, while achieving a positive success in CBMs, soon transferred politically sensitive issues regarding territorial and jurisdictional contentions to other formal mechanisms, in particular, the ASEAN Regional Forum (ARF), and limited its activities to the legal and technical arenas, where it found itself most active and productive. In 1994, the ASEAN and its dialogue partners, plus China and Russia (then not yet ASEAN dialogue partners), Vietnam and Laos (then not yet ASEAN members), and Papua New Guinea (an ASEAN observer), initiated the ARF for consultation on regional political and security issues. The ARF was East Asia's first formal multilateral security dialogue (Track 1 dialogue).[32] Participants included countries outside of the South China Sea region with increased interests in the South China Sea.[33] As it turned out, the ARF gradually took up the role of an influential multilateral institution managing the SCS dispute.[34]

During the first meeting in Bangkok in 1994, the ARF reached consensus that the situation in the SCS was one of the flashpoints of potential conflict in the region. Yet, China's negative attitude towards the multilateral approach in dealing with the SCS issue did not change much. Beijing was uneasy about the likelihood that the ASEAN might use the forum to internationalize the Spratly Islands dispute and take a united stance against it, because the ARF included among its participants some powerful states from outside the region, particularly, the United States.[35] As a result, during this meeting Beijing consistently refused to bring up the SCS matter for discussion.[36] This concern over internationalizing the SCS dispute was promptly reflected in domestic academic discourse. Before 1994, there had been no mention in major Chinese academic journals of "internationalizing" the SCS dispute. Academic writings on the SCS dispute from 1990 to 1994 continued in line with the previous reasoning, focusing on China's superior claims supported by historic evidence of discovery and effective occupation.[37] Starting in 1994, some writers began to talk about the trend of "internationalizing" the SCS dispute, worrying that it might adversely affect China, and exploring available options to respond. Zhao Lihai, a prominent Chinese specialist on maritime law, warned the government that the ASEAN intended to "internationalize" the dispute and challenged from the legal standpoint the validity of "internationalizing" the SCS dispute.[38]

The first ARF meeting was a critical moment in two senses. First, the fact that China's stance clashed with those of other participants in the ARF demonstrated that up to this point, China had not been prepared to allow the sovereignty dispute in the SCS to be included in any formal multilateral institutional agenda. Second, China felt a considerable amount of pressure from the other participating states that it had not previously experienced and could not ignore. It was reported that the environment of the first few meetings was quite tense and that Chinese officials were upset by the push.[39]

It is important to note that this push highlighted a growing trend of interaction of power pressure and institutional dynamics in regional political engagements in the 1990s. Power politics could not operate effectively on its own. The USA was a great power in the ARF, but it was not directly involved in the dispute. Other claimants in the SCS were relatively weaker compared to China, which imposed restraints on them in bilateral engagement. Therefore, the powerful push China felt in the ARF stemmed from a coordinated pressure exerted through institutionalized channels of interaction made available by the ARF.

Throughout the Cold War period, China's interactions with ASEAN states were conducted solely on a bilateral basis, and no institutionalized link was formally forged between China and regional organizations.[40] This situation changed with the attendance of then Chinese Foreign Minister Qian Qichen at the opening session of the 24th ASEAN Ministerial Meeting (AMM) in July 1991 as a guest of Malaysia.[41] Following the AMM, the ASEAN began to expand its Post-Ministerial Conference (PMC): external dialogues which included four new dialogue partners, one of which was China. Since the establishment of the ASEAN-China framework, more institutionalized and regularized interactions began to take place, including the ASEAN-China Senior Official Consultations (ASEAN-China SOC), the ASEAN-China Joint Cooperation Committee meetings, the ASEAN Plus China framework (alongside the APT process), and regular ASEAN-China summits.[42] Outside the ASEAN-China framework, there were the SCS workshop, the ARF, the Asia-Pacific Economic Cooperation (APEC), and the "ASEAN Plus Three" (China, Japan, and South Korea) (APT) meetings, each of which included China. The unprecedented growth of multilateral regional arrangements regularized inter-state interactions in the SCS region, and wove a dense policy space. As Keohane argued, "The denser the policy space, the more highly interdependent different issues."[43] Facilitated by China's expanded participation in the dense policy space of the regional multilateral architecture, negotiation on the SCS dispute was able to take place in various institutional venues and other member states found new institutional venues and leverage to either pressure or persuade China, something not available in the traditional state-to-state engagement dominated purely by power politics.

The first ASEAN-China forum and the second ARF meeting following the Mischief Incident in 1995 clearly illustrate this point. As mentioned earlier, in February 1995, China was reported to be building facilities on the Mischief

Reef (Meiji Jiao), a land feature also claimed by the Philippines. China's move strained the Sino-Filipino relations and raised concerns throughout the SCS region. There are competing explanations as to why China chose to advance to the Mischief Reef at this particular point in time.[44] Some view China's move to the Mischief Reef as a move aimed to broaden the scope of waters over which it could claim effective control, but many suggest that the occupation might have been conducted by the PLA Navy without the authorization of central leadership.[45] Regardless of the actual motivation, China's action in effect caught the Philippines and the ASEAN in general off guard. Before the Mischief Reef Incident, it was the tacit belief among the ASEAN members that China would not take on claimants other than Vietnam.[46] The immediate reaction of the ASEAN countries to the discovery of China's construction on the Mischief Reef was shock, and hence the other nations did not have a clear idea how to deal with it.

The Philippines began to work on building an ASEAN consensus to be presented at the first China-ASEAN Forum in Hangzhou, an annual forum covering various kinds of issues between China and the ASEAN countries. On the eve of the formal sessions, ASEAN and Chinese officials held an informal meeting solely to discuss the issue. The leader of the ASEAN delegation told the Chinese side that the Mischief Reef Incident had had a negative impact on the stability of the Asia-Pacific region, and that the issue should be settled peacefully in accordance with the 1992 Manila Declaration.[47] The meeting was characterized by one participant as "hectic, direct, and quite unsettling to the Chinese."[48] Later, during the second ARF meeting, delegations from the United States and the Philippines played a pivotal role, taking advantage of the forum provided by the ARF to persuade and push other participants to arrive at a consensus to request the SCS dispute be included on the ARF agenda.[49] The ASEAN members also raised the issue with China in a consultative session before formal talks began.

ASEAN's unity and concerted action in pressuring China during the second ARF meeting and through the China-ASEAN framework caught Beijing by surprise, forcing a reassessment of the regional consequences of its action, which in turn led to a remarkable compromise on the Chinese side.[50] China conceded to discussing the SCS issues in this multilateral setting and signaled further willingness to cooperate in relation to a limited range of issues. During this meeting, participants discussed the Mischief Reef case and other aspects of the SCS issue. The meeting also concluded with the ARF Concept Paper that outlined a three-stage process for the forum: (1) promotion of CBMs; (2) preventive diplomacy (PD) mechanisms; and, finally, (3) elaboration of approaches to conflict.[51] It was especially significant that Qian Qichen publicly pledged for the first time that competing claims should be resolved on the basis of the UNCLOS.[52] While Beijing had already signaled acceptance of the LOSC as legal bedrock for staking claims in the SCS, this time Qian's remarks indicated Beijing's further acceptance of the new LOS as the legal basis for resolving conflicting sovereign claims. In addition, he promised that at an appropriate time, China would be prepared to publish a Defense White Paper as one of its contributions to the confidence building process. Changes in China's perception and behavior continued to unfold. Regular interactions between China and the littoral countries and extra-regional countries through multilateral mechanisms at all levels gradually transformed the atmosphere of dialogues and negotiations into a more relaxed and constructive space. Issues that were previously deemed sensitive were now raised freely and discussed in a comfortable manner.[53] The following years witnessed China's further widening of involvement in the ARF forum. In April 1996, Beijing offered to co-chair with Manila the next ARF inter-sessional support group (ISG) meeting on CBMs. In 1997, China sent representatives to take part in the first meeting of Defense College chiefs held in Manila. It also hosted a meeting on CBMs in Beijing that same year. In 2001, the ARF made substantive progress. All participants reached consensus on preventive diplomacy (PD), which signified an important achievement in the transitional process as the ARF moved from confidence-building measures to preventive diplomacy. In November 2002, ten years of multilateral engagement bore one of its biggest fruits, as the ASEAN and China signed a Declaration on the Conduct of Parties in the SCS (hereafter referred to as the DOC).

The 2002 DOC

The 2002 Declaration on the Conduct of Parties in the SCS is based on a multilateral framework as well as on a convergence of views on managing the contentious SCS disputes in a peaceful manner. The notion of a code of conduct was not alien to the littoral SCS states. In August 1995, in the wake of the Mischief Reef conflict, pressed by a united ASEAN through multiple institutional networks, China and the Philippines issued a Joint Statement on the SCS and Other Areas of Cooperation, in which the two sides rejected the use of force and pledged to conform to specific principles for a code of conduct in accordance with the 1982 UNCLOS in the disputed Spratly area. Later in the same year, the Philippines and Vietnam reached a similar joint agreement, which provided for "basic principles for a code of conduct in the contested areas."[54] These two agreements on managing the SCS dispute were both bilateral in nature.

The idea of a multilateral code of conduct was first introduced in the ASEAN Ministerial Meeting in 1996. Then, the ASEAN began to engage China through several multilateral venues. During the seventh SCS workshop meeting in Batam in December 1996, participants from the ASEAN initiated discussion on a possible code of conduct.[55] China resisted the ASEAN's proposal on the grounds that previous bilateral agreements between China and the ASEAN member countries already embodied the commitment to a peaceful resolution of disputes. The ASEAN countries raised the issue again in ASEAN-China annual consultative meetings in 1997. China argued that the 1997 China-ASEAN joint statement on twenty-first-century cooperation made such a code unnecessary. In 1998, under the pressure of the ASEAN's persistence, China agreed to work for a regional code of conduct to prevent further escalation of the SCS conflict.

The drafting process on a code of conduct accelerated during the annual ASEAN-China SOC in 1999.[56] In 2000, the SOC established a working group to explore the possibility of creating a code of conduct in the disputed area. After three years of painstaking negotiations, China and the ASEAN members signed the Declaration on Conduct in the South China Sea in November 2002.[57]

In the negotiation stage, Beijing expressed strong preference for a non-binding multilateral code of conduct limited to the Spratlys, while the ASEAN expected a legally binding pact for the SCS. On March 15, 2000, during senior official meetings in Thailand, China and ASEAN members reached a compromise that the incoming DOC would mainly serve as an instrument of confidence building applied to the SCS, and would not be legally binding.

The 2002 DOC consists of a preamble and ten primary paragraphs which include several commitments by the parties, such as reaffirming their adherence to related international instruments (e.g., those of the UN Charter and the UNCLOS) and other recognized international legal principles (e.g., the Treaty of Amity and Cooperation and the "five principles of peaceful-coexistence"); exploring ways for building trust and confidence; and committing to the freedom of navigation on the SCS and flight above the South China Sea.[58] There were no guidelines and no enforcement provisions in the DOC.[59]

The signing of the DOC had at least two crucial implications. First, in spite of the rightful criticism of its lack of sufficient legal teeth, the DOC still proscribed stringent specifications to the signatories regarding the types of acceptable behavior for parties involved in the SCS. In particular, three commitments were made in the statement. The first was undertaking to "refrain from action of inhabiting on the presently uninhabited islands, reefs, shoals, cays, and other features," which meant a freeze on the status quo of occupations in the SCS. The second commitment was a pledge to continue regular consultations on the observance of the declaration, "for the purpose of promoting good neighborliness and transparency … and facilitating peaceful resolution of disputes." In other words, the DOC offered mechanisms of consultation that the ASEAN members and China could always fall back on. Finally, the parties agreed to work for the eventual adoption of a genuine and binding code of conduct (as opposed to a declaration) on the basis of consensus, setting a new benchmark that the parties should strive to attain.[60]

Second, by signing the DOC, the first formal multilateral agreement on the SCS, Beijing acknowledged the multilateral nature of the disputes and that bilateral solutions might not always be sufficient.[61] Years of interaction with the maritime regime cultivated a view of multilateralism in China's policy-making circles as not only a practical approach but also a norm in dealing with the SCS issue. This normative change, as discussed further in the following chapters, showed a notable resilience in later years, even though considerable changes took place in the geostrategic environment.

Throughout the whole of the 1990s, China made three incremental steps in terms of modifying its approach to political engagement with claimant countries and extra-regional countries concerned with the dispute. It started from an insistence on the traditional type of bilateral exchanges and moved to participation in multilateral institutional networks in Track 2 discussions on a limited range of non-political maritime issues in the SCS. Then, it further modified its position from blocking political negotiation of disputes over sovereignty from any multilateral dialogues to conceding to allow the dispute to be brought up in Track 1 fora in which not only regional countries but also extra-regional ones participated. Finally, in 2002, Beijing took the third step: a formal commitment to a multilateral arrangement, the DOC, in managing the SCS issue. As demonstrated above, this prolonged process through which China adapted to multilateralism was pushed by a combination of political pressure and normative institutional forces, which will be thoroughly elaborated in the final section.

Policy practices of maritime governance in the SCS

This section examines China's policy practices in dealing with the everyday use of the SCS waters. There are three major changes in this aspect of China's SCS policy. First, China's acceptance of the LOSC as the legal basis for constructing the SCS issue led to changes in its actual practices concerning fisheries in the SCS. Second, China's continued engagement with the maritime regime at both regional and international levels resulted in the internalization of the norm of sustainability in its marine practices in the SCS. Third, some international organizations helped China identify and define problems in the SCS that required cooperative action and provided the Chinese leadership with policy-related knowledge and funding resources, hence eliciting China's cooperation in regional cooperative projects.

Changes in fishery practices: distant-water fishing

The first change identified in China's marine practices in the 1990s was its increasing participation in international multilateral distant-water fishing arrangements. This trend, according to a leading Chinese specialist on fisheries law, was largely developed in response to the substantial restriction of access to China's traditional offshore fishing grounds.[62] Under the new LOSC, many of the most highly productive fishing grounds in which Chinese fishermen traditionally had fished were either enclosed in the EEZ of China's maritime neighbors or located in the SCS waters under dispute. In response, China sought to develop distant-water fishing capabilities and joined international distant-water fishing organizations and arrangements. This shift to distant-water fishing was part of China's adjustment of its SCS policy in line with the

LOSC. It also reflects the fact that legal developments of the maritime regime not only changed China's legal position but also its actual practices in the SCS.

Sustainable development

As mentioned in Chapter 4, the concept of sustainable development was first introduced to China in the 1980s when China participated in the Brundtland Commission. This concept was placed in the global spotlight during the United Nations Conference on Environment and Development (UNCED) in 1992. This conference, also known as the Earth Summit, highlighted the impending challenges of environmental degradation and climate change on a worldwide basis and urged collaborative efforts on sustainable development to cope with these challenges. The conference produced the Rio Declaration on Environment and Development, a set of 27 principles designed to commit governments to global collaboration on environmental protection and the implementation of sustainable development throughout the world.[63]

One of the main foci of the conference was integrating the norm of sustainability in ocean development. Chapter 17 of Agenda 21, an action plan produced by the Conference, is entitled "Protection of the oceans, all kinds of seas, including enclosed and semi-enclosed seas, and coastal areas and the protection, rational use and development of their living resources." This chapter in particular brings the 1982 UNCLOS into scope by claiming that:

> The marine environment – including the oceans and all seas and adjacent coastal areas – forms an integrated whole that is an essential component of the global life-support system and a positive asset that presents opportunities for sustainable development. International law, as reflected in the provisions of the United Nations Convention on the Law of the Sea 1/, 2/ referred to in this chapter of *Agenda 21*, sets forth rights and obligations of States and provides the international basis upon which to pursue the protection and sustainable development of the marine and coastal environment and its resources.[64]

By doing so, this UN conference injected new dynamics into the international ocean regime, accelerating multilateral cooperation in protecting marine environments and implementing sustainable development around the world.

Following the 1992 Earth Summit, China began to implement the norm of sustainability in its own oceanic development agenda. It acceded to a number of ocean environment-related treaties and non-binding legal instruments coming out of the 1992 Rio Conference. It ratified the Convention on Biological Diversity on January 5, 1993. It signed the Agenda 21, and to fulfill the obligation required by the Agenda 21, started the process of developing a National Agenda 21: White Paper on China's Population, Environment and Development in the 21st Century. To this end, a Leading Group co-chaired by a deputy minister of the State Science and Technology Commission and a deputy minister of the State Planning Commission was quickly established in August 1992 to organize and coordinate the formulation and implementation of the National Agenda 21, which was approved by the State Council in March 1994. In 1996, China adopted Ocean Agenda 21 following the 1992 Rio Agenda 21. In 1998, for the first time in history the central government in Beijing issued a White Paper on the development of marine affairs.

Sustainability in the area of marine environment protection

The growing emphasis on sustainable development influenced China's marine practices in mainly two policy arenas: marine environment protection and fisheries. In the area of environment protection, the 1992 Rio Conference triggered a series of revisions of the London Convention. As a party to the 1972 London Convention, China followed these revisions and implemented them through domestic legislation. At the 16th Consultative Meeting of the Treaty Parties to the London Convention in 1993, China accepted three resolutions concerning disposal at sea of radioactive wastes, incineration at sea of industrial wastes and sewage sludge, and sea disposal of industrial wastes, as amendments to the Annexes to the London Convention: Doc LC.51 (16) (1993), Doc LC. 50 (16) (1993), and Doc LC.49 (16) (1993).[65] It also participated in the negotiations of the 1996 Protocol to London Convention. To fulfill these new obligations, China amended the 1982 Marine Environmental Protection Law in 1999 (the 1999 MEPL).[66] The 1999 MEPL substantially expanded the 1982 MEPL from the original 8 chapters to 10 and from 48 clauses to 98. It incorporated the principle of "sustainable development" in prescribing the purpose of the Law (Article 1). Based on the sustainability principle, the law adopted a more stringent and proactive approach in pollution control. For example, it established concrete mechanisms for controlling the total quantity of pollution discharged in important sea areas and placed caps on the main pollutants allowed to be discharged according to pollution sources.[67]

These domestic commitments were made as ways to implement the norm of sustainable development as well as the LOS Convention.[68] They also further raised awareness of sustainable development and environment protection in Chinese policy-making circles, paving the way for China's participation in concrete projects of regional multilateral cooperation on marine environment protection.

In the 1990s, two large projects funded by the Global Environment Facility (GEF) were introduced into the SCS for the purpose of marine management and protection. Since the GEF's intervention in the East Asia Seas region in December 1993 and its reconstruction in 1994 following the Earth Summit, considerable emphasis has been placed on the prevention and management of marine pollution.[69] Subsequently, two international multilateral projects funded by GEF were established, focusing on the marine environment in the South China Sea.

The first major project was the GEF Project on Marine Pollution Prevention in the East Asian Seas (MPP-EAS). Implemented by the United Nations Development Programme (UNDP) and executed by the International Maritime

Organization (IMO), the MPP-EAS project was signed by representatives from the IMO, UNDP, Cambodia, the PRC, the Philippines, Thailand, and Vietnam on November 13, 1993. The MPP-EAS was based on the integrated coastal management (ICM) approach. Following this approach, China set up one of the first two integrated coastal management (ICM) pilot sites in Xiamen the following year.[70] The successful completion of the pilot phase of the project in September 1999 led to the second phase of the project: Partnerships in Environmental Management for the Seas of East Asia (PEMSEA) launched in October 1999, focusing on building intergovernmental, interagency, and multi-sector partnerships in environmental management.[71]

The second project was developed in 1996, entitled "Reversing Environmental Degradation Trends in the SCS and Gulf of Thailand," also known as the UNEP/GEF SCS Project. This project will be addressed later, as it serves as a useful case illustrating the linkages between different actors and processes within the regime and how they interacted and connected with each other in influencing China's policy-making and eliciting cooperative behavior.

Sustainability in the area of fisheries

The second trend was the internalization of the norm of sustainability in fishery practices. The most notable effort at the international level in promoting sustainable fisheries in the 1990s was found in three pieces of fishery legislation: (1) the Agreement for the Implementation of the Provisions of the UNCLOS of December 10, 1982 Relating to the Conservation and Management of Straddling Fish Stocks and Highly Migratory Fish Stocks (the UN Fish Stocks Agreement); (2) the 1993 FAO Agreement to Promote Compliance with International Conservation and Management Measures by Fishing Vessels on the High Seas (the FAO Compliance Agreement); and (3) the FAO Code of Conduct for Responsible Fisheries.[72]

China signed the 1995 Fish Stocks Agreement on November 6, 1996. Upon signature, the Chinese government affirmed:

> The [said Agreement] is an important development of the United Nations Convention on the Law of the Sea. This Agreement will have a significant impact on the conservation and management of living marine resources, especially fish resources in the high seas as well as on the international cooperation in fishery.[73]

As regards the FAO Compliance Agreement, although not a formal member of the Agreement, China participated in a number of international and regional fisheries management organizations bound by the Agreement. Hence, China's fishery practices were also indirectly influenced by the principle of sustainable fishery of the Agreement. As Xue Guifang points out, given the international normative pressure and China's growing interest in distant-water fishing, ratification of the UN Fish Stocks Agreement and the Compliance

Agreement was just a matter of time.[74] Unlike the above two Agreements, the FAO Code of Conduct for Responsible Fisheries was a voluntary non-binding instrument. Hence, no specific action by States is required for it to take effect. However, its provisions may be used as a basis for domestic action, whether in the form of policy initiatives or even in shaping specific legislative provisions.[75] In fact, relevant principles and provisions on sustainable and responsible fishing were incorporated into the revised Chinese Fisheries Law promulgated in 2000.[76]

In the 1990s, following its increasing activities in distant-water fishing, China sought to participate in a host of international and regional fisheries management organizations. It entered the International Commission for the Conservation of Atlantic Tunas (ICCAT) and the Indian Ocean Tuna Commission (IOTC) in 1996 and 1998 respectively. In 2001, the Chinese delegation was sent to attend the 12th ICCAT special conference, the 5th IOTC annual conference, and the International Whaling Commission (IWC). In addition, it participated in the Convention on International Trade in Endangered Species of Wild Fauna and Flora (CITES) and the North Pacific Anadromous Fish Commission (NPAFC).[77] These international fishery arrangements were established in line with international instruments such as the UNCLOS and the FAO Code of Conduct for Responsible Fisheries. Participation in these commissions and conventions made China more familiar with international customary law and norms regarding fishery practices.

At the regional level, China co-established fishery organizations with neighboring countries. From 1994 to 2000, China attended all seven sessions of the Multilateral High Level Conferences for drafting the Convention on the Conservation and Management of Highly Migratory Fish Stocks in the Western and Central Pacific (the WCPF Convention) as well as the establishment of the Commission (WCPFC). The Convention represented the first regional multilateral effort to implement the UN Fish Stocks Agreement. With regard to existing fishery management mechanisms, China sought to enhance its level of participation in the Asia-Pacific Fishery Commission (APFIC). While China was one of the original members of the APFIC founded in 1948, it was not involved in most activities until the 1980s. The APFIC revised the APFIC Agreement in 1993 to incorporate the norm of sustainable development and made further amendments in 1996, paving the way for the Commission to play a more active role in fishery management and sustainable development.[78] Beijing chaired the 26th session of the APFIC from 1997–1998. During this session, Zhuo Youzhan, Director-General of the Fishery Administration of China, stated that China had experienced many problems, such as the depletion of coastal fishery resources, water pollution, fish diseases, and wastage of bycatch. Zhou attached great value to the APFIC works, acknowledging that the FAO/DFID Expert Consultation on Bycatch Utilization in Tropical Fisheries had provided useful strategies for addressing these problems.[79] Table 5.1 summarizes China's membership in fishery-related organizations in the 1990s. Note that many regional environmental preservation organizations also covered fisheries management:

Table 5.1 China's membership in fishery-related organizations in the 1990s

Organization	*Year founded*	*Members*	*China's membership*	*Role and responsibilities*
Asia-Pacific Fishery Commission (APFIC)	1948	Australia, Bangladesh, Cambodia, China, France, India, Indonesia, Japan, Korea (Rep. of), Malaysia, Myanmar, Nepal, New Zealand, Pakistan, the Philippines, Sri Lanka, Thailand, UK, USA, Vietnam	1948	Promote cooperation in fisheries development and management among its members including policy and planning; promote and advise on fishery research and exchange of information and statistics; and promote post-harvest technology development
Asia-Pacific Economic Cooperation (APEC)	1989	Australia, Brunei, Canada, Chile, China (including Taiwan), Hong Kong SAR, Indonesia, Japan, Korea (Rep. of), Malaysia, Mexico, New Zealand, Papua New Guinea, Peru, the Philippines, Russia, Singapore, Thailand, USA, Vietnam	1991	Promote conservation and sustainable use of fishery resources and sustainable aquaculture; enhance food safety/quality of fish products; and promote trade liberalization, investment, and facilitation of trade
Indian Ocean Tuna Commission (IOTC)	1996	Australia, China, Eritrea, the European Community, France, India, Japan, Korea (Rep. of), Madagascar, Malaysia, Mauritius, Pakistan, Seychelles, Sri Lanka, Sudan, Thailand, UK	1996	Promote cooperation among members to ensure the conservation and optimum use of tunas and tuna-like fishes through appropriate management; and encourage sustainable development of fisheries on such stocks

Organization	*Year founded*	*Members*	*China's membership*	*Role and responsibilities*
Network of Aquaculture Centres in Asia and the Pacific (NACA)	1990	Australia, Bangladesh, Cambodia, China, Korea (DPR), Hong Kong SAR, India, Myanmar, Nepal, Pakistan, Sri Lanka, Thailand, Vietnam Participating governments: Indonesia, Laos, the Philippines, Iran, Korea (Rep. of), Japan, Singapore	1990	Assist members in accelerating aquaculture development through TCDC in order to improve food security, rural income, and better economies
WCPF Convention	1994	The Philippines, China (including Taiwan), Indonesia, Vietnam, Thailand	1994	The Conservation and Management of Highly Migratory Fish Stocks in the Western and Central Pacific Ocean
Coordinating Body on the Seas of East Asia (COBSEA)	1994	China, Cambodia, Malaysia, Indonesia, the Philippines, Singapore, Thailand, Vietnam, Australia, Korea (Rep. of)	1994	Coordinate and implement the COBSEA Action Plan and other regional projects concerning the environment and fisheries
Partnerships in Environmental Management for the Seas of East Asia (PEMSEA)	1999	Brunei, Cambodia, Malaysia, Indonesia, the Philippines, China, Singapore, Thailand, Vietnam, DPR Korea, Japan, and Korea (Rep. of)	1999	Building intergovernmental, interagency, and multi-sector partnerships in environmental management and sustainable fishing

Multilateral engagements and international cooperation infused into China's fishery practices the norm of "sustainable development." Starting in mid-1990s, the issue of fishing capacity control was pushed to the top of the domestic agenda of fisheries management.[80] In 1997, the ninth Five-Year Plan (a detailed outline designed every five years to chart the country's economic goals) enacted policies of "double control on fishing capacity," controlling both the number and power of fishing vessels. Starting in 1998, the Chinese government expanded the summer fishing moratorium to the area to the north of 12°N in the South China Sea (including the Gulf of Tonkin) from noon on June 1 to noon on August 1.[81]

More importantly, in view of the priority placed on sustainable development and responsible fishing, Beijing came to realize that the national Fisheries Law promulgated in 1986 needed revision to address new issues surfacing from the changing environment. The overall aim of the 1986 Fisheries Law was to promote the development of fisheries. It did not provide powerful enough penalties to tackle the problems of unsustainable use of fisheries resources and non-compliance. This resulted in the failure to deter illegal and unregulated fishing.[82] As the conservation of fisheries resources and marine ecosystems became a growing concern for fisheries management, China moved quickly to address these issues,[83] reflected in the Amendment to Fisheries Law passed on October 31, 2000 and resulting in the 2000 Fisheries Law.[84]

The UNEP/GEF SCS Project

The South China Sea is located in what the UNEP defines as the "East Asian Seas Region." As early as the 1970s, the UNEP established the EAS program. In 1981, it adopted the "Action Plan for the Protection and Development of the Marine Environment and Coastal Areas of the East Asian Seas Region" (the EAS Action Plan), stimulated by concerns about the effects and sources of marine pollution. In the initial stage, the EAS Action Plan involved the marine environment and coastal areas of only five states (Indonesia, Malaysia, the Philippines, Singapore, and Thailand), primarily located in the South China Sea and the Gulf of Thailand. In the aftermath of the 1992 Rio conference, the EAS Action Plan was revised in 1994 into the "Action Plan for the Protection and Sustainable Development of the Marine and Coastal Areas of the East Asian Region."[85] The 1994 Action Plan made a paradigmatic shift from oil pollution to ecosystems, emphasizing the importance of marine ecosystem management, which was driven by the changing perception of marine environmental problems at the global level including biodiversity, climate change, desertification, and biotechnology.[86] China joined this revised program along with four other states (Australia, Cambodia, the Republic of Korea, and Vietnam) in 1994, expanding the total membership to 10. It also served in the Coordinating Body on the Seas of East Asia (COBSEA), an agency steering the implementation of the EAS Action Plan.

The UNEP/GEF SCS Project was the first large-scale multilateral intergovernmental initiative on marine environmental protection, involving all the major countries of the SCS and covering the entirety of SCS waters. Funded by the GEF and implemented by the UNEP, the project was intended primarily to design an appropriate multi-state intervention to address the agreed-upon priority issues among marine environmental problems in the South China Sea and the Gulf of Thailand.[87] With a total of $32 million in funding, the project aimed to reverse the environmental degradation trend in the SCS, targeting components including mangroves, coral reefs, sea grass, wetlands, land-based pollution, and fisheries. Given the sensitivity of the ocean space covered under this project, China's initial response was negative, but eventually Chinese leaders accepted the project, which officially started in 2000. Below is outlined the process through which the UNEP secured approval from China. This process serves as a useful case illustrating the links between different actors and processes within the regime and how they interacted and connected with each other in influencing China's policy-making and eliciting cooperative behavior.

Prior to the inception of the SCS workshop, China was not a member of the UNEP's EAS Action Plan, and largely stayed aloof from regional cooperative projects in the SCS. As mentioned earlier, the SCS workshop provided the first-ever venue in which all the claimants could sit down and address common maritime issues. Over the years, various working groups were established within the workshop to tackle problems in the SCS waters in need of cooperative action. China's involvement in these working groups, however preliminary, helped bolster China's experience in participating in multilateral cooperative measures targeting issues regarding everyday maritime governance in the SCS.

During the first workshop, various areas of possible cooperation were discussed and a series of technical and scientific issues were identified as potential areas for future cooperation. These issues included: protection of the marine environment, safety of navigation, marine scientific research, and developing institutional mechanisms to facilitate cooperation. By the third workshop, a decision had been made by the working group to establish two Technical Working Groups (TWGs), one on marine scientific research and the other on resource assessment and the means of development. As the informal workshops identified more technical issues for cooperation, three other TWGs were formed to discuss cooperation on these issues, including marine environmental protection, safety of navigation and communication, and legal matters. The outputs and results of these TWGs were reported in the annual informal working group meetings.

Years of involvement in this workshop had three major impacts on China's policy towards cooperation on environmental protection.[88] First, China became familiar with the norm of multilateralism as well as a sense of regional cooperation. Institutionalized communication contributed to the trust and confidence building among the littoral countries necessary for further regional cooperation. Second, the Chinese became more comfortable discussing with their ASEAN counterparts technical and scientific issues regarding the use of the SCS waters in this multilateral venue and joining related cooperative initiatives, which explains why China had no problem joining the aforementioned East Asia Action Plan and the COBSEA, whose members up to China's entry had been purely ASEAN countries. Chinese participants also came to realize that many maritime issues are transnational in nature and thus in need of a coordinated regional response. Third, the workshop also introduced international organizations into the cooperative projects organized by the workshop. Many of the participants were from epistemic communities who either had working experiences in relevant international organizations or had links with them, including experts and officials of the East Asia Action Plan. This progress built through the workshop process paved the way for China's later involvement in formal inter-governmental environmental cooperation initiated by the UNEP in the SCS.[89]

Following the workshop's group activities, the UNEP initiated the development of the UNEP/GEF SCS project. It aimed to make ground-breaking progress in formalizing regional marine environmental cooperation and undertaking substantive cooperative activities to address marine environmental problems. China was a member of the SCS Project together with six SCS littoral counterparts: Cambodia, Indonesia, Malaysia, the Philippines, Thailand, and Vietnam. The other two littoral countries, Brunei and Singapore, were not participants because they were not eligible for funding from the GEF. During the preparatory stage, China was quite responsive and published the National Report for the Transboundary Diagnostic Analysis in 1998 as required by the UNEP.[90] The UNEP provided all participating countries with the format for the collection of data and information and the procedures of causal chain analysis. China's national report was formulated strictly following the UNEP's guidelines.[91] After the gathering of national reports was completed, the project document was drafted and the project brief dispatched to the GEF National Operation Focal Points of the participating countries for written endorsement in March 1999. Except for China whose initial response was negative, the other six countries sent their endorsement letters within one month. UNEP officials met with the Chinese delegation during the GEF Council meeting in April 1999 and got the impression that China stood extremely firm on this issue. During the discussion, the UNEP officials approached the Chinese delegation with a combined "soft" and "hard" strategy. On the one hand, they stressed the importance of China's participation, and expressed the UNEP's wish for China's support and participation; on the other hand, they informed the delegates that the project would go ahead with or without China's participation. After the discussion, there was a slight softening of China's position, and the delegation indicated a willingness to reconsider the decision.[92]

After the April discussion, the UNEP realized that the main obstacle came from the Ministry of Foreign Affairs, whose leaders were not well educated about marine environmental issues and were worried that participation in such a project would create implications for China's sovereignty claims and uncertainty beyond China's control.[93] Consequently, the UNEP undertook a strategy of allying with its window agency in China: the State Environment Protection Agency (SEPA) through which it leveraged its influence during domestic inter-ministerial meetings.[94] Several SEPA officials had already cultivated personal relationships at regional meetings in the preparatory stage leading up to the project and a sense of regional cooperation had been fostered. These SEPA officials felt obliged to push for the approval of the project. Second, personal relationships had been established between SEPA and UNEP officials and other members of the associated epistemic community. All of this assured that UNEP's teachings and other forms of support on technical and scientific matters could be communicated effectively to SEPA officials and helped the SEPA present a convincing case before the MFA and answer the questions of other domestic agencies with overlapping responsibilities, especially the State Oceanic Administration (SOA).

In the meantime, backed by its prestigious status as a well-funded international organization from the giant UN family, the UNEP directly confronted the MFA. It formulated a case combining both normative and material incentives. Normatively, the UNEP persuaded China that non-participation in an UN project would incur the cost of de-legitimization of its sovereign claims in the SCS and damage its reputation as a responsive power before the ASEAN[95] and in the international environmental regime.[96] As for the material incentives, the UNEP officials indicated that exclusion from the project meant the loss of information and the opportunity for Beijing to enunciate its opinion. As a Chinese official explained in an interview conducted by UNEP official Sulan Chen:

> The Chinese government was afraid that other South China Sea countries would discuss the issues behind the Chinese government, and China would not have any control over the agenda or issues they discuss excluding China. This will be an even worse situation.[97]

The UNEP also formed a case of issue-linkage tying China's decision regarding the UNEP/GEF project to future allocation of other GEF-funded environmental protection projects as well as other UN projects, since China was the biggest recipient of GEF funding. In addition to pressuring the MFA, the UNEP also took advantage of the negotiation process to teach MFA officials that marine environmental cooperation was possible and important for Chinese sustainable economic development without necessarily infringing on politically sensitive problems.[98]

The UNEP's efforts eventually paid off when China sent a letter to the UNEP proposing several principles with regard to the project. This represented a turning point in Beijing's attitude, given its original refusal without explanation. Since these principles were designed to stem any potential ramifications to China's claims associated with participation, the UNEP staff quickly incorporated them without imposing many changes to the project. Official approval of the UNEP/GEF South China Sea Project was achieved in 2000. Since its launch, China has been reported to be playing a leading role in implementing the project, with strong support from both the central government and local governments and executing agencies.[99]

These three changes observed in China's marine practices in the 1990s were clearly products of China's participation in the maritime regime. Development of distant-water fishing was a domestic policy adjustment made by the Chinese policy-makers in view of the potential shrinking of traditional fishing grounds in the SCS. This policy response demonstrates that the internalization of the LOSC not only affected China's legal stance but also its concrete practices. The second finding, China's incorporation of sustainable development into marine governance highlights the fact that the maritime regime also influences the concrete ways through which sovereignty is expressed and exercised in the SCS. As we will see in Chapter 6, implementation of sustainable policies in the SCS and the related law enforcement activities have an undeniable impact on China's exercise of sovereignty in the SCS. For example, the practice of encouraging sustainable fisheries was deployed in a larger area in the SCS and became a new tool for China to assert its sovereignty in the disputed SCS waters in the 2000s. As regards the UNEP/GEF project on marine environment protection in the SCS, China's cooperation in this project was also proved to be connected to the normative pressure and material incentives provided by the UNEP. This finding offers a number of insights in terms of formulating effective regional cooperation projects and exploring innovative forms of co-governance in the SCS conducive to a peaceful management and resolution of the SCS issue, which will be discussed in detail in the Conclusion.

China's position on solutions for the dispute: continuing to push for joint development

It was shown in Chapter 4 that the Chinese leadership began to embrace the idea of joint development in the 1980s as a proposal to cope with the new nature of the SCS dispute, pending a final resolution. Entering the 1990s, Beijing sought to propose joint development to a broader audience in multilateral settings.

In 1990, Li Peng, the then Chinese Premier, put forward the approach of "shelving the disputes and developing jointly" to the Malaysians during a state visit to Kuala Lumpur. The Chinese leaders also brought up the idea in multilateral settings. During the 25th AMM held in July 1992, Chinese Foreign Minister Qian Qichen raised the joint development proposal, saying that "the Chinese government proposes 'shelving disputes and going for joint development.' If the conditions for negotiations are not yet ripe, then we should shelve the dispute and start joint development of the area." During the second ARF in 1995, the PRC's Foreign Minister Qian Qichen reiterated that the sovereignty question should be shelved and efforts made to begin the joint development of resources.[100]

These efforts soon garnered a welcome from the littoral countries, and a consensus on the principle of joint development was formed, although no concrete projects were proposed. In May 1994, Premier Li Peng and Prime Minister Mahathir of Malaysia endorsed this approach. On November 26, 1996, China's President Jiang Zemin, in talks with his Filipino counterpart, Fidel Ramos, agreed that China and the Philippines should "shelve differences" over the Spratly Islands and work together to build confidence and develop the disputed area jointly.

Concurrent with the official endorsements, Chinese scholars and governmental officials worked on exploring the jurisprudence, technical, and practical aspects of this concept. In 1991, the Chinese Society of the Law of the Sea and the Hainan Association of SCS Research (which later evolved into the Hainan Institute for the South China Sea Research) jointly held a conference on the SCS in Hainan, China, where altogether five papers presented were concerned with joint development in the SCS. These papers discussed the joint development issue from military, economic, legal, political, and regional perspectives.[101] It marked the first time that joint development in the SCS has been deeply and widely discussed in Chinese epistemic community. As will be discussed in Chapter 6, in the 2000s, the Chinese domestic discourse continued to borrow insights from international discourse and practices to formulate more effective policy proposals to inform and guide official practice of joint development.

Analysis

While unilateralism and confrontation characterized the 1980s period, China's SCS policy in the 1990s experienced a sea change. China's increasing engagement with the international maritime regime resulted in multiple changes unfolding on both legal and policy fronts.

The maritime regime played several roles in the unfolding of these policy changes. First, the maritime regime redefined the legal nature of the SCS dispute (role 1 in Chapter 1). Because of the snowballing ratifications of the UNCLOS worldwide and the expanding number of multilateral institutions within the maritime regime appealed to image-conscious Chinese leaders, this influence was quickly codified through a series of domestic legislation. Such a normative internalization paved the way for subsequent changes in other aspects of China's SCS policy.

Second, the maritime regime informed China of policy-related norms, principles, and knowledge in terms of the practice of maritime governance in the SCS. Some international institutions initiated cooperative projects and elicited China's participation to tackle problems identified in the everyday usage of the SCS (roles 2 and 5 in Chapter 1). These changes in marine governance resulted from China's engagement with the maritime regime and had repercussions on and added new dynamics to the development of the SCS issue in the 2000s.

Third, the intricate interaction between geopolitics and normative institutional forces yielded a multilateral turn in China's approach to political engagement in the SCS region in the 1990s (role 3 in Chapter 1). The key elements and the process through which this multilateral turn was accomplished are explained here.

The first key element is obviously the advent of the norm of multilateralism in the beginning of the 1990s. This normative innovation is essentially a product of and a response to the transformative influence of the maritime regime which restructured the SCS dispute. It is for this reason that multilateral engagement did not appear in the 1960s and 1970s. At that time bilateral engagement was sufficient for dealing with the SCS dispute which belonged to the conventional type of territorial disputes. The emergence of multilateralism had nothing to do with geopolitics, although geopolitics influenced the attitudes of the relevant countries, including China, to this norm.

The second key force is the restructuring of the geopolitical environment following the end of the Cold War. This geopolitical restructuring cast a shadow of uncertainty over the strategic theater of the Southeast Asia region. Such uncertainty consisted of three facets interlinked in a triangular shape. The USA, the ASEAN, and China each occupied a corner of the triangle, suspicious of the intentions of the players standing at the other two corners (see Figure 5.1).

In this triangle, the end of bipolar rivalry left the United States the dominant power in the world, forcing it to reprioritize its strategic posture in Asia and directing its attention to emerging regional trends and potential areas of conflict, which included in particular the rise of China and the troubled waters of the SCS. The ASEAN countries were concerned with the political and security uncertainty surrounding the new US role in the region. They also watched with caution China's military modernization and activities in the SCS.[102] In the third corner stood China, whose leaders focused on the ASEAN's plans for expanded membership and the creation of new regional fora like the ARF. Beijing perceived these moves as ways for smaller powers to "gang up on China," which would simultaneously work to the advantage of the USA in containing China and dictating regional agendas.[103]

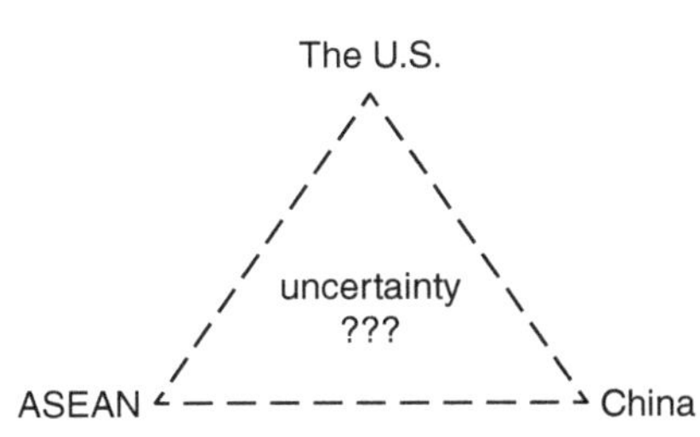

Figure 5.1 A strategic triangle: ASEAN, China, and the USA in the 1990s

This new geostrategic environment, as Ba has argued, opened opportunities and created incentives for these countries to reconsider the foundations of their relations and to engage one another in different ways.[104] In other words, the new geostrategic environment made the option of engaging in the multilateral institutional environment for constructive social interactions attractive to the three poles above. It also alleviated the initial hesitation each side might have had (especially China) about entering a socializing setting which provided opportunities for participation, persuasion, and reassurance. Venues such as the SCS workshop and the ARF, for example, once created, found themselves welcomed by SCS border countries, the United States, and other countries with vested interests in the SCS, as places where they could sit down and talk out their concerns. These institutionalized and regularized venues allowed states to bargain and negotiate over possible ways to implement the new maritime order and approach conflicts of interest in the SCS while maintaining peace and stability.

Yet, geopolitical flux alone did not determine the final results of policy changes. Rather, it worked with normative and institutional dynamics through the regime structure. While the changes in the geopolitical environment in the early 1990s provided the initial impetus for regional countries to enter into the multilateral institutional architecture, they were insufficient to sustain such an interest in multilateralism. Without productive and conscious argumentation directed at fostering an inter-subjective consensus of shared identity and converging expectations, upheld by effective institutional arrangements, countries could have simply treated the discussions as merely a talking shop yielding no meaningful benefits.

The success of the conscious argumentation in the multilateral social interactions to a large extent could be attributed to the "ASEAN Way," which refers to a set of diplomatic norms shared by ASEAN members, characterized by an informal and consensus-based approach to cooperation through lengthy consultation and dialogue.[105] ASEAN's quiet informality and particular brand of regionalism contain three ASEAN rules: (1) exchanges remain private; (2) agreement is by consensus; and (3) internal affairs are excluded.[106]

Geopolitical realities constrained ASEAN countries in terms of their approach to engagement. As Alexander Wendt argues, smaller powers may be more inclined at the outset to consider or adopt a non-coercive, diplomatic approach.[107] Faced with the power difference between themselves and China, ASEAN countries chose an informal and incremental style of engagement, which was the ASEAN Way.

The ASEAN Way of argumentation was used in the SCS workshop and in other dialogues and mechanisms with a SCS mandate, such as the ARF. The aim of the conscious yet non-coercive argumentation was to communicate a basic understanding to China that many of the extant rules and norms were not antithetical to China's interests and that China could even take an active role in helping design the rules and norms of these institutions.[108] This helped eased China's initial suspicion of any multilateral forum regarding the issue of the SCS and fostered a sense of regional identity. After several years' involvement in the workshop meetings, Chinese government officials, experts, and scholars found that "ASEAN countries aren't that scary, and that people are fairly reasonable."[109] The open and inclusive style of engagement helped persuade China to reconsider its views regarding regional multilateralism and the ASEAN.[110] The attitudinal and policy change towards multilateralism was best epitomized by the agreement Beijing reached with other disputant parties: the 2002 DOC. As Aileen S. P. Baviera comments on the completion of the DOC:

> It was the first formal multilateral agreement entered into by China on the SCS, indicating acknowledgment of the multilateral nature of the disputes and that bilateral solutions, while desirable especially at the initial stages, may no longer be sufficient.[111]

The emerging multilateral institutional arrangements offered a medium through which the balance of power could exert its influence in a more flexible manner. In a dispute where the USA was not directly involved, it was difficult for US leaders to elicit desired policy changes from China through bilateral state-to-state engagements, even though it was the dominant power in the region with military preponderance. For each of the countries directly involved in the dispute, China was the most powerful competitor, which also meant that Southeast Asian countries might not always have been able to influence China's policy-making through bilateral engagements. The creation of various new institutional venues and leverage following China's expanded and deepened participation in multilateral institutional networks solved this problem. The state-regime-state engagements enabled the ASEAN countries and the USA to effectively leverage pressure and persuade China and elicited the aforementioned three-step modification of its approach, an accomplishment not possible in traditional state-to-state engagement dominated by power politics.

Notes

1 "The Struggle Around the LOS Convention," *People's Daily*, December 12, 1982.
2 Interview, Haikou, August 2012, interviewee requested anonymity.
3 Interview with Dr. Wu Shicun, Haikou, August 2012.
4 Interview, Beijing, August 2012, interviewee requested anonymity.
5 Qing Ling, *From Yan'an to the United Nations* (Fujian, China: Fujian Renmin Press, 2008), 169.
6 Ibid., 166–167.
7 Yann-Huei Song and Keyuan Zou, "Maritime Legislation of Mainland China and Taiwan: Developments, Comparison, Implications, and Potential Challenges for the United States," *Ocean Development and International Law* 31, no. 4 (2000): 308.
8 Interview, Haikou, August 2012, interviewee requested anonymity.
9 Nong Hong, *UNCLOS and Ocean Dispute Settlement: Law and Politics in the South China Sea* (New York: Routledge, 2012), 148–149.

10 Additional benefits of ratification, pointed out by Li Zhaoxing, included: it was conducive to preserving and protecting the PRC's maritime rights and interests, enlarging the PRC's maritime jurisdiction, and helped to maintain the substantive status of the PRC as a "pioneer investor" in deep seabed resource exploration activities, thus fulfilling the PRC's long-term interests.
11 See Appendix B.
12 See Appendix C.
13 Article 57 of UNCLOS stipulates that the exclusive economic zone shall not extend beyond 200 nautical miles from the baselines from which the breadth of the territorial sea is measured.
14 Article 2 of the Law on EEZ and CS stipulates that:

> The continental shelf of a coastal State comprises the seabed and subsoil of the submarine areas that extend beyond its territorial sea throughout the natural prolongation of its land territory to the outer edge of the continental margin, or to a distance of 200 nautical miles from the baselines from which the breadth of the territorial sea is measured where the outer edge of the continental margin does not extend up to that distance.

See Appendix C.
15 I use "historic claims," "the historic regime," and "the historic concept" interchangeably and under this term I place historic bays, historic rights, historic waters, which are the terms used by China (including Taiwan) when invoking the historic concept. It is unnecessary for this book and difficult to define each term individually because these terms to date remain under-defined and the Chinese government has not clarified its own position with respect to the specific meaning of each.
16 The origin and legal definition of the historic concept are elaborated in Chapter 4.
17 "Editorial," *People's Daily*, September 23, 1957.
18 For details of these two cases, see Keyuan Zou, "Historic Rights in International Law and in China's Practice," *Ocean Development and International Law* 32, no. 2 (2001): 156–157.
19 E. C. Farrell, *The Socialist Republic of Vietnam and the Law of the Sea: An Analysis of Vietnamese Behavior within the Emerging International Oceans Regime* (The Hague: Martinus Nijhoff Publishers, 1998), 70, Wanxiu Yang, "The Sovereignty Dispute on Xisha and Nansha in China-Vietnam Relations," in *Prospects for the China-Southeast Asian Relations Around 2000*, ed. Southeast Asian Institute (Guangzhou: Zhongshan University Press, 1991), 135, in Chinese. Also see Keyuan Zou, "Maritime Boundary Delimitation in the Gulf of Tonkin," *Ocean Development and International Law* 30, no. 3 (1999): 238.
20 The Mischief Reef Incident will be further elaborated in the next section, as it also influenced the political engagements among the SCS countries and extra-regional countries.
21 Nayan Chanda, "Territorial Imperative," *Far Eastern Economic Review*, February 23, 1995, 15.
22 Hong, *UNCLOS and Ocean Dispute Settlement*, 189.
23 Hasjim Djalal, "Indonesia and the South China Sea Initiative," *Ocean Development and International Law* 32, no. 2 (2001): 99.
24 In East Asia, Track 2 diplomacy typically involves academics, journalists, and occasionally politicians, as well as civilian and military officials acting in their "private" or "unofficial" capacities. For the role of Track 2 diplomacy in East Asia politics, see Brian Job, "Track 2 Diplomacy: Ideational Contribution to the Evolving Asian Security Order," in *Asian Security Order: Instrumental and Normative Features*, ed. M. Alagappa (Stanford, CA: Stanford University Press,

2003), 241–279, Hiro Katsumata, "The Role of ASEAN Institutes of Strategic and International Studies in Developing Security Cooperation in the Asia-Pacific," *Asian Journal of Political Science* 11, no. 1 (2003): 93–111, Amitav Acharya, "How Ideas Spread: Whose Norms Matter? Norm Localization and Institutional Change in Asian Regionalism," *International Organization* 58, no. 2 (2004): 239–275, Alice D. Ba, "On Norms, Rule-Breaking and Security Communities: A Constructivist Response," *International Relations of the Asia-Pacific* 5, no. 2 (2005): 255–266, and David Capie, "When Does Track Two Matter? Structure, Agency and Asian Regionalism," *Review of International Political Economy* 17, no. 2 (2010): 291–318.

25 M. Singgih Hadipranowo *et al.* eds., *The Second Workshop on Managing Potential Conflicts in the South China Sea* (Jakarta, Indonesia: Research and Development Agency, 1991), 75.

26 Hasjim Djalal, "Dispute Settlement and Conflict Management in the SCS," *Strategic Review*, available at: www.sr-indonesia.com/this-months-issue/indonesia-360/170-dispute-settlement-and-conflict-management-in-the-south-china-sea (accessed March 1, 2014).

27 Djalal, "Indonesia and the South China Sea Initiative," 100.

28 *ASEAN Declaration on the South China Sea 1992.*

29 Adopted at the first ASEAN Summit held in Bali in 1976, the Treaty of Amity and Cooperation constitutes a norm-based code of conduct that enunciates the ASEAN's core principles, including the respect for sovereignty and non-interference in the affairs of other states. The text of the Treaty of Amity and Cooperation is available at ASEAN, www.asean.org/news/item/treaty-of-amity-and-cooperation-in-southeast-asia-indonesia-24-february-1976-3 (accessed March 2014).

30 Rodolfo C. Severino, "ASEAN and the South China Sea," *Security Challenges* 6, no. 2 (2010): 42.

31 Kwa Chong Guan and John K. Skogan, eds., *Maritime Security in Southeast Asia* (New York: Routledge, 2007), 55.

32 While Track 2 diplomacy typically involves academics, journalists, and occasionally politicians, as well as civilian and military officials acting in their "private" or "unofficial" capacities, Track 1 diplomacy refers to a formal governmental level of diplomatic engagement.

33 Alice D. Ba, "Who's Socializing Whom? Complex Engagement in Sino-ASEAN Relations," *The Pacific Review* 19, no. 2, (2006): 163.

34 Djalal, "Indonesia and the South China Sea Initiative," 101.

35 Cheng-Chwee Kuik, "Multilateralism in China's ASEAN Policy: Its Evolution, Characteristics, and Aspiration," *Contemporary Southeast Asia* 27, no. 1 (2005): 107.

36 Ibid., 108.

37 See, for instance, Liyu Wang, "Preliminary Discussion on the Legal Implications of China's Discovery and Effective Occupation of the Islands in the SCS," *Ocean and Coast Zone Development* 8, no. 4 (1991): 39–44; Qiwu Zhu, "The Problem of Ownership of the Spratly Islands Discussed from the Viewpoint of International Law (Parts One and Two)," *The Forum of Political Science and Law – Journal of China University of Political Science and Law* 6 (1990): 7–12 and 1 (1991): 7–15; Lihai Zhao, "Understanding China's Undisputable Ownership of the Islands in the South China Sea from the Viewpoint of International Law," *Journal of Beijing University* 3 (1992): 30–40. All are in Chinese.

38 See Lihai Zhao, "Several Legal Issues Concerning the SCS Islands," *Rule of Law and Social Development* 4 (1995): 50–63, in Chinese.

39 Kuik, "Multilateralism in China's ASEAN Policy," 108.

40 Ibid., 103.

41 Ibid.

42 Ba, "Who's Socializing Whom?" 163.

43 Robert O. Keohane, "The Demand for International Regimes," *International Organization* 36, no. 2 (1982): 339–340.

44 American scholar Allen Whiting's interviews with officials and academic specialists in several ASEAN countries suggest that prior to 1995, there was general confidence that Beijing might attack Vietnamese installations but would not move against an ASEAN member, see Allen S. Whiting, "ASEAN Eyes China," *Asian Survey* 37, no. 4 (1997): 300.

45 M. Taylor Fravel, *Strong Borders, Secure Nation: Cooperation and Conflict in China's Territorial Disputes* (Princeton, NJ: Princeton University Press, 2008), 297, Ian J. Storey, "Creeping Assertiveness: China, the Philippines and the South China Sea Dispute," *Contemporary Southeast Asia* 21, no. 1 (1999): 100, and Whiting, "ASEAN Eyes China," 312.

46 Whiting, "ASEAN Eyes China," 311.

47 Storey, "Creeping Assertiveness," 107–108.

48 During the first consultative meeting between senior officials of ASEAN and China in 1995, ASEAN officials confronted China over the Mischief Incident. See Whiting, ASEAN Eyes China," 319.

49 Rosemary Foot, "China in the ASEAN Regional Forum: Organizational Processes and Domestic Modes of Thought," *Asian Survey* 38, no. 5 (1998): 429–435.

50 Whiting, "ASEAN Eyes China," 320.

51 See Kuik, "Multilateralism in China's ASEAN Policy," 107. In the original proposal, China had no problem with the first two stages, but voiced its objections to the third, which was "development of conflict resolution mechanisms." The Chinese representative insisted that the ARF is only a dialogue forum and hence should not be designed as a formal institution that aimed to resolve conflicts. Therefore, the third process was replaced by "elaboration of approaches to conflict."

52 Foot, "China in the ASEAN Regional Forum," 433 and M. Taylor Fravel, "China's Strategy in the South China Sea," *Contemporary Southeast Asia* 33, no. 3 (2011): 300.

53 Kuik, "Multilateralism in China's ASEAN Policy," 108.

54 Nguyen Hong Thao, "Vietnam and the Code of Conduct for the South China Sea," *Ocean Development and International Law* 32, no. 2 (2001): 127.

55 Djalal, "Indonesia and the South China Sea Initiative," 100.

56 As mentioned earlier, the ASEAN-China SOC was one of the mechanisms created under the ASEAN-China framework, hence one of the platforms to discuss the SCS issue.

57 Zhiguo Gao, "SCS: Turning Suspicion into Mutual Understanding and Cooperation," in *ASEAN-China Relations: Realities and Prospects*, ed. Saw Swee-Hock, Sheng Lijun and Chin Kin Wah (Singapore: Institute of Southeast Asian Studies, 2005), 332.

58 ASEAN, *Declaration on the Conduct of Parties in the South China Sea*, available at: www.asean.org/asean/external-relations/china/item/declaration-on-the-conduct-of-parties-in-the-south-china-sea (accessed March 1. 2014).

59 Also see Nguyen Hong Thao and Ramses Amer, "A New Legal Arrangement for the South China Sea?" *Ocean Development and International Law* 40, no. 4 (2009): 341.

60 Aileen S. P. Baviera, "SCS after 2002: Beyond Confidence-Building," in Saw, Sheng and Chin, *ASEAN-China Relations: Realities and Prospects*, 348–349.

61 Ibid., 352.

62 Guifang Xue, *International Fisheries Law and China's Practice* (Qingdao: China Ocean University Press, 2008), 137, in Chinese.

63 United Nations (1992), *Rio Declaration on Environment and Development*, available at: www.un.org/documents/ga/conf151/aconf15126-1annex1.htm, Report of

the United Nations Conference on Environment and Development, Annex I (accessed February 12, 2014).

64 See United Nations (1992) *Agenda 21*, paragraph 17.1, available at: http://sustainabledevelopment.un.org/content/documents/Agenda21.pdf (accessed February 12, 2014).

65 See Keyuan Zou, "Regulation of Waste Dumping at Sea: the Chinese Practice," *Ocean and Coastal Management* 52, no.7 (2009): 384.

66 Ministry of Land and Resources of China, 1999 MEPL (English), available at: www.mlr.gov.cn/mlrenglish/laws/200710/t20071012_656329.htm (accessed January 1, 2014).

67 Ibid.

68 Keyuan Zou, "The Establishment of a Marine Legal System in China," *The International Journal of Marine and Coastal Law* 13, no. 1, (1998): 23.

69 For a brief overview of the GEF's reconstruction in the 1994 and its shifting focus in the 1990s, see Global Environment Facility, "What is GEF?," available at: www.thegef.org/gef/whatisgef (accessed March 1, 2014).

70 The other ICM pilot project was established in the Batangas Bay, in the Philippines.

71 For the introduction of the evolution of the MPP-SEA project, see PEMSEA, available at: www.pemsea.org/about-pemsea/history (accessed March 1, 2014).

72 For a brief overview of the development of international legislation promoting sustainable fishery, see Food and Agriculture Organization of the United Nations, *FAO Compliance Agreement*, available at: www.fao.org/fishery/topic/14766/en (accessed February 12, 2014).

73 For the complete statement upon signature, see United Nations, available at: http://treaties.un.org/Pages/ViewDetails.aspx?src=TREATY&mtdsg_no=XXI-7&chapter=21&lang=en#EndDec. It has to be pointed out that China has not yet ratified this agreement, mainly due to China's objection to the provisions regarding the "use of force," see Xue, *International Fisheries Law and China's Practice*, 153.

74 Xue, *International Fisheries Law and China's Practice*, 153.

75 *FAO Compliance Agreement*.

76 Xue, *International Fisheries Law and China's Practice*, 141.

77 Ibid., 159.

78 See Deb Menasveta, "APFIC – Its Changing Role," available at: www.apfic.org/apfic_downloads/pubs_APFIC/2000-05%20APFIC%20-%20its%20changing%20role.pdf (accessed March 1, 2014).

79 Asia-Pacific Fishery Commission, *Report of the Twenty-six Session of the Asia-Pacific Fishery Commission*, available at: www.apfic.org/apfic_downloads/pubs_APFIC/%2326%20Session%20APFIC.pdf (accessed March 1, 2014).

80 Wenlu Guo and Shuolin Huang, "A Discussion on the Challenges and Countermeasures of Fishing Capacity Control in China's Marine Fisheries," *Shanghai Fisheries University Journal* 10, no. 2 (2001): 133.

81 The Ministry of Agriculture of China, *Circular on the Enforcement of the Summer Moratorium in the South China Sea*, 1999.

82 Zheng Liu, "How to Establish and Improve the Fisheries Legal System in China," *Chinese Fisheries Economics* 4 (1999): 19, in Chinese.

83 Xue, *International Fisheries Law and China's Practice*, 104.

84 The Fishery Law was first adopted on January 20, 1986 and amended on October 31, 2000. English text of the 1986 Law is available in State Oceanic Administration of China, Office of Policy, Law, and Regulation, *Collection of the Sea Laws and Regulations of the People's Republic of China* (Beijing: Ocean Press, 1998), 222–232. For the text of the 2000 amended law, see *Gazette of the Standing Committee of the National People's Congress of the People's Republic of China,* 6 (2000): 608–615, in Chinese.

85 For details of the revised Action Plan, see COBSEA, available at: www.cobsea.org/documents/action_plan/ActionPlan1994.pdf (accessed March 1, 2014).

86 Ibid., 174–175.

87 UNEP, *Repository Documents of the UNEP/GEF SCS Project*, available at: www.unepscs.org/remository.html (accessed March 1. 2014).

88 On this point, Martha Finnemore has an excellent study investigating external influences shaping states' interests and policy preferences. She finds that states' preferences and interests are not necessarily inherent and unproblematic. Rather, they are malleable and subject to external influences from regional and international society, especially the powerful UN institutions. In particular, teaching is a very important mechanism through which the influence of international society or a specific organization is exerted on a state's policy formulation. See Martha Finnemore, *National Interests in International Society* (Ithaca, NY: Cornell University Press, 1996).

89 Sulan Chen, "Instrumental and Induced Cooperation: Environmental Politics in the South China Sea" (PhD diss., University of Maryland, 2005), 224.

90 UNEP, *China's National Report on the UNEP/GEF SCS Project*, available at: www.unepscs.org/remository/Download/01_-_Project_Development/PDF-B_Phase/National_Reports.html (accessed March 1, 2014).

91 Chen, "Environmental Politics in the South China Sea," 225, 232.

92 Ibid., 239.

93 Ibid., 241.

94 In China, the Central Government designates a "window agency" for each International Organization. The "window agency" of an IO deals with activities related to that IO. For example, the Ministry of Finance is the "window agency" of the World Bank and IMF. The SEPA is the window agency for UNEP.

95 China in the 1990s formulated a policy called the "good neighbor policy," aiming to cement closer relationships with Southeast Asian countries. For the origin and evolution of the "good neighbor policy," see Suisheng Zhao, "China's Periphery Policy and its Asian Neighbors," *Security Dialogue* 30, no. 3 (1999): 335–346.

96 China had tried to build an image as a cooperative actor in solving regional and global environmental problems. See Jimin Zhao and Leonard Ortolano, "The Chinese Government's Role in Implementing Multilateral Environmental Agreements: The Case of the Montreal Protocol," *China Quarterly* 175 (2003): 708–725.

97 Chen, "Environmental Politics in the South China Sea," 243.

98 Ibid., 244.

99 Ibid., 208.

100 The earlier proposal refers to Li Peng's joint development proposal in 1990.

101 For relevant papers, see China Institute for Marine Development Strategy, *Selected Papers Presented to the Academic Conference on the SCS Islands* (Beijing, March 1992), in Chinese.

102 Ba, "Who's Socializing Whom?," 163.

103 Michael Swaine and Ashley Tellis, *Interpreting China's Grand Strategy* (Santa Monica, CA: Rand Corporation, 2000).

104 Ba, "Who's Socializing Whom?," 163.

105 Hiro Katsumata, "Reconstruction of Diplomatic Norms in Southeast Asia: The Case for Strict Adherence to the 'ASEAN Way,'" *Contemporary Southeast Asia* 25, no. 1 (2003): 104.

106 Ba, "Who's Socializing Whom?," 169.

107 Alexander Wendt, "Anarchy Is What States Make of It: The Social Construction of Power Politics," *International Organization* 46, no. 2 (1992): 415.

108 Alastair I. Johnston, *Social States: China in International Institutions, 1980–2000* (Princeton, NJ: Princeton University Press, 2008), 148.

109 Chen, "Environmental Politics in the South China Sea," 224.
110 Ibid., 168–169.
111 Baviera, "SCS after 2002: Beyond Confidence-Building," 352.

Bibliography

Acharya, A. 2004. "How Ideas Spread: Whose Norms Matter? Norm Localization and Institutional Change in Asian Regionalism," *International Organization*, vol. 58, no. 2, pp. 239–275.

Alagappa, M. (ed.) 2003. *Asian Security Order: Instrumental and Normative Features*, Stanford University Press, Stanford, CA.

ASEAN. 2002. *Declaration on the Conduct of Parties in the South China Sea*, available at: www.asean.org/asean/external-relations/china/item/declaration-on-the-conduct-of-parties-in-the-south-china-sea (accessed March 1, 2014).

Asia-Pacific Fishery Commission. 2000. *Report of the Twenty-six Session of the Asia-Pacific Fishery Commission*, available at: www.apfic.org/apfic_downloads/pubs_APFIC/%2326%20Session%20APFIC.pdf. (accessed March 1, 2014).

Ba, A.D. 2005. "On Norms, Rule-Breaking and Security Communities: A Constructivist Response," *International Relations of the Asia-Pacific*, vol. 5, no. 2, pp. 255–266.

Ba, A.D. 2006. "Who's Socializing Whom? Complex Engagement in Sino-ASEAN Relations," *The Pacific Review*, vol. 19, no. 2, pp. 157–179.

Capie, D. 2010. "When Does Track Two Matter? Structure, Agency and Asian Regionalism," *Review of International Political Economy*, vol. 17, no. 2, pp. 291–318.

Chanda, N. 1995. "Territorial Imperative," *Far Eastern Economic Review*, vol. 23, pp. 14–16.

Chen, S.L. 2005. "Instrumental and Induced Cooperation: Environmental Politics in the South China Sea," PhD diss., University of Maryland.

China Institute for Marine Development Strategy. 1992. *Selected Papers Presented to the Academic Conference on the SCS Islands*, China Institute for Marine Development Strategy, Beijing (in Chinese).

China Ministry of Agriculture. 1999. *Circular on the Enforcement of the Summer Moratorium in the South China Sea*, Chinese Ministry of Agriculture, Beijing.

Djalal, H. 2012. "Dispute Settlement and Conflict Management in the SCS," *Strategic Review*, available at: www.sr-indonesia.com/this-months-issue/indonesia-360/170-dispute-settlement-and-conflict-management-in-the-south-china-sea (accessed March 1, 2014).

Farrell, E.C. 1999. *The Socialist Republic of Vietnam and the Law of the Sea: An Analysis of Vietnamese Behavior within the Emerging International Oceans Regime*, Martinus Nijhoff Publishers, the Hague.

Finnemore, M. 1996. *National Interests in International Society*, Cornell University Press, Ithaca, NY.

Fravel, M.T. 2008. *Strong Borders, Secure Nation: Cooperation and Conflict in China's Territorial Disputes*, Princeton University Press, Princeton, NJ.

Fravel, M.T. 2011. "China's Strategy in the South China Sea," *Contemporary Southeast Asia*, vol. 33, no. 3, pp. 292–319.

Foot, R. 1998. "China in the ASEAN Regional Forum: Organizational Processes and Domestic Modes of Thought," *Asian Survey*, vol. 38, no. 5, pp. 425–440.

Guo, W.L. and Huang, S.L. 2001. "A Discussion on the Challenges and Countermeasures of Fishing Capacity Control in China's Marine Fisheries," *Shanghai Fisheries University Journal*, vol. 10, no. 2, pp. 132–139 (in Chinese).
Hadipranowo, M.S. (ed.) 1991. *The Second Workshop on Managing Potential Conflicts in the South China Sea*, Research and Development Agency, Jakarta, Indonesia.
Hong, N. 2012. *UNCLOS and Ocean Dispute Settlement: Law and Politics in the South China Sea*, Routledge, New York.
Johnston, A.I. 2008. *Social States: China in International Institutions, 1980–2000*, Princeton University Press, Princeton, NJ.
Katsumata, H. 2003a. "The Role of ASEAN Institutes of Strategic and International Studies in Developing Security Cooperation in the Asia-Pacific," *Asian Journal of Political Science*, vol. 11, no. 1, pp. 93–111.
Katsumata, H. 2003b. "Reconstruction of Diplomatic Norms in Southeast Asia: The Case for Strict Adherence to the 'ASEAN Way'," *Contemporary Southeast Asia*, vol. 25, no. 1, pp. 104–121.
Keohane, R.O. 1982. "The Demand for International Regimes," *International Organization*, vol. 36, no. 2, pp. 325–355.
Kuik, C.C. 2005. "Multilateralism in China's ASEAN Policy: Its Evolution, Characteristics, and Aspiration," *Contemporary Southeast Asia*, vol. 27, no. 1, 102–122.
Kwa, C.G. and Skogan, J.K. (eds.) 2007. *Maritime Security in Southeast Asia*, Routledge, New York.
Ling, Q. 2008. *From Yan'an to the United Nations*, Fujian Renmin Press, Fujian, China.
Liu, Z. 1999. "How to Establish and Improve the Fisheries Legal System in China," *Chinese Fisheries Economics*, vol. 4, pp. 18–20 (in Chinese).
National People's Congress of the People's Republic of China. 2000. *Gazette of the Standing Committee of the National People's Congress of the People's Republic of China*, vol. 6, pp. 608–615 (in Chinese).
Saw, S.H., Sheng, L.J. and Chin, K.W. (eds.) 2005. *ASEAN-China Relations: Realities and Prospects*, Institute of Southeast Asian Studies, Singapore.
Severino, R.C. 2010. "ASEAN and the South China Sea," *Security Challenges*, vol. 6, no. 2, pp. 37–47.
Song, Y.H. and Zou, K.Y. 2000. "Maritime Legislation of Mainland China and Taiwan: Developments, Comparison, Implications, and Potential Challenges for the United States," *Ocean Development and International Law*, vol. 31, no. 4, pp. 303–345.
Southeast Asian Institute. 1991. *Prospects for the China-Southeast Asian Relations Around 2000*, Zhongshan University Press, Guangzhou, China (in Chinese).
State Oceanic Administration of China, Office of Policy, Law, and Regulation. 1998. *Collection of the Sea Laws and Regulations of the People's Republic of China*, Ocean Press, Beijing, China.
Storey, I.J. 1999. "Creeping Assertiveness: China, the Philippines and the South China Sea Dispute," *Contemporary Southeast Asia*, vol. 21, no. 1, pp. 95–118.
Swaine, M.D. and Tellis, A. 2000. *Interpreting China's Grand Strategy*, Rand Corporation, Santa Monica, CA.
Thao, N.H. 2001. "Vietnam and the Code of Conduct for the South China Sea," *Ocean Development and International Law*, vol. 32, no. 2, pp. 105–130.
Thao, N.H. and Amer, R. 2009. "A New Legal Arrangement for the South China Sea?," *Ocean Development and International Law*, vol. 40, no. 4, pp. 333–349.

UNEP. 2007. *China's National Report on the UNEP/GEF SCS Project*, available at: www.unepscs.org/remository/Download/01_-_Project_Development/PDF-B_Phase/National_Reports.html (accessed March 1, 2014).

UNEP. n.d. *Repository Documents of the UNEP/GEF SCS Project*, available at: www.unepscs.org/remository.html (accessed March 1, 2014).

United Nations. 1992a. *Agenda 21*, available at: http://sustainabledevelopment.un.org/content/documents/Agenda21.pdf (accessed February 12, 2014).

United Nations. 1992b. *Rio Declaration on Environment and Development, Report of the United Nations Conference on Environment and Development*, Annex I, available at: www.un.org/documents/ga/conf151/aconf15126-1annex1.htm. (accessed February 12, 2014).

United Nations. 1993. *FAO Compliance Agreement*, available at: www.fao.org/fishery/topic/14766/en (accessed February 12, 2014).

Wang, L.Y. 1991. "Preliminary Discussion on the Legal Implications of China's Discovery and Effective Occupation of the Islands in the SCS," *Ocean and Coast Zone Development*, vol. 8, no. 4, pp. 39–44 (in Chinese).

Wendt, A. 1992. "Anarchy Is What States Make of It: The Social Construction of Power Politics," *International Organization*, vol. 46, no. 2, pp. 391–425.

Whiting, A.S. 1997. "ASEAN Eyes China," *Asian Survey*, vol. 37, no. 4, pp. 299–322.

Xue, G.F. 2008. *International Fisheries Law and China's Practice*, China Ocean University Press, Qingdao, China (in Chinese).

Zhao, J.M. and Ortolano, L. 2003. "The Chinese Government's Role in Implementing Multilateral Environmental Agreements: The Case of the Montreal Protocol," *China Quarterly*, vol. 175, pp. 708–725.

Zhao, LH. 1992. "Understanding China's Undisputable Ownership of the Islands in the South China Sea from the Viewpoint of International Law," *Journal of Beijing University*, vol. 3, pp. 30–40.

Zhao, L.H. 1995. "Several Legal Issues Concerning the SCS Islands," *Rule of Law and Social Development*, vol. 4, pp. 50–63 (in Chinese).

Zhao, S.S. 1999. "China's Periphery Policy and Its Asian Neighbors," *Security Dialogue*, vol. 30, no. 3, pp. 335–346.

Zhu, Q.W. 1990. "The Problem of Ownership of the Spratly Islands Discussed from the Viewpoint of International Law: Part One," *The Forum of Political Science and Law – Journal of China University of Political Science and Law*, vol. 6, pp. 7–12 (in Chinese).

Zhu, Q.W. 1991. "The Problem of Ownership of the Spratly Islands Discussed from the Viewpoint of International Law: Part Two," *The Forum of Political Science and Law – Journal of China University of Political Science and Law*, vol. 1, pp. 7–15 (in Chinese).

Zou, K.Y. 1998. "The Establishment of a Marine Legal System in China," *The International Journal of Marine and Coastal Law*, vol. 13, no. 1, pp. 23–46.

Zou, K.Y. 1999a. "Implementing Marine Environmental Protection Law in China: Progress, Problems and Prospects," *Marine Policy*, vol. 23, no. 3, pp. 207–225.

Zou, K.Y. 1999b. "Maritime Boundary Delimitation in the Gulf of Tonkin," *Ocean Development and International Law*, vol. 30, no. 3, pp. 235–254.

Zou, K.Y. 2001a. "China's Exclusive Economic Zone and Continental Shelf: Developments, Problems, and Prospects," *Marine Policy*, vol. 25, no. 1, pp. 71–81.

Zou, K.Y. 2001b. "Historic Rights in International Law and in China's Practice," *Ocean Development and International Law*, vol. 32, no. 2, pp. 149–168.

Zou, K.Y. 2005. *China's Marine Legal System and the Law of the Sea*, Martinus Nijhoff, Leiden.

Zou, K.Y. 2009. *China-ASEAN Relations and International Law*, Chandos Publishing, Oxford.

6 The 2002–2013 period

Changes and continuities

This chapter consists of five sections. The first section focuses on the development of China's legal position in the SCS in the period 2002–2013. The 2009 deadline to submit information regarding the continental shelf to the Commission on the Limits of Continental Shelf (CLCS) sparked a new round of legal battles between SCS-bordering countries and resulted in clarifications to the Chinese legal position. The second section considers geopolitical flux and regional normative institutional dynamics in the SCS. While multilateral political engagement among claimants and between SCS countries and extra-regional countries remained consistent in face of geopolitical flux, policy results varied, depending on the interaction of the geostrategic environment and the normative institutional dynamics in the SCS. The third section examines developments in China's maritime governance policy practices. The Chinese government has continued to internalize modern maritime governance through detailed domestic legislation. Chinese policy has at the same time been placing greater emphasis on enhancing governance over the waters within the nine-dash line. The fourth section explores China's attitude to dispute resolution. The Sino-Vietnamese Agreement on Maritime Boundary Delimitation in the Gulf of Tonkin is an example of successful dispute resolution in the SCS. The delimitating efforts underscored China's determination to comply with contemporary maritime order. The 2002–2013 period also witnessed substantial progress in China's efforts to implement joint development as a provisional solution to manage the SCS issue. The final section summarizes the developments of China's SCS policy in the past decade and analyzes how different forces have sculpted the contours of China's SCS policy.

The CLCS submissions and the nine-dash line

Entering the new millennium, the Chinese government continued to formalize its legal position in line with the new maritime order. China made a notable legal clarification in 2009 in response to Malaysian and Vietnamese submissions to the CLCS. This move, as explained later in this section, was the product of direct pressure created by the CLCS deadline and an integral part of the incremental modifications China made to its legal position under the sustained influence of the maritime regime.

China's Notes Verbales in 2009

On May 6, 2009, Malaysia and Vietnam made a joint submission to the CLCS regarding a portion of the continental shelf between the two states in the southern South China Sea.[1] The area of the extended continental shelf is between the 200 nautical mile limits of these two states measured from the baselines along the mainland coast of Vietnam and the East Malaysian states of Sarawak and Sabah (see Figure 6.1). The submission informed the

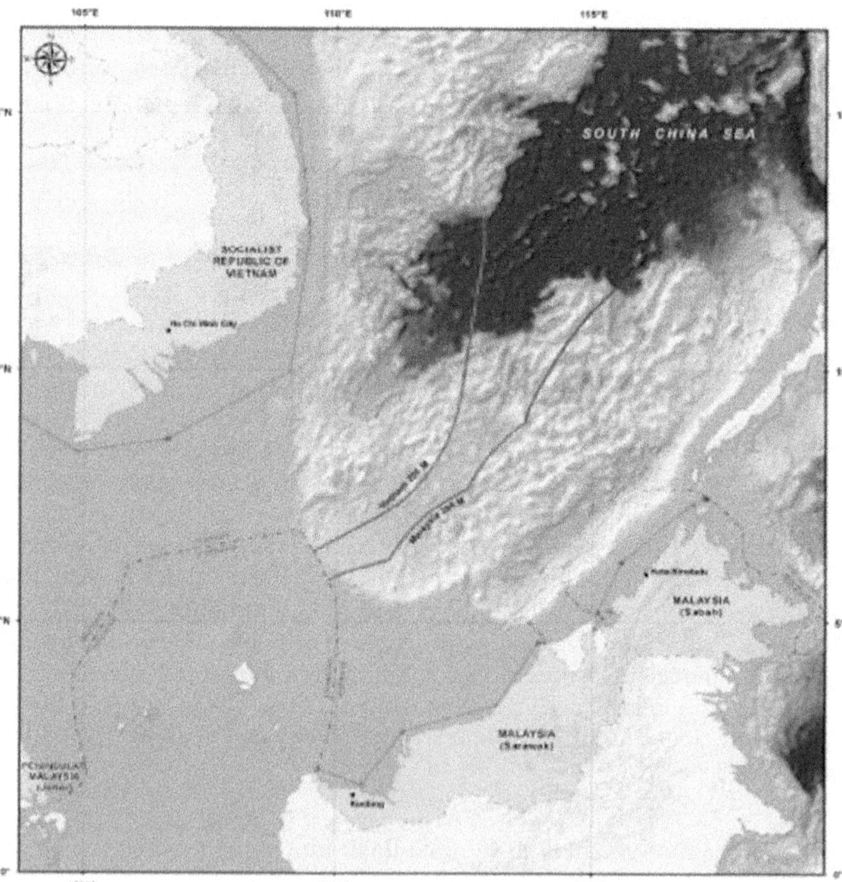

Figure 6.1 Joint Outer Continental Shelf Submission by Malaysia and Vietnam
CLCS, "Joint Submission of Malaysia and the Socialist Republic of Vietnam," May 6, 2009, available at: www.un.org/Depts/los/clcs_new/submissions_files/mysvnm33_09/mys_vnm2009excutivesummary.pdf, 5 (accessed March 1, 2014).

Commission of the existence of unresolved boundary disputes in the defined area and made assurances that to the extent possible, the submission would not prejudice matters relating to the delimitation of boundaries between states with opposite or adjacent coasts in the area.[2] On May 7, 2009, Vietnam made a separate submission to the CLCS regarding the area north of its joint submission with Malaysia. The northern boundary in this submission is an equidistant line measured from the baselines of Vietnam and China.[3]

On May 7, 2009, the day following the joint submission of Vietnam and Malaysia and the same day of Vietnam's separate submission, China submitted two similar Notes Verbales to the UN Secretary-General, the main body of which reads:

> China has indisputable sovereignty over the islands in the South China Sea and the adjacent waters, and enjoys sovereign rights and jurisdiction over the relevant waters as well as the seabed and subsoil thereof (see attached map). The above position is consistently held by the Chinese Government, and is widely known by the international community.
>
> The continental shelf beyond 200 nautical miles as contained in the Joint Submission by Malaysia and the Socialist Republic of Viet Nam has seriously infringed China's sovereignty, sovereign rights and jurisdiction in the South China Sea. In accordance with Article 5(a) of Annex I to the Rules of Procedure of the Commission on the Limits of the Continental Shelf, the Chinese Government seriously requests the Commission not to consider the Joint Submission by Malaysia and the Socialist Republic of Viet Nam. The Chinese Government has informed Malaysia and the Socialist Republic of Viet Nam of the above position.[4]

A map of the South China Sea marked by China's nine-dash line was attached to both documents (Figure 6.2). On this map, the line encloses almost the entire South China Sea.

The enclosure of the nine-dash line map in Beijing's Notes Verbales to the UN was the first time China officially had used the nine-dash line to defend its claims in the South China Sea. To understand the legal implication of China's 2009 Notes, it is necessary to first explore the historic evolution of the nine-dash line.

The nine-dash line

The nine-dash line has several names, including "the U-shaped line," "nine-interrupted lines," "the nine-dashed intermittent line," "the dotted line," or "the traditional maritime boundary line." It is a loose boundary line appearing in various Chinese maps and atlases, first noted in a December 1914 map compiled by Hu Jinjie, a Chinese cartographer.[5] Due to domestic turmoil in the 1910s and 1920s, Chinese authorities were unable to undertake new fieldwork. Most of the maps produced in this period were reproductions of older

Figure 6.2 The nine-dash map included in China's Note Verbale, May 7, 2009
CLCS, "Joint Submission of Malaysia and the Socialist Republic of Vietnam," May 6, 2009, available at: www.un.org/Depts/los/clcs_new/submissions_files/mysvnm33_09/mys_vnm2009excutivesummary.pdf, 5 (accessed March 1, 2014).

maps or foreign-produced maps and only enclosed the Pratas and the Paracels.[6] The southernmost end of the demarcation was located at about 15°and 16° north latitude. In 1933, in reaction to the French occupation of nine small islands in the Spratly archipelago, the Republic of China (led by the Nationalist Party) formed a Land and Water Maps Inspection Committee to work on demarcating China's sovereignty in the SCS. In April 1935, the committee finally authorized a publication detailing China's maritime sovereignty in the SCS which included all four South China Sea archipelagos. This publication included the names of 132 islets and reefs belonging to the four archipelagos as well as an annexed map which marked the southernmost James Shoal at the location of about 4° north latitude and 112° east longitude.[7]

In response to the end of Japanese occupation in the SCS after World War II, the central government sent naval officers and survey teams to the South China Sea to map the various islands and islets. In November 1947, the Ministry of Interior renamed the islands in the South China Sea on the basis of their geographic location and promulgated the new names.[8] The Geography Department printed *The Location Map of the South China Sea Islands*. On this map, the Pratas Islands, the Paracel Islands, the Macclesfield Bank, and the Spratly Islands were shown as being part of China with the use of an eleven-dotted line. The southernmost end of Chinese claims was located at 4° north latitude, including the James Shoal. This map was attached to the *Atlas of Administrative Areas of the Republic of China,* officially published by the Nationalist government in February 1948.[9] Immediately following the founding of the People's Republic of China in 1949, the map was adopted by the Communist government in Beijing. In 1953, as the anti-French War in Vietnam quickly escalated, two segments of the line marking the Gulf of Tonkin were eliminated by the PRC for the purpose of providing North Vietnam additional strategic depth. The line thus became the nine-dash line used in PRC practice ever since.[10]

Prior to the mid-1990s, this nine-dash line appeared regularly in various publications of Chinese maps and atlases, encountering little complaint or objection from neighboring countries. Despite these appearances, the Chinese government never publicly invoked the line as the legal ground for its own claims. As explained in previous chapters, the legal justification given by the Beijing government over the years was essentially historical, drawing on ancient archives and records dating back as far as the Song dynasty to prove China's first discovery and occupation. The line did not appear in the 1958 Declaration on Territorial Sea, the most authoritative maritime legislation in the pre-1990s period, nor did it appear in Chinese diplomatic protests against other claimants. In 1992, Beijing signed a lease with the Crestone Energy Corporation to explore oil in a 7347 square nautical mile area between the Vanguard Bank (Wan'an Tai) and the Prince of Wales Bank, 160 nautical miles off Vietnam's coast. The exploration team soon withdrew in face of bitter protests and naval harassment from the Vietnamese side. In response to Vietnam's protest, the spokesman from the Chinese Foreign Ministry claimed that China had "indisputable sovereignty" over the Nansha and Xisha Islands and the contiguous waters so that the exploitation by China's oil company was irreproachable. Again, the Chinese government did not invoke the line to legitimize its exploration activities.

This brief review of the nine-dash line shows that in the course of over four decades (from the 1950s to the early 1990s), the nine-dash line had never been linked to historic claims in official pronouncements. The silence on the nine-dash line points to the rather consistent nature of China's legal position towards SCS disputes: that is, up to the early 1990s, China's claims focused exclusively on islands in the SCS, and were not concerned with territorial seas. It might have seemed to the leadership in Beijing that available evidence was already sufficient to legitimize its island claims under the general international law on territorial acquisition.

An important change began to unfold in Beijing's official position in mid-1990s when claims of historic rights became important in China's legal stance regarding its sovereign rights in the SCS. As explained previously, such an adjustment was part of China's attempts to adapt to the legal reconstruction of the SCS dispute and the new LOS. It was essentially a legal solution permitted under the framework of the new LOS to meet the legal challenge posed by complying with new maritime rules.

At this point, the exact content of China's claimed historic rights and its legal reasoning remained unclear. In the years leading up to the 2009 CLCS submission, despite mounting criticism from other SCS countries and scholarly speculation surrounding the potential connection between the historic claims and the nine-dash line, Beijing remained silent, taking no further steps to publicly clarify the issue.

Clarification finally came in 2009 when the nine-dash line was put on the table of the CLCS by the Chinese government in response to the submissions lodged by Vietnam and Malaysian. It marked the first time that the Chinese government officially used the line in defending its sovereign claims in the South China Sea:

> China has indisputable sovereignty over the islands in the South China Sea and the adjacent waters, and enjoys sovereign rights and jurisdiction over the relevant waters as well as the seabed and subsoil thereof (see attached map).[11]

First, the Note indicated that not all the waters enclosed within the nine-dash line were viewed by Beijing as historic waters or internal waters. In this Note, Beijing distinguished between claims of full sovereignty over islands and their adjacent waters and claims of relevant sovereign rights and jurisdiction, suggesting that beyond islands and territorial seas it perceived itself enjoying not full sovereignty but some kind of sovereign or jurisdictional rights.[12] Second, by attaching the map to the clause "sovereign rights and jurisdiction over the relevant waters as well as the seabed and subsoil thereof," Beijing alluded to the possibility that the nine-dash line might be able to legitimately generate certain sovereign rights and jurisdiction, although the content of these rights and jurisdiction remained unclarified. As discussed in Chapter 5, Beijing might have envisaged traditional fishery rights as part of the rights associated with historic claims.

Two years later, China indicated its intention to use the nine-dash line to legitimize some kind of historic rights in another Note Verbale submitted to the UN. In response to the Philippines' diplomatic note dated April 5, 2011, China emphasized in its Note Verbale, dated April 14, 2011, that "China's sovereignty and *related rights* and jurisdiction in the South China Sea are supported by abundant *historical and legal evidence*" (emphasis added).[13] In contrast to China's previous official claims, two new terms appeared in this sentence: the first is "related rights and jurisdiction," and the second, "legal evidence." These two new terms taken together indicated that China envisaged some rights and jurisdiction not exactly the same as sovereign rights and jurisdiction but supported by historical and legal evidence. As some legal scholars observe, the term "related rights" was deliberately used rather than the term "sovereign rights" to refer to something either different or broader than sovereign rights.[14] Otherwise there would be no need for this new term. The claim to "legal evidence" in an official proclamation was also a departure from Chinese official reasoning in previous decades, well known for its consistent historical rhetoric. The legal evidence to which China was referring very likely included the nine-dash line map. In other words, in this Note Verbale, China intended to rely on the nine-dash map as a legal basis to support its claims to "related rights," which seemed to be historic rights.[15]

In this Note, Beijing also attempted to clarify its official position on the issue of possible maritime entitlements to the Nansha (Spratly) Islands:

> In addition, under the relevant provisions of the 1982 United Nations Convention on the Law of the Sea, as well as the Law of the People's Republic of China on the Territorial Sea and the Contiguous Zone (1992) and the Law on the Exclusive Economic Zone and Continental Shelf of the People's Republic of China (1998), China's Nansha Islands are fully entitled to Territorial Sea, Exclusive Economic Zone (EEZ) and Continental Shelf.[16]

From China's official standpoint, the Nansha Islands should be qualified to generate the EEZ and the CS and the waters nearby were not viewed as historic waters. This view coincides with the argument of a senior scholar from the State Oceanic Administration (SOA), who had suggested a model of the EEZ and CS regime plus historic claims for the Spratly Islands, and corroborates earlier views of a few prominent Chinese legalists that the waters enclosed by the nine-dash line would not be treated by Beijing as internal waters.[17] As we will see soon, such corroboration is not an unintentional coincidence; it is an important phenomenon relating to the evolution of China's legal position.

China's clarification of the nine-dash line conveyed through the UN diplomatic Notes rid the Chinese government of potential benefits associated with maintaining an ambiguous position. China made public in the UN that it did not perceive the waters enclosed in the nine-dash line as historic waters, a position from which China could hardly retreat in the future. This elimination of ambiguity surrounding China's legal stance was a necessary step towards forming a common ground for future negotiations.

The CLCS deadline

The timing of Beijing's decision to further clarify its sovereign claims has much to do with the CLCS's deadline of submission. It was this deadline that put direct pressure on China to take action and set in motion a series of diplomatic exchanges in the SCS region.

Under Article 4 of Annex II to the 1982 UNCLOS, a coastal state that wishes to claim that it has a continental shelf that extends beyond 200 nautical miles and establish the outer limits to its continental shelf beyond 200 nautical miles is obligated to submit information of such limits to the CLCS, along with supporting scientific and technical data within 10 years of the entry into force of the Convention for that state. During the 11th meeting of the UNCLOS 1982 States Parties (SPLOS), developing states expressed concern regarding the difficulty of complying with the 10-year time limit in light of the significant resources, capacity, and expertise required in order to include scientific and technical data with the submission. Consequently, the time frame was amended. Pursuant to a decision adopted by the meeting (SPLOS/72) of May 19, 2001, for any state for which UNCLOS entered into force before May 13, 1999,[18] the date of commencement of the 10-year time limit for making submissions would be set at May 13, 2009.[19] The effect of this decision was to move the deadline for making submissions to the CLCS for all disputants in the SCS to May 13, 2009.

Several SCS-bordering states, including Indonesia, Malaysia, Vietnam, and the Philippines, made moves on submitting particulars to the CLCS in order to meet the May 13, 2009 deadline. The motivation was clear: the CLCS offered a great opportunity for claimant countries to assert and publicize their claims. The CLCS has significant potential power as a universally recognized, neutral, and authoritative inter-governmental institution. By using the CLCS as a venue to express their official positions, countries sought to obtain additional credentials for their claims, potentially legitimizing their respective positions before an international audience. As Sam Bateman and Clive Schofield rightly point out:

> On the face of it, these submissions seem to be provocative moves … That said, Malaysia and Vietnam, along with many other states worldwide, were faced with a deadline (agreed among parties to UNCLOS) of 13 May 2009 to make such submissions or risk losing their rights.[20]

Vietnam and Malaysia's submissions put direct pressure on China. Originally, Chinese leaders might not have decided to take any action ahead of the approaching deadline, since the leadership had been quite prudent when it came to fulfilling international obligations, as in the process of ratifying the UNCLOS and the UNEP projects. After all, despite the benefits discussed above, making a proactive submission was bold and risky, given the already contentious situation and the amicable relationship between China and the

ASEAN. However, the Beijing government was equally cautious about any activity that might potentially challenge its position. Hence, Beijing responded in an immediate and affirmative manner, protesting the joint submission by Vietnam and Malaysia and the separate submission by Vietnam. Beijing's two Notes Verbales submitted to the UN had two effects. First, they helped mitigate the de-legitimization caused by Vietnam and Malaysia's actions, since Beijing did not initially submit its own claim to the continental shelf in the area. Second, Beijing used this opportunity not only to publicize the nine-dash line but also make important legal clarifications directed at the international community through the venue of the UN.

Although directly prompted by the CLCS deadline, China's legal clarification was not a hasty response to Vietnam and Malaysia's CLCS submissions. Rather, it was crafted in line with the LOSC and constituted a further step in the Chinese government's continuous and consistent effort to reconstruct the legal basis of its SCS sovereignty in conformity with the new maritime law.

Over the past two decades, the Chinese government had taken four steps to modify its legal position in the SCS. First, starting in the 1990s, China began to utilize historic claims as part of its attempt to solve the legal dilemma posed by the application of the new maritime law to the SCS, as discussed in Chapter 5. Since the statement of historic rights only appeared in the Law on the EEZ and CS and not in the Law on Territorial Sea, the Chinese government seemed to imply that China was not intending to claims historic waters within which it could enjoy full sovereignty, rather, the application of historic rights would only affect the application of EEZ and CS rights. Following this change to China's official position, the second step was prompting an evolution in the domestic discourse on the issue of the nine-dash line. In the years leading up to the 2009 CLCS deadline, leading scholars in China (many of whom were connected to the government) appeared to share similar views on the nine-dash line as delineating ownership of islands rather than historic waters.[21]

The late Professor Zhao Lihai of Peking University,[22] a well-known Chinese scholar of international law and legal counselor to the Foreign Ministry, wrote in 1996 that:

> In April 1947, in its official correspondence to the Guangdong Provincial government, the Ministry of Internal Affairs wrote straightforwardly that the dotted line was "to confirm and publicize the geographical scope of and sovereignty over Paracel and Spratly island groups," which clearly explained the legal meaning of the dotted line. In other words, the dotted line explicitly demarcates our country's territorial sovereignty over the South China Sea islands … Therefore, the dotted line is meant to show that the enclosed islands and their adjacent waters belong to China. It does not mean that the entire waters within the line are China's internal waters.[23]

Zou Keyuan, another professor from Peking University, stated in 1999 that "it seems that China does not claim everything within the line as can be seen from its diplomatic notes, relevant laws and public statements. What China claims are the islands and their adjacent waters within the line."[24] Gao Zhiguo, Director of the China Institute for Marine Affairs of State Oceanic Administration, also viewed the nine-dotted line as delineating ownership of the islands rather than a maritime boundary enclosing all the waters as Chinese territorial waters.[25] He wrote, "Careful study of Chinese documents reveals that China never has claimed the entire water column of the South China Sea, but only the islands and their surrounding waters within the lines."[26] Jia Yu, Deputy Director of the China Institute for Marine Affairs of State Oceanic Administration, shared a similar view that according to the history of the nine-dotted line, the line was used to delineate the islands in the South China Sea.[27] She concluded, "The Chinese government had never laid claims of sovereignty over the entire waters enclosed in the nine-dash line."[28]

These legal specialists also explored the link between the nine-dash line and historic rights. Some scholars believe that the map entitles China to the natural resources within the line.[29] Some allude to fishery rights.[30] Still others remain ambiguous about the exact content of the rights supported by the nine-dash line, and believe the final result depends on state practice.[31]

China's official use of the nine-dash line in support of its claims in the SCS in 2009 constitutes the third step. It confirmed that the waters enclosed within the line were not historic waters and suggested a possible linkage between the line and some types of historic rights.

After 2009, academic discussion on the nine-dash line continued to flourish. In July 2013, the National Institute for South China Sea Studies, a think tank affiliated with the Ministry of Foreign Affairs, held a three-day seminar in which the legal status of the nine-dash line in the SCS and related issues were widely discussed.[32] An expansive corpus of publications appeared, including academic journal articles and books, deliberating the historical, legal, and practical aspects of the nine-dash line.[33] Many of these studies converge on the view that the nine-dash line could be used to support possible historical rights and that the current ambiguity helps create room for future negotiation.[34] Researchers with official backgrounds also became more vocal about the linkage between the nine-dash line and certain historic rights within the waters enclosed by the line. For example, in a leading Chinese legal journal, the aforementioned scholar Jia Yu reviewed the history of China's practice within the nine-dash line and argued that China should enjoy relevant historic rights, including historical fishery rights and traditional navigation rights in the South China Sea.[35] She also articulated her opinions through a number of media outlets.[36] The Chinese government itself also adopted a more proactive approach in dealing with the issue of nine-dash line. A senior scholar from National Academy of Social Sciences acknowledged that his research team in recent years has been submitting circulars on this issue to the central government for review on a regular basis.[37] Another researcher revealed that the central government had been summoning scholars nationwide to work on forming an official explanation of the nine-dash line.[38]

Overall, the period 2002–2013 witnessed a continuous evolution of China's legal position in the SCS. The legal modifications China made to its position resulted from the sustained influence of the new maritime order and were precipitated by the CLCS deadline. These changes in China's SCS policy have had a profound impact on maritime governance, as expressed through practical changes in that area. As we will see in the third section, to strengthen its claims of historic rights, the Chinese government implemented a number of policies to expand and consolidate its presence in the waters enclosed by the nine-dash line in the SCS.

Political engagement in the 2002–2013 period

America's return-to-Asia strategy, unveiled in 2009, marked a major change in the geostrategic environment of Asia. This geopolitical shift divided the 2002–2013 into two stages. While multilateralism continued to dominate China's approach to political engagement in the SCS region both before and after 2009, the actual effects of multilateral engagement among relevant parties varied depending on the interaction between the global geopolitical environment and regional multilateral architecture.

2002–2008

Given the complexity of the SCS issue, multilateralism is a mandatory approach to regional engagement over the management and resolution of the dispute. As elaborated previously, the 1990s witnessed the emergence of a multilateral institutional maritime architecture based on a series of increasingly shared norms about interstate relations and security in the SCS. Beijing gradually integrated into this dense web of multilateralized, institutionalized, and regularized political and policy interactions among relevant parties in the SCS. The most significant fruit of such interactions is the Declaration on the Conduct of Parties (DOC) in the SCS in 2002.

In the years following the promulgation of the DOC, China continued to participate in multilateral regional dialogues and frameworks and exercised restraint compatible with the spirit of the DOC. This commitment to multilateralism was achieved in the absence of obvious material incentives.[39] First, as Asia entered the new millennium, the strategic environment became more stable. Geopolitical uncertainties which had emerged in the immediate aftermath of the end of the Cold War, providing powerful motivation for China's adaptation to multilateral political engagement in the 1990s, gradually waned. Second, after the September 11, 2001 terrorist attacks, the US leadership was preoccupied with global counter-terrorism. Consequently, it was difficult for the USA to maintain its previous active participation in Asian multilateral engagement processes. In the face of a new geostrategic environment unable to maintain the same level of pressure present in the 1990s, what accounted for China's continuous practice of multilateral engagement in the 2000s? The answer is the uninterrupted functioning of the multilateral institutional maritime architecture. This architecture demonstrated a lock-in effect on China and other concerned parties, all of whom continued down the path of multilateralism.

A lock-in effect, as explained in Chapter 1, is often observed in a situation where a state's continuous participation leads to institutionalized and habitual interaction which helps to maintain a certain level of compliance even in the absence of original incentives. In the 2002–2013 period, although the geopolitical impetus had become less powerful, the diverse multilateral exchange mechanisms did not cease functioning, largely because all the major SCS countries were locked into this dense web of institutionalized and regularized political and policy interactions.

This multilateral architecture had two leverages operating independently of geopolitical flux which secured Beijing's continuous participation. First, as discussed in Chapter 5, the ASEAN countries consciously adopted "the ASEAN Way" of constructive non-coercive argumentation when engaging China in the 1990s, cementing a basic understanding among the Chinese elite that many of the extant rules and norms were not antithetical to China's interests and that China could even take an active role in helping design the rules and norms of these institutions. It took years for Beijing to establish such a normative understanding of multilateral engagement. Yet once established, it was resilient, upholding Beijing's continuous involvement in regional multilateral engagement.

Second, the web of political and policy interactions in which China was locked was an intricate network weaving together not only maritime policies but also a wide range of political, economic, and security issues. As Robert Keohane argues, "The denser the policy space, the more highly interdependent different issues."[40] Such a dense policy space was created alongside the evolving China-ASEAN framework (which included ASEAN-China senior official consultations, ASEAN-China Joint Cooperation Committee meetings, and regular ASEAN-China summits) and related multilateral arrangements, such as the "ASEAN Plus Three" (China, Japan, and South Korea) (APT). Interactions through these venues were not limited to maritime issues; negotiations were often linked to the dynamics of other policy arenas, such as expanding trade and investment. For example, the China-ASEAN framework crafted the China-ASEAN Free Trade Agreement (CAFTA), which expanded to encompass East Asia in 2004 through the APT mechanism. The APT not only addressed economic issues; it was also used by participants to formulate a coordinated regional response to address maritime piracy.[41]

In October 2003, the PRC acceded to the Treaty of Amity and Cooperation in Southeast Asia (TAC) and established a strategic partnership for peace and prosperity, becoming the first non-ASEAN country to do so. The TAC formally commits China to enforcing the principles of non-aggression and non-interference, as well as a variety of other conflict resolution mechanisms.[42] Chinese leaders also expressed willingness to strengthen the military dimension of the multilateral engagement. At the 11th ASEAN Regional Forum (ARF) foreign ministers' meeting, China proposed an expansion of the ARF to include the participation of defense officials as well as strengthening military cooperation in counter-terrorism and other transnational non-traditional security issues. It then hosted the ARF security policy meeting, which for the first time gathered senior defense officials to discuss security issues. During the 2006 ASEAN-China Summit, Chinese Premier Wen Jiabao reaffirmed that China was prepared to expand its cooperation with the ASEAN states to include a military dimension.[43] In 2007, China for the first time sent to the Shangri-La Dialogue top-level military officials, led by Deputy Chief of the General Staff of the PLA Lieutenant-General Zhang Qinsheng. In 2008, Deputy Chief of the General Staff Lieutenant-General Ma Xiaotian led Beijing's delegation.

In the years between 2002 and 2008, the stabilized geopolitical environment and the US reduced involvement had two effects on regional multilateral engagement. On the one hand, since there was no abrupt change in the geostrategic environment to obstruct the lock-in effect, this stable geopolitical environment was in effect conducive to those positive developments in regional political engagement mentioned above as well as successful maintenance of a relatively peaceful and cooperative environment in the SCS. On the other hand, this stabilized environment was unable to produce powerful pressure or incentives to work with regional institutions to elicit major progress, especially in negotiating on a formal binding Code of Conduct (the COC). This situation began to change after 2009.

2009–2013

In 2009, soon after his inauguration as the new US president, Barack Obama initiated a fundamental rebalancing of the US global strategy towards Asia, also called the "Asia Pivot," and made Southeast Asia his first target. The Obama administration was determined to end decades of "benign neglect"[44] of Southeast Asia, placing the Asia-Pacific region at the top of the US global agenda.[45] In his speech delivered on November 13, 2009 in Tokyo, Obama promised at the Suntory Hall to be the first "Pacific President."[46] On July 21, 2009, during her second trip to Asia as Secretary of State, Hillary Clinton declared "the United States is back" upon arriving in the Thai capital of Bangkok, a Southeast Asian country and also a state bordering the SCS.[47] The idea of an "Asia Pivot," that the USA would assume a central role in Asia, the region determining the future of politics, was further fleshed out in Hillary Clinton's high-profile article in the November 2011 edition of *Foreign Policy* magazine, underscoring Washington's determination to refocus on the Asia-Pacific region.[48]

Obama's strategic rebalancing towards the Asia-Pacific created new dynamics into the SCS region. The USA wanted to make clear to countries in the SCS region its interest in the freedom of navigation of the Sea Lanes of Communication (SLOCs) in the SCS, its deep concern over the dispute, and its willingness to play an active role in the dispute's resolution. This message was first conveyed in the ASEAN Regional Forum held in Laguna Phuket, Thailand. in July 2009. US Secretary of State Hillary Clinton recalled, "We worked with a lot of the ASEAN countries who are directly impacted and 12 of us raised it at the ARF last July to make it clear that issues like that have to be resolved in accordance with the rule of law."[49] It was also during this ARF that the USA signed the TAC, a move showcasing US determination to stake an upgraded presence in the region.[50]

The fact that this high-profile diplomacy was carried out within the ARF, one of the major multilateral political-security institutions in regional diplomacy, revealed an important approach employed by the Obama administration in its shifting focus towards Asia: that is, strengthening the US relationship with the ASEAN organizations and expanding its involvement in regional multilateral institutional structures.

This approach was underscored by the inauguration of the US-ASEAN summit. In November 2009, in Singapore, Obama and leaders of the ASEAN member countries held the inaugural US-ASEAN Leaders' Meeting. It was during this summit that the USA expressed its plans to open a US Mission to the ASEAN in Jakarta and named the first ambassador for ASEAN Affairs.[51] More importantly, the USA signaled its intent to increase its presence in the regional multilateral architecture. The joint statement explicitly stated that the USA and the ASEAN

> shared a vision of a regional architecture that is inclusive, promotes shared values and norms, and respects the diversity within the region. We agreed to work closely together in building this regional construction, and were ready to study initiatives of this nature.[52]

As one Southeast Asia watcher assessed the first US-ASEAN summit:

> The key outcome is that President Obama will now have a direct link with ASEAN leaders. The fundamental reality is that the United States must stay engaged in Asia, and therefore it must be part of any regional architecture that is going to succeed and be sustained.[53]

Obama echoed this approach again in his opening remarks at the second US-ASEAN summit held in New York on September 24, 2010. He said:

> As President, I've, therefore, made it clear that the United States intends to play a leadership role in Asia. So we've strengthened old alliances; we've deepened new partnerships, as we are doing with China; and we've reengaged with regional organizations, including ASEAN.[54]

Active US involvement added new weight to the influence of existing regional maritime fora in dealing with the SCS dispute. After the 2009 ARF, the USA made statements in multiple multilateral fora concerning the issue of navigational freedom, objection to use or threat of force in the SCS dispute, and the need for a multilateral approach in handling the dispute. At the Shangri-La Dialogue in June 2010, US Secretary of Defense Robert Gates publicly raised the SCS issue. He stated that Washington did not take sides in sovereignty disputes, yet it opposed any action that could threaten the navigational freedom in the SLOCs in the South China Sea. A month later, at the ARF meeting in Hanoi, US Secretary of State Clinton directly confronted China over the latter's handling of the territorial disputes and offered to facilitate multilateral talks through the ASEAN on the islands' future. Clinton mentioned the dispute once again at the ARF meeting in Bali in July 2011, this time encouraging the ASEAN and China to conclude a COC over the issue.

The USA also expanded its presence into some newly established multilateral dialogues, increasing their ability to play a constructive role in the management of the SCS issues. One of such new dialogue mechanisms established in the 2000s is the East Asia Summit (EAS), established in 2005. Its participants were expansive, involving many new user states and concerned parties such as Russia, Australia, and New Zealand.[55] Originally, the USA did not take part in the EAS. It was not until 2010 that the USA attended the 5th EAS as a guest of the chair and obtained formal membership in the 6th EAS on November 19, 2011.[56] During the 6th EAS in Bali in November 2011, the USA aired concerns over the South China Sea question.[57] US President Obama stated:

> While we are not a claimant in the South China Sea dispute, and while we do not take sides, we have a powerful stake in maritime security in general, and in the resolution of the South China Sea issue specifically – as a resident Pacific power, as a maritime nation, as a trading nation and as a guarantor of security in the Asia Pacific region.[58]

The USA also gave explicit support to the idea of an expanding ASEAN Defense Ministers Meeting Plus (ADMM-Plus), welcomed by the ASEAN. The ADMM-Plus issue was first deliberated during the first US-ASEAN summit, where the ASEAN was assured of US support for its creation.[59] The ADMM-Plus process is a tool intended to engage the ASEAN dialogue partners and encourage cooperation on defense and security matters. The inaugural ADMM-Plus was convened in Hanoi, Viet Nam, on October 12, 2010. During this meeting, defense ministers agreed on five areas of practical cooperation to pursue under this new mechanism: maritime security, counter-terrorism, disaster management, peacekeeping operations, and military medicine.[60]

The influence of America's rebalancing strategy exerted through the multilateral institutional maritime architecture put pressure on China, in particular with regard to implementing the DOC and negotiating a formal binding COC, a crucial element of multilateral political management of the SCS dispute.

The ASEAN and China reached agreement on the DOC in 2002, which is closer to a political consensus than a formal binding code of conduct. The two sides agreed to go on to explore the possibility and the terms of a COC, as the DOC specifically calls on the parties to develop a formal code of conduct for the South China Sea. In the years between 2002 and 2008, while parties to the DOC demonstrated considerable self-restraint in maintaining peace in the SCS, no real progress was made in terms of negotiating a binding COC. This situation changed in 2010, as the USA and other countries pressured China through regional multilateral fora, such as the Shangri-La Dialogue and the ARF. On October 1, 2010, three months after the confrontation between Beijing and Washington in the ARF, the Chinese ambassador in Manila, Liu Jianchao signaled China's willingness to start negotiating a formal code of conduct with the ASEAN countries based on the 2002 DOC.[61] After months of negotiations, Beijing eventually decided to work with the ASEAN as a group in July 2011 at the China-ASEAN Foreign Ministers Meeting. In the 2011 the ARF held in Bali, Indonesia, China and the ASEAN countries agreed on the Guidelines on the Implementation of the Declaration on the Conduct of Parties in the South China Sea.[62] The USA responded positively to this progress. In contrast to the thorny remarks at the ARF meeting in 2010 in Vietnam, US Secretary of State Hillary Clinton hailed the process during the 2011 ARF, saying, "This is an important first step toward achieving a COC and reflects the progress that can be made through dialogue and multilateral diplomacy."[63]

Chinese leaders also made additional attempts to reaffirm their peaceful intentions and commitment to fulfill the obligations of the DOC, including the COC negotiation. In June 2011, Chinese Defense Minister and State Councilor General Liang Guanglie led the Chinese delegation participating in the 10th Shangri-La Dialogue. This was the highest rank of Chinese delegations over the years. General Liang reiterated the policy of "be a good neighbor and good partner," and that China always participated in regional security cooperation in a sincere, candid, and constructive manner. He said China was committed to maintaining "peace and stability" in the Asia-Pacific and "actively keeping dialogues and consultations" with the ASEAN on implementing the DOC.[64] During the 6th East Asia summit in 2011, Chinese Premier Wen Jiabao, when confronted by the USA and other attendees, responded by reaffirming the freedom of navigation principle and calling for a peaceful resolution to the South China Sea disputes.[65] Chinese officials also proposed to host a workshop on freedom of navigation in the South China Sea to address concerns particularly from the USA and other user states. On December 14–15, 2011, the workshop "Implementing DOC: Maintaining Freedom and Safety of Navigation in the SCS" was held in Haikou, Hainan.[66] On October 5, 2013, the Expanded ASEAN Maritime Forum was established, attended by government and non-government delegates from the EAS participating countries. At this forum, China pledged to provide RMB 3 billion (US$ 474 million) to set up a China-ASEAN maritime cooperation fund.[67]

While the US reengagement with regional multilateral architecture has been effective in rejuvenating the COC negotiation, it is associated with a potential problem. The way the US rebalancing strategy was implemented raised serious concern and suspicion among the Chinese leaders who perceived it as brash and lack of due respect to China's legitimate interests. Since 2009, Chinese leaders felt directly confronted by US representatives on multiple occasions. At the Hanoi Summit in 2010, for example, when the USA challenged China in front of an Asian audience in Vietnam, the Chinese Foreign Minister reportedly walked out, enraged.[68] Many Chinese analysts seem to be convinced that America's active diplomacy in multilateral dialogue venues followed a "divide and conquer" strategy and that supporting countries that have territorial disputes with China is part of Washington's strategy.[69] They believe that in the ARF, the EAS, and other multilateral fora, the Chinese were frequently caught by an orchestrated united voice challenging China's behavior in the SCS. They point out that in the 2010 ARF, US Secretary of State Clinton first held closed-door meetings in relation to the SCS issue with selected ASEAN countries before meeting with China. In the 2011 EAS, Obama let other attendees voice their concerns to China before he finally came out expressing his agreement with them.[70]

Adding to this suspicion of American containment were renewed efforts to build bilateral defense relationships between the USA and regional countries. In June 2009, US Defense Secretary Robert Gates visited the Philippines and met with his counterpart, Filipino Defense Secretary Gilberto Teodoro. The two defense secretaries talked about how to move forward on building the capacity of Filipino armed forces, which forms "a fundamental tenet of American foreign policy in the new administration." Washington had shifted hundreds of millions of dollars into the 2010 fiscal budget for such partner-nation capacity building.[71] A senior US defense official also added that the Pentagon would continue to support Filipino forces fighting terrorist groups, "while currently looking at ways to go beyond that help."[72]

It was against this background that China became concerned about the possibility of US support for the Philippines in a tense standoff in the vicinity of the Scarborough Shoal (in Chinese: Huangyan Dao) in April 2013. The Scarborough Shoal is a disputed territory in the SCS claimed by both China and the Philippines. Fishing vessels from both China and the Philippines have been exploiting the lagoon, fisheries, and other marine livestock in the surrounding waters for decades. The shoal is particularly valuable because there are several rocks on the reef. The largest one, South Rock (Nanyan), is above water at high tide (1.8m high), possibly meeting the definition of an "island" under the 1982 UNCLOS and hence generating expansive maritime jurisdiction.[73]

The incident began after China blocked an attempt by the Filipino Navy frigate BRP *Gregorio del Pilar* to arrest Chinese fishermen operating in the vicinity of the shoal on April 10, 2013. In response, the Philippines' leaders sent additional vessels to the shoal area. Subsequently, both Beijing and Manila based non-military vessels at the shoal to "effectively administer" their rights, resulting in a standoff. In receipt of Manila's appeal to add the Scarborough Shoal into the coverage of the 1951 Mutual Defense Treaty, the USA first remained careful not to release any official statement confirming or denying this request. Then on May 13, the USA stationed the nuclear-powered fast attack submarine *USS North Carolina* in Subic port. A month later, another nuclear-powered attack submarine, the *USS Louisville*, docked in Subic Bay. Although routine port calls, the wide publicity surrounding the dockings was viewed as an implicit sign from the Obama administration indicating that it would not stand idle if the Philippines were threatened by armed aggression.[74]

The Scarborough incident ended with Beijing's control of the Scarborough Shoal. This incident had two successive consequences in relation to the ongoing COC negotiation. Immediately after the Scarborough standoff, the Philippines tried to use the ASEAN to form a united position on the SCS dispute through the 45th ASEAN AMMs in Phnom Penh, Cambodia. The Philippines wanted the communiqué routinely concluded at the end of the meeting to include a reference to the Scarborough confrontation and reflect that the ministers had discussed the confrontation between the Philippines and China at Scarborough Shoal. In response, the Chinese leaders pressured Cambodia, which chaired the meeting and had a more neutral position on the dispute, not to cater to Manila's demand.[75] As a result, the ASEAN Foreign Ministers failed to issue a joint communiqué, which was unprecedented in its 45-year history.[76]

The disarray of the 2013 AMM highlighted the internal disparity within the ASEAN and forced the ASEAN leaders to rethink their approach to China, resulting in a more coordinated and determined position to engage China concerning the COC negotiation in 2013. In 2013, Brunei assumed the ASEAN chair and Vietnamese diplomat Le Luong Minh became the new ASEAN Secretary General. Both are claimant nations of the SCS and pledged to place priority on kick-starting discussions with China on a COC.[77] In the meantime, Thailand proceeded to raise the South China Sea issue informally with Beijing and Cambodia ceased its obstruction of ASEAN efforts to forge a unified position.[78]

China responded accordingly. On April 2, at the 19th ASEAN-China Senior Officials Consultation, Chinese diplomats expressed their willingness to commence discussions with the ASEAN on a COC later in the year. Later in that month, Brunei issued the post-summit chair's statement that declared, "We tasked our Ministers to continue to work actively with China on the way forward for the early conclusion of a Code of Conduct in the South China Sea (COC) on the basis of consensus."[79] During his visit to Southeast Asia in late April and early May, the new Chinese Foreign Minister, Wang Yi confirmed to his hosts that the COC would be discussed at the next meeting of the ASEAN-China Joint Working Group on the DOC.

However, the progress in the ASEAN-China negotiation was overshadowed by the Philippines' decision to initiate an international arbitration process at the beginning of 2013, which took China and other ASEAN countries by surprise. China publicly refused to take part in the arbitration process, and concern was expressed by Chinese Foreign Minister Wang Yi. In August 2013, during his visit to Vietnam, Wang Yi told the press that to maintain peace and stability in the SCS region, China and the ASEAN had agreed to push for the COC negotiation in the framework of the 2002 DOC. He then signaled caution concerning the negotiation by raising four points. The third point called on relevant countries to eliminate interferences and create the necessary conditions and atmosphere, not going the opposite way, which presumably was referring to the Philippines' recent action to invoke dispute settlement procedures of the LOSC.[80] These four points were raised again during the 6th high-level official meeting on implementing the DOC in September 2013 in Suzhou, China.[81] This meeting adopted a work plan for 2013–2014, approved an eminent persons group to offer technical advice, and agreed to meet in Thailand in the first quarter of 2014.

In face of the pressure of the COC negotiation, the Chinese leadership realized that it needed to increase maritime governance exercises and speed up attempts to develop resources in the SCS in order to create a favorable position at the negotiation table. As we will see in the next two sections, China increased its maritime governance activities in disputed waters, especially along the nine-dash line, in an effort to help support China's legal position conveyed through its UN Notes Verbales. China also pushed for exploration of resources in the SCS to enhance effective control of the disputed waters. This effort would also help create conditions for joint development and mitigate China's disadvantaged position compared to its competitors caused by its limited resource exploration projects in the SCS.

Policy practices of maritime governance in the SCS

In the post-2000 period, Chinese marine practices in the SCS have been characterized by major policy developments in the areas of fisheries and environmental protection. Changes to Chinese fishery practices in the SCS are consistent with the modifications China made to its legal position elaborated earlier. In other words, these changes were designed by the Chinese leadership to reflect and exercise the sovereignty and related rights it perceived ti had in the SCS. With regard to environmental protection, China continued to transfer relevant international instruments into domestic legislation, and to improve the domestic marine-governance system to meet the contemporary standards of international maritime governance. These efforts have substantial implications for China's increasing law enforcement activities in the SCS.

Historic fishery rights in the waters enclosed by the nine-dash line

In the period 2002–2013, China's fisheries practices in the SCS consisted of two main building blocks. First, following the trend of the 1990s, Chinese fishery practices continued to be influenced by the principle of sustainability. Second, concurrent with the legal adjustments of China's position in the SCS, the Chinese leadership developed various policies to consolidate Chinese fishery rights in the waters enclosed by the nine-dash line.

With regard to sustainable fishing, the Chinese government continued to implement and strengthen fishing ban policies in the SCS in the new millennium. Fishing bans during the summer moratorium of the South China Sea were first implemented in 1999. Entering the 2000s, the government expanded the fishing ban to include new types of fishing methods. In 1999, only trawling and purse seining were banned from fishing during the summer moratorium. In 2001, the government added light seining to the list. In 2009, all fishing methods were banned except single layered gillnets and simple angling.[82] Moreover, based on experience accumulated in the first ten years of implementing the fishing ban (1999–2008), the Ministry of Agriculture (MOA) observed new developments in fishery resources and breeding environments in the SCS to which the fishing ban policy needed to be adjusted accordingly. For example, in 2008, an official from the Fisheries Administration Bureau of the South China Sea Region pointed out that climate change had moved up the maturing period of many fisheries from the summer to late spring.[83] The MOA subsequently revised the fishing ban policy in February 2009. The new policy moved up the starting date of the fishing ban from June 1 to May 16. As a result, since 2009, the SCS fishing ban has spanned two and half months.[84] The new policy also extended the fishing ban to include foreign fishing boats,[85] out of concern that the effect of protecting fishery resources would be discounted by increasing foreign fishing activities in the same period if the fishing ban were only imposed on Chinese fishermen.[86]

It is worth noting that apart from the concern over protection of fishery resources, the imposition of the fishing ban on foreign fishing boats has another goal: increasing effective control in the SCS. This goal is more relevant to the second component of Chinese SCS fishery policy in this period, which is expanding and consolidating Chinese fishing activities within the nine-dash line.

In 1985, the Chinese government adopted a policy called "exploring the Spratly, starting with fisheries." For the most part of the 1980s and 1990s, this policy was implemented mainly for economic benefits. Entering the 2000s, China began to consciously expand the scope of fishing operations in the SCS and diversify fishery practices. In 2000, the South China Sea Fisheries Research Institute of China initiated a program to explore the possibility of marine aquaculture in Mischief Reef. Mischief was chosen not only for its ideal marine environment for aquaculture but also with the aim that fishery practices in the Mischief Reef would help strengthen China's presence in the Spratlys.[87] After years of laboratory research, Chinese marine scientists began experiments in Mischief Reef in 2007 and achieved success in 2009. In early 2010, to add nongovernmental presence and increase productivity, the MOA introduced a private company into Mischief Reef to begin commercial aquaculture production.[88]

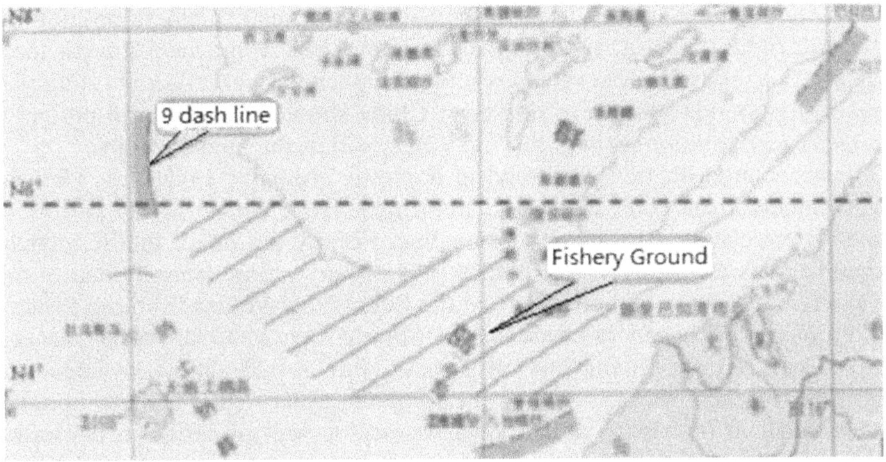

Figure 6.3 Location of trawl fishery grounds in the Southern South China Sea
Jianwei Zou, "An Analysis on the Development Status of Trawl Fishery Grounds in the Southern Part of the South China Sea," *Modern Fisheries Information* 12 (2011): 3. The image is reproduced with the kind permission of Jianwei Zou.

The Chinese authorities also attempted to increase fishery operations in the southern part of the SCS near the southernmost segment of the nine-dash line, north of Natuna Islands and James Shoal (see Figure 6.3). Due to limitation on technical capacity, operations of Chinese fishermen in this area used to be occasional and on a small scale. From 2005, with government encouragement, Chinese fishermen began to acquire the new generation of fishing trawlers with larger tonnage and suitable for long distance fishing. Since then, fishing in the southern part of the SCS has been conducted more frequently throughout the year.[89]

Expansion and diversification of fishery operations in a larger area of the SCS are driven by obvious economic concerns. Chinese fishermen need to explore new fishery resources due to overexploitation of near shore fisheries and the shrinking of traditional fishery grounds in the Gulf of Tonkin after the implementation of the Sino-Vietnamese Fishery Agreement in the Gulf of Tonkin.[90] More importantly, these new fishery practices are linked with dynamics in the legal and political aspects of China's SCS policy. For China, fishery management has become an effective means to strengthen its claims of historic rights within the nine-dash line. Although not publicly articulated by the Chinese government, this motive has been widely circulated in the domestic epistemic community, especially after 2009, correlating with China's move to publicize the nine-dash line map in the UN. In several leading Chinese journals on fisheries, scholars converge on three opinions. First, they view that China enjoys traditional fisheries rights because Chinese fishermen have been conducting fisheries in the SCS since ancient times. Second, they believe that traditional fisheries rights are an essential part of China's historic rights in the SCS and should be used as the basis to formulate Chinese position on historic rights.[91] Third, they argue that active fishery practices are an ideal approach to consolidate sovereignty and strengthen the legal effect of traditional maritime boundary lines. In this view, China should maintain and protect a large-scale operation throughout the waters within the nine-dash line.[92]

Concurrent with this new trend in domestic academic circles, the Chinese government from 2009 worked to implement more active fishery patrols in the waters enclosed by the nine-dash line. Fishery patrols in the SCS could date back as far as the 1970s. Before 1994, fishery patrols were limited to the vicinity of China's main coast and in the Beibu Gulf. Vessels from the Fishery Administration began to cruise in the Spratly area in 1994, when *Yuzheng 311* departed from Guangzhou on April 20 and crossed almost 19 degrees in latitude to reach near 4 °N.[93] Yet before 2009, fishery patrols in the Spratlys were small in both scale and frequency and focused primarily on patrolling the islands to collect relevant information.[94]

Also starting from 2009, the government substantially increased investment in upgrading fishery monitoring facilities. In March 2009, a retired Chinese navy rescue vessel with a water displacement of 4500 tons was reconstructed into *China Yuzheng 311* to curb illegal fishing in the SCS.[95] In November 2010, *Yuzheng 310* was commissioned and started patrolling in the SCS. With a displacement of 2500 tons, *Yuzheng 310* is the fastest and most advanced patrol ship in China and can carry two Z-9A helicopters. In this same period, the Chinese leadership shifted the focus of missions and increased the patrolling frequency.[96] Before 2010, fishery patrols cruised according to pre-assigned schedules and along default routes, although they would come to the rescue of Chinese fishermen when requested. This style of patrolling changed in 2010. To strengthen and effectively protect fishing activities in the Spratlys, vessels of the Fishery Administration have been dispatched to directly escort Chinese fishing fleets operating in the fishing grounds in the Spratlys throughout the year.[97]

Developing modern management of marine environment protection

The legal regime of marine environmental protection has proven to have a sustained influence on China's practices of marine environmental protection, mainly through defining the parameters of Chinese regulation of marine environmental protection. In the post-2000 period, the Chinese government continues to transfer elements of the international legal regime into domestic legislation and bring marine environment governance in line with the latest legal and practical developments.

Given the tremendous volume of sea-borne transportation through the SLOCs, a major challenge to the marine environment in the SCS comes from vessels. Vessel source pollution is governed by various conventions adopted by the IMO. China has been supportive of a large number of IMO conventions tackling marine pollution. In the 2000s, the IMO continued to revise the legal regime of marine pollution to meet new challenges. For example, the IMO amended the 1989 Basel Convention, resulting in the 2001 Basel Ban Amendment, and revised the MARPOL by adding Annexes IV and VI in 2006, both of which have been ratified by China. In 2011, China acceded to the International Convention on the Control of Harmful Anti-Fouling Systems on Ships (Anti-Fouling Convention). These new developments need to be transferred into domestic legislation for them to take full effect and guide China's practices in the SCS.

Consequently, China has taken incremental steps in the period 2002–2013 to incorporate these new trends into domestic management of marine pollution and promulgate more detailed implementation guidelines (see Table 6.1). This domestic legislation is applicable to China's internal waters, territorial sea, contiguous zone, the EEZ, and other sea areas under China's jurisdiction, forming the legal basis for relevant Chinese law enforcement activities in the SCS. It is unknown whether China has conducted law enforcement patrols in the disputed sea areas in the SCS, as annual national reports on sea patrols published by the State Oceanic Administration refrain from specifying the sea areas that Chinese sea patrols have covered.[98] However, considering the emerging trend of expanding and enhancing maritime governance in the waters enclosed by the nine-dash line, the professionalization of marine environment management seems to indicate similar trends and might have a potential impact on China's future policy practices in the SCS.

At the regional level, China continued to participate in regional cooperative initiatives tackling marine environment issues. With regard to the UNEP/GEF SCS Project, after the UNEP successfully secured official approval from China in 2000, the project became fully operational on January 21, 2002. The implementation stage was divided into two phases: the preparatory phase (Feb. 2002–June 2004), and the operational phase (July 2004–Dec. 2007). During the preparatory phase, the project mainly focused on collecting,

Table 6.1 China's laws and regulations relating to the protection of the marine environment in the 2000s period

Laws/regulations	*Date of promulgation*
Law on the Management of Sea Area Use	October 27, 2001
Provisional Provisions on the Management of Abandoned Offshore Oil Platforms	June 24, 2002
Provisional Measures on the Management of Dumping Sites	November 14, 2003
Regulations on the Management of the Prevention of Pollution Damage to the Marine Environment by Marine Construction Projects	August 30, 2006
Provisions on the Management of Sea Area Use Rights	October 13, 2006
Regulation on the Prevention and Control of Marine Pollution from Vessels	March 1, 2010

compiling, and consolidating data and information at both national and regional levels to prioritize sites for interventions. In the past, data and information were collected and compiled mostly at the national level, and regional exchange of information was conducted on an individual and personal basis.[99] The implementation of the project in the preparatory phase provided a first-time experience for SCS countries to exchange data and information on the status of marine environmental problems in the region, resulting in the production of four regional booklets regarding the regional status of mangroves, coral reefs, sea grass, and wetlands.[100] The potential value of this achievement will be explained in the policy recommendation section of the concluding chapter.

China's practice of dispute resolution

The period examined in this chapter witnessed two important breakthroughs in the area of dispute resolution. One is the final resolution of the Sino-Vietnamese dispute over the Gulf of Tonkin. The Tonkin dispute is part of the SCS dispute. China and Vietnam reached agreements on the issues of delimitation and fisheries in the Gulf area in 2000 and 2004, respectively. As the first and only resolution of an SCS issue, this settlement reveals useful information on China's attitude, principles, and practice of dispute resolution regarding the SCS issue which, as demonstrated below, are highly consistent with the new LOSC and relevant customary practices in international maritime delimitation exercises.[101] The discussion below illustrates the process through which the new maritime order reconstructed the negotiation agenda and shaped the final agreement on maritime governance in the Gulf of Tonkin.

The other major achievement is related to joint development. In 2005, China, Vietnam, and the Philippines conducted the first tripartite seismic survey in the disputed waters of the SCS to fulfill the obligations of the 2002 DOC. This survey is also the first substantive step China took to implement the idea of joint development. Following the conclusion of this project, the government encouraged and funded domestic research to draw lessons from this experience and explore more effective means to push forward joint development in the SCS. The tripartite survey and the ensuing progress in domestic discourse underscore China's unabated interest in joint development as the tentative solution for the SCS dispute.

Delimitation of the Gulf of Tonkin

China and Vietnam reached a delimitation agreement on the Gulf of Tonkin (Beibu Gulf in Chinese and Bac Bo Gulf in Vietnamese) on December 15, 2000. This agreement constitutes China's first successful effort in delimiting part of the SCS and highlights the normative influence on the two countries' practice of dispute resolution.

The Gulf of Tonkin is a semi-enclosed gulf surrounded by the northern part of Vietnam to the west, China's Guangxi Province and the Leizhou Peninsula to the north, and Hainan Island to the east. The gulf measures 170 nautical miles at the widest and has two outlets: the Qiongzhou Strait between Hainan Island and the Leizhou Peninsula, approximately 19 nautical miles in width; and the major passage to the south, 125 nautical miles wide at its narrowest point.[102] It ranges an area of approximately 128,000 square kilometers and is rich in hydrocarbon reserves and fishery resources. The Gulf provides the livelihood of hundreds of thousands of fishermen.[103]

The dispute started in August 1974. The Vietnamese government planned to grant an Italian oil company access to an area in the Gulf of Tonkin for oil exploration, and proposed to China to launch bilateral negotiations on the maritime boundary of the Gulf.[104] Brief negotiation was brought up again in 1977–1978, but no agreement was reached and the process was completely halted as the Sino-Vietnam relationship quickly deteriorated at the end of the 1970s. It was not until the normalization of the Sino-Vietnamese relationship in 1992 that the two sides resumed official negotiations.

The negotiations in the 1990s were starkly different from the 1970s. Legal and practical developments in the maritime governance regime changed the new round of negotiations in three aspects. First, the new maritime order reshaped the legal basis of the dispute. Before the 1970s, there was not much conflict over the Gulf except sporadic friction over fishing practices. The Chinese and Vietnamese (North Vietnam) governments had signed two fishery agreements, one in 1957 and the other in 1963.[105] In the first agreement, each side agreed to focus on managing fishing within territorial seas of 6 nautical miles' width. The two sides renewed the agreement in 1961, with a supplementary protocol stipulating that the offshore limit should extend from 6 nm to 12 nm.[106] The second agreement signed in 1963 was similar to the previous one. In all these agreements, the area beyond territorial seas was treated as high sea for free-fishing.[107] In 1974, Hanoi's proposal of to delimit the Gulf of Tonkin caught China by surprise. At that time China still considered the area beyond territorial seas as dispute-free high sea and was not prepared to modify its position. On the Vietnamese side, Hanoi's claim was purely influenced by the conception of historic title and used as the maritime boundary line the meridian line contained in the 1887 Sino-French Treaty. There was no sign showing influence of the newly emerging developments such as the CS and EEZ regimes on Hanoi's position.

However, when the Chinese and Vietnamese governments initiated negotiations in 1992, both sides embraced the entire LOSC framework. Consequently, the LOSC added two focal points to the content of negotiation: delimitation of the EEZ and delimitation of the continental shelf, which were reflected in the title of the Agreement – the *Agreement on the Delimitation of the Territorial Seas, the Exclusive Economic Zones and Continental Shelves in the Beibu Gulf* (hereafter referred to as the Agreement). Applying the new LOS in delimiting the Gulf of Tonkin, the two countries found that the whole body of water as well as the land underwater of the Tonkin Gulf fell under overlapping claims, because the maximum width of the whole Gulf did not exceed 180 nautical miles. This change was acknowledged by Wang Yi, then Deputy Foreign Minister and head of the negotiation delegation. During an interview in June 2004, he explained the impact of the new maritime order and said: "Entering the 1980s, due to the new ocean order that was taking shape, the disputed area in the Gulf of Tonkin enlarged to enclose the whole Gulf area."[108] This view was echoed by Xiao Jianguo, a senior official from the Department of Treaty and Law of the Chinese Foreign Ministry, who commented in an interview in 2004 that:

> Since the 1970s, the development of modern ocean governance has given rise to new problems in terms of delimiting the Gulf of Tonkin. According to the modern maritime law anchored by the UNCLOS, concluded in 1982, and entering into force in 1994, coastal countries may have territorial seas of 12 nm, the EEZ of 200 nm and a continental shelf of up to 350 nm.[109]

Second, emerging customary practices influenced China and Vietnam to use a single maritime boundary line to delimit different maritime zones (the EEZ and the CS). The practice of a single maritime boundary line was a relatively new development in the maritime regime. During the years between the advent of the Truman Proclamation embodying the concept of CS and the emergence of the concept of EEZ in the 1970s, the two legal regimes (the EEZ and the CS) were treated separately.[110] Prior to the 1982 UNCLOS, the fundamental principle of delimitation of the continental shelf was the principle of natural prolongation, set out in the 1958 Convention on the Continental Shelf and developed in case law. But this criterion is inapplicable to the superjacent water column. In the 1969 North Sea case, the court determined that:

> The doctrine of the just and equitable share was wholly at variance with the most fundamental of all the rules of law relating to the continental shelf, namely, that the rights of the coastal State in respect of the area of continental shelf constituting a *natural prolongation of its land territory* under the sea existed *ipso facto* and *ab initio,* by virtue of its sovereignty over the land.[111]
>
> (emphasis added)

While scholarly opinion is divided as to whether the CS and the EEZ are unitary or dual regimes, a degree of integration between the EEZ and CS regimes was achieved (or at least initiated) in the 1982 UNCLOS.[112] This legal development is believed to have influenced the 1984 Gulf of Maine case before the International Court of Justice. While cases decided by international tribunals prior to 1984 focused only on the continental shelf, the Gulf of Maine case constituted the first international judicial determination of boundaries dividing jurisdiction over both the continental shelf and the water column beyond the territorial sea. In this case, a single maritime boundary line was adopted in light of the integrating nature of the two legal regimes.[113] Since then, the single line principle became the new customary international law in delimiting practices.[114]

Third, the legal framework of the LOSC also shaped the bilateral fishery arrangement in the Gulf of Tonkin (Figure 6.4), another major issue in the negotiation between Beijing and Hanoi.[115]

The Beibu Gulf is known for abundant marine living resources. The gulf enjoys nutrient-rich sediments from numerous river systems and year-round warm water temperatures. The waters contain ample plankton and other organisms numbering up to 1150 types. These favorable conditions form an ideal environment for fish to spawn, breed, feed and mature.[116] Accordingly, it has been a traditional fishing ground for both Chinese and Vietnamese fishermen. In the 1990s, China had a slightly larger population of fishermen operating in the Gulf, reportedly over 500,000 each year, compared to the Vietnamese side,

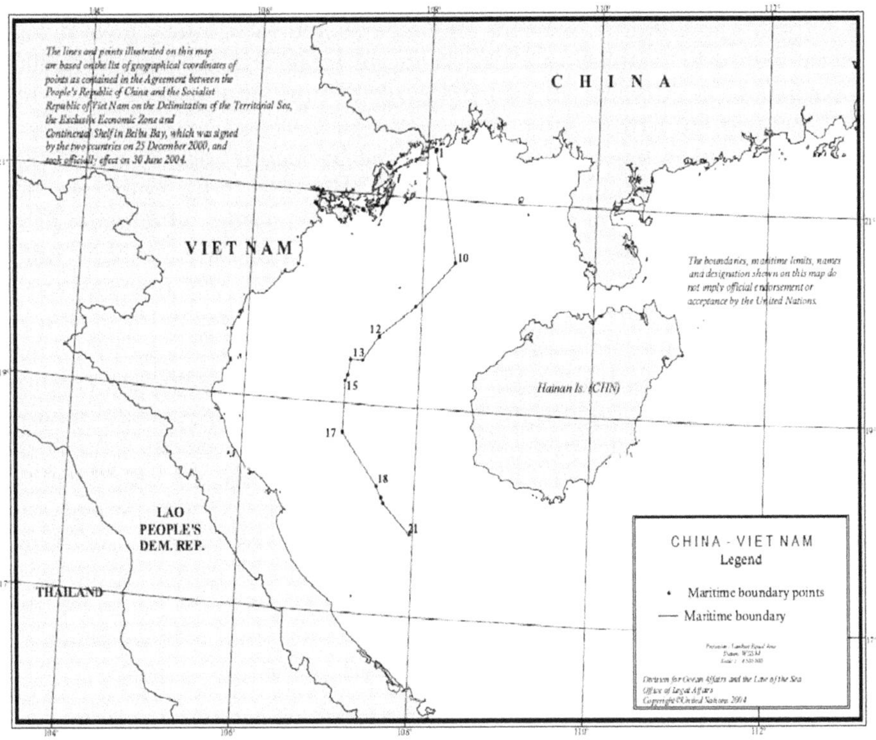

Figure 6.4 Map of the boundary points and boundary lines of the Gulf of Tonkin United Nations, *Law of the Sea Bulletin,* no. 56:138. All the *Law of the Sea Bulletins* are available on the UN website at: www.un.org/Depts/los/doalos_publications/los_bult.htm.

which had around 330,000 fishermen.[117] Annually the catch of Chinese fishermen composed 82% of the total catch of the Gulf, leaving the Vietnamese side with 18%.[118] Partly due to this disparity in fishing capability, the Chinese government originally proposed to negotiate the cooperation of fishery management and the maritime boundary delimitation issue as a "package deal" in hope of gaining at least partial recognition of Chinese traditional fishing rights from the Vietnamese. Vietnam initially refused China's request. The Vietnamese emphasized the importance of resolving the issue of the EEZ demarcation line, arguing that the conservation and utilization of the fisheries should be considered only after resolution of the boundary delimitation. In 1998, China and Vietnam reached consensus on discussing the fishery issue in the context of the negotiation of the Beibu boundary delimitation, which resulted in the maritime delimitation agreement and a general agreement on fishery cooperation in 2000. The two countries spent another three years negotiating details of regulating fisheries in the Gulf area under the 2000 agreements. Their negotiation finally resulted in the Supplementary Protocol on Fishery in April 2004.

The fishery arrangements stipulated in these two agreements were consistent with the LOSC framework and underscored the Chinese government's determination to establish modern ocean governance in the Gulf of Tonkin. In particular, the Chinese government made a substantial concession by fully implementing the EEZ regime.

Originally, the Chinese delegation insisted in negotiations on the recognition of traditional fishing rights of Chinese fishermen in the Gulf area. This was a very practical concern since hundreds of thousands of Chinese fishermen had a long history of operating freely in a large area of the Gulf of Tonkin beyond the 6 nm of territorial sea. However, the area covered by traditional fishing rights, had it been fully recognized, inevitably overlapped with the EEZ regime in some parts of the Gulf. The Chinese government took two steps to resolve this problem. First, in favor of fully implementing the EEZ regime in fishery governance, the Chinese government removed explicit reference to traditional fishing rights in the agreement texts. As the new EEZ regime in the Gulf of Tonkin inevitably altered the traditional free fishing pattern of local economy on the Chinese side, the governments took a second step to mitigate the negative impact on the interests of Chinese fishermen. A transitional arrangement spanning four years was set up by the Fishery Agreement so that the Chinese side could gradually phase out their own fisheries activities (see Figure 6.5). The transitional arrangements contained in the Fishery Agreement implied traditional fishing rights,[119] but as a legal scholar commented,

> It should be borne in mind that even the transitional arrangements made under the Agreement may only last four years after the entry into force of the Agreement. When the period of four years expires, the Chinese traditional fishing rights in Vietnam's EEZ may be taken away totally.[120]

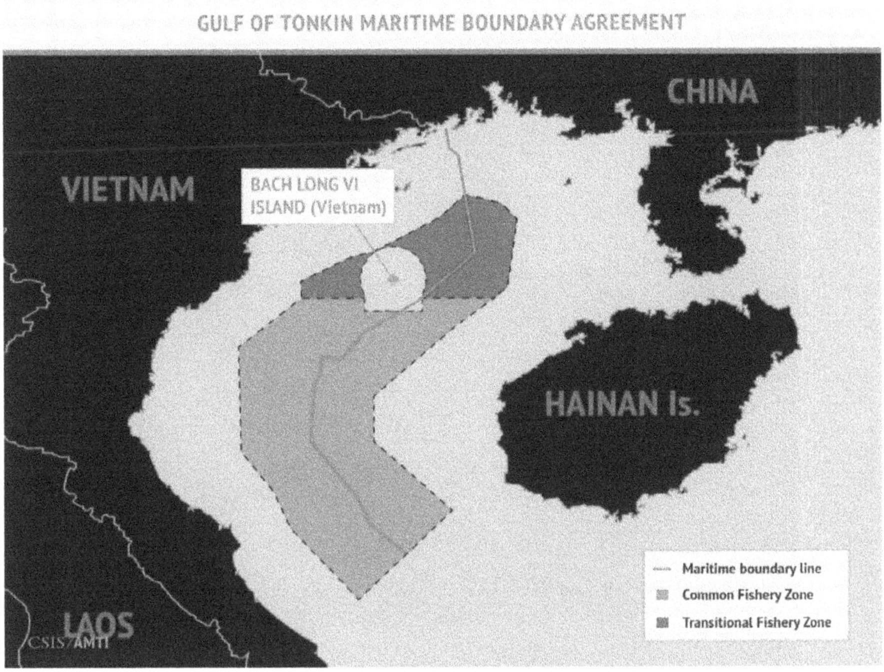

Figure 6.5 Fisheries arrangements in the Gulf of Tonkin
Asia Maritime Transparency Initiative, "The Evolution of Asia's Contested Waters," available at: http://amti.csis.org/maritime-disputes/ (accessed July 1, 2017).

As of 2009, five years after the Fishery Agreement took effect, more than a 100,000 fishermen had been transferred to other sectors of the local economy.[121]

In addition, China and Vietnam established a Common Fishery Zone, a joint mechanism of cooperation and co-management of resources under the new EEZ regime (see Figure 6.5).[122] Both parties pledged to work towards long-term fishery cooperation in the Common Fishery Zone in the spirit of mutual benefit. In April 2004, the two governments signed the Protocol for the Conservation and Management of Fisheries Resources of the Joint Fishing Zone, focusing primarily on sustainable development and marine environment protection. A Joint Fishery Committee was also established as a permanent bilateral body tasked with managing fishery issues in the Gulf of Tonkin.[123] So far, a number of activities have been undertaken, including joint regular surveys, a joint venture on exploration, and joint navy patrols.[124]

Joint development

The 2002–2013 period witnessed a major achievement in the area of joint development: the 2005 joint seismic survey project carried out by oil

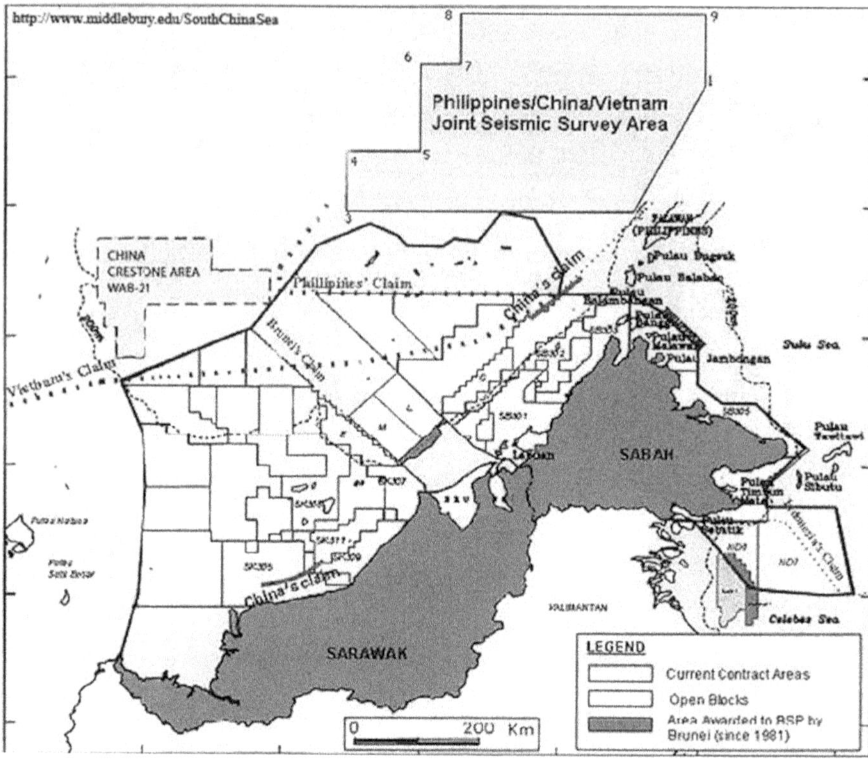

Figure 6.6 The Philippines/China/Vietnam Joint Seismic Survey Area
Leszek Buszynski and Iskandar Sazlan, "Maritime Claims and Energy Cooperation in the South China Sea," *Contemporary Southeast Asia* 29, no. 1 (2007): 167. This image is reproduced with the kind permission of Dr. Leszek Buszynski.

companies from the Philippines, China, and Vietnam in part of the disputed waters of the SCS (see Figure 6.6). Extolled as a major practical breakthrough, this tripartite joint exploration project was designed to fulfill the obligations of the DOC and in the spirit of the DOC and the LOSC.

On March 14, 2005, the oil companies from the Philippines, China, and Vietnam signed a Tripartite Agreement for Joint Marine Seismic Undertaking in the Agreement Area in the South China Sea (JMSU). It was the first time the three major claimant countries had engaged in cooperative practice in a disputed area of the SCS. In a joint statement, the three parties affirmed that the signing of the Agreement would contribute to the transformation of the South China Sea into an area of peace, stability, cooperation, and development in accordance with the 1982 UNCLOS and the 2002 DOC.[125]

The project was first agreed to by Beijing and Manila. The two countries planned to conduct seismic studies in the SCS to identify areas for oil and gas exploration. The agreement, known as the Joint Marine Seismic Undertaking (JMSU), was signed during Filipino President Gloria Macapagal Arroyo's state visit to the PRC in the beginning of September 2004, and provided for a three-year study to be undertaken by the Philippines' state owned oil company Philippine National Oil Company (PNOC) and the Chinese National Offshore Oil Corporation (CNOOC). Manila emphasized that the JMSU was a "pre-exploration" study and would not involve any drilling in disputed waters. According to Manila, the JMSU could be classified as "marine scientific research" and was therefore covered by paragraph five of the DOC.[126] Later on, Vietnam entered into negotiations with the Philippines and China, and on March 14, 2005 the three state-owned oil companies, the Chinese National Offshore Oil Corporation (CNOOC), the Philippines National Oil Company (PNOC), and the Vietnam Oil and Gas Corporation (PetroVietnam) signed a new JMSU to jointly prospect for oil and gas in the SCS.[127] The JMSU proposed to survey and research an area of over 143,000 km^2, which included part of the disputed waters. The three national oil firms shared the costs involved in conducting the research equally, which eventually totaled approximately $7.14 million.[128] The joint exploration project expired in 2008 as scheduled and was unable to be renewed due to increasing domestic pressure from the Philippines' side.

Alongside this practical progress, the academic discourse surrounding joint development continued to develop in the new millennium. While discussions in the 1990s focused primarily on the legality and suitability of joint development as a tentative solution for the SCS dispute, scholarly deliberation in the 2000s paid more attention to lessons and experiences, potential obstacles, and concrete models.[129]

In 2002, the National Institute for the South China Sea Studies held a national conference on SCS to discuss the concept of joint development. The conference reaffirmed that while joint development was unable to solve the territorial disputes of the Spratly Islands, it could be a useful provisional measure to solve maritime jurisdictional disputes. Given the official background of the participants and host organization of this conference, the deliberation suggested the positive attitude of the Chinese government to joint development.

During this conference, a SOA official suggested China should select some areas in which to create conditions for joint development.[130] The following disputed areas were suggested as potential areas: Reed Bank (in Chinese: Lile Tan), Brunei-Shaba Basin and James Shoal Basin, North and West Vanguard Bank Basins (in Chinese: Wan'an Bei and Wan'an Xi).[131]

The conclusion of the JMSU in 2008 further boosted the already-flourishing domestic research. A large body of research projects in the post-2008 period were encouraged and directly funded by the Chinese government, out of three concerns. China perceived itself as falling behind other disputant parties in terms of the development of resources in the SCS. The goal of strengthening the Chinese presence in the waters within the nine-dash line required the Chinese government to increase exploration and exploitation activities. Additionally, the Chinese leaders have since 2009 faced increasing pressure to engage more actively in the negotiation of a COC. A legally binding COC, once agreed, would secure other littoral countries' resource development activities while locking China into its current infancy status. The Chinese government realized that, doing more to develop resources in the SCS would benefit the Chinese position at the negotiation table. Finally, after two decades of practice in joint development, Chinese policy-makers and researchers have accumulated the knowledge and experience in terms of the lessons and obstacles necessary to pursue successful joint development.

These three concerns are reflected in the burgeoning domestic discourse in the post-2008 period, distinguished by its funding sources and its newly broader focus. At this time, a considerable portion of the academic publications on joint development was funded by national-level governmental grants, from three major sources in particular: the National Social Science Fund of China, the Ministerial Level Research Projects of Chinese Law Society, and the Social Science Fund of Ministry of Education. While previous studies tended to concentrate on jurisprudence and international cases of joint development, research projects in the post-2008 period cover a diverse spectrum of aspects of joint development. These include: joint development from bilateral and multilateral approaches, the designation of areas for joint development, joint fisheries development, cross-strait cooperation towards joint development, the institutionalization of joint development, lessons from Southeast Asian practices, comparisons of various models, and suggestions on how to cope with current obstacles.[132] These two features suggest that Chinese leaders now have a more pragmatic approach to joint development and a better understanding of existing obstacles confronting implementation. It is for this reason that they have determined to boost domestic academic research to help inform China's practices.

Many of these studies share a positive appraisal of the tripartite joint exploration between China, Vietnam, and the Philippines and urge the central government to adopt a more proactive approach to joint development. They tend to converge on the following views:

1 The absence of resource development activities in the SCS puts China in a disadvantaged position relative to other disputants, and accounts for the tepid attitude of other countries to China's joint development proposals. For that reason, many researchers suggest that China select some areas to start independent exploitation so as to create conditions for joint development. Nanwei Tan (Riflemen Bank) is suggested as an ideal place to begin China's own oil and gas activities, since it is located beyond the continental shelf limits claimed by Brunei, Indonesia, and Malaysia, beyond the 200-mile EEZ limit claimed by Vietnam and beyond the "Kalayaan" claimed by the Philippines.[133]
2 Based on the lessons drawn from international and regional practices, China could start with bilateral joint development to reduce the potential for conflict. Candidate areas include Reed Bank (with the Philippines),

Brunei-Shaba Basin and James Shoal Basin (with Malaysia or Brunei), North and West Vanguard Bank Basins (in Chinese: Wan'an Bei and Wan'an Xi) (with Vietnam).[134] This view echoes one of the conclusions of the conference hosted by the National Institute of South China Sea Studies in 2002 mentioned earlier.

3 China should come up with more concrete, step-by-step roadmaps for joint development. It needs to work on the institutionalization of a joint development regime and promote the rule of law in regional cooperation.[135]

Some of the suggestions proffered by these researchers have been adopted by the Chinese government. For example, on May 9, 2013, China National Offshore Oil Corporation (CNOOC), the country's largest offshore oil producer, sent China's first deep-water drilling rig, CNOOC-981, to begin operation in Liwan, an undisputed area of the South China Sea 320km southeast of Hong Kong. A week later, CNOOC sent a newly-built crane ship, CNOOC-201, to the South China Sea to cooperate with CNOOC-981 in carrying out deep water pipe-laying operations.[136] In June 2013, CNOOC designated nine offshore blocks in the SCS available for cooperative exploration with foreign oil companies.[137] Most of these blocks are located in the suggested Nanwei Tan (Riflemen Bank) and West Vanguard Bank.[138]

Analysis

In the period 2002–2013, the maritime regime played several roles in unfolding policy changes with regard to Chinese SCS policy. In the legal realm, the new maritime order generated continuous pressure on China to modify its legal position. This modification process proceeded incrementally and was driven by the pre-determined deadline of the CLCS.

In the area of political engagement, the maritime regime has demonstrated a lock-in effect, ensuring uninterrupted political engagement among all the relevant countries in regional multilateral institutional settings despite geopolitical changes. In this period, the influence of geopolitical flux on China's SCS policy continued to interact with and work through regional multilateral institutional structures. The effects of such interaction on Chinese SCS policy varied depending on the actual composition of geopolitical and regime dynamics. This pattern is most obvious in the post-2009 period. While the US strategic reorientation towards Asia remained constant, the result on China's policy varied and followed three stages.

From 2009 to 2011, active US engagement provided a powerful jump-start for the COC negotiation, although China was concerned about America's confrontational approach in regional multilateral dialogues. At the same time, America increased its efforts to consolidate defense relationships with its traditional allies, especially the Philippines. While America's high profile activities were very effective in strengthening its own presence in Asia, it nevertheless raised considerable suspicion among the foreign policy circle in China that containing China and supporting opposite claimants was a major part of the US return to Asia policy. Following the 2013 Sino-Filipino confrontation over the Scarborough Shoal, the COC negotiation temporarily stalled as China attempted to leverage the internal disunity of the ASEAN to counter the Philippines' efforts to forge a united ASEAN position on the issue. In 2013, the SCS situation experienced three new developments. First, the disunity highlighted by the failure to issue a joint communiqué for the 45th AMM forced the ASEAN leaders to rethink their approach, resulting in a more unified and determined ASEAN in revitalizing engagement with China concerning the COC negotiation, which in turn elicited positive responses from China. Second, the routine institutional rotation of the ASEAN governance placed Brunei and Vietnam as Chair and Secretary General of ASEAN, giving these two claimants administrative leverage in setting the COC negotiation agenda. These two developments have resulted in positive signs for the forward movement of COC negotiations.

The third development is related to the Philippines' decision to bring China before an Arbitral Tribunal under Article 287 and Annex VII of the LOSC, regarding the dispute over the Scarborough Shoal. China rejected Manila's request for arbitration, and implicitly expressed dissatisfaction through its release of four points on the COC negotiation. Nevertheless, the actual effect of such action on the COC negotiation and the SCS dispute in general is not necessary negative. First, the invocation of international arbitration brought the SCS dispute into the international spotlight. The ensuing international pressure on China could potentially create momentum for the ongoing COC negotiation. Second, although China refused to participate in the arbitral proceedings, the arbitral panel might decide to go forward with the arbitration or provide advisory opinions. In either case, the legal deliberation of the arbitral panel will have repercussions for the Scarborough dispute and the SCS dispute in general. The Philippines' statement mentioned several issues, three of which were of particular legal significance: (1) the validity of the nine-dash line; (2) the definition of rock; and (3) the status of submerged reefs.[139] Legal deliberation of these three issues might bring new clarity to the indeterminacy associated with the claimed boundaries in the SCS dispute. Moreover, other claimants might be encouraged by the Philippines' action and consider using dispute settlement procedures for their respective claims. Fear of the possibility of successive actions might generate additional pressure on China to be more pragmatic in the COC negotiation. How the combination of US involvement, the ASEAN's engagement, and these new arbitration procedure developments influence the COC negotiation remains to be seen.

Changes in the legal and political aspects of China's SCS policy are linked with other aspects of China's SCS policy. First, in order to support its historic claims based on the nine-dash line, the Chinese government has consciously taken measures to enhance and expand practices of maritime governance to cover the waters enclosed by the line. Second, the desire to enhance the legal effect of the nine-dash line and the urgent need to create favorable conditions for the COC negotiation together have forced the Chinese government to push for tangible progress in implementing joint development. Specifically, in the past few years, the Chinese government has increased financial support for research on joint development and started to implement concrete projects suggested by domestic research.

With regard to China's practice of dispute resolution, the delimitation of the Gulf of Tonkin is the first successful instance of dispute resolution between China and its neighboring countries in the SCS. Notwithstanding the intensive diplomatic exchanges between the two governments over nearly three decades, the 1990s delimitation negotiation process and its guiding principles, such as the principle of equity, the embrace of the EEZ and CS regimes, the use of a single boundary line, and sophisticated arrangements for shared fisheries transforming a traditional free fishing regime into the EEZ regime, have demonstrated a high degree of conformity with the LOSC and evolving customary law and practices. Moreover, this Gulf of Tonkin case is a bilateral delimitation practice. While it is generally thought that China could exert its might in bilateral negotiations, the Gulf of Tonkin case suggests the opposite, as the equity principle dominated the bilateral arrangement. Therefore, it is reasonable to infer that this principle will not be easily abandoned in future negotiations.

Notes

1 Commission on the Limits of the Continental Shelf, *Joint Submission of Malaysia and the Socialist Republic of Vietnam*, May 6, 2009, available at: www.un.org/Depts/los/clcs_new/submissions_files/mysvnm33_09/mys_vnm2009excutive summary.pdf (accessed March 1, 2014).
2 Ibid.
3 Ibid.
4 Commission on the Limits of the Continental Shelf, *Note of China No. CML/17/2009*, May 7, 2009, available at: www.un.org/Depts/los/clcs_new/submissions_files/mysvnm33_09/chn_2009re_mys_vnm_e.pdf (accessed March 1, 2014,
5 The map was called "The Chinese territorial map before the Qianglong-Jiaqing period (1736–1820) of the Qing Dynasty," in *New Geographical Atlas of the Republic of China*. See Zhenhua Han, ed., *A Compilation of Historical Archives of China's South China Sea Islands* (Beijing: Oriental Press, 1988), 355, in Chinese.
6 Jinming Li and Dexia Li, "The Dotted Line on the Chinese Map of the South China Sea: A Note," *Ocean Development and International Law* 34, no. 3–4 (2003): 287.
7 Keyuan Zou, "Historic Rights in International Law and in China's Practice," *Ocean Development and International Law* 32, no. 2 (2001): 33.
8 Han, *Historical Archives of China's South China Sea Islands*, 12.
9 Zou, "Historic Rights," 33.
10 Yu Jia, "On the Legal Status of the Dotted Line of the South China Sea," *China's Borderland History and Geography Studies* 15, no. 2 (2005): 113, in Chinese.
11 *Note of China, No. CML/17/2009*.
12 Robert Beckman, "South China Sea: Worsening Dispute or Growing Clarity in Claims?," *RSIS Commentaries* 16, August 2010.

13 Commission on the Limits of the Continental Shelf, *Philippines' Note Verbale No. 000228*, April 5, 2011, available at: www.un.org/Depts/los/clcs_new/submissions_files/mysvnm33_09/phl_re_chn_2011.pdf (accessed March 1, 2014).

14 Nguyen-Dang Thang and Ngueyn Hong Thao, "China's Nine Dotted Lines in the South China Sea: The 2011 Exchange of Diplomatic Notes Between the Philippines and China," *Ocean Development and International Law* 43 (2013): 43–44.

15 It is highly debatable as to whether the nine-dash line is of any legal value and to what extent the Chinese historic claims can rely on this line. For example, in 2002, the ICJ rejected the map submitted by Indonesia as containing legal value for supporting its claims to Ligitan and Sipadan Islands. See *Sovereignty Over Pulau Ligitan and Pulau Sipadan (Indonesia v. Malaysia),* I.C.J. Reports (2002). However, the controversy does not negate the fact that the use of the nine-dash line to support relevant historical claims amounts to a change or modification of China's legal position in the 2000s.

16 Commission on the Limits of the Continental Shelf, *Note of China No. CML/8/2011*, April 14, 2011, available at: www.un.org/depts/los/clcs_new/submissions_files/vnm37_09/chn_2011_re_phl_e.pdf (accessed March 1, 2014).

17 Jia, "Legal Status of the Dotted Line," 120. The author is Deputy Director of the China Institute for Marine Affairs under the State Oceanic Bureau.

18 The starting point being set for May 1999 is tied to the fact that the scientific and technical guidelines for measuring the continental shelf were promulgated in May 1999.

19 United Nations, *Final Report of the Eleventh SPLOS Meeting*, available at: http://daccess-dds-ny.un.org/doc/UNDOC/GEN/N01/387/64/PDF/N0138764.pdf?OpenElement (accessed October 30, 2013).

20 Sam Bateman and Clive Schofield, "Outer Shelf Claims in the South China Sea," *RSIS Commentaries* 65 (2009).

21 Zhiguo Gao, "The South China Sea: From Conflict to Cooperation," *Ocean Development and International Law* 25, no. 3 (1994): 345–359; Li and Li, "The Dotted Line on the Chinese Map," Keyuan Zou, "The Chinese Traditional Maritime Boundary Line in the South China Sea and Its Legal Consequences for the Resolution of the Dispute over the Spratly Islands," *International Journal of Marine and Coastal Law* 14, no. 1 (1999): 27–55, and Tingting Luo, "Exploring the Legal Status of the Nine-Dash Line – Four Schools of Arguments," *China Review of the Science of Maritime Law* 1 (2008): 56–64, in Chinese.

22 Lihai Zhao was elected one of the first 21 judges of the ITLOS in 1996.

23 Lihai Zhao, *Studies of the Law of the Sea Issues* (Beijing: Peking University Press, 1996), 37–38, in Chinese.

24 Zou, "Chinese Traditional Maritime Boundary," 52.

25 Gao Zhiguo was elected as a Judge of the ITLOS in 2008 and re-elected in 2011.

26 Gao, "From Conflict to Cooperation," 346.

27 Jia, "Legal Status of the Dotted Line," 112–120.

28 Ibid., 120. Similar views have been expressed by a number of Chinese scholars. For example, see Jinming Li, "A Study of the Nine-Dash Line and Related Issues," *China's Borderland History and Geography Studies* 11, no. 2 (2001): 15–16, in Chinese. Also see Yongzhi Wang, "A Comprehensive Discussion on the Dotted Line in the SCS," *Journal of Ocean University of China (Social Science)* 3 (2008): 1–5, in Chinese.

29 Jia, "Legal Status of the Dotted Line," 120.

30 Zhao, *Studies of the Law of the Sea Issues*, 38.

31 Zou, "Historic Rights," 160.

32 The issue of the nine-dash line was discussed in the section "Cross-strait Legal Studies of the SCS and Cooperation on Law Enforcement." The agenda and video recordings of this seminar are available on the National Institute for South

China Sea Studies, available at: www.nanhai.org.cn/zt.asp (accessed October 30, 2013).

33 Yongming Jin, "The Nature of the SCS Dotted Line and the Legal Status of the Enclosed Waters," *China Legal Science* 6 (2013): 38–50, Yu Jia, "Legal Principle of the South China Sea Disputes," *China Legal Science* 6 (2013): 26–35, Wei Huang, "China's Historic Rights over 'the Other Waters' within the U-shaped Line of South China Sea," *Journal of Ocean University* 3 (2011): 36–40, Jianting Wang, "On the Jurisprudential Foundation and Demonstrative Evidence of Historic Rights," *Pacific Journal* 19, no. 3 (2011): 87–96, Chongmin Wang and Kui Zhang, "A Study on the Legal Status of U-shaped Line in the South China Sea," *Journal of Henan Administration Institute* 5 (2010): 106–109. All are in Chinese.

34 See, for example, Huang, "China's Historic Rights over 'the Other Waters'," 37, Wang and Zhang, "A Study on the Legal Status of U-shaped Line in the South China Sea," 109, and Wang, "On the Jurisprudential Foundation and Demonstrative Evidence of Historic Rights." It is worth noting that these three research projects are funded by government grants.

35 Jia, "Legal Principle," 26.

36 For example, Yu Jia, "The Past and Present of the Dotted Line," *Liao Wang Dong Fang Weekly* 30 (2013), and State Ocean Administration, "Defending Maritime Interests, Exploring Room for Development: Interview with Jia Yu," available at: www.soa.gov.cn/xw/dfdwdt/jsdw_157/201311/t20131107_6776.html (accessed December 30, 2013).

37 Interview, Beijing, August 2013, interviewee requested anonymity.

38 Interview, Beijing, August 2013, interviewee requested anonymity.

39 Ralf Emmers, "The De-escalation of the Spratly Dispute in Sino-Southeast Asian Relations," paper presented to the Conference "The South China Sea: Towards a Cooperative Management Regime," Singapore, May 2007.

40 Robert O. Keohane, "The Demand for International Regimes," in *International Regimes*, ed. Stephen D. Krasner (Ithaca, NY: Cornell University Press, 1983), 339–340.

41 In October 2001, Japanese Prime Minister Junichiro Koizumi proposed at the APT summit the Regional Cooperation Agreement on Combating Piracy and Armed Robbery against Ships in Asia (ReCAAP) to address maritime security. After three years of negotiations, regional countries finalized the Agreement on November 11, 2004, in Tokyo which came into force on September 4, 2006.

42 David Shambaugh, "China Engages Asia: Reshaping the Regional Order," *International Security* 29, no. 3 (2004/05): 75.

43 Michael Richardson, "Sovereignty Tussle Key to China-ASEAN Ties," *Straits Times*, November 9, 2006.

44 See Diane K. Mauzy and Brian L. Job, "U.S. Policy in Southeast Asia: Limited Re-engagement after Years of Benign Neglect," *Asian Survey* 47, no. 4 (2007): 622–641.

45 Geoff Dyer, "Obama Declares Asia a 'Top Priority,'" *Financial Times*, November 18, 2011.

46 White House, "Remarks by President Barack Obama at Suntory Hall," available at: www.whitehouse.gov/the-press-office/remarks-president-barack-obama-suntory-hall (accessed October 30, 2013).

47 "U.S. Is Back in Asia, Secretary of State Hillary Clinton Declares," *Daily News*, July 21, 2009, available at: www.nydailynews.com/news/world/u-s-back-asia-secretary-state-hillary-clinton-declares-article-1.429381 (accessed March 1, 2014).

48 Hillary R. Clinton published an article entitled "America's Pacific Century," in *Foreign Policy*, in which Clinton declared that "The future of politics will be decided in Asia, not Afghanistan or Iraq, and the United States will be right at the center of the action." See Hillary R. Clinton, "America's Pacific Century,"

available at: www.foreignpolicy.com/articles/2011/10/11/americas_pacific_century, *Foreign Policy*, November 2011 (accessed October 30, 2013).

49 Interview with Greg Sheridan of *The Australian*, Hillary Rodham, Secretary of State, Melbourne, Australia, Nov. 8, 2010, cited in Carlyle A. Thayer, "Recent Development in the South China Sea: Grounds for Cautious Optimism," *RSIS Working Paper* 220, Dec 2010, 4, footnote 10.

50 "We've had a series of very productive sessions here in Phuket, and I've had the opportunity for the first time to engage with the nations of ASEAN and our regional partners on issues of common concern, to sign the Treaty of Amity and Cooperation, and to lay the groundwork for even stronger partnerships as we move forward." See U.S. Department of State, "Remarks at the ASEAN Regional Forum," July 23, 2009, available at: www.state.gov/secretary/20092013clinton/rm/2009a/july/126373.htm (accessed April 14, 2014).

51 White House, *U.S.-ASEAN Leaders Joint Statement*, November 2009, available at: www.whitehouse.gov/the-press-office/us-asean-leaders-joint-statement (accessed October 30, 2013).

52 Ibid.

53 Ernest Bower, "U.S.-ASEAN Summit: President Obama Engages Southeast Asia," *Center for Strategic and International Security Publication*, November 9, 2009, available at: http://csis.org/publication/us-asean-summit-president-obama-engages-southeast-asia (accessed October 30, 2013).

54 White House, "Remarks by President Obama and President Triet of Vietnam at Opening of U.S.-ASEAN Leaders Meeting," September 24, 2010, available at: www.whitehouse.gov/the-press-office/2010/09/24/remarks-president-obama-and-president-triet-vietnam-opening-us-asean-lea (accessed October 30, 2013).

55 The United States formally joined EAS in 2011.

56 One of the requirements for membership in the EAS is accession to the TAC. The USA acceded to the TAC in 2009, so only after 2009 was the USA eligible to officially participate in the EAS as a formal member.

57 Jackie Calmes, "Obama and Asian Leaders Confront China's Premier," *New York Times*, November 19, 2011.

58 Ibid.

59 US active engagement in the ADMM-Plus was further acknowledged by ASEAN leaders during the second US-ASEAN summit. See Joint Statements of the 1st and 2nd US-ASEAN Leaders Meeting. The texts are available at the White House, www.whitehouse.gov/the-press-office/us-asean-leaders-joint-statement and www.whitehouse.gov/the-press-office/2010/09/24/joint-statement-2nd-us-asean-leaders-meeting (accessed October 30, 2013).

60 A brief introduction to the ADMM-Plus meeting, available at: www.asean.org/communities/asean-political-security-community/category/asean-defence-ministers-meeting-admm (accessed October 30, 2013).

61 "Liu Jianchao: China Officially Starts Negotiation on a Formal COC with ASEAN," *Phoenix News*, October 1, 2010 available at: news.ifeng.com/mainland/special/zhongmeijiaofeng/zhongguo/detail_2010_10/01/2685930_0.shtml (accessed October 30, 2013).

62 "China ASEAN Reach Consensus on Implementing DOC," *China Daily*, July 20, 2011, available at: www.chinadaily.com.cn/china/2011-07/20/content_12944715.htm (accessed October 30, 2013).

63 The full text of Clinton's Statement on South China Sea is available at the US Embassy, http://iipdigital.usembassy.gov/st/english/texttrans/2011/07/20110723125330su0.9067433.html#axzz2vEIeCT00 (accessed March 6, 2014).

64 Xuegang Zhang, "'Shangri-La Dialogue' Should Focus on Cooperation," *Chinese Daily*, June 3, 2011, available at: www.chinadaily.com.cn/opinion/2011-06/03/content_12639436.htm (accessed October 30, 2013).

65 "Premier Wen Jiabao Expounds China's Position on the SCS Disputes," *Xinhua News*, November 19, 2011, available at: http://news.xinhuanet.com/world/2011-11/19/c_111180192.htm (accessed October 30, 2013).
66 Meidyatama Suryodiningrat, "ASEAN Regional Forum 2011: China and the United States," *Asia Pacific Bulletin* 127 (August 2011).
67 ASEAN-China Center, "Wen Jiabao: China Provides 3 Billion to Promote Maritime Cooperation," available at: http://service.aseanchinacenter.org/investment/information/2011/3020.html (accessed October 30, 2013).
68 Mark J. Valencia, "The South China Sea: Back to the Future?" *Global Asia* 54 (December 2010).
69 Daojiong Zha, "South China Sea Diplomacy: More Needs to Be Done," *RSIS Commentaries* 102 (2011) and Mingjiang Li, "Chinese Debates of South China Sea Policy: Implications for Future Developments," *RSIS Working Paper* 239 (2013).
70 Calmes, "Obama and Asian Leaders Confront China."
71 Fred W. Baker III, "Gates Visits Philippines to Reaffirm US Commitment," *American Forces Press Service*, June 1, 2009, available at the U.S. Department of Defense, www.defenselink.mil/news/newsarticle.aspx?id=54569 (accessed October 30, 2013).
72 Ibid.
73 For the potential value of the Scarborough Shoal in the delimitation of maritime boundary in the SCS between China and the Philippines, see Keyuan Zou, "Scarborough Reef: A New Flashpoint in Sino-Philippine Relations?" *Boundary and Security Bulletin* 7 (1999): 71–81.
74 Alec Almazan, "U.S. N-sub in Subic a Strong Signal to China: Routine Visit Comes amid Reports China Is Mobilizing Fleet for Philippines Ops," *Business Times*, May 18, 2013, and Renato Cruz de Castro, "Future Challenges in U.S.-Philippine Alliance," *Asia-Pacific Bulletin* 168 (June 26, 2013): 1.
75 Luke Hunt, "ASEAN Summit Fallout Continues," *The Diplomat*, July 20, 2013, http://thediplomat.com/asean-beat/2013/07/20/asean-summit-fallout-continues-on/ (accessed October 30, 2013).
76 Ernest Z. Bower, "China Reveals Its Hand on ASEAN in Phnom Penh," *CSIS Southeast Asia Program* 3, no. 14 (2013): 2.
77 Carlyle A. Thayer, "New Commitment to a Code of Conduct in the South China Sea?" *The National Bureau of Asian Research Commentary*, October 9, 2013, available at: http://nbr.org/research/activity.aspx?id=360#.Uxk0E84z3KQ (accessed March 6, 2014).
78 Ibid.
79 ASEAN, "Chairman's Statement of the 22nd ASEAN Summit, 'Our People, Our Future Together,'" April 24–25, 2013, available at: www.asean.org/news/asean-statementcommuniques/item/chairmans-statement-of-the-22nd-asean-summit-ourpeople-our-future-together (accessed March 6, 2014).
80 The four points are as follows:

1. *Reasonable expectations.* Some countries are talking about "quick fix," like reaching consensus on COC within one day. It is an attitude neither realistic nor serious. COC involves multilateral interests from different parties, and its formulation is a process of sophisticated and complex coordination.
2. *Consensus through negotiations.* We should refer to the experience of reaching DOC to move forward COC, to seek consensus as broadly as possible and to keep the comfort of all parties in mind. Wills of individual countries or of a few countries should not be imposed on other countries, as an old Chinese saying, nothing forcibly done is going to be agreeable.

3. *Elimination of interference.* China and the ASEAN countries tried several times to hold discussions on COC before, but got stuck due to interference. All parties concerned should do more to help move forward the process of COC, and create the necessary conditions and atmosphere, not going the opposite way.
4. *Step-by-step approach.* The formulation of COC is stipulated in DOC. COC is not to replace DOC, much less ignore DOC and go its own way. The top priority now is to continue to implement DOC, especially promoting maritime cooperation. In this process, we should formulate the road map for COC through consultations, and push it forward in a step-by-step approach.

See Chinese Foreign Ministry, "Foreign Minister Wang Yi on Process of 'Code of Conduct in the South China Sea," August 5, 2013, available at: www.fmprc.gov.cn/eng/zxxx/t1064869.shtml (accessed March 6, 2014).

81 "Pragmatically Carry Forward the COC Negotiation," *People's Daily*, September 16, 2013, available at: www.people.com.cn/24hour/n/2013/0916/c25408-22927936.html (accessed January 1, 2014).

82 Yanming Chen, "A Study on Fishing Bans during Summer Moratorium of Chinese Seas," *Hebei Fisheries* 9 (2010): 48, in Chinese.

83 Zhuang Wu, "The Tenth Anniversary of Fishing Ban: A Review and Reflection," *China Fisheries* 8 (2008), in Chinese.

84 "Fishing Ban of the South China Sea Region Extends to 77 Days in 2009," *Xinhua News*, April 22, 2009, available at: www.gx.xinhuanet.com/dtzx/2009-04/22/content_16329712.htm (accessed January 2, 2014).

85 Michael D. Swaine and M. Taylor Fravel, "China's Assertive Behavior – Part Two: The Maritime Periphery," *China Leadership Monitor* 35 (2011): 5.

86 Bin Che and Tao Xiong, "Impact of the South China Sea Dispute on Fisheries and Countermeasures," *Research of Agricultural Modernization* 30, no. 4 (2009): 416, in Chinese.

87 South China Sea Fisheries Research Institute, "Aquaculture in Mischief Lagoon Got Harvest," December 3, 2009, available at: www.southchinafish.ac.cn/gnyydt/200912/t20091203_7363.htm (accessed March 1, 2014).

88 "Sea Farming in Mischief for Both Aquaculture Far from Sea and Sovereignty Consolidation," *Chinese Aquaculture Network*, July 24, 2013, available at: www.shuichan.cc/news_view-96382.html (accessed January 3, 2014).

89 Jianwei Zou, "An Analysis on the Development Status of Trawl Fishery Grounds in the Southern Part of the South China Sea," *Modern Fisheries Information* 12 (2011): 3, in Chinese.

90 Zou, "Development Status of Trawl Fishery Grounds," 3.

91 See, for example, Shaoyang Chen and Zhenyan Cheng, "Discussion on the Future of China's SCS Policy and Measures of Safeguarding Rights," *Chinese Fisheries Economics*, no. 6 (2013): 13, in Chinese.

92 See, for example, Fuchen Bai and Peng Luo, "Developing Marine Fisheries in the Spratlys: Challenges and Countermeasures," *Chinese Fisheries Economics* 4 (2011): 6–7, Shuolin Huang, "Fisheries Rights are Essential Part of Maritime Rights," *China Legal Science* 6 (2013): 74–76, and Qingyin Wang, *et al.*, "Contemplation on Maintaining Chinese Fishery Interests in the South China Sea," *Fishery Information and Strategy* 1 (2013): 15. All are in Chinese.

93 Tianrong Liu, "A Historical Cruise – Documenting First Mission of *Yuzheng 31* to the Spratlys," *China Fisheries* 12 (1994): 13, in Chinese.

94 "Fishery Patrols Manifesting Sovereignty – Interview of Liu Tianrong, Deputy Director of Regional Bureau of South China Sea Fishery Management," April 28, 2010, available at: http://news.163.com/10/0428/10/65BNEDER00011MTO.html (accessed January 3, 2014).

95 Xin Zhang, "2nd Ship to Patrol South China Sea," *China Daily*, March 28, 2009, available at: www.chinadaily.com.cn/china/2009-03/28/content_7625985.htm (accessed January 3, 2014). Also see Chinese Government Official Web Portal, "Chinese Fishery Administration Vessel Begins Patrol in South China Sea," March 17, 2009, available at: http://english.gov.cn/2009-03/17/content_1261548.htm (accessed January 3, 2014).

96 Mingshuang Li, "Yuzheng 310 Joins Fishery Patrol Ranks and Starts Patrol Mission," *China Fisheries* 12 (2010): 13, in Chinese.

97 "Fishery Patrols Manifesting Sovereignty."

98 China Oceanic Information Network, *National Reports on Marine Administrative Law Enforcement (2001–2010)*, available at: www.coi.gov.cn/gongbao/xingzheng/ (accessed January 1, 2014).

99 Sulan Chen, "Instrumental and Induced Cooperation: Environmental Politics in the South China Sea" (PhD diss., University of Maryland, 2005), 247.

100 See UNEP 2004. *Mangroves in the South China Sea*. UNEP/GEF/SCS Technical Publication No. 1.; *Coral Reefs in the South China Sea*. UNEP/GEF/SCS Technical Publication No. 2.; *Seagrass in the South China Sea*. UNEP/GEF/SCS Technical Publication No. 3.; and *Wetlands Bordering the South China Sea*. UNEP/GEF/SCS Technical Publication No. 4.

101 Many scholars believe the Gulf of Tonkin sets a precedent for maritime delimitation in the South China Sea. See Zhirong Zhang, "Sino-Vietnamese Maritime Delimitation in the Beibu Gulf and Its Implication for Maritime Dispute Resolution," *International Forum* 7, no. 2 (2005): 29–33, in Chinese, and Keyuan Zou, "The Sino-Vietnamese Agreement on Maritime Boundary Delimitation in the Gulf of Tonkin," *Ocean Development and International Law* 36, no. 1 (2005): 13–24.

102 Ewan W. Anderson, *An Atlas of World Political Flashpoints: A Sourcebook of Geopolitical Crisis* (London: Pinter Reference, 1993), 211.

103 The actual size of the Gulf differs in different sources. The size defined here is according to the Agreement on the Delimitation of the Territorial Seas, the Exclusive Economic Zones and Continental Shelves in the Beibu Gulf.

104 Wei Wu, "Beibu Gulf Delimitation is a Win-Win Solution and Guideline for the Spratly Issue: Interview with Xiao Jianguo," *Xin Jing Bao*, August 4, 2004.

105 Guifang Xue, *International Fisheries Law and China's Practice* (Qingdao: China Ocean University Press, 2008), 221, in Chinese.

106 Keyuan Zou, "Maritime Boundary Delimitation in the Gulf of Tonkin," *Ocean Development and International Law* 30, no. 3 (1999): 245–247.

107 Wu, "Interview with Xiao Jianguo."

108 "Beibu Gulf Delimitation: Interview with Deputy Foreign Minister Wang Yi," *Xinhua News*, June 30, 2004.

109 Wu, "Interview with Xiao Jianguo."

110 L. H. Legault and Blair Hankey, "From Sea to Seabed: The Single Maritime Boundary in the Gulf of Maine Case," *American Journal of International Law* 79, no. 4 (1985): 979.

111 ICJ Reports, *North Sea Continental Shelf (Federal Republic of Germany/Netherlands)*, February 20, 1969, available at: www.icj-cij.org/docket/index.php?sum=295&code=cs2&p1=3&p2=3&case=52&k=cc&p3=5 (accessed May 28, 2013).

112 Legault and Hankey, "Gulf of Maine Case," 980.

113 ICJ Reports, *Case Concerning Delimitation of the Maritime Boundary in the Gulf of Maine Area*, October 12, 1984, available at: www.icj-cij.org/docket/index.php?sum=346&code=cigm&p1=3&p2=3&case=67&k=6f&p3=5 (accessed May 28, 2013).

114 For example, the single line was applied in the 1989 Maritime Boundary Delimitation Agreement Between the GDR and Poland, see Erik Franckx, "The

1989 Maritime Boundary Delimitation Agreement Between the GDR and Poland", *International Journal of Estuarine and Coastal Law* 4, no. 4 (1989): 237.

115 Xue, *International Fisheries Law and China's Practice*, 182.

116 See Shicun Wu, "Sustainable Exploitation of the Fishery Resources of the Beibu Bay (the Gulf of Tonkin)," paper presented at the Conference "Human and Regional Security around the South China Sea", University of Oslo, Oslo, Norway, June 2000, 2.

117 Shuolin Huang and Yonglan Huang, "Preliminary Analysis of the Impact of the Sino-Vietnam Beibu Gulf Fishery Agreement on the Fishery Industry of Our Coastal Provinces," *Journal of Shanghai Fishery University* 3, (2001): 223–228.

118 Xue, *International Fisheries Law and China's Practice*, 219.

119 Article 11 of the Sino-Vietnamese Fishery Agreement provides that:

> Each Contracting Party shall make transitional arrangements for the existing fishing operations of the other Contracting Party in its exclusive economic zone north of the Common Fishery Zone (measured from 20° N). The transitional arrangements shall be implemented from the date of the entry into force of this Agreement. The other Contracting Party shall take measures to reduce such fishing operations year by year. The transitional arrangements will end within four years from the date of the entry into force of this Agreement. The extent of the water area and management measures for the transitional arrangements shall be made by the Contracting Parties in the form of a supplementary protocol, which shall constitute an integral part of this Agreement. Each Contracting Party, upon the end of the transitional arrangements, shall give priority, under the same conditions, to the other party for fishing operations in its exclusive economic zone.

120 Keyuan Zou, *Law of the Sea in East Asia: Issues and Prospects.* Vol. 5 (New York: Routledge, 2005), 103.

121 Yusong Liu, "Five Years of Implementing the Fisheries Agreement," *Chinese Fisheries* 7 (2009): 4–6, in Chinese.

122 Xue, *International Fisheries Law and China's Practice*, 226.

123 According to Article 13 of the Sino-Vietnamese Fishery Agreement, the following functions are granted to the Joint Fishery Committee: (1) to consult on relevant matters relating to the preservation and sustainable utilization of fishery resources in the Agreed Water Area, and to make proposals for the two sides; (2) to consult on relevant matters relating to fishery co-operation between the two countries in the Agreed Water Area, and to make proposals for the two sides; (3) to adopt regulations and implementing measures on preservation and management of fishery resources in the Common Fishery Zone in pursuance to Article 5 of the Agreement; (4) to determine the quantity of fishing vessels of each party entering into the Common Fishery Zone annually in pursuance to Article 6 of the Agreement; (5) to consult and decide on other matters relating to the Common Fishery Zone; (6) to carry out the functions in accordance with the supplementary protocol on transitional arrangements; (7) to settle disputes of fishing activities occurring in the buffer zone for small fishing boats; (8) to guide the settlement of fishery disputes and maritime accidents within its prescribed capacity; (9) to evaluate the situation of implementing this Agreement and report to the two Governments; (10) to propose to the two Governments any amendment or revision of the Agreement, annexes, and supplementary protocols; and (11) to consult on other matters within common concern of the two parties.

124 Xue, *International Fisheries Law and China's Practice*, 238.

125 Chinese Foreign Ministry, "Joint Statement," available at: www.fmprc.gov.cn/eng/wjb/zwjg/zwbd/t187333.htm (accessed March 5, 2014).

126 "Philippines, China to study potential oil deposits in South China Sea," *Agence France Presse*, September 2 2004.

127 "Three Nations Sign Pact for Joint Spratlys Survey," *Straits Times*, March 15, 2005.

128 Abigail L. Ho, "RP, China, Vietnam Pursue Spratlys Project," *The Inquirer*, November 2, 2007, available at: http://business.inquirer.net/money/topstories/view/20070211-48824/RP,_China,_Vietnam_pursue_Spratlys_project?ModPagespeed=off (accessed March 1, 2014).

129 For example, Jianguo Xiao, an official from the Department of Treaty and Law of Foreign Ministry, has a series of academic publications deliberating existing international practices of joint development. See Jianguo Xiao, "The Concept of Joint Development and Its Characteristics in International Law," *Foreign Affairs Review* 2 (2003): 58–63, and *Joint Exploration of Oil in International Maritime Boundaries* (Beijing: Ocean Press 2006). Jinming Li, professor at Xiamen University and a legal advisor to the Foreign Ministry, made several proposals and compared their practicality in the SCS region. See Jinming Li, "Oil Resources around the Nansha Islands: Development and Prospects of Dispute Handling," *Journal of Xiamen University* 4 (2002): 52–59. Also see Guoqiang Li, "The Analyses of Some Proposals of Resolving Sovereign Disputes of Nansha Islands," *China's Borderland History and Geography Studies* 10, no. 3 (2000): 79–88, Zaiwen Tan, "International Political Economy of the Joint Development in South China Sea," *Southeast Asian Affairs* 3 (2005): 9–13, Song Guan, "Models of Joint Development: The Solution for the SCS Dispute," *Chinese Fisheries Economics* 5 (2005): 71–74, Meili Wang, "Shelving Disputes Joint Developing: A New Method for Solving International Disputes," *Journal of Yunnan University* 15, no. 2 (2002): 81–86, and Guoxuan Li, "Institutionalization of Joint Development in the SCS: Connotation, Preconditions and Restraints," *Southeast Asian Affairs* 1 (2008): 61–68. All are in Chinese.

130 See Jinzhe Liang, "Reflections on Certain Issues of Developing Disputed Areas in the SCS," in *Proceedings of the SCS Workshop (2002)*, ed. Tianxiang Zhong, Jia Han and Huaifeng Ren (Hainan: Hainan Institute for the SCS, 2002), 102, in Chinese.

131 Ibid., 111–112.

132 Examples of research funded by National Social Science Fund of China are: Miao He, "Analyses on the Current Joint Development of Oil and Gas Resources over the Nansha Islands Waters," *Academic Exploration* 8 (2011): 18–26, Yingmin An, "A Discussion of Possible Models for Joint Development of Gas and Oil Resources in Contested Waters in the South China Sea," *Journal of Contemporary Asia-Pacific Studies* 6 (2011): 124–140, Hongxia Quan, "Exploring the Legal Mechanisms for Joint Development of Fisheries Resources in the South China Sea," *Theory Monthly* 10 (2010): 161–163, Yingmin An and Tao Jiang, "The Issue of Joint Development of Hydrocarbon Resources in the Contested Area of the South China Sea and Possible Models," *The New Orient* 4 (2011): 28–32, Jianping Shao, "Challenge of South China Sea Dispute on China's 'Good Neighbor' Policy and Response," *Journal of Guangxi University* 35, no. 3 (2013): 12–18, and Lina Zhang, "On the Joint Development of Oil and Gas Resources in the Contested Waters in the South China Sea: Its Predicament and Way Out," *Journal of Hainan University* 4, no. 31, (2013): 13–20. Examples of research funded by Ministerial Level Research Projects of the Chinese Law Society are: Xiaojun Zhang, "Exploring the Legal Mechanism of Implementing 'Shelving Disputes, Jointly Developing' Strategy," *Journal of Jinan University* 2 (2011): 75–81, and Zewei Yang, "The Principle of 'Shelving Disputes and Joint Development:' Dilemma and Way Out," *Journal of Jiangsu University* 13, no. 3 (2011): 70–75. Examples of research funded by Ministry of Education are:

Guoqiang Luo, "An Analysis of Joint Development Policy And its Practical Effect in Solving Maritime Disputes: Analysis and Prediction," *Law Science Magazine* 4 (2011): 14–17, Guoqiang Luo and Wei Guo, "Analyzing Two Joint Development Cases in the South China Sea," *Southeast Asian Affairs* 2 (2013): 45–55, Yan Li and Qingbo Huang, "A Study of Establishing International Cooperative Mechanisms for Marine Resources Development," *Intertrade* 6 (2013): 21–25, and Hao Xu and Le Yang, "A Review of Joint Development Theories and Cases and A Study of Development Trend in the South China Sea," *Journal of Hainan Normal University* 5 (2013): 100–105. All are in Chinese.

133 See, for example, He, "Current Joint Development of Oil and Gas Resources," 13, Shao, "Promoting Joint Development in the South China Sea," 158, and An, "Possible Models for Joint Development," 137.

134 See, for example, Luo, "Cooperative Mechanisms for Joint Development," 4–5, Zhang, "Joint Development: Predicament and Way Out," 19, and Shao, "Promoting Joint Development in the South China Sea," 158.

135 See, for example, Li and Huang, "International Cooperative Mechanisms for Marine Resources Development," 23; Zhang, "Legal Mechanism of Implementing 'Shelving Disputes, Jointly Developing' Strategy," 79; Quan, "Legal Mechanisms for Joint Development of Fisheries Resources," 161–163; and Zhang, "Joint Development: Predicament and Way Out," 19.

136 "CNOOC Sends Deepwater Crane Ship to South China Sea," *Xinhua News*, May 15, 2013, available at: news.xinhuanet.com/english/china/2013-05/15/c_131589480.htm (accessed January 2, 2014).

137 "CNOOC to Offer 9 Blocks in S. China Sea for Joint Exploration," *Global Times*, June 27, 2013, available at: www.globaltimes.cn/content/717464.shtm (accessed January 2, 2014).

138 Xiangqian Lu, "CNOOC-981 Starts Drilling, South China Sea Oil Blocks Offered for Foreign Bids, Maintaining Chinese Maritime Rights and Quickening Exploration Pace," *International Petroleum Economics* 1 (2013): 50, in Chinese.

139 Department of Foreign Affairs of the Philippines, "Notification and Statement of Claim," available at: www.dfa.gov.ph/index.php/2013-06-27-21-50-36/unclos (accessed March 1, 2014).

Bibliography

Anderson, E.W. 1993. *An Atlas of World Political Flashpoints: A Sourcebook of Geopolitical Crisis*, Pinter Reference, London.

Bateman, S. and Schofield, C.H. 2009. "Outer Shelf Claims in the South China Sea," *RSIS Commentaries*, no. 65.

Beckman, R. 2010. "South China Sea: Worsening Dispute or Growing Clarity in Claims?," *RSIS Commentaries*, no. 16.

Bower, E.Z. 2009. "U.S.-ASEAN Summit: President Obama Engages Southeast Asia," *Center for Strategic and International Security Publication*, vol. 9, available at: http://csis.org/publication/us-asean-summit-president-obama-engages-southeast-asia. (accessed Oct. 30, 2013).

Bower, E.Z. 2013. "China Reveals Its Hand on ASEAN in Phnom Penh," *CSIS Southeast Asia Program*, vol. 3, no. 14, pp. 1–4.

Buszynski, L. and Sazlan, I. 2007. "Maritime Claims and Energy Cooperation in the South China Sea," *Contemporary Southeast Asia*, vol. 29, no. 1, pp. 143–171.

Castro, R.C.D. 2012. 'Future Challenges in U.S.-Philippine Alliance," *Asia-Pacific Bulletin*, no. 168.

Chen, S.L. 2005. "Instrumental and Induced Cooperation: Environmental Politics in the South China Sea," PhD diss., University of Maryland.

Chen, Y.M. 2010. "A Study on Fishing Bans during the Summer Moratorium of Chinese Seas," *Hebei Fisheries*, vol. 9, pp. 46–56 (in Chinese).

China Oceanic Information Network. 2010. *National Reports on Marine Administrative Law Enforcement (2001–2010)*, available at: www.coi.gov.cn/gongbao/xingzheng/ (accessed Jan. 1, 2014).

Clinton, H.R. 2011. "America's Pacific Century," *Foreign Policy*, available at: www.foreignpolicy.com/articles/2011/10/11/americas_pacific_century (accessed Oct. 30, 2013).

Commission on the Limits of the Continental Shelf. 2009a. *Joint Submission of Malaysia and the Socialist Republic of Vietnam*, 6 May, available at: www.un.org/Depts/los/clcs_new/submissions_files/mysvnm33_09/mys_vnm2009excutivesummary.pdf (accessed March 1, 2014).

Commission on the Limits of the Continental Shelf. 2009b. *Note of China No. CML/17/2009*, 7 May, available at: www.un.org/Depts/los/clcs_new/submissions_files/mysvnm33_09/chn_2009re_mys_vnm_e.pdf (accessed March 1, 2014).

Commission on the Limits of the Continental Shelf. 2011a. *Philippines' Note Verbale No. 000228*, 5 April, available at: www.un.org/Depts/los/clcs_new/submissions_files/mysvnm33_09/phl_re_chn_2011.pdf (accessed March 1, 2014).

Commission on the Limits of the Continental Shelf. 2011b. *Note of China No. CML/8/2011*, 11 April, available at: www.un.org/depts/los/clcs_new/submissions_files/vnm37_09/chn_2011_re_phl_e.pdf. (accessed March 1, 2014).

Emmers, R. 2007. "The De-escalation of the Spratly Dispute in Sino-Southeast Asian Relations," paper presented at the Conference of The South China Sea: Towards a Cooperative Management Regime, Singapore, May 2007.

Franckx, E. 1989. "The 1989 Maritime Boundary Delimitation Agreement Between the GDR and Poland," *International Journal of Estuarine and Coastal Law*, vol. 4, no. 4, pp. 237–251.

Fuchen Bai, F.C. and Luo, P. 2011. "Developing Marine Fisheries in the Spratlys: Challenges and Countermeasures," *Chinese Fisheries Economics*, no. 4, pp. 6–7 (in Chinese).

Gao, Z.G. 1994. "The South China Sea: From Conflict to Cooperation," *Ocean Development and International Law*, vol. 25, no. 3, pp. 345–359.

Gau, M.S.T. 2012. "The U-Shaped Line and a Categorization of the Ocean Disputes in the South China Sea," *Ocean Development and International Law*, vol. 42, no. 1, pp. 57–69.

Han, Z.H. (ed.) 1988. *Collection of Historical Materials on Our Country's South China Sea Islands*, Dongfang Publishing House, Beijing (in Chinese).

Huang, W. 2011. "China's Historic Rights over 'the Other Waters' within the U-shaped Line of South China Sea," *Journal of Ocean University*, vol. 3, pp. 36–40 (in Chinese).

Huang, Y. and Huang, M.M. 2013. "Implementation of the Sino-Vietnamese Fishery Agreement: Mainly Chinese Perspective," *Beijing Law Review*, vol. 4, no. 3, pp. 103–119.

I.C.J. 1969. *Report: North Sea Continental Shelf (Federal Republic of Germany/Netherlands)*. ICJ, Brussels.

I.C.J. 1984. *Report: Case Concerning Delimitation of the Maritime Boundary in the Gulf of Maine Area*. ICJ, Brussels.

I.C.J. 2002. *Report: Sovereignty over Pulau Ligitan and Pulau Sipadan (Indonesia v. Malaysia)*. ICJ, Brussels.

Jensen, Ø, 2014. *The Commission on the Limits of the Continental Shelf-Law and Legitimacy*, Brill, Leiden.

Jia, Y. 2005. "On the Legal Status of the Dotted Line of the South China Sea," *China's Borderland History and Geography Studies*, vol. 15, no. 2, pp. 112–120 (in Chinese).

Jia, Y. 2011. "Legal Principle of the South China Sea Disputes," *China Legal Science*, vol. 6, pp. 26–35 (in Chinese).

Jia, Y. 2012. "The Past and Present of the Dotted Line," *Liao Wang Dong Fang Weekly*, vol. 30. pp. 24–27.

Keohane, R.O. 1982. "The Demand for International Regimes," *International Organization*, vol. 36, no. 2, pp. 325–355.

Legault, L.H. and Hankey, B. 1985. "From Sea to Seabed: The Single Maritime Boundary in the Gulf of Maine Case," *American Journal of International Law*, vol. 79, no. 4, pp. 961–991.

Li, J.M. 2001. "A Study of the Nine-Dash Line and Related Issues," *China's Borderland History and Geography Studies*, vol. 11, no. 2, pp. 15–16 (in Chinese).

Li, J.M. and Li, D.X. 2003. 'The Dotted Line on the Chinese Map of the South China Sea: A Note," *Ocean Development and International Law*, vol. 34, no. 3–4, pp. 287–295.

Li, M.J. 2013. "Chinese Debates of South China Sea Policy: Implications for Future Developments," *RSIS Working Paper*, no. 239.

Li, M.J. and Lee, D.M. (eds.) 2011. *China and the Strategic Dynamics in East Asia: The Shaping of a New Regional Order*, Lexington Books, Lanham, MD.

Luo, T.T. 2008. "Exploring the Legal Status of the Nine-Dash Line – Four Schools of Arguments," *China Review of the Science of Maritime Law*, no. 1, pp. 56–64 (in Chinese).

Mauzy, D.K. and Job, B.L. 2007. 'U.S. Policy in Southeast Asia: Limited Re-engagement after Years of Benign Neglect," *Asian Survey*, vol. 47, no. 4, pp. 622–641.

Shambaugh, D. 2004. "China Engages Asia: Reshaping the Regional Order," *International Security*, vol. 29, no. 3, pp. 64–99.

State Ocean Administration. 2012. "Defending Maritime Interests, Exploring Room for Development: Interview with Jia Yu," 4 June, available at: www.soa.gov.cn/xw/dfdwdt/jsdw_157/201311/t20131107_6776.html (accessed Dec. 30, 2013).

Swaine, M.D. and Fravel, M.T. 2011. "China's Assertive Behavior – Part Two: The Maritime Periphery," *China Leadership Monitor*, no. 35, pp. 1–32, available at: http://101.96.10.63/carnegieendowment.org/files/Swaine_Fravel_CLM_35_0624111.pdf (accessed July 31, 2017).

Thang, N.D. and Thao, N.H. 2012. "China's Nine Dotted Lines in the South China Sea: The 2011 Exchange of Diplomatic Notes Between the Philippines and China," *Ocean Development and International Law*, vol. 43, no. 1, pp. 35–56.

Thayer, C.A. 2010. 'Recent Development in the South China Sea: Grounds for Cautious Optimism," *RSIS Working Paper*, no. 220.

United Nations. 2012. Final Report of the Eleventh SPLOS Meeting, available at: http://daccess-dds-ny.un.org/doc/UNDOC/GEN/N01/387/64/PDF/N0138764.pdf?OpenElement (accessed Oct. 30, 2013).

Wang, C.M. and Zhang, K. 2010. "A Study on the Legal Status of the U-shaped Line in the South China Sea," *Journal of Henan Administration Institute*, vol. 5, pp. 106–109 (in Chinese).

Wang, J.T. 2011. "On the Jurisprudential Foundation and Demonstrative Evidence of Historic Rights," *Pacific Journal*, vol. 19, no. 3, pp. 87–96 (in Chinese).
Wang, Y.Z. 2008. "A Comprehensive Discussion on the Dotted Line in the SCS," *Journal of Ocean University of China (Social Science)*, vol. 3, pp. 1–5 (in Chinese).
Wang, Z. 2015. "Chinese Discourse on the 'Nine-Dashed Line': Rights, Interests, and Nationalism," *Asian Survey*, vol. 55, no. 3, pp. 502–524.
Wu, S.C. 2000. "Sustainable Exploitation of the Fishery Resources of the Beibu Bay (the Gulf of Tonkin)," paper presented at the Conference of Human and Regional Security around the South China Sea, University of Oslo, Oslo, Norway, June 2000.
Wu, S.C. 2013. *Solving Disputes for Regional Cooperation and Development in the South China Sea: A Chinese Perspective*, Chandos Publishing, Oxford.
Wu, S.C. and Hong, N. (eds.) 2014. *Recent Developments in the South China Sea Dispute: The Prospect of a Joint Development Regime*, Routledge, New York.
Wu, S.C. and Zou, K.Y. (eds.) 2009. *Maritime Security in the South China Sea: Regional Implications and International Cooperation*, Routledge, New York.
Wu, Z. 2008. "The Tenth Anniversary of the Fishing Ban: A Review and Reflection," *China Fisheries*, no. 8, pp. 4–6 (in Chinese).
Xiao, J.G. 2003. "The Concept of Joint Development and Its Characteristics in International Law," *Foreign Affairs Review*, no. 2, pp. 58–63 (in Chinese).
Xiao, J.G. 2006. *Joint Exploration of Oil in International Maritime Boundaries*, Ocean Press, Beijing (in Chinese).
Xue, G.F. 2008. *International Fisheries Law and China's Practice*, China Ocean University Press, Qingdao, China (in Chinese).
Yongming Jin, Y.M. 2013. "The Nature of the SCS Dotted Line and the Legal Status of the Enclosed Waters," *China Legal Science*, vol. 6, pp. 38–50 (in Chinese).
Zha, D.J. 2011. "South China Sea Diplomacy: More Needs to Be Done," *RSIS Commentaries*, no. 102.
Zhang, Z.R. 2005. "Sino-Vietnamese Maritime Delimitation in the Beibu Gulf and Its Implications for Maritime Dispute Resolution," *International Forum*, vol. 7, no. 2, pp. 29–33 (in Chinese).
Zhao, L.H. 1996. *Studies of the Law of the Sea Issues*, Peking University Press, Beijing (in Chinese).
Zhong, T.X., Han, J. and Ren, H.F. (eds.) 2002. *Proceedings of the SCS Workshop*, Hainan Institute for the SCS, Haikou, China.
Zou, J.W. 2011. "An Analysis on the Development Status of Trawl Fishery Grounds in the Southern Part of the South China Sea," *Modern Fisheries Information*, no. 12, pp. 3–24 (in Chinese).
Zou, K.Y. 1999a. "Maritime Boundary Delimitation in the Gulf of Tonkin," *Ocean Development and International Law*, vol. 30, no. 3, pp. 235–254.
Zou, K.Y. 1999b. "The Chinese Traditional Maritime Boundary Line in the South China Sea and Its Legal Consequences for the Resolution of the Dispute over the Spratly Islands," *International Journal of Marine and Coastal Law*, vol. 14, no. 1, pp. 27–55.
Zou, K.Y. 2001. "Historic Rights in International Law and in China's Practice," *Ocean Development and International Law*, vol. 32, no. 2, pp. 149–168.
Zou, K.Y. 2005. "The Sino-Vietnamese Agreement on Maritime Boundary Delimitation in the Gulf of Tonkin," *Ocean Development and International Law*, vol. 36, no. 1, pp. 13–24.

Zou, K.Y. 2006. “Joint Development in the South China Sea,” *International Journal of Marine and Coastal Law*, vol. 21, pp. 83–109.

Zou, K.Y. 2009. “Recent Chinese Practice in the Maintenance of Maritime Security and the European Experience,” *The European Union and China*, vol. 27, pp. 275–289.

Zou, K.Y. 2012. “China’s Ocean Policymaking: Practice and Lessons,” *Coastal Management*, vol. 40, no. 2, pp. 145–160.

Zou, K.Y. 2017. “Navigation in the South China Sea: Why Still an Issue?,” *International Journal of Marine and Coastal Law*, vol. 32, no. 2, pp. 243–267.

7 The South China Sea arbitration case and beyond

This chapter examines the most recent changes in China's policy towards the SCS since 2013. On January 22, 2013, the Philippines initiated the SCS Arbitration case against China. This case has important bearings on China's legal position and elicited a new round of legal deliberation by the Chinese government of its SCS claims, which will be explored in the first section. On the political front, the post-2013 period has seen heightened tensions in the SCS, partly due to increasing involvement and mobilization of the United States and its security allies in the SCS issue. Geopolitical dynamics and the normative pressure generated by the SCS Arbitration case pressured China to upscale its commitment to political engagement with its regional neighbors, a process that yielded some positive progress, in particular, towards a legally binding Code of Conduct (COC). The third section assesses China's policy practices of maritime governance and finds that the trend of consolidating jurisdiction through enhancing governance continued, with even greater efforts. Some of these policy practices have been quite controversial and invoked a strong response from other claimants. In the meantime, it is also observed that, absent of direct external pressure, the Chinese epistemic community were self-conscious in defending and implementing the modern standard in China's practices of marine governance. The fourth section looks at China's attitude to joint development, while joint development remained China's preferred approach to managing and resolving the SCS dispute interests, the post-2013 period also witnessed the emergence of new proposals for SCS governance inspired by China's global participation in the maritime regime. The final section summarizes the developments of China's SCS policy in the post-2013 period and analyzes the concrete roles of the LOS regime in shaping the latest contours of China's SCS policy.

Development of China's legal position

Overview of the procedures of the South China Sea Arbitration case and China's reaction and responses

On January 22, 2013, the Philippines government under the Aquino III administration initiated arbitral proceedings against China under Article 287 and Annex VII of 1982 UNCLOS. The Filipino government submitted the Notification and Statement of Claim which outlined the Philippines' grievances against China and the legal basis for its claims.[1]

The Philippines' action set in motion a chain of critical dates, directing pressure on China to respond (see Table 7.1). The latter took a series of actions in line with the legal framework as set out in the UNCLOS. The first action, in response to the Philippines' initial notification, took place within less than a month. On February 19, 2013, the government of China sent a Note Verbale to the Filipino government in which it rejected the Philippines' initiation of arbitral proceedings and called for dispute resolution through bilateral negotiations.[2]

Upon the Philippines' request, a five-member Tribunal was established on May 27, 2013, composed of Judge Thomas A. Mensah as the presiding arbitrator, Judge Jean-Pierre Cot, Judge Stanislaw Pawlak, Professor Alfred H. A. Soons and Judge Rudiger Wolfrum. On July 12, 2013, the Tribunal issued Administrative Directive No. 1 and provided it to the Chinese and Philippines governments for comments, along with draft Rules of Procedures and other relevant documents. In response, China returned those documents and uttered a position of non-acceptance and non-participation in its Note Verbale dated July 29, 2013 addressed to the Permanent Court of Arbitration, which served as the Registry in this Arbitration.

On August 27, 2013, the Tribunal issued Procedural Order No. 1, by which it fixed March 30, 2014 as the date for the Philippines to submit a Memorial that "shall fully address all issues including matters relating to jurisdiction, admissibility, and the merits of the dispute." On March 30, 2014, the Philippines submitted its Memorial and accompanying annexes, copies of which were sent to the Embassy of the PRC in the Kingdom of Netherlands. The same day, the Spokesperson of Chinese Foreign Ministry Hong Lei commented on the Philippines' submission, arguing that at the heart of the matter were the disputes between the two sides on the sovereignty over islands and reefs and delimitation of maritime boundaries, which had already been excluded from arbitration procedures through China's declaration in 2006 pursuant to the UN Convention on the Law of the Sea (UNCLOS).[3]

On June 2, 2014, the Tribunal issued Procedural Order No. 2 in which December 15, 2014 was set as the date by which China could submit a Counter-Memorial. Consequently, on December 7, 2014, the Ministry of Foreign Affairs of the PRC published a *Position Paper of the Government of the People's Republic of China on the Matter of Jurisdiction in the South China Sea Arbitration Initiated by the Republic of the Philippines* (hereafter the Position Paper).[4] On December 8, 2014, the Chinese Embassy in the Kingdom of Netherlands deposited with the PCA a Note Verbale in which the position of non-acceptance and non-participation was reiterated and requested China's Position Paper to be forwarded to the members of the Tribunal.[5]

On December 16, 2014, the Tribunal issued Procedural Order No. 3 in which it fixed March 16, 2015 as the date for the Philippines to file a

Table 7.1 Timetable of the South China Sea arbitration case

Critical dates	*Legal proceeding*		*China's response*	
Jan. 22, 2013	Statement of Claim (the Philippines)	→	Feb. 19, 2013	Note Verbale
July 12, 2013	Administrative Directive No. 1 of the Tribunal	→	July 29, 2013	Note Verbale
Aug. 27, 2013	Procedural Order No.1 (fixing March 30, 2014 for the Philippines to submit Memorial)	→	March 30, 2014	Press Conference
March 30, 2014	Memorial (the Philippines)			
June, 2, 2014	Procedural Order No.2 (fixing 15 December 2014 for China to submit Counter-Memorial)	→	Dec. 7, 2014	Position Paper
Dec. 16, 2014	Procedural Order No.3 (fixing 16 March 2015 for the Philippines to file supplemental submission and 16 June 2015 for China to respond)	→	Feb. 6, 2015	First Ambassador Letter
		→	March 16, 2015	Supplemental Written Submission (the Philippines)
Apr. 21, 2015	Procedural Order No.4 (setting 7 July 2015 to convene Hearing on Jurisdiction)	→	July 1, 2015	Second Ambassador Letter
July 7–13, 2015	Hearing on Jurisdiction and Admissibility	→	July 7/ July 14/ Aug. 24, 2015	Press Conferences
Oct. 29, 2015	Award on Jurisdiction and Admissibility	→	Oct. 30, 2015	Statement on the Award on Jurisdiction
Nov. 24–30, 2015	Hearing on Merits	→	Nov. 24/ Dec. 1/ Dec. 21, 2015	Press Conferences

Critical dates	*Legal proceeding*		*China's response*	
May–June 2016	External investigation (the Tribunal)	→	May 12, 2016	Media Briefing by Xu Hong
		→	May–Jun 2016	1. Four Letters from the New Ambassador; 2. Press Conferences
July12, 2016	Final Award	→	July 12, 2016	1. Statement on the Award of July 12, 2016; 2. Statement on China's Territorial Sovereignty and Maritime Rights and Interests in the SCS
		→	July, 13, 2016	Statement: China Adheres to the Position of Settling Through Negotiation the Relevant Disputes Between China and the Philippines in the SCS

Supplemental Written Submission and June 16, 2015 as the date by which China could provide comments in response. On February 6, 2015, the Chinese Ambassador to the Netherlands wrote a letter to the members of the Tribunal which described China's Position Paper as having "comprehensively explained why the Tribunal … manifestly has no jurisdiction over the case" and expressed China's "firm opposition" to some of the procedural issues raised in the PCA's correspondence, such as "intervention by other states," "*amicus curiae* submissions" and "site visit[s]."[6] On March 16, the Philippines submitted its Supplemental Written Submission and accompanying annexes. A month later, the Tribunal issued Procedural Order No. 4 on April 21, 2015, in which it considered that the communications by China, including notably the Position Paper of December 7, 2014 and the Ambassador Letter of February 6, 2015, "effectively constitute a plea concerning the Tribunal's jurisdiction," and decided to convene a Hearing on Jurisdiction on July 7, 2015.[7]

On July 1, 2015, a few days before the Hearing on Jurisdiction was scheduled to be convened, China's Ambassador to the Netherlands sent a second letter to the members of the Tribunal. The letter recalled China's "consistent policy and practice of [resolving] the disputes related to territory and maritime rights and interests with States directly concerned through negotiation and consultation," reaffirmed the official position elaborated in the Position Paper, and emphasized China's "legitimate right" under the Convention not to accept unilateral resorting to a third-party settlement nor any arbitral arrangements, including the hearing procedures.

The Hearing on Jurisdiction commenced on July 7,2015 as scheduled and lasted until July 13, 2015. Vietnam, Malaysia, Thailand, and Japan sent delegations as observers to the hearing. The Tribunal invited the Philippines to submit by July 23, 2015 written responses to certain questions posed during the hearing and set the date of August 17, 2015 by which China could comment on any matter raised during or after the Hearing on Jurisdiction. China expressed its position through three regular press conferences on July, 7, July 14, and August 24, respectively, and did not respond to the August 17, 2015 deadline for comment.[8]

On October 29, 2015, the Tribunal published its Award on Jurisdiction and Admissibility, declaring that the Tribunal was properly constituted, had jurisdiction to consider the Philippines' Submissions No. 3, 4, 6, 7, 10, 11 and 13, and preserved consideration of its jurisdiction to rule on Submissions No. 1, 2, 4, 5, 9, 12, and 14 to the merits phase.[9] The following day, China's Foreign Ministry issued the *Statement on the Award on Jurisdiction and Admissibility of the South China Sea Arbitration by the Arbitral Tribunal Established at the Request of the Republic of the Philippines* (hereafter Statement on the Award on Jurisdiction) reiterating, again, China's policy of non-acceptance and non-participation and the legal reasoning behind its position.[10]

The Hearing on the Merits took place on November 24–30, without China's appearance and on the last day of the hearing, the Tribunal set January 1, 2016 as the date by which China could comment on anything said during the Hearing on the Merits or submitted subsequently. Similar to its reaction to the Hearing on Jurisdiction and Admissibility, the government of China responded to the Hearing through three press conferences, on the opening day of the Hearing (November 24), the day following the conclusion of the Hearing (December 1) as well as the day the verbatim of the Hearing was released (December 21).

Following the Hearing, the Tribunal began to draft external experts to do further investigations on issues related to the case. Some of the issues under investigation were quite controversial, and evoked reactions from China. For example, on May 12, 2016, the Director-General of the Department of Treaty and Law of the Chinese Ministry of Foreign Affairs, Xu Hong, gave a "Briefing on the South China Sea Arbitration Initiated by the Philippines," expounding China's position from the perspective of international law. On May 20, 2016, the new Chinese Ambassador to the Netherlands delivered a letter to the PCA to be presented to members of the Tribunal. In the letter, the Ambassador made clear again China's policy towards this Arbitration case and enclosed a statement from Foreign Ministry Spokesperson Hua Chunying of May 20, 2016.[11] In the statement Hua emphasized that China disagreed with the Philippines' claim that arbitration was its last resort after exhausting all the bilateral means and that "before unilaterally initiating the arbitration in January, 2013, the Philippine government failed to have any consultation or negotiation with the Chinese side on relevant items, still less exhaust all the bilateral means for the settlement of disputes."[12]

In light of the Tribunal's ongoing investigation of Itu Aba (Taiping Dao in Chinese), the new Chinese Ambassador sent a second letter to the members of the Tribunal on June 3, 2016, enclosing a statement from Foreign Ministry Spokesperson Hua Chunying concerning the status of Itu Aba. Hua confirmed the Itu Aba (Taiping Dao) was an "island" completely capable of sustaining human habitation or economic life of its own and argued that the Philippines' attempt to characterize it as a "rock" was for the purpose of denying China's sovereignty over Nansha Islands and relevant maritime rights and interests.[13]

On June 8, 2016 and June 10, 2016, respectively, the Chinese Ambassador presented to the members of the Tribunal the third and fourth letters summarizing the major points of China's policy towards the SCS Arbitration case. In the fourth letter was enclosed a statement by the Chinese Society of International Law, entitled "the Tribunal's Award in the 'South China Sea Arbitration' Initiated by the Philippines is Null and Void," which opined on the legal issues raised in the Award on Jurisdiction.[14]

On July 12, 2016, the Tribunal issued the final award on the South China Sea Arbitration case. According to the Award, of all the 15 submissions on which the Philippines requested the Tribunal to adjudge, the Tribunal ruled on No. 1 to No. 13 and No. 14 (d) in favor of the Philippines. In particular, with regard to controversial issues such as China's claim of the nine-dash line and the status of some of the maritime features in the SCS, the Arbitral

Tribunal agreed to the Philippines' position as expressed in the latter's submissions.

China was quick to respond. On July 12, the same day the Final Award came out, the Ministry of Foreign Affairs promulgated two official documents. The first document is *Statement of the Ministry of Foreign Affairs of the People's Republic of China on the Award of 12 July 2016 of the Arbitral Tribunal in the South China Sea Arbitration Established at the Request of the Republic of the Philippines* (hereafter Statement on the Award), in which the government rebuked the Tribunal's judgment.[15] The second document, entitled "Statement of the Government of the People's Republic of China on China's Territorial Sovereignty and Maritime Rights and Interests in the South China Sea" (hereafter the 2016 Statement of Sovereignty and Maritime Rights) clarified China's claims of sovereignty and related maritime rights.[16] The following day, China published a lengthy statement entitled "China Adheres to the Position of Settling Through Negotiation the Relevant Disputes Between China and the Philippines in the South China Sea", expounding on the details of all the major diplomatic exchanges between China and the Philippines concerning the SCS dispute.

China's legal position on the South China Sea dispute

As illustrated in Table 7.1, the unfolding of the Arbitration cases, over a time span of three and a half years, set more than 10 critical dates to which the government of China was pressured to react, resulted in six Ambassador letters, a handful of diplomatic Notes Verbales, publication of various official statements, as well as numerous press conferences of the Foreign Ministry regarding specific issues raised during the arbitral proceedings. Together these documents demonstrate China's mastery of sophisticated skills of legal deliberation and sound knowledge of the Convention.

These documents fall into three categories. The first category is China's preference for the means through which the SCS dispute is to be resolved; the second category is China's position on the Arbitral Tribunal instituted at the request of the Philippines; falling in the last category is a comprehensive elaboration of China's claims to the SCS, including its claims of sovereignty and related maritime interests.

First, the Chinese government made it clear that it viewed political consultations and negotiations as the preferable approach to resolve disputes with the Philippines. This preference was further elaborated in Part III of China's Position Paper released on December 7, 2014 as well as the official statement "China Adheres to the Position of Settling Through Negotiation the Relevant Disputes Between China and the Philippines in the South China Sea" published on July 13, 2016.

Second, China has repeatedly expressed its attitude to the five-member Tribunal established at the request of the Philippines, that is, this Tribunal had no jurisdiction over the case and hence China would not accept nor participate in this Arbitration. The legal reasoning behind China's position of non-acceptance and non-participation, elaborated most comprehensively in the Position Paper, can be summarized as two basic points. First, the Chinese government emphasized that at the heart of the subject-matter of this Arbitration was the territorial sovereignty over several maritime features in the South China Sea, which was therefore beyond the scope of the Convention and did not concern the interpretation or application of the Convention.[17] Second, China argued that the Philippines had split up the dispute of maritime delimitation into discrete issues and selected a few of them for arbitration. These issues presented by the Philippines for arbitration constituted an integral part of maritime delimitation between China and the Philippines and, according to China's 2006 declaration, should be excluded from compulsory settlement procedures under the Convention.[18]

Falling in the third category are documents that present a comprehensive elaboration of China's claims to the SCS, including its claims of sovereignty and related maritime interests. In the 2016 Statement of Sovereignty and Maritime Rights, China's legal position on its claims to and rights in the South China Sea contains four layers as listed in the following:

1 China has sovereignty over Nanhai Zhudao, consisting of Dongsha Qundao, Xisha Qundao, Zhongsha Qundao and Nansha Qundao.
2 China has internal waters, territorial sea and contiguous zone, based on Nanhai Zhudao.
3 China has an exclusive economic zone and a continental shelf, based on Nanhai Zhudao.
4 China has historic rights in the South China Sea.

The first layer of China's legal claims to the SCS concerns territorial sovereignty of four groups of islands: Dongsha, Xisha, Zhongsha, and Nansha; The second layer to China's SCS claims is related to the sovereignty over some part of the water column in the SCS; the third layer concerns the establishment of an exclusive economic zone and a continental shelf; and finally, a claim to historic rights in the areas enclosed in the Dashed Line adds the fourth layer to China's legal position on the SCS.

China's claims to the EEZ and CS is supplemented by Chinese Foreign Ministry Spokesperson Hua Chunying's remarks concerning the status of Itu Aba. Hua's remarks were two-fold. On the one hand, she confirmed the Itu Aba (Taiping Dao) was an "island" completely capable of sustaining human habitation or economic life of its own. On the other hand, she argued that China had, based on the Nansha Islands as a whole, territorial sea, exclusive economic zone and continental shelf.[19]

What is also worth noting is China's legal position on the nine-dash line. Based on the legal deliberations of the Chinese government in response to the Arbitration case, it is reasonable to infer that the nine-dash line is not a line of historic title. When China submitted to the UN the nine-dash line map in

2009, a popular speculation was that the line demarcated a historical title to the waters enclosed within the line. However, the fact that China refrained from invoking "historical title" in paragraph 1 (a) (i) of Article 298 to reject the case demonstrates that China does not treat the nine-dash line as a line of historic title. Throughout the course of the proceedings of the Arbitration case, China reiterated over and over again that the subject-matter of the case was disputes concerning territorial sovereignty over several maritime features and maritime delimitation which, according to China's opt-out declaration in 2006, had been excluded from compulsory dispute settlement procedures. In other words, although China's 2006 declaration excludes all three types of disputes, Beijing carefully chose "sovereignty" and "boundary delimitation", rather than "historical title", as the basis for its opt-out position, even though the nine-dash line was directly challenged by the Philippines in its submissions No. 1 and 2. This notable silence on historic title in China's legal response to the Arbitration case further confirms that China does not treat the nine-dash line as a line of historic title.

The impact of the South China Sea Arbitration case on China's legal claims

At this point, it is necessary to make a comparison between the PRC's original claims to the SCS in the 1950s and China's latest position on the SCS elaborated in the *Statement of Sovereignty and Maritime Right* in 2016. The difference between these two positions marks the long journey which the PRC has traveled over the past six decades, from a simple claim of sovereignty covering land features in the South China Sea to a well-structured, four-layered and multi-dimensional claim to the South China Sea.

The PRC's legal position on the SCS experienced four major developments, in the 1970s, the 1990s, 2009 and 2016, respectively (see Table 7.2). As demonstrated in previous chapters, the first three developments were all influenced by concurrent developments of the LOS regime. It was shown in Chapter 2 that the PRC's original sovereign claims to the South China Sea mainly focused on land features. Beijing classified these land features into four groups of islands – Dongsha Qundao, Xisha Qundao, Zhongsha Qundao, and Nansha Qundao. The government did not pay much attention to or carefully think through, in legal terms, what the vast area of waters enclosed in the dashed line meant to its South China Sea claims, nor did the government invoke the line to justify or support its legal claims.

Beijing began to expand its legal claims in the SCS to include "adjacent waters" in the 1970s, a move informed by its participation in the UNCLOS III Conference. China's claims to the SCS experienced substantial development in the 1990s, when the government promulgated two pieces of national legislation: the Law on Territorial Sea and the Law on EEZ and CS in 1998. The legislation introduced two changes to China's legal claims. One is the incorporation of the regimes of the Territorial Sea, the Contiguous Zone, the EEZ, and the CS. The other change is the mentioning of China's historical rights.

Table 7.2 Four major legal developments of China's SCS claims

Period	*Claims of sovereignty to land features*	*Maritime Claims (sovereign and jurisdictional rights)*	*Claims to historical rights*	*Dashed line*
1. 1950s	yes	Territorial seas of 12 nautical miles	N/A	Not invoked
2. 1970s	yes	Adjacent sea areas, natural resources, nearby waters	N/A	Not invoked
3. 1990s	yes	Contiguous Zones, Exclusive Economic Zones, Continental Shelf	A general claim	Not invoked
4. 2009	yes	Sovereign rights and jurisdiction over the relevant waters as well as the seabed and subsoil thereof	Not explicit	Officially invoked by submission to the UN
5. 2013-	yes	CZ, EEZ, CS and internal waters (treating each island group as a whole for measurement)	Explicit assertion in the SCS	Invoked in the 2016 Statement of Sovereignty and Maritime Rights

These two changes, as analyzed in Chapter 5, were the product of Beijing's two-stage efforts to reconstruct its legal position in the context of the UNCLOS, which it ratified in 1996. The first step, China accepted the LOSC as the legal basis for its SCS claims and internalized the Convention through a series of domestic legislation. The second step, in face of the potential negative impact of the UNCLOS on its legal position, China came up with a legal solution – adding a new claim of historic rights – to strengthen its position.

The third stage of development of China's legal claims to the SCS was unfolded in 2009, marked by China's submission to the UN of the dashed line map along with a Note Verbale explaining its legal position. It was China's first official attempt at invoking the line to develop and support its SCS claims in light of the UNCLOS. As discussed in Chapter 6, China's submission was an immediate response aroused by Vietnam's and Malaysia's submissions on the limits of continental shelf in the SCS. While this move was consistent with and formed an integral part of Beijing's continuous efforts to reconstruct its legal position on the SCS, the timing of this move was directly triggered by the deadline for filing continental shelf applications set by the UNCLOS. However, during this stage, no further attempts were made by the Chinese government to specify how the EEZ and CS in the SCS should be determined. The government also left it speculative as to what kind of historical rights were claimed and whether they were applicable to the SCS.

Finally, legal deliberations made by the Chinese government from 2013 to 2016 in response to the Arbitration case brought the two latest developments in China's SCS claims. One development is, for the first time, Beijing clarified that each of the four island groups should be treated as a whole when measuring maritime entitlements, including the territorial sea, the contiguous zone, the EEZ, and the CS. This would also mean that China claimed internal waters in at least some, if not all, of the four island groups. The second development is related to the claim of historical rights. When China asserted historical rights in the 1990s, it was quite a general claim. It was unclear whether historical rights were applicable in the SCS. In the 2016 Statement of Sovereignty and Maritime Rights, China explicitly asserted historical rights in the SCS.

Similar to previous legal developments, China's latest move to assert and clarify its SCS claims is the result of the functioning of the LOSC regime into which China found itself, like it or not, deeply locked. As analyzed earlier in this chapter, the move was made under direct pressure of a series of critical dates spinning off from the operation of Annex XII, a compulsory dispute settlement procedure in the LOS Convention initiated by the Philippines. In the meantime, these two developments outlined above amount to the latest attempt by the Beijing government to reconstruct and balance its SCS claims in the context the UNCLOS.

Political engagement in the post-2013 period

In the post-2013 period, a combination of geopolitical dynamics and the normative pressure arising from the South China Sea Arbitration case gave a new boost to the multilateral mechanisms of political engagement among China, the ASEAN and other concerned parties. In particular, China upscaled its degree of engagement with the ASEAN concerning the implementation of the DOC, the process of which yielded the China-ASEAN agreement on a formal framework of Code of Conduct in June 2017.[20]

As explored in Chapter 6, starting in 2009, geopolitical dynamics stirred up by the Obama Administration through the so-called "Asia rebalancing" strategy added new weight to the multilateral institutional architecture concerning maritime issues in the SCS, pressurizing China to make further commitment to its participation in it. Consequently, China started to formally work with the ASEAN as a group on implementing the DOC. During the 2011 ARF held in Bali, Indonesia, China and the ASEAN countries agreed on the Guidelines on the Implementation of the DOC, including the negotiation on a COC.

In the post-2013 period, geopolitical tensions continued to escalate. First, the USA and Japan intensified their efforts to consolidate the US-Japan alliance and the US-led security network in Asia. The Abe administration published *The National Security Strategy* in 2013, in which the US-Japan alliance was highlighted as a core element of Japan's security policy. In October 2013, the USA and Japan started negotiations on a new *Guidelines for U.S.-Japan Defense Cooperation* to replace the 2002 *Guidelines for U.S.-Japan Defense Cooperation*. This new revision aimed at gearing up deterrence by establishing seamless defense cooperation, intelligence sharing and co-development of defense equipment between the USA and Japan.[21] To strengthen the US-led alliance network in Asia, Japan began to participate in a number of major military exercises held by the USA and its Asian allies. For instance, in 2014 alone, Japan joined PHIBLEX, previously a bilateral amphibious landing exercise between the USA and the Philippines,[22] and participated in the Pacific-Partnership in 2014, a multilateral exercise of humanitarian assistance, in which it transported a group of the US-Australian joint force to the SCS region.[23] The USA. and Japan also actively expanded maritime cooperation with regional countries outside the US-led alliance system. Since 2013, the USA has increased its defense engagement in Vietnam and Indonesia and contributed, financially and materially, to the military build-up of these two countries. In 2014, the Obama Administration lifted the arms embargo to Vietnam and later fully removed it in 2016.[24] Japan soon followed suit, donating patrol boats and vessels to Vietnam and Indonesia and providing training and technology transfer to help these two countries with capacity building in the maritime domain.[25] These activities aimed at strengthening cooperation among the US security alliance in Asia were viewed by China as intending to counter and contain China.

Second, in the post-2013 period, other extra-regional countries like Australia and India sought to exert greater influence in the SCS, raising alarm in China about their possible cooperation with the USA in containing China. As a traditional ally of the USA., Australia increased its presence in the SCS and deepened its ties with the USA and other US allies. India is another extra-regional country showing a strong interest in the SCS. In particular, the Modi government actively sought cooperative opportunities with Vietnam in the SCS. For example, in October 2014, during the Indian Prime Minister's visit to Vietnam, the two countries agreed to cooperate through their national energy companies, the Oil and Natural Gas Corporation of India and Petro-Vietnam, to conduct joint development of oil and gas in two designated blocks in the SCS. The deal was later renewed in July 2017.[26] Besides energy cooperation, India was also keen to expand its security ties with Vietnam and other regional countries and intensified defense cooperation with extra-regional countries, in particular, the United States and Japan. In the post-2013 period, India has conducted several joint naval drills with Vietnam in the SCS and offered financial aid and defense equipment to support Vietnam's defense build-up. In September 2016, India and Vietnam concluded an agreement which allowed India to build four high-speed patrol vessels for the Vietnam Coast Guard and offer US$500 million credit to assist Vietnam's defense procurement from India.[27] In the meantime, India actively sought to tighten cooperation with the USA and Japan. A good example is the Malabar exercise. The Malabar exercise was traditionally a bilateral exercise between India and the USA. Japan participated in this exercise a few years ago and in consideration of the protest from China, India rejected Japan's request to participate in the following years. However, the Modi administration changed this position and granted Japan a seat as an observer in the Malabar exercise in 2014 despite China's strong protest. Starting in 2015, Japan became a permanent participant in the Malabar exercise, turning this bilateral exercise into a trilateral one.[28] In 2017, the trilateral Malabar exercise, involving carriers from each of the three navies, focused on anti-submarine warfare, which seems to suggest a posture against China's growing submarine capabilities.[29] In China's view, the move was a clear signal of the Modi government's desire and willingness to join the USA and Japan in forging a defense alliance to contain China.

Third, on the part of China, a number of controversial policies were initiated in the SCS in the post-2013 period, further escalating tensions in the region. The most controversial policy carried out in the SCS by the Chinese government was land reclamation projects on seven features in the Spratly area that are under China's control. These include the Subi, Mischief, Gaven, Johnson, Cuarteron, Fiery Cross and McKennan Reefs. The project started in 2013 and by July 2015, most of the land reclamation construction works were completed.[30] It is estimated that about 3.9 million square meters of land have been reclaimed. On these reclaimed features are new facilities and equipment have been constructed, such as wooden barracks, communications arrays, and helipads and airstrips. China's decision to undertake these constructions at an unprecedented pace rang alarm bells among regional countries as well as extra-regional countries. The USA and Japan, on many multilateral and international diplomatic occasions, criticized China's action as destabilizing and changing the status quo of the geostrategic theater in the SCS. For example, during the 2015 G7 summit, participant countries, under the coordinated pressure of the USA and Japan, "strongly opposed … any unilateral actions that seek to change the status quo, such as large scale land reclamation."[31] The USA and Japan perceived China's construction as intending to militarize these features. The Ministry of Defense of Japan for the first time published a White Paper in 2015 on "China's Activities in the South China Sea," in which Japan highlighted the possibility of militarization on China's reclaimed lands in the Spratly islands.[32] The tensions revolving around China's reclamation activities hiked up when the USA decided to conduct what it called "Freedom of Navigation Operations" (FONOPs) in the SCS. In October 2015, the guided-missile destroyer *USS Lassen* transited inside 12 nautical miles of five maritime features in the Spratly Islands – Subi Reef, Northeast Cay, Southwest Cay, South Reef, and Sandy Cay – to directly challenge China's claim of territorial limits around the Subi Reef.[33] In response, the Chinese authorities monitored, followed and warned the US warship *USS Lassen* and summoned the US ambassador to protest.[34]

These geopolitical dynamics in the post-2013 period further fueled suspicion and concern in China. In the view of many scholars, the increasing presence of extra-regional countries and their deepened cooperation with regional countries in the SCS are directed towards an emerging alliance of containment against China.[35] This concern certainly put pressure on China to rethink its

SCS policy and its political engagement. Consequently, in front of China were two choices, staying in the multilateral architecture of political engagement, or walking away from it.

As it turned out, China chose to stay in, rather than walking away from, the multilateral architecture of political engagement, in which it has been involved for over two decades. From 2013 on, the Chinese government demonstrated greater dedication to the China-ASEAN mechanisms regarding the implementation of the DOC and expedited the negotiation on a formally binding COC. In August 2014, when attending the China-ASEAN Foreign Ministers' Meeting, Chinese Foreign Minister Wang Yi proposed a "dual-track approach" in managing the SCS issues. The "dual-track" approach envisioned: (1) relevant disputes being addressed by countries directly concerned through friendly consultations and negotiations in a peaceful way; and (2) peace and stability in the South China Sea being jointly maintained by China and the ASEAN countries.[36] This approach was later confirmed by Chinese Premier Li Keqiang during the ASEAN summit series held in November 2014.[37]

Negotiations on the implementation of the DOC by China and the ASEAN are conducted through two interlinked venues: one is the China-ASEAN Joint Working Group (JWG on DOC), the other is the China-ASEAN Senior Officials' Meeting on the implementation of the DOC (SOM on DOC). As illustrated in Table 7.3 and Table 7.4, negotiations on the implementation of the DOC between China and the ASEAN accelerated in the post-2013 period. The first China-ASEAN Senior Officials' Meeting on the implementation of the DOC was convened in 2004. Between 2004 and 2012, there were only five

Table 7.3 Chronology of meetings of SOM on DOC

Year	*SOM on DOC*	*Location*
2004	1st SOM	Malaysia
2007	2nd SOM	China
2011	3rd SOM	Indonesia
2012	4th SOM (January) 5th SOM (June)	China Vietnam
2013	6th SOM	China
2014	7th SOM (April) 8th SOM (October)	Thailand Thailand
2015	9th SOM (July) 10th SOM (October)	China China
2016	11th SOM (April) 12th SOM (June) 13th SOM (August)	Singapore Vietnam China
2017	14th SOM	China

Table 7.4 Chronology of meetings of JWG on DOC

Year	*JWG on DOC*	*Location*
2005–2011	1st–5th JWG	
2011	6th JWG	Indonesia
2012	7th JWG (January) 8th JWG (June)	China Vietnam
2013	9th JWG	China
2014	10th JWG (March) 11th JWG (June) 12th JWG (October)	Singapore Indonesia Thailand
2015	13th JWG (March) 14th JWG (July) 15th JWG (October)	Cambodia Malaysia China
2016	16th JWG (March) 17th JWG (June) 18th JWG (August)	the Philippines Vietnam China
2017	19th JWG (February) 20th JWG (March) 21st JWG (May)	Indonesia Cambodia China

SOM on DOC meetings. In contrast, from 2013 to 2017, China and the ASEAN convened nine SOM on DOC meetings, three taking place in 2016.

A similar pattern is identified in the China-ASEAN Joint Working Group meetings (see Table 7.4), which are the preparatory meetings for the SOM on DOC. The first JWG on DOC meetings was held in 2005. Of all the 21 JWG on DOC meetings, 13 meetings were convened in the post-2013 period.

China's dedication to political engagement was also reflected in the positive result of these engagement activities. Since 2013, China and the ASEAN have held a number of seminars on issues related to regional marine studies, freedom of navigation in the SCS, marine disaster prevention and mitigation, marine surveillance technology, and marine ecology and biodiversity in the SCS. China and the ASEAN also worked on the establishment of three technical committees on search and rescue (SAR), combating transnational crime and marine scientific research and environment protection.[38] Two hotlines have been set up as part of the Early Harvest Measures – the Hotline Platform on Search and Rescue among China and the ASEAN Member States and the Senior Officials' Hotline Platform in Response to Maritime Emergencies among Ministries of Foreign Affairs of China and ASEAN Member States. Other Early Harvest Measures regarding the implementation of DOC included the Table-Top Exercise of SAR among China and ASEAN Member States.[39] In addition, China and the ASEAN are preparing an Eminent Persons and Experts Group to support the official consultations.[40]

The most prominent fruit yielded from the political consultations concerning the implementation of the DOC is the agreement on the framework text of the COC concluded in May 2017. Official negotiation on COC kicked off during the 6th SOM on DOC held in Suzhou, China, in 2013. After two rounds of SOM on DOC negotiations, China and the ASEAN agreed on the first list of Commonalities in Developing the COC during the 8th SOM on DOC in August 2014. In July 2015, parties to the 9th SOM on DOC agreed that, by concluding the second list of Commonalities for the COC consultations, the consultation had entered a new stage. In the 10th SOM on DOC, delegations from China and the ASEAN discussed and formulated two preliminary leaving documents, namely, the list of crucial and complex issues and the list of elements for the outline of a COC, and mandated the JWG to further review and study the two lists.[41]

China and the ASEAN further hastened the COC consultation in the second half of 2016. On July 25, 2016, China and the ASEAN issued the *Joint Statement of the Foreign Ministers of ASEAN Member States and China on the Full and Effective Implementation of the Declaration on the Conduct of Parties in the South China Sea*, in which China and the ASEAN reaffirmed that "the adoption of a code of conduct in the South China Sea would further promote peace and stability in the region and agree to work, on the basis of consensus, towards the eventual attainment of this objective."[42] During the 13th SOM on DOC held in August 2016, one month following the issuance of the Tribunal's final award on the South China Sea Arbitration case, vice foreign ministers from China and the ASEAN countries agreed to speed up consultations on the COC. During the meeting, Liu Zhenmin, the Chinese Vice Foreign Minister, pledged China's commitment to a draft COC framework to be completed by mid-2017. The meeting adopted two outcome documents, *Guidelines for Hotline Communications among Senior Officials of the Ministers of Foreign Affairs of ASEAN Member States and China in Response to Maritime Emergencies at Sea* and *Joint Statement on the Application of the <Code for Unplanned Encounters at Sea> in the South China Sea*. The latter was officially issued during the China-ASEAN Summit in September 2016. In March 2017, China and the ASEAN reached a consensus on the first draft of the framework for the COC during the 20th JWG on DOC. The draft text was officially approved during the 14th SOM on DOC in May 2017, which is a crucial step closer to the conclusion of a COC.

The aforementioned efforts taken by China to uphold its commitment to the political architecture of the maritime regime cannot be attributed to the rising geopolitical pressure alone. As demonstrated in previous chapters, geostrategic pressure alone does not necessarily lead to China's engagement or compliance with the maritime regime. For example, in the period 2008–2012, the US strategic adjustment in the Asia-Pacific introduced new dynamics into the geopolitical environment in the SCS and gave a jump-start to the DOC implementation process in the regional political arena. However, when the geostrategic pressure in the SCS continued to simmer to the brink of serious confrontation, as reflected in the case of the Scarborough Shoal Incident, the COC negotiation stalled. In other words, there is always the possibility that rising geostrategic pressure may backfire and obstruct the political engagement process when China feels the pressure is too much to bear and forcing it to a corner. Indeed, to a large extent, China's decision to undertake reclamation activities in the SCS on features under its control is a counter-weight move to the increasing pressure imposed by the changing geostrategic environment.

In the post-2013 period, while geopolitical dynamics maintained a high pressure on China to carefully tread the path of political engagement, it is the lock-in effect of the maritime regime that glued China to the institutions of political engagement in which it had participated for more than two decades, and it is the normative pressure generated by the proceedings of the South China Arbitration case that forced China to uphold its commitment to political consultations and upgrade its attempts at engagement. As regards the lock-in effect, similar to what we observed in the 2008–2012 period, the fact that China chose to stay in the multilateral architecture of political engagement despite rising challenges from the regional countries in coordination with extra-regional countries is a vivid illustration of the resilience effect of the multilateral political architecture of the maritime regime with which China found itself deeply intertwined. China has been locked into this architecture to such an extent that it is inappropriate and unthinkable to opt out.

The South China Sea Arbitration case generated additional normative pressure on China to deepen its political engagement with the regional countries concerning the SCS dispute. As analyzed earlier in this chapter, China adopted a position of non-acceptance and non-participation regarding this Arbitration case. Despite this position, Chinese calculated all the responses to the Arbitration case to fit into the legal framework set out in Part XV of the UNCLOS and consciously undertook a series of political actions to support and strengthen its legal argumentation. According to China's Position Paper, published in December 2014, the legal reasoning behind this position was elaborated on three pillars: (1) the exclusion of jurisdiction over territorial sovereignty from compulsory settlement procedures; (2) the exclusion of jurisdiction over maritime delimitation from compulsory settlement procedures; and (3) the agreement between China and the Philippines on settling disputes through political negotiations. To support and fulfill with actual practice the third pillar of its argument – settling disputes through political negotiations – the Chinese government upgraded its dedication and commitment to the political engagement concerning the implementation of the DOC and concluded with the ASEAN the framework text for the COC.

Maritime governance practices

In the post-2013 period, China's marine governance in the SCS continued to concentrate on two tasks: (1) transferring the practices of international marine governance into its maritime legislation and governance in the SCS; and (2) using marine governance practices to consolidate its sovereignty and jurisdiction over the claimed waters in the SCS.

In recent years, the LOS regime developed a number of multilateral maritime treaties and instruments governing activities related to the world's oceans, which were quickly transferred into Chinese domestic legislation. For example, the International Labor Organization promulgated the *Maritime Labour Convention 2006*, a single, coherent instrument embodying up-to-date standards of labour protection for seafarers.[43] This Convention entered into force in August 20, 2013. Nine days later, the National Peoples' Congress of China approved the ratification of this Convention.[44]

As regards practices of marine governance, the State Oceanic Administration prioritized three issues areas – management of maritime space and islands, marine environment protection, and maritime law enforcement.[45] These three areas are chosen to promote the development of the maritime space and, at the same time, reinforce state sovereignty and jurisdiction over the seas. For the management of maritime space and islands, the Chinese government enacted *Island Protection Law of the People's Republic of China* in 2009. Since then, the government has enhanced the protection of offshore islands and invested heavily in improving environment surveillance, economic development and infrastructure on these islands. In 2016, the SOA published the *Statistical Communiqué of the People's Republic of China on Offshore Islands*, compiling information on the scientific studies of the conditions on offshore islands and the implementation of protection measures of islands.[46]

In the area of marine environment protection, the SOC promulgated the *Opinion Paper on Establishing and Implementing the Marine Eco-Redline System,* along with *The Technical Guidelines for the Delimitation of the Marine Eco-Redline* in 2016. The Marine Eco-Redline system was established in the background of growing awareness at both the government and public levels about the serious challenge imposed by marine environmental degradation in China's surrounding seas. According to the bills proposed by delegations of the National People's Congress, land-based pollution has been identified as a major source of marine pollution and set as the primary area to tackle.[47] Protection of environment protection was also carried out through multilateral cooperation, such as the aforementioned seminars on marine biodiversity and ecosystems co-organized by SCS countries.

What is worth noting is the active role of the Chinese epistemic community in assessing and dealing with the potential environmental impact of the government's reclamation activities. In Chapter 5, it was illustrated that interactions with relevant international organizations in the LOS regime cultivated knowledge of marine environment protection and infused a sense of cooperation in the Chinese epistemic community, which later became ardent supporters of integrating these norms and knowledge into China's marine governance practices. This time, when confronted with the challenges to the marine environment surrounding the Spratly features under China's reclamation construction, Chinese marine scientists offered quite diversified yet candid and objective observations and assessments. Some Chinese marine scientists, after conducting a scientific survey on the reclaimed features, pointed out that the negative impact on marine environment should not be exaggerated, for construction works were mostly carried out on the rim of dead reefs, leaving the live ones largely intact.[48] Some scientists criticized the government for not conducting an environmental impact assessment report (EIA report) before the construction, thus failing to fulfill its international obligation.[49] Other scientists, using their political leverage as delegations to the People's Congress in Sansha city, urged the government to take measures to restore and rebuild the marine environment as friendly to the reproduction of coral reefs and other species.[50] These efforts demonstrated that the Chinese epistemic community had internalized the norms, standards, and practices of the LOS regime and, this time without external pressure, consciously pushed for the effective implementation in Chinese marine practices of these norms, rules and popular practices of the LOS regime.

In the post-2013 period, law enforcement activities continued to be employed by China as an effective tool for consolidating China's sovereign and jurisdictional rights in the SCS. As mentioned in Chapter 6, China started to regularize law enforcement patrols in the SCS in 2008. In recent years, the Chinese government gradually increased financial, personnel, and other policy support to develop a modernized air-sea coordinative law enforcement system.[51] In the meantime, faced with the challenge posed by the Arbitration case, China used law enforcement activities as a flexible tool to defend its maritime interests in the SCS. For example, in December 2014, the government of Hainan Province promulgated a new amendment to implement the *Fisheries Law of the People's Republic of China*, tightening control over fishing activities by foreigners and fishing boats in waters designated as under Hainan's jurisdiction.[52] In August 2016, China's Supreme Court issued a regulation concerning the judicial interpretation of China's jurisdiction over its territorial seas, a legal means to nullify the Tribunal's verdict on the South China Sea. Under the same consideration, the scope of China's law enforcement activities has been expanded from purely law enforcement to humanitarian assistance and marine environment protection in the SCS, as a way to demonstrate to the international community that, as a responsible power and a signatory to the DOC, China is committed to fulfilling its obligations such as humanitarian assistance and advancing regional welfare in the SCS. For example, in November 2016, the Chinese Coast Guard 3501 picked up two Filipino fishermen whose fishing boat had run aground.[53] The Aerial Law Enforcement Group of the South China Sea Division of China Marine Surveillance carried out a series of scientific survey and reconnaissance activities on the mangroves in the SCS, in an attempt to support marine environment protection projects in the SCS.[54]

Best practices: joint development and more

In the post-2013 period, discussions on possible solutions to the SCS disputes, including tentative arrangements pending the final resolution, continued to be aimed at the idea of joint development. In the meantime, this period also witnessed the emergence of some new proposals drawn from China's accumulated experience and knowledge of global maritime governance.

At the government level, in spite of rising tensions in the region, the Chinese government continued to express their faith in joint development as a preferable tentative arrangement for managing the SCS dispute. The Chinese leaders used many bilateral and international occasions to reaffirm and reassure their commitment to promoting joint development projects in the SCS. For example, during his official visit to Brunei in October 2013, Chinese Premier Li Keqiang and his Brunei counterpart issued a *Joint Statement between the PRC and Brunei Darussalam*, in which the two countries agreed to increase maritime cooperation and promote joint development. In this Statement, joint development is touted as a practical path towards exploring the resolution of the SCS dispute and conducive to maintaining peace and stability in the region.[55]

The post-2013 period witnessed some progress in pushing for the implementation of joint development projects in disputed areas in the SCS, thanks to the normative pressure generated by the Arbitration case on China to live up to its promises and its commitment to the joint development proposal which was first brought up by China in the 1980s. On July 13, 2016, the day after the Tribunal delivered the final award on the SCS Arbitration case, the Chinese government issued a statement entitled "China Adheres to the Position of Settling Through Negotiation the Relevant Disputes Between China and the Philippines in the South China Sea." In this statement. China pointed out that in April 1988, when meeting with Philippine President Corazón Aquino, Deng Xiaoping proposed that "for the sake of the friendship between our two countries, we can shelve the issue for now and pursue joint development." China claimed that it would continue to pursue joint development and make every effort to explore joint development projects in areas such as fishery, oil and gas, so as to uphold peace and stability in the South China Sea region and create conditions for the final settlement of disputes[56]

As to concrete projects of joint development, the most recent progress was made by China and the Philippines through a bilateral consultation mechanism established in early 2017. In January 2017, China and the Philippines reached a consensus on establishing a bilateral consultation mechanism to directly negotiate on their disputes concerning the SCS. In May 2017, back to back with the 13th SOM on DOC meeting, the China-Philippines Bilateral Consultation Mechanism (BCM) was officially established and the first meeting of the BCM was convened. During this meeting, the two countries exchanged views on current and other issues of concern and discussed the promotion of next-step practical maritime cooperation and the possible establishment of relevant technical working groups. The meeting also explored the possibility of joint development projects in the SCS.[57] It was decided during the meeting that the BCM would be convened every 6 months. A few days after the BCM meeting, Philippine President Rodrigo Duterte's special envoy Jose de Venecia Jr, while attending the One Belt and One Road Forum[58] in Beijing, proposed the joint development of oil and natural gas resources by China and the Southeast

Asian countries in the disputed South China Sea.[59] Philippine President Duterte, after returning from the One Belt and One Road Forum, also announced that he was open to restoring an earlier agreement with China and Vietnam for joint development of the rich resources in the South China Sea.[60] As discussed in Chapter 5, this trilateral agreement was reached in 2005 to conduct a seismic survey in the SCS, a three-year project as a preparatory step to joint development and exploitation of resources. On July 24, 2017, right before Chinese Foreign Minister Wang Yi's official visit to the Philippines, Duterte mentioned in his State of the Nation Address that the Philippines and China were working on entering a joint exploration agreement regarding natural gas deposits in the disputed South China Sea.[61] Undoubtedly, negotiating details of such a joint development agreement would top the agenda during Wang Yi's visit to Manila starting on July 25, 2017.

At the academic level, Chinese scholars' enthusiasm on joint development and related issues goes on unabated in the post-2013 period. A wide range of issues related to joint development has been explored. The main issues include a legal framework and principles, the role of third parties, international practices and cases of joint development, situating joint development in the SCS in the context of the One Belt and One Road initiative, site-choosing for joint development projects, and choosing resources type for joint development.[62] In the meantime, some new proposals have emerged to manage and resolve the SCS dispute. In particular, the Mediterranean Sea governance model, the Antarctic governance Model and the Arctic Model have been proposed by Chinese scholars. These new proposals are inspired by the experience and knowledge accumulated through China's participation in the global maritime regime. For instance, one proposal is that the SCS governance may follow the model of Arctic governance. China has long expressed a strong interest in participating in the Arctic governance and, after years of engagement, was accepted as observer in the Arctic Council in 2013 along with India, Italy, Japan, South Korea, and Singapore. Supported by the government, the Arctic governance model and the implications of the observer status have been thoroughly studied in Chinese scholarship.[63] It was China's experience in the Arctic governance that inspired Chinese scholars to assess the Arctic Model and its applicability in resolving the SCS dispute.

The Arctic governance is dominated by the Arctic Council, a high level inter-governmental forum composed of eight Arctic-bordering countries (Canada, the Kingdom of Denmark, Finland, Iceland, Norway, the Russian Federation, Sweden, and the United States), six indigenous permanent participant organizations, and observers. Observer status in the Arctic Council is open to non-Arctic states, along with inter-governmental, inter-parliamentary, global, regiona, and non-governmental organizations that can contribute to the work. Arctic Council Observers primarily contribute through their engagement in the Council at the level of Working Groups.[64] Gao Zhiguo, a leading Chinese scholar on LOS, suggests that the SCS region may draw from the Arctic experience and establish the South China Sea Cooperation Council.

He proposes that in terms of organization design, the SCS Cooperation Council might be composed of member states and observers. Similar to the Arctic Council, member states are countries bordering the SCS. Observer status can be granted to other countries in the SCS region and later on may expand to include other extra-regional countries as well as inter-governmental and non-governmental organizations. In his view, in the beginning, the SCS Cooperation Council may be designed to meet for member states' cooperation once a year and hold ministerial-level meetings every two years. For concrete cooperation activities, Gao suggests the SCS Cooperation Council establish five working groups on: (1) marine environment protection working group; (2) joint development working group; (3) confidence building measures working group; (4) sustainable development working group; and (5) prevention and emergency response working group.[65]

Analysis

In the post-2013 period, the LOS regime exerted its influence in shaping China's SCS policy through a number of ways. With regard to China's legal claims to the SCS, the proceedings of the South China Sea Arbitration case generated direct pressure on China to rethink and reconstruct its legal position on the SCS dispute. This pressure has two major components. One component is the pressure of deadlines to which China was forced to respond (role 4 in Chapter 1). Throughout the proceedings, the Arbitral Tribunal set over a dozen deadlines requesting China take responsive legal actions. Consequently, the Chinese government carefully formulated its responses and articulated its position through sophisticated legal language in the form of Note Verbales, Ambassador's letters, press conferences and publicists' writings. More importantly, the final award of this case elicited from the Chinese government new clarifications on its legal position on the SCS. For the first time, Beijing made it an official position that the four island groups should be treated as a whole when delimiting internal waters, territorial seas, the EEZ and the CS, and that they should enjoy historical rights in the SCS.

The other component of the pressure created by the South China Sea Arbitration case is the normative pressure on China to uphold its commitment and obligations. This normative pressure is part of the lock-in effect (role 6 in Chapter 1). A locked-in country in the regime would feel it appropriate to behave in certain ways and comply with certain rules and norms, that is, acting in the "logic of appropriateness."[66] When expounding its legal reasoning for not accepting the Tribunal's jurisdiction, China offered an alternative approach – political consultations – as the preferred means to resolve its dispute with the Philippines, and called upon the Philippines to return to the negotiation table. Consequently, China felt the pressure of demonstrating to the international community its commitment to political negotiation and proving to the world the effectiveness of political negotiation in resolving the SCS dispute. This normative pressure, along with rising geopolitical tensions in the region, pushed China and other countries in the region to expedite the implementation of the DOC process, including the COC negotiation.

The impact of the LOS regime runs even deeper than what has been observed in the nuanced changes and continuity in China's legal position. China's participation in various issue-arenas of the global LOS governance regime gave the Chinese leadership and the epistemic community new knowledge, new experience, new approaches, and new ideas of marine governance and dispute management (role 5 in Chapter 1). Through decades of participation in the international maritime regime, decision-makers and policy pundits in China have gradually internalized the norms, standards, and principles developed in the LOS regime and, consequently, they become self-conscious in complying and implementing them in China's policy practices. As we have seen in this chapter, China's participation in Arctic governance inspired the Chinese epistemic community to consider the possible application of the Arctic Model to the SCS governance. China's marine scientists, in the absence of direct external pressure, judged China's land reclamation activities against the norms and standards of marine environment protection.

Indeed, it is this internalization of these LOS norms, principles, and the maritime order that has kept intact China's faith in UNCLOS at a time when the negative effect of UNCLOS on China's maritime interests was greatly augmented by the SCS Arbitration case. The South China Sea Arbitration case presented a critical test of the lock-in effect/resilience of the LOS regime (role 6 in Chapter 1). This case evoked a heated debate in China among policy practitioners and the general public concerning the legitimacy and effectiveness of the UNCLOS. In the wake of the issuance of the final award, national sentiment against the UNCLOS quickly arose. Many questioned the fairness of the UNCLOS compulsory settlement regime and proposed the government undertake a complete withdrawal of China from the UNCLOS.[67] The Chinese government closely watched this sentiment and felt pressured to present a clear position to the public on this matter. During the press conference held on July 12, 2016, a journalist raised the following question: "Chinese media reports said that China might consider quitting UNCLOS if the award goes against China's interests. What is your comment on that?" In response, the Chinese Foreign Ministry spokesperson reaffirmed that China would remain in UNCLOS and emphasized that "ever since we approved UNCLOS in 1996, China have been faithfully implementing and upholding the Convention."[68]

The official position of staying in and being committed to upholding the UNCLOS was echoed by all major leading Chinese scholars on the SCS issue. For example, Wu Shicun and Zhu Feng argued that in spite of the illegitimate and unfair rulings of the SCS Arbitration case, China would not consider withdrawing from the UNCLOS. China values its nine-year contribution to the UNCLOS III and the advent of the Convention. China could and ought to play an important role in upholding and promoting order and the stability of the world's oceans as envisaged by the UNCLOS.[69] Jia Yu, a leading Chinese scholar on the LOS and Director of the China Institute for Marine Affairs under the SOA, argued that China was one of the founding states of the Convention and the modern maritime order. It has benefited from the Convention and would continue to play a constructive role in advancing world maritime welfare.[70] Many scholars considered the SCS Arbitration case an invaluable lesson for China to deepen understandings of the comprehensiveness and nuances of the UNCLOS. The Arbitration case gave rise to a booming interest in the LOS among young Chinese students of International Law in the post-2013 period.[71]

In the political arena, a trend of continuity dominated China's engagement with the regional countries, despite heightened tensions in the SCS region. In the face of rising tensions and the pressure arising from the SCS Arbitration case, China demonstrated greater commitment to political engagement, particularly to the process of the implementation of the DOC.

The post-2013 period witnessed a spike of confrontations in the geopolitical environment in the SCS. Under the US "Asia Pivot" strategy, the US-led security alliance architecture was further consolidated and diversified, turning the traditional hub-and-spoke system into a complex web of security relationships.[72] Defense exchanges and cooperation between regional countries such as Vietnam and the Philippines and extra-regional countries, including the USA, Japan, India and Australia, were tightened and quickly expanded. The Philippines' decision to initiate arbitration proceedings caught China by surprise and made China suspect that it was a move by the USA, Japan and the Philippines as part of their containment strategy.

However, rising geopolitical pressure alone does not necessary lead to China's further commitment to political engagement. Rather, from China's perspective, it reinforced China's growing suspicion of a containment circle being forged by the USA and its allies in the SCS. This growing suspicion threatened to put a sudden stop to the COC negotiation in 2013. What gave the negotiation process a renewed boost was the progress of the SCS Arbitration case. The case effectively pressured China and created a sense of urgency within the Chinese leadership to demonstrate to the international community its commitment to deepening engagement and cooperation through political consultations regarding the SCS dispute.

In conclusion, the SCS situation in the post-2013 period was driven by two sources of influence: geopolitical dynamics and the unfolding of the SCS Arbitration case. Decades of active participation in the international maritime regime not only showed the Chinese decision-makers and the epistemic community the relevant knowledge, norms, principles and standards of modern maritime governance but also cultivated a perspective of a global maritime power in which China started to reconsider and recalculate its maritime interests and related practices.

Notes

1 Government of the Republic of the Philippines, *Notification*, available at: www.gov.ph/documents/20147/151042/20130122-Notification-and-Statement-of-Claim

-on-West-Philippine-Sea.pdf/abb0b2eb-1749-e006-ceb5-7d212ef27fa4?version=1.0andpreviewFileIndex=1, and *Statement of Claim*, www.gov.ph/documents/20147/151042/20130122-Notification-and-Statement-of-Claim-on-West-Philippine-Sea.pdf/abb0b2eb-1749-e006-ceb5-7d212ef27fa4?version=1.0andpreviewFileIndex=2 (accessed July 31, 2017).

2 For the Note Verbale from the Embassy of the PRC in Manila to the Department of Foreign Affairs of the Republic of the Philippines, No. (13) PG-039, see Annex 3 of the Award on Jurisdiction and Admissibility of the South China Sea Arbitration of 29 October 2015, the whole text of the Award is available at Permanent Court of Arbitration, at: www.pcacases.com/web/sendAttach/1506 (accessed July 31, 2017).

3 Chinese Foreign Ministry, "Remarks by Foreign Ministry Spokesperson Hong Lei on the Philippines' Submission of a Memorial to the Arbitral Tribunal in Relation to Disputes with China in the South China Sea," 30 March 2014, available at: www.fmprc.gov.cn/mfa_eng/xwfw_665399/s2510_665401/2535_665405/t1142356.shtml (accessed July 31, 2017).

4 The official text of the Summary of the Position Paper is provided in Appendix D, available at Chinese Foreign Ministry, www.fmprc.gov.cn/mfa_eng/zxxx_662805/t1217149.shtml (accessed July 31, 2017).

5 Award on Jurisdiction and Admissibility of October 29, 2015, para. 56.

6 In addition, the Chinese ambassador's letter stated that the Chinese government "holds an omnibus objection to all procedural applications or steps that would require some kind of response from China." China's non-participation and non-response to any issue raised by the Tribunal "shall not be understood or interpreted by anyone in any sense as China's acquiescence in or non-objection to any and all procedural or substantive matters already or might be raised by the Arbitral Tribunal." See Award on Jurisdiction and Admissibility, para. 64.

7 Ibid., para. 68.

8 The three press conferences of the Chinese Foreign Ministry were held on the first day of the Hearing, the day after the Hearing was concluded and the day the verbatim and records of the Hearing were circulated.

9 Award on Jurisdiction and Admissibility, para. 413.

10 Chinese Foreign Ministry, *Statement of the Ministry of Foreign Affairs of the People's Republic of China on the Award on Jurisdiction and Admissibility of the South China Sea Arbitration by the Arbitral Tribunal Established at the Request of the Republic of the Philippines*, October 30, 2015, available at: www.fmprc.gov.cn/mfa_eng/zxxx_662805/t1310474.shtml (accessed July 31, 2017). The full text of this statement is provided in Appendix E.

11 See Award on the South China Sea Arbitration, para. 97. The whole text is available at Permanent Court of Arbitration, https://pcacases.com/web/sendAttach/2086 (accessed July 31, 2017).

12 Chinese Foreign Ministry, "Foreign Ministry Spokesperson Hua Chunying's Regular Press Conference," May 20, 2016, available at: www.fmprc.gov.cn/mfa_eng/xwfw_665399/s2510_665401/2511_665403/t1365237.shtml (accessed July 31, 2017).

13 Chinese Foreign Ministry, "Foreign Ministry Spokesperson Hua Chunying's Remarks on Relevant Issue about Taiping Dao," June 3, 2016, available at: www.fmprc.gov.cn/mfa_eng/xwfw_665399/s2510_665401/2535_665405/t1369189.shtml (accessed July 31, 2017).

14 Chinese Foreign Ministry, "The Tribunal's Award in the 'South China Sea Arbitration' Initiated by the Philippines Is Null and Void," June 10, 2016, available at: www.fmprc.gov.cn/mfa_eng/zxxx_662805/t1371363.shtml (accessed July 31, 2017).

15 Chinese Foreign Ministry, *Statement of the Ministry of Foreign Affairs of the People's Republic of China on the Award of 12 July 2016 of the Arbitral Tribunal in the South China Sea Arbitration Established at the Request of the Republic of the*

Philippines, July 12, 2016, available at: www.fmprc.gov.cn/mfa_eng/zxxx_662805/t1379492.shtml (accessed July 31, 2017). The full text of the Statement on the Award is provided in Appendix F.

16 Chinese Foreign Ministry, *Statement of the Government of the People's Republic of China on China's Territorial Sovereignty and Maritime Rights and Interests in the South China Sea*, July 12, 2016, available at: www.fmprc.gov.cn/mfa_eng/zxxx_662805/t1379493.shtml (accessed July 31, 2017). The full text of the 2016 Statement of Sovereignty and Maritime Rights is provided in Appendix G.

17 See Part II of the Position Paper.

18 See Part IV of the Position Paper.

19 "Foreign Ministry Spokesperson Hua Chunying's Remarks on Relevant Issue about Taiping Dao."

20 "China, ASEAN Countries Agree on COC framework," *Xinhua News*, May 18, 2017, available at: http://news.xinhuanet.com/english/2017-05/18/c_136295814.htm (accessed July 31, 2017).

21 See Ministry of Foreign Affairs of Japan, *The Interim Report on the Revision of the Guidelines for Japan-U.S. Defense Cooperation*, available at: www.mofa.go.jp/files/000055169.pdf (accessed July 31, 2017).

22 "SDF Observes Island Defense Exercise in Philippines, Aimed at Countering China," *Asahi Shimbun*, October 3, 2014, available at: http://ajw.asahi.com/article/behind_news/politics/AJ201410030061 (accessed July 31, 2017).

23 US Navy, "Pacific Partnership 2014 Kicks Off in Vietnam," June 6, 2014, available at: www.navy.mil/submit/display.asp?story_id=81496 (accessed July 31, 2017).

24 "United States Lifts Vietnam Arms Embargo," *The Diplomat*, October 3, 2014, http://thediplomat.com/2014/10/united-states-lifts-vietnam-arms-embargo-with-a-catch/ (accessed July 31, 2017).

25 Martin Petty, "Japan Offers Vessels to Vietnam to Boost Its Sea Strength," *Reuters*, August 1, 2014, available at: www.reuters.com/article/2014/08/01/us-vietnam-japan-idUSKBN0G13EA20140801; CogitAsia of CSIS, "Japan's Pivot Should Be Sustained: View from Southeast Asia," October 8, 2013, available at: http://cogitasia.com/japans-pivot-should-be-sustained-view-from-southeast-asia/ (accessed July 31, 2017).

26 "'Strategic Move': Vietnam Renews India Oil Deal in Tense South China Sea," *Times of India*, July 6, 2017, available at: http://timesofindia.indiatimes.com/business/india-business/strategic-move-vietnam-renews-india-oil-deal-in-tense-south-china-sea/articleshow/59478405.cms (accessed July 31, 2017).

27 Ibid.

28 "India Shuns China, Allows Japan in Malabar Naval Drill," *Times of India*, July 13, 2015, available at: http://timesofindia.indiatimes.com/india/India-shuns-China-allows-Japan-in-Malabar-naval-drill/articleshow/48047379.cms (accessed July 31, 2017).

29 "India-Japan-US Malabar 2017 Naval Exercises Kick Off with Anti-Submarine Warfare in Focus," *The Diplomat*, July 10, 2017, available at: http://thediplomat.com/2017/07/india-japan-us-malabar-2017-naval-exercises-kick-off-with-anti-submarine-warfare-in-focus/ (accessed July 31, 2017).

30 Chinese Foreign Ministry, "Foreign Ministry Spokesperson Lu Kang's Remarks on Issues Relating to China's Construction Activities on the Nansha Islands and Reefs," June 16, 2015, available at: www.fmprc.gov.cn/mfa_eng/xwfw_665399/s2510_665401/2535_665405/t1273370.shtml (accessed July 31, 2017).

31 White House, *G-7 Leaders' Declaration*, June 8, 2015, available at: https://obamawhitehouse.archives.gov/the-press-office/2015/06/08/g-7-leaders-declaration (accessed July 31, 2017).

32 See the Ministry of Defense of Japan, *China's Activities in the South China Sea*, December 22, 2015, available at: www.mod.go.jp/j/approach/surround/pdf/ch_d-act_20151222e.pdf (accessed July 31, 2017).

33 The U.S. Naval Institute, "SECDEF Carter Clarifies South China Sea Freedom of Navigation Operation in Letter to McCain," January 5, 2016, available at: https://news.usni.org/2016/01/05/secdef-carter-clarifies-south-china-sea-freedom-of-naviga tion-operation-in-letter-to-mccain (accessed July 31, 2017).

34 Chinese Foreign Ministry, "Foreign Ministry Spokesperson Lu Kang's Regular Press Conference on 27 October 2015," available at: www.fmprc.gov.cn/mfa_eng/xwfw_665399/s2510_665401/t1309625.shtml (accessed July 31, 2017).

35 See, for example, Zhu Feng, ed., *In-depth Analysis of the SCS Situation – 2014* (World Affairs Publishing House, 2016), in Chinese.

36 Chinese Foreign Ministry, "Wang Yi: Handle the South China Sea Issue through the 'Dual-track' Approach," August 9, 2014, available at: www.fmprc.gov.cn/mfa_eng/zxxx_662805/t1181523.shtml (accessed July 31, 2017).

37 The State Council of the People's Republic of China, "China, ASEAN Identify Dual-track Approach to South China Sea Issue," November 13, 2014, available at: http://english.gov.cn/premier/news/2014/11/13/content_281475009489708.htm (accessed July 31, 2017).

38 Chinese Foreign Ministry, "The Sixth Senior Officials Meeting and the Ninth Joint Working Group Meeting on the Implementation of the 'Declaration on Conduct of Parties in the South China Sea' Are Held in Suzhou," September 15, 2013, available at: www.fmprc.gov.cn/mfa_eng/zxxx_662805/t1079289.shtml (accessed July 31, 2017).

39 China and ASEAN agreed on Early Harvest Measures during the 8th SOM on DOC held in October 2014 in Thailand. The Early Harvest Measures agreed also include the first text on Commonalities in Developing the COC.

40 Ministry of Foreign Affairs of the Kingdom of Thailand, "Press Releases: The 10th ASEAN-China Joint Working Group on the Implementation of the Declaration on the Conduct of Parties in the South China Sea (JWG on DOC)," March 19, 2014, available at: www.mfa.go.th/main/en/media-center/14/44171-The-10th-ASEAN-China-Joint-Working-Group-on-the-Im.html (accessed July 31, 2017).

41 Chinese Foreign Ministry, "Tenth Senior Officials Meeting on the Implementation of the Declaration on the Conduct of the Parties in the South China Sea Held in Chengdu," October 20, 2015, available at: www.fmprc.gov.cn/mfa_eng/wjbxw/t1307573.shtml (accessed July 31, 2017).

42 Chinese Foreign Ministry, *Joint Statement of the Foreign Ministers of ASEAN Member States and China on the Full and Effective Implementation of the Declaration on the Conduct of Parties in the South China Sea*, July 25, 2016, available at: www.fmprc.gov.cn/nanhai/eng/zcfg_1/t1384245.htm (accessed July 31, 2017).

43 International Labor Organization, *Maritime Labour Convention 2006*, available at: www.ilo.org/wcmsp5/groups/public/@ed_norm/@normes/documents/normativein strument/wcms_090250.pdf (accessed July 31, 2017).

44 "*Maritime Labour Convention 2006* Officially Entered into Force in China," *China Ocean Online*, November 15, 2016, available at: www.oceanol.com/content/201611/15/c59351.html (accessed July 31, 2017).

45 See State Oceanic Administration, *Focal Points for Works on National Maritime Law and Regulations 2014*, July 2, 2014, available at: www.soa.gov.cn/xw/hyyw_90/201407/t20140702_33009.html and State Oceanic Administration, *Focal Points for Works on National Maritime Law and Regulations 2016*, April 4, 2016, available at: www.soa.gov.cn/bmzz/jgbmzz2/zcfzydyqys/201604/t20160414_50947.html (accessed July 31, 2017).

46 "SOA Published the First Annual Statistical Communiqué of the People's Republic of China on Offshore Island," *China Ocean Online*, December 28, 2016, available at: www.oceanol.com/zhuanti/201612/28/c59999.html (accessed July 31, 2017).

47 "Marine Environment Protection Hotly Debated among Delegations to National Annual Plenary Sessions," *China Oceanic Information Network*, March 13, 2017, available at: www.coi.gov.cn/news/guonei/201703/t20170313_35380.html (accessed July 31, 2017).

48 Interview with Dr. Ge Chendong, Deputy Director of Department of Coastal and Marine Science, School of Geographic and Oceanographic Sciences, Nanjing University, Nanjing China, May 2017.

49 Remarks made at the Seminar on the Implications of the South China Sea Arbitration Case and China's Responses held on July 25, 2016. Quoted scholars requested anonymity.

50 "Turning Coral Reefs into Colorful Underwater Marine Ranch," *Hainan Daily*, April 7, 2015, available at: http://hnrb.hinews.cn/html/2015-04/07/content_5_1.htm (accessed July 31, 2017).

51 "China Marine Surveillance SCS Corps Conducted Air-Sea Coordination Exercise," *China Ocean Online*, December 25, 2015, available at: www.oceanol.com/zhifa/201512/25/c57603.html (accessed July 31, 2017).

52 "Hainan Implemented New Regulation on SCS Fisheries, Tightening Control and Supervision," *China News*, December 19, 2014, available at: www.hi.chinanews.com/zt/2014/1219/44999.html (accessed July 31, 2017).

53 "China Marine Surveillance SCS Corps Law Enforcement Division: Marine Governance by Rule of Law and Enhancing the Reputation of China," *China Ocean Online*, February 10. 2017, available at: www.oceanol.com/zhifa/201702/10/c61252.html (accessed July 31, 2017).

54 "Watching over the South China Sea through 'Eagle Eye' – the Aerial Law Enforcement Group of the South China Sea Division of China Marine Surveillance," *China Ocean Online*, November 4, 2016, available at: www.oceanol.com/zhifa/201611/04/c59055.html (accessed July 31, 2017).

55 "Joint Statement between the PRC and Brunei Darussalam", *China News*, October 11, 2013, available at: www.chinanews.com/gn/2013/10-11/5366494.shtml (accessed July 31, 2017).

56 See Chinese Foreign Ministry, *China Adheres to the Position of Settling Through Negotiation the Relevant Disputes Between China and the Philippines in the South China Sea*, July 13, 2016, available at: www.fmprc.gov.cn/nanhai/eng/snhwtlcwj_1/t1380615.htm (accessed July 31, 2017).

57 Chinese Foreign Ministry, "Joint Press Release for the First Meeting on the China-Philippines Bilateral Consultation Mechanism on the South China Sea," May 19, 2017, available at: www.fmprc.gov.cn/mfa_eng/wjdt_665385/wshd_665389/t1463538.shtml (accessed July 31, 2017).

58 Chinese President Xi Jingping proposed the initiative of The Silk Road Economic Belt and the 21st-century Maritime Silk Road in 2013. It is often shortened to the Belt and Road initiative or OBOR. Although the initiative is often seen a quite a vague idea and so far the Chinese government has not provided a clear definition and description of this initiative. At the basic level it is safe to say that the Belt and Road initiative is a development strategy comprising a collection of interlinking trade deals and infrastructure projects throughout Eurasia and the Pacific. For brief introductions, see "Xi's Strategic Conception of 'One Belt and One Road' Has Great Significance," *China Radio International*, October 11, 2014, available at: http://english.cri.cn/12394/2014/10/11/53s847421.htm and Center for Strategic and International Studies, "Building China's 'One Belt, One Road,'" April 3, 2015, available at: www.csis.org/analysis/building-china%E2%80%99s-%E2%80%9Cone-belt-one-road%E2%80%9D (accessed July 31, 2017).

59 "De Venecia Proposes Joint Exploration, Development in Spratlys," *The Inquirer*, May 15, 2017, available at: http://globalnation.inquirer.net/156618/de-venecia-proposes-joint-exploration-development-spratlys (accessed July 31, 2017).

60 "Duterte Open to Joint Sea Exploration," *Manila Times*, May 17, 2017, available at: www.manilatimes.net/duterte-open-joint-sea-exploration/327591/ (accessed July 31, 2017).

61 "Duterte: Joint Gas Exploration Deal in Disputed Sea May Be Forged with China," *Philstar*, July 25, 2017, available at: www.philstar.com/headlines/2017/07/25/1721372/duterte-joint-gas-exploration-deal-disputed-sea-may-be-forged-china (accessed July 31, 2017).

62 See, for example, Wang Zheng, "Maritime Delimitation, Ownership and Joint Development: Exploring Concrete Proposals for Future Settlement of the South China Sea Dispute," *Asia-Pacific Security and Maritime Affairs*, no. 1 (2015): 39–51; Xu Hao, "The Realistic Dilemma and Game Theory Solution in the Joint Development of South China Sea Oil and Gas Resources," *Southeast Asian Studies*, no. 4 (2014): 18–27; Li Jinming, "An Analysis on the Prospect of China-Philippines 'Joint Development' of Reed Bank's Oil and Gas Resources," *Pacific Journal*, no. 5 (2015): 78–83; Yang Zewei, "On Identification of the Zone of Joint Development in Sea," *Present-day Law Science*, no. 3 (2014): 3–10; Sun Zelin, "Keypoint of the 21st-Century Maritime Silk Road Strategy: Joint Development in the South China Sea," *Reform and Opening*, no. 13 (2016): 5–6; Li Guoqiang, "Policy Adjustment in Resources Development in the South China Sea," *International Studies*, no. 6 (2014): 104–115; Li Guoxuan, "The Dilemma of the Joint Development of the South China Sea: A Perspective of the Supply of the Regional Public Good," *Southeast Asian Affairs*, no. 1 (2017): 84–94; Deng Yingying, "Promoting Tourism Cooperation in South China Sea with the Ocean Park as the Mode of Cooperation," *Humanities and Social Sciences Journal of Hainan University*, no. 5 (2014): 43–49; Zhang Lina, "Legal Countermeasures for Promoting Joint Development of Oil and Gas Resources in South China Sea," *The Journal of South China Sea Studies*, no. 1 (2015): 82–88. All are in Chinese.

63 For example, Guo Peiqing and Sun Kai, "'Nuuk Criteria' of the Arctic Council and China's Road to the Arctic," *World Economics and Politics*, no. 12 (2013): 118–139; Liu Huirong and Song Xin, "Fishery Legal Regulation in the Central Arctic Ocean: Status, Future, and China's Participation," *Northeast Asia Forum*, no. 4 (2016): 86–94; Xiao Yang, "Exclusivity Open: 'Monroe Doctrine' Logic of the Arctic Council," *Pacific Journal*, no. 9 (2014): 12–19; Liu Huirong, Chen Yitong and Dong Yue, "Analysis and Prospects of Legal Path in Arctic Environmental Governance," *Journal of Ocean University of China (Social Sciences Edition)*, no. 2 (2011): 1–4; Sun Kai and Zhang Yu, "Myth and Reality of Arctic Governance: Rational Thinking on Arctic Governance," *Journal of Ocean University of China (Social Sciences Edition)*, no. 3 (2016): 1–5. All are in Chinese.

64 Arctic Council, "The Arctic Council: A Backgrounder," available at: http://arctic-council.org/index.php/en/about-us (accessed July 31, 2017).

65 Gao Zhiguo, "Review and Prospect of the Security Cooperation Mechanisms in the South China Sea," *Journal of Boundary and Ocean Studies*, no. 2 (2016): 5–10, in Chinese.

66 The term "logic of appropriateness" is explained in Chapter 1. It is a term often expounded by constructivists to describe patterns of states' behavior. It stipulates that behaviors are guided by norms and identities suggesting *appropriate* action in given situations.

67 Remarks made at the Seminar on the Implications of the South China Sea Arbitration Case and China's Responses, held on July 25, 2016. Quoted scholars requested anonymity.

68 Chinese Foreign Ministry, "Foreign Ministry Spokesperson Lu Kang's Regular Press Conference, on 12 July, 2016," available at: www.fmprc.gov.cn/mfa_eng/xwfw_665399/s2510_665401/2511_665403/t1380374.shtml (accessed July 31, 2017).

69 See "Scholars: Illegitimate Ruling of the SCS Arbitration Case Would Not Lead to China Withdrawal from the UNCLOS Simply Because of the Judgment," *China News*, July 7, 2016 available at:, www.chinanews.com/gn/2016/07-07/7930350.shtml (accessed July 31, 2017).

70 Jia Yu, "Should China Withdraw from the UNCLOS?," *China Ocean Online*, December 19, 2015, available at: www.oceanol.com/redian/shiping/2015-12-09/54107.html (accessed July 31, 2017).

71 Research Professor at the National Institute for South China Sea Studies Hong Nong's remarks on "The 4th Asia Maritime Security Forum: Revisiting and Innovating Maritime Security Order in the Asia-Pacific," Nanjing, China, November, 2016.

72 The transition from the hub-and-spoke system to a complex web system and the trend of multilateralization of the US security alliance system have been well explored by a number of scholars. See, for example, Jae Jeok Park, "The US-led Alliances in the Asia-Pacific: Hedge against Potential Threats or an Undesirable Multilateral Security Order?" *Pacific Review* 24, no. 2 (2011): 137–158, David Brewster, "The Australia–India Framework for Security Cooperation: Another Step Towards an Indo-Pacific Security Partnership," *Security Challenges* (2015): 39–48; Victor D. Cha, "Complex Patchworks: U.S. Alliances as Part of Asia's Regional Architecture," *NBR Asia Policy*, no. 11 (2011): 27–50; Takashi Inoguchi, G. John Ikenberry and Yoichiro Sato, eds., *The U.S.-Japan Security Alliance: Regional Multilateralism* (New York: Palgrave Macmillan, 2011).

Bibliography

Cha, V.D. 2011. "Complex Patchworks: U.S. Alliances as Part of Asia's Regional Architecture," *NBR Asia Policy*, no. 11, pp. 27–50.

Chinese Foreign Ministry. 2014. *Position Paper of the Government of the People's Republic of China on the Matter of Jurisdiction in the South China Sea Arbitration Initiated by the Republic of the Philippines*, 7 December, available at: www.fmprc.gov.cn/mfa_eng/zxxx_662805/t1217147.shtml (accessed July 31, 2017).

Chinese Foreign Ministry. 2015. *Statement of the Ministry of Foreign Affairs of the People's Republic of China on the Award on Jurisdiction and Admissibility of the South China Sea Arbitration by the Arbitral Tribunal Established at the Request of the Republic of the Philippines*, 30 October, available at: www.fmprc.gov.cn/mfa_eng/zxxx_662805/t1310474.shtml (accessed July 31, 2017).

Chinese Foreign Ministry. 2016a. *The Tribunal's Award in the "South China Sea Arbitration" Initiated by the Philippines Is Null and Void*, 10 June, available at: www.fmprc.gov.cn/mfa_eng/zxxx_662805/t1371363.shtml (accessed July 31, 2017).

Chinese Foreign Ministry. 2016b. *Statement of the Government of the People's Republic of China on China's Territorial Sovereignty and Maritime Rights and Interests in the South China Sea*, 12 July, available at: www.fmprc.gov.cn/mfa_eng/zxxx_662805/t1379493.shtml (accessed July 31, 2017).

Chinese Foreign Ministry. 2016c. *Statement of the Ministry of Foreign Affairs of the People's Republic of China on the Award of 12 July 2016 of the Arbitral Tribunal in the South China Sea Arbitration Established at the Request of the Republic of the Philippines*, 12 July, available at: www.fmprc.gov.cn/mfa_eng/zxxx_662805/t1379492.shtml (accessed July 31, 2017).

Chinese Foreign Ministry. 2016d. *China Adheres to the Position of Settling Through Negotiation the Relevant Disputes Between China and the Philippines in the South*

China Sea, 13 July, available at: www.fmprc.gov.cn/nanhai/eng/snhwtlcwj_1/t1380615.htm (accessed July 31, 2017).

Gao, Z.G. 2016. "Review and Prospect of the Security Cooperation Mechanisms in the South China Sea," *Journal of Boundary and Ocean Studies*, no. 2, pp. 5–10 (in Chinese).

Gao, Z.G. and Jia, B.B. 2016. *The Nine-Dash Line in the South China Sea: History, Status and Implications*, Ocean Press, Beijing (in Chinese).

Guo, P.Q. and Sun, K. 2013. "'Nuuk Criteria' of the Arctic Council and China's Road to the Arctic," *World Economics and Politics*, no. 12, pp. 118–139 (in Chinese).

Inoguchi, T., Ikenberry, G.J. and Sato, Y. (eds.) 2011. *The U.S.-Japan Security Alliance: Regional Multilateralism*, Palgrave Macmillan, New York.

Kong, L.J. (ed.) 2016. *On Decided Territorial Dispute Cases*. Social Sciences Academic Press, Beijing (in Chinese).

Li, G.X. 2017. "The Dilemma of the Joint Development of the South China Sea: A Perspective of the Supply of the Regional Public Good," *Southeast Asian Affairs*, no. 1, pp. 84–94 (in Chinese).

Li, J.M. 2015. "An Analysis on the Prospect of China-Philippines 'Joint Development' of Reed Bank's Oil and Gas Resources," *Pacific Journal*, no. 5, pp. 78–83 (in Chinese).

Liu, H.R. and Song, X. 2016. "Fishery Legal Regulation in the Central Arctic Ocean: Status, Future, and China's Participation," *Northeast Asia Forum*, no. 4, pp. 86–94 (in Chinese).

March, J.G. and Olsen, J.P. 1989. *Rediscovering Institutions: The Organizational Basis of Politics*, Free Press, New York.

Ministry of Defense of Japan. 2015. *China's Activities in the South China Sea*, December 22, available at: www.mod.go.jp/j/approach/surround/pdf/ch_d-act_20151222e.pdf (accessed July 31, 2017).

Ministry of Foreign Affairs of Japan. 2015. *The Interim Report on the Revision of the Guidelines for Japan-U.S. Defense Cooperation*, available at: www.mofa.go.jp/files/000055169.pdf(accessed July 31, 2017).

Park, J.J. 2011. "The US-led Alliances in the Asia-Pacific: Hedge against Potential Threats or an Undesirable Multilateral Security Order?," *Pacific Review*, no. 2, pp. 137–158.

Permanent Court of Justice. 2015. *Award on Jurisdiction and Admissibility of the South China Sea Arbitration*, 29 October, available at: www.pcacases.com/web/sendAttach/1506 (accessed July 31, 2017).

Permanent Court of Justice. 2016. *Award on the South China Sea Arbitration*, 12 July, available at: https://pcacases.com/web/sendAttach/2086 (accessed July 31, 2017).

Talmon, S. and Jia, B.B. (eds.) 2014. *The South China Sea Arbitration: A Chinese Perspective*, Hart Publishing, Oxford.

The Chinese Society of International Law. 2016. *The Chinese Yearbook of International Law: Special Volume on the Jurisdiction over the South China Sea Arbitration Case*, Law Press, Beijing (in Chinese).

Wang, Z. 2015. "Maritime Delimitation, Ownership and Joint Development: Exploring Concrete Proposals for Future Settlement of the South China Sea Dispute," *Asia-Pacific Security and Maritime Affairs*, vol. 1, no. 1, pp. 39–51 (in Chinese).

Wu, S.C., Valencia, M. and Hong, N. (eds.) 2015. *UN Convention on the Law of the Sea and the South China Sea*, Routledge, New York.

Wu, S.C. and Zou, K.Y. (eds.) 2016. *Arbitration Concerning the South China Sea: Philippines Versus China*, Ashgate Publishing Limited, Farnham.

Xiao, Y. 2014. “Exclusivity Open: ‘Monroe Doctrine’ Logic of the Arctic Council,” *Pacific Journal*, no. 9, pp. 12–19 (in Chinese).

Xu, H. 2015. “The Realistic Dilemma and Game Theory Solution in the Joint Development of South China Sea Oil and Gas Resources,” *Southeast Asian Studies*, no. 4, pp. 18–27 (in Chinese).

Zhu, F. (ed.) 2016. *In-depth Analysis of the SCS Situation – 2014*, World Affairs Publishing House, Beijing (in Chinese).

Zou, K.Y. 2009. “China’s Antarctic Policy and the Antarctic Treaty System,” *Ocean Development and International Law*, vol. 24, no. 3, pp. 237–255.

Zou, K.Y. 2010. “The International Tribunal for the Law of the Sea: Procedures, Practices, and Asian States,” *Ocean Development and International Law*, vol. 41, no. 2, pp. 131–151.

Zou, K.Y. 2015. “Managing Biodiversity Conservation in the Disputed Maritime Areas: The Case of the South China Sea,” *Journal of International Wildlife Law and Policy*, vol. 18, no. 2, pp. 97–109.

Zou, K.Y. 2016. “Historic Rights in the South China Sea Arbitration Case: A Preliminary Reflection,” *Asia-Pacific Journal of Ocean Law and Policy*, vol. 1, no. 2, pp. 268–272.

Zou, K.Y. 2017. “Navigation in the South China Sea: Why Still an Issue?,” *International Journal of Marine and Coastal Law*, vol. 32, no. 2, pp. 243–267.

Zou, K.Y. and Liu, X.C. 2015. “The Legal Status of the U-shaped Line in the South China Sea and Its Legal Implications for Sovereignty, Sovereign Rights and Maritime Jurisdiction,” *Chinese Journal of International Law*, vol. 14, pp. 57–77.

Zou, K.Y. and Ye, Q. 2017. “Interpretation and Application of Article 298 of the Law of the Sea Convention in Recent Annex VII Arbitrations: An Appraisal,” *Ocean Development and International Law*, vol. 48, pp. 1–14.

8 Conclusion

The concluding chapter is comprised of four sections. The first section summarizes the major findings and answers the research questions raised in the Introduction. The debate over China's rising is revisited in light of the findings of this research in the second section. In the third part, several policy recommendations are proposed, based on the findings of this research. The final section explores three areas for future investigation.

The influence of the IMR and its interaction with geopolitics

A thorough evaluation of China's SCS policy needs to answer three basic questions: (1) What are the components of China's SCS policy?; (2) How has China's SCS policy evolved over the past six decades?; and (3) What are the factors shaping the evolving path of the Chinese SCS policy? This research is devoted to answering these questions and providing a comprehensive, accurate, and up-to-date understanding of the evolution of Chinese SCS policy.

This research contends that existing studies often have a narrow and simplified conception of Chinese policy regarding the SCS dispute. The omission of some important aspects of the SCS policy could lead to an inaccurate assessment of China's policy stance. Failure to identify changes and the forces behind them will misinform our understanding of the trajectory of China's SCS policy and yield ineffective policy proposals.

This research identifies four major components of China's SCS policy: (1) China's legal position; (2) the political interaction with other disputants and user states; (3) marine practices regarding everyday uses of the SCS; and (4) practices of tentative arrangements and final resolution. The research finds that changes in the legal and political aspects of China's SCS policy are often linked to practical aspects of China's SCS policy. In other words, China's legal and political positions are expressed through and supported by concrete marine practices. This pattern has become increasingly notable, as Chinese SCS policy continues to expand and becomes more sophisticated. For example, the legal connection between the nine-dash line and historic claims in the 2000s has resulted in China consciously taking measures to enhance and expand practices of maritime governance to cover the waters enclosed by the line. The desire to enhance the legal effect of the nine-dash line and the urgent need to create favorable conditions for the COC negotiations together have forced the Chinese government to push for tangible progress in implementing joint development through increased financial support for domestic research and by conducting concrete trial projects.

This research argues that the maritime regime has been a unique and influential factor shaping these four aspects of China's SCS policy, exerting its influence in two broad ways. First, it (re)constructs the legal foundation of the SCS dispute, which in turn (re)shapes China's legal conceptualization of its claims and related exercises of marine governance in the SCS. Second, the normative and institutional dynamics of the maritime regime interact with the broader geostrategic environment, offering an integrative combination of motivations and pressure in shaping the calculus of the Chinese leadership. More concretely, this research identifies six roles that the maritime regime has played in this process:

1, (re)defining the rules of the game;
2, providing the playground and institutional benefits for disputants to interact with each other and with maritime institutions;
3, offering new venues for multilateral political engagements;
4, setting critical deadlines for states to meet;
5, teaching policy-related knowledge;
6, locking states into institutionalized and habitualized interactions.

China's legal claims

With regard to the first component of China's SCS policy, this research arrives at three observations. First, China's legal position has undergone a series of modifications in accordance with the evolving international maritime order. Second, changes in China's legal claims to sovereignty in the SCS were not completed overnight. Rather, the process has been incremental. Third, legal and normative developments of the maritime regime have been responsible for those observed changes in China's legal position.

The maritime regime has played two roles in this process. The first role is redefining the SCS dispute by placing the dispute within the legal framework of the new maritime order (role 1). The SCS dispute in the 1950s and 1960s was a bilateral territorial dispute between China and Vietnam over a clearly defined area, in which both sides grounded their claims in general principles of international law on territorial acquisition. Starting from the 1970s, as China began to formally participate in the maritime regime, a new maritime order emerging on the international stage gradually transformed the SCS dispute into a multilateral dispute over an enlarged area whose boundaries and related sovereign rights and duties are associated with considerable indeterminacy. This transformation greatly intensified the disputes in the SCS, altering not only the number of claimants but also the content of their respective legal claims.

For China, changes in its legal position have unfolded in four incremental steps. During the negotiation stage of the UNCLOS in the 1970s, the Chinese government began to indicate its interests in incorporating new maritime entitlements into its claims. These maritime entitlements were not justified by evidence of discovery and acquisition but granted by the new maritime law. In the face of the snowballing ratification of the LOSC worldwide in the early 1990s, the Chinese government followed the trend and transferred the LOSC into domestic legislation. Subsequently, China accepted the new LOS as the legal bedrock not only for its own claims to sovereignty in the SCS but also for resolving disputes in the area. The Chinese government realized that complying with the new maritime order might adversely affect its interests in the SCS. To mitigate the potential negative impact on its claims in the SCS, the Chinese government modified its legal position in two steps by asserting historic rights in the SCS and then adding a new claim of historic rights to strengthen its position.

The third stage of development of China's legal claims to the SCS unfolded in 2009, marked by China's submission to the UN of the dashed line map along with a Note Verbale explaining its legal position, a move triggered by Vietnam's and Malaysia's submissions on the limits of continental shelf in the SCS. It was China's first official attempt at invoking the line to develop and support its SCS claims in light of the UNCLOS. At this stage, a few important issues concerning China's legal position still remained unspecified: how should the EEZ and CS in the SCS be determined? What kind of historical rights were claimed by the Chinese government? Were historical rights applicable to the SCS?

Finally, legal deliberations by the Chinese government from 2013 to 2016 in response to the Arbitration case introduced the two latest developments to China's SCS claims. One development is the clarification that China views each of the four island groups as a whole when measuring maritime entitlements, including the territorial sea, the contiguous zone, the EEZ and the CS. This also gives rise to the possibility that China would claim internal waters in at least some, if not all, of the four island groups. The second development is related to the claim of historical rights. In the 2016 *Statement of Sovereignty and Maritime Right*, China explicitly assert historical rights in the SCS.

The second tool the maritime regime used to influence changes in China's legal position is as the body vested with the authority to set critical dates by which states feel pressured to respond (role 4). The CLCS set May 13, 2009 as the deadline for coastal states to make submissions of claims to the outer limits of the continental shelf. Given the authoritative status of the CLCS, the CLCS deadline represented both an opportunity for SCS claimants to publicize and potentially legitimize their claims, and direct pressure to which they must carefully respond in order to avoid any negative impact on their respective positions. This deadline ignited a chain of reactions among the SCS countries, resulting in important legal clarifications on the issue of the nine-dash line, an integral part of the ongoing modification of China's SCS claims.

Similarly, in the South China Sea Arbitration case initiated by the Philippines, the arbitral tribunal issued more than ten deadlines for China to respond to the legal proceedings, creating a momentum of normative pressure on China to take further efforts to clarify its legal claims to the SCS. This Arbitration case also taught China a fresh lesson about compulsory settlement designed in Part VX of the UNCLOS. When signing the UNCLOS in 1982, China did express concern and reservations about the compulsory settlement regime, yet it was not a well-informed position for two reasons. First, to a large extent, this reservation was motivated by China's long-standing suspicion of the international adjudication and arbitration. No further research was conducted on the potential implications of the compulsory settlement regime on China's maritime interests. Second, the LOS regime is an evolving entity. It was not until 1994, when the UNCLOS came into force, that the compulsory settlement regime began to operate and knowledge of this regime started to develop. The Arbitration case was the first case that challenged China under the compulsory settlement regime. Through its interaction with the arbitration case, China accumulated practical knowledge and field experience of the operation of compulsory settlement regime. Although China declared that the page of the South China Sea arbitration should be and had been turned over,[1] a review and assessment of the pros and cons of China's strategy and responses to the case continue to date at both governmental and academic levels, as the Chinese leadership is aware that there exists a real possibility of a similar challenge from other claimants in the future and that China needs to be better prepared for it.

Political engagement

With regard to the second aspect of China's SCS policy, China's approach to political engagement, this research finds that China's political interaction with relevant parties involved in the SCS dispute has been the product of the interaction of geopolitical flux and the normative and institutional dynamics of the maritime regime. The interactive relationship between geopolitics and the maritime regime has experienced four distinctive stages.

The first stage was during the 1970s and 1980s. Legal developments in the international maritime order greatly complicated the territorial dispute in the SCS and emboldened countries bordering the SCS to occupy land features in the SCS. In the midst of regional escalation, geopolitical flux pulled the trigger on the military showdown between China and the RVN, producing the 1974 Paracel clash. The pullback of US forces from Indochina and the looming collapse of the RVN regime in Vietnam in 1973 were perceived by China as the ideal time to strike back. In the years leading up to 1988, all claimants except China had quickly consolidated their respective presence in the Spratlys. While China was preparing to insert its own presence into the region, the intense Sino-Vietnamese relationship dipping to an all-time-low in the late 1980s fueled the military confrontation between these two countries.

The second stage ranges from the early 1990s to 2002. During this stage, a regional multilateral network for political engagements gradually developed, and the trend of geopolitics working with and through the venues of this network became more obvious. In the early 1990s, leaders in the SCS region came to realize that in light of the new nature of the SCS dispute, the traditional bilateral approach was insufficient to facilitate effective political engagement aimed at conflict prevention and dispute resolution. Consequently, multilateralism was proposed as both a norm and an approach for political interaction concerning the dispute. When multilateralism was first introduced by ASEAN countries, it was unclear whether this approach would succeed and be welcomed by other countries, especially China. The uncertainty in the geostrategic environment of the SCS region created by the end of the Cold War provided the initial impetus for China to participate in multilateral engagement mechanisms. Consequently, a multilateral institutional architecture flourished across the region, encompassing the SCS Workshop, a series of dialogues and venues under the ASEAN-China and the ASEAN +3 frameworks, the ARF, and others. These institutionalized interactive arrangements offered new venues and leverage for states to successfully elicit China's cooperation in discussing the SCS dispute on a multilateral basis, something not available in traditional state-to-state engagement (role 3). The ASEAN Way argumentation infused in these multilateral settings alleviated China's suspicion of the pressure it felt from other member states. In 2002, multilateral engagements bore one of its biggest fruits, the conclusion of the DOC.

The third stage spans from 2002 to 2008. In this stage, due to America's preoccupation with counter-terrorism, the geostrategic environment of the SCS region was characterized by relative stability and lacked the same level of pressure observed in the 1990s. This geostrategic environment was conducive to the operation of the multilateral institutional architecture in continuing to lock China into institutionalized and regularized interactions, yielding a relatively peaceful and cooperative environment in the SCS (role 6). However, this stabilized environment was unable to produce powerful pressure and incentives to work with regional institutions to elicit major progress, especially in respect to negotiating a binding COC.

The fourth stage, the post-2009 period, is defined by the USA rebalancing towards Asia. America's active re-engagement revitalized multilateral institutional networks and formed a new impetus to propel the COC negotiation on a multilateral basis. This process temporarily stalled in the immediate aftermath of the Scarborough standoff in 2012. In 2013, the institutional rotation of the ASEAN leadership positions and the Philippines' decision to bring the Scarborough dispute before international arbitration introduced a new dynamics into the process. These institutional and legal dynamics converged to fuel and expedite the negotiations between China and the ASEAN on the implementation of the DOC including the formulation of the COC.

Maritime practices

In the area of marine governance, the maritime regime has served as both the playground in which China interacted with relevant international institutions and regional countries and the classroom in which China's leaders learned the necessary knowledge regarding technology and policy options to tackle issues concerning the everyday usage of the SCS (roles 2 and 5). This research observes that the maritime regime initiated and facilitated the regional cooperation necessary to tackle transnational issues such as the protection of marine environments (role 3). For example, the UNEP has played a leading role in forging a regional response to environment degradation in the SCS. Engagement with international organizations of the maritime regime has helped the Chinese government to establish a comprehensive legal and institutional maritime system in line with modern maritime governance. The improvement and modernization of marine management systems define the policy parameters and enhance the capability of Chinese maritime law enforcement activities, which have been expanding in recent years to promote the effective administration of the waters enclosed by the nine-dash line and to probe possible forms of historic rights that China might claim.

Practices of dispute resolution

The fourth aspect of China's SCS policy is related to practices of provisional arrangements and permanent dispute resolutions. The delimitation of the Gulf of Tonkin is an example of the successful resolution of part of the SCS dispute. As it turned out, this practice was entirely grounded in the legal framework of the new LOS. During the negotiation stage in the 1990s, the Chinese government (and the Vietnamese government) focused on implementing newly established regimes such as the EEZ and the CS in the Gulf of Tonkin. To solve the potential conflict between traditional fishery activities and the EEZ regime, the two countries established joint fishery arrangements consistent with the spirit of the new LOS and held regular joint patrols to facilitate the implementation of these arrangements. The maritime regime also inspired China with regard to the concept of joint development as a provisional measure to solve the SCS disputes. This concept emerged in the 1970s in international maritime practices. The Chinese government first embraced joint development in the 1980s. In the 1990s, China began to propose this concept as a promising measure to manage the SCS dispute on multilateral basis. Its efforts achieved a major breakthrough in 2005, when China, Vietnam, and the Philippines conducted a tripartite joint seismic survey in the disputed waters of the SCS. In the meantime, burgeoning domestic research concentrates on studying the latest developments in the international arena on joint development in an attempt to inform Chinese practices. Some of the research recommendations have materialized in recent years.

Table 8.1 The geopolitics and regime influence on China's SCS policy

Policy dimensions	*Maritime regime*		*Geopolitics*
	Influence	*Mechanisms/Roles*	*Influence*
1. Legal position	Independent	(Re)defining (role 1) Critical dates (role 4)	General
2. Political engagement	Co-determining	Venues for external pressure (role 3) Lock-in (role 6)	Co-determining
3. Practices of governance	Independent	Playground and institutional incentives (role 2) Teaching (role 5)	General
4. Practice of best solutions	Independent	Teaching/informing (role 5)	General

Table 8.1 summarizes the regime influence and the influence of geopolitics on China's SCS policy. While geopolitical influence is most salient in policy dimension 2, it is worth noting that geopolitics also affects policy dimensions 1, 2, and 3, mostly in an indirect manner. With regard to the legal dimension of China's SCS policy, geopolitics played a significant role in shaping the new international maritime order which in turn influenced China's legal position in the SCS. Geopolitics could also affect regional political trust which conditions regional cooperation and the final resolution of the dispute. As an essential element of international relations, geopolitics has a general bearing on the development of China's SCS policy, but such influence is often indirect and the final outcome of its effect also depends on the normative and institutional dynamics of the maritime regime which shape the parameters and concrete practices of China's SCS policy. As we have seen in the case of delimiting the Gulf of Tonkin, while the political environment was favorable for negotiations between China and Vietnam, it was the knowledge and experience accumulated through decades of engagement with the maritime regime that determined the final content of the bilateral agreements.

The big debate revisited: status quo or revisionism?

As elaborated in the Introduction, in the context of the theoretical debate over the rise of China, the South China Sea dispute presents a useful case to test support for the status quo versus revisionism in China's foreign policy institutions. In the face of a conflict of interests like the South China Sea disputes, a revisionist power is tempted to resort to force. Military means represent the most direct way of settling the dispute, allowing a state to annex the disputed territory and increase its national power. Since a revisionist power is dissatisfied with the existing international order and eager to increase its own power, it would find peaceful negotiation under the framework of international law unattractive, as such an approach entails a degree of compromise and conformity with international order.

Contrary to realist pessimist expectations, the evolving path of China's policy in the South China Sea dispute does not fit the characterization of a revisionist power, nor does it amount to a challenge to the existing international and regional orders. Rather, China's handling of the SCS issue to a large extent is characterized by a pattern of self-adjustment to fit international law and order, as demonstrated in the incremental modification of its legal position, the delimitation practice in the Gulf of Tonkin, and the institutionalization of domestic maritime governance in line with international standards of modern ocean governance. Moreover, although the pace of constructive engagement has varied over time, political interaction between China and other countries with conflicting interests has so far been carried out within the regional institutional architecture. This observation coincides with the pattern of system maintainer identified in other areas of China's foreign policy.

Policy recommendations

Before turning to concrete policy recommendations, it is necessary to first clarify the goals to which the following policy suggestions are devoted. There are generally three kinds of policy orientations: (1) maintaining peace; (2) reaching an equitable resolution; and (3) maximizing the interests of a specific country. The third policy orientation is in conflict with the first two and is not the focus of this policy recommendation. Although not necessarily incompatible, the first two policy goals can sometimes be in conflict. Preferring absolute peace to a fair distribution of interests in the SCS may result in an unfair loss of legitimate interests for a particular state and incur new instability. Therefore, the policy recommendation proposed here endeavors to maintain a balance between these two policy objectives.

Preparing a common ground for negotiation towards final resolution

China's legal position in the SCS has been reflective of the international maritime order. Modification of Chinese claims to sovereignty, domestic internalization of the maritime legal regime, and the resolution of the Gulf of Tonkin dispute highlight China's willingness to be bound by the modern international maritime order and comply with the spirit of the law. This implies that a fair resolution of the dispute consistent with the LOSC is desirable and possible. To this end, it is necessary to first promote and prepare a common ground for negotiation. Policy-makers should not count solely on power politics to push to reach a common ground for negotiation. In fact, power politics are ineffective in this regard, given the legal complexity of the SCS dispute. Relevant states should take advantage of a number of legal means and practical tools.

SCS claimants should encourage the international legal epistemic community to work on the clarification of several legal issues on which states have conflicting views. As put forward in Chapter 4, one of the core issues concerning the SCS dispute is the indeterminacy associated with maritime boundaries and shares of interests. Due to the transition of the international maritime order and the legal ambiguities of the new LOS on a number of issues, states have both uncertain and conflicting views about their respective shares of maritime interests in the SCS. This indeterminacy is a major obstacle keeping states from arriving at a common ground, and removing it is a prerequisite for any constructive negotiation towards final resolution.

For the international maritime law community, the main task is to reach consensus on the elaboration and interpretation of those issues challenging the SCS-bordering countries. Major issues include the island regime, the concept of historic rights, and the legal effect of map publications. To this end, policy-makers of SCS-claimant countries need to provide funding and other resources to facilitate relevant legal research.

Using the dispute settlement regime provided by the UNCLOS generates additional impetus for international deliberations on specific LOSC provisions. The Philippines have done just this recently by initiating the South China Sea Arbitration case. The Philippines requested that the arbitration panel rule over several issues, two of which are especially pertinent to the SCS dispute in its entirety: the nine-dash line and the island regime. Despite the controversy surrounding the ruling, in particular with regard to the status of Itu Aba (Taiping Dao), the case renewed discussions within the international law community on these thorny and unresolved legal issues and, more importantly, affected China's legal claims and resulted in new clarifications to China's position.

Finally, for policy-makers of the claimant states, it is pragmatic at this stage to focus on works that (1) help clarify the vague contents of their claims; and (2) help create an amicable atmosphere for cooperation and consultation. One of the most important works is the collection of scientific data and information about the SCS. Scientific information and data are crucial for determining the exact content of the claim of each country, finding common ground for negotiation, and designing provisional measures and cooperative projects. Scarcity of relevant information may cause unnecessary uncertainty and oversensitivity among the disputants. To date, the region still lacks accurate geological information and scientific data about the oceanographic and geologic conditions of the features, fishery resources, hydrocarbon potentials, and environmental degradation. Apart from the sensitivity of the dispute, constraints on domestic capability and weak regional cooperative institutions also account for the slow progress in this respect. Therefore, countries bordering the SCS should strengthen regional cooperative institutions in order to jointly conduct scientific research and gather relevant information to overcome domestic resource constraints and cultivate a spirit of regional cooperation.

International institutions could take a more active role in this process. This research demonstrates that international institutions have considerable influence in terms of promoting regional cooperation in the SCS. The UNEP and

GEF have played an active role in forging regional cooperation on environmental issues in the SCS. Their efforts have resulted in the establishment of a regional system for information sharing and exchange. For a region lacking the tradition of regional cooperation and inter-state information sharing and exchange, the institutionalization of a cross-regional network of information sharing and exchange is the first step towards more sophisticated cooperation. In future, international organizations should continue to take the lead in fostering regional cooperation on scientific research and exploration. In the meantime, SCS countries need to set aside the dispute and respond more positively to international organizations' initiatives. Through participation, countries can take advantage of the funding, technology, and resources provided by the international organizations to collect scientific data in the SCS without necessarily damaging their claims. Cooperation also creates the political trust and momentum conducive to reaching common ground for negotiations.

Regional countries should make further efforts to push for tentative arrangements of cooperation such as joint research, joint exploration, joint exercises of search and rescue and humanitarian assistance. In recent years, China and the ASEAN have established a number of joint cooperation programs during the DOC implementation negotiations. On a bilateral level, China and the Philippines resumed a bilateral fishery committee and carried out several fishery cooperation projects. The two countries also set up a bilateral consultation mechanism in 2017 which will be used as the venue to push for joint development in disputed areas in the SCS on a bilateral and possibly a multilateral level. While keeping the current momentum and amicable atmosphere of maritime cooperation, countries bordering the SCS should also consider using the newly reclaimed features and the facilities installed on these features to develop and support joint marine cooperation projects. The Chinese government explained that one of the purposes of the construction work was to better perform "China's international responsibility and obligation in maritime search and rescue, disaster prevention and mitigation, marine science and research, meteorological observation, environmental protection, navigation safety, fishery production service and other areas."[2] Regional countries could consider using these facilities to promote the implementation of the DOC in future DOC negotiations and urge the Chinese government to fulfill its promise of advancing regional welfare in the maritime domain.

Pushing for the DOC and COC negotiation

Considering that achieving a final resolution to the SCS dispute is a long process, a parallel negotiation on the DOC and COC, aimed at conflict prevention and management, is absolutely necessary. The COC negotiation achieved quite positive progress in 2017 with the conclusion of a framework text, a critical step towards the final agreement on a legally binding COC. A political momentum seems to be emerging. The COC, once concluded, will become an important pillar upholding regional stability.

To build on this precious political momentum and carry the COC negotiation forward, China should continue deliberating on its own principles of the COC negotiation and keep open lines of effective communication with the ASEAN to avoid any misunderstanding or misperception. It also needs to refrain from expanding its law enforcement activities in the contested waters.

Meanwhile, the findings of this research suggest that maintaining a balanced mixture of geopolitical pressure and normative pressure would help to keep up the current momentum on the COC negotiation and the DOC negotiation in general between China and the ASEAN. On the one hand, as shown in previous chapters, geopolitical pressure has contributed to the advances in the COC negotiations. The ASEAN's determination to put priority on pushing for progress on the COC discussion, together with America's active involvement in the existing multilateral institutional architecture in the past few years, has boosted the COC negotiations. In the future, the ASEAN should continue to take the lead in cooperative and active engagement with China, while refraining from activities that may further escalate regional tensions.

On the other hand, normative pressure has played a quite constructive role in eliciting regional countries' commitment to regional negotiation and cooperation. In the future, regional countries should encourage and support research and deliberation in the regional legal community to promote future clarification of those legal issues on which states have conflicting views, which will introduce new normative dynamics conducive to regional negotiations concerning the SCS disputes.

To make sure that the aforementioned efforts do not backfire or cause unnecessary regional tensions, the USA and the ASEAN need to take four additional measures to alleviate China's suspicion and potential frustration. While these measures are employed only for a temporary period in order to maintain the current political momentum, they may also be used for a longer time, depending on the development of the DOC and COC negotiations.

First, the USA should modify its confrontational posture when engaging China in multilateral settings. Much of the coordination work could be done beforehand within the ASEAN-US framework rather than holding closed-door meetings immediately before coming out to engage China, as has happened in the past. This will save face for China and alleviate suspicion and wariness.

Second, the USA should be more cautious in implementing its so-called Freedom of Navigation Operations (FONOPs). FONOPs have been used by the USA to challenge China's maritime claims in the SCS. Starting from October 2016, the USA has conducted several FONOPs in the SCS, and the scope and content of the FONOPs are gradually expanding. FONOPs are designed to be an effective means to demonstrate the US. commitment to regional security. Given the controversial military nature of the FONOPs, if not used cautiously, these activities may cause undesirable tensions in the region. China has been quite concerned about these activities, given their military nature, and has used the existence of these operations to legitimize China's deployment of defense capabilities on the recently reclaimed features.

The USA could also slow down its defense cooperation with other Asian nations. While it may not be in America's interest to slow the pace of consolidating traditional allies in Asia, it could at least postpone high-profile engagement with new Asian partners, such as Vietnam. After all, while the real policy objectives of the USA in Asia are debatable, at the current stage a peaceful environment in the SCS region conducive to continued COC negotiation is definitely not against US interests.

The fourth measure is that the USA could also give at least partial respect to China's legitimate claims of interests when necessary, especially when regional tension is on the rise. Given the influential status of the USA in Asia, its respect for China's legitimate interests will serve as an effective painkiller for China's frustration. This way will also help build the US image as an objective facilitator.

In future negotiations on the COC, DOC, and SCS disputes more generally, the USA should continue acting as a reliable deterrent, pre-empting military showdowns caused by potential escalations in regional tensions. This deterrent not only applies to countering China's assertiveness, but also to discouraging the risky advances of America's traditional allies aimed at testing and spoiling the US guarantee of protection. The USA also needs to keep a vigilant eye on the SCS region, promptly transferring potential crises into windows of opportunity conducive to making breakthroughs in future negotiations between direct claimants and between China and the ASEAN.

Policy response to compulsory settlement procedures

At present, China has actively participated in the COC negotiations. China could also push forward a parallel negotiation aimed at permanently resolving the dispute. This will discourage other claimants from considering settling the dispute through legal means. Meanwhile, as discussed in Chapter 7, the Chinese leadership and the epistemic community have come to realize that the issue of compulsory settlement is a growing challenge that must be dealt with in the future.

Compulsory dispute settlement would appeal to states because of the impact of the availability of these procedures on the political dynamic of a dispute.[3] Moreover, the binding nature of the regime gives less powerful states equal standing before the law. Faced with a China growing militarily and economically, third-party arbitration appears increasingly attractive to the Southeast Asian claimants. By ratifying the UNCLOS, China has in effect consented in advance to the system of compulsory settlement in the Convention. China made a declaration under Article 298 of the UNCLOS on August 25, 2006 to exclude certain categories of disputes from compulsory procedures, but such exclusion is not "self-judging." A party to the UNCLOS cannot determine whether the exclusions made in the written declaration under Article 298 apply to a given case, because according to Article 288 (4), in the event of a dispute as to whether a court or tribunal has jurisdiction, the matter shall be settled by the decision of that court or tribunal.

So far, China has not been well prepared for the growing probability of the SCS dispute being brought before international arbitration, for three interrelated reasons. First, it is traditionally suspicious of international arbitration. Second, it lacks and fears it lacks the necessary experience and expertise. Third, it does not like the idea of internationalizing the dispute. It was not until very recently that the domestic discourse began to explore issues related to this dispute settlement mechanism.

To prepare for possible international litigation in the near future and to defend its own position, it is urgent that Chinese leaders change their mindsets and substantially increase support for domestic research on this subject.[4] The research finds that this trend has already started in the post-2013 period and is likely to continue. The leadership must accept that all claimants, including China, have legitimate rights to use dispute settlement mechanisms, and that China could even benefit from this process, if it is well prepared. The Chinese government should stop interpreting such moves as attempts to internationalize the dispute, as leveling such charges brings no benefit, instead tarnishing its image as a responsible party to the LOSC as well as a responsible power in the eyes of the international community. Dropping such charges will also reduce the political sensitivity of this issue, granting more freedom to relevant domestic research.

Future research

The findings of this book suggest three areas for future investigation. The first area is located at the domestic level. This research shows that a large portion of the influence of the maritime regime has been transferred into domestic dynamics. The domestic epistemic community has been influential in the process of SCS policy formation. For example, the consensus that Chinese legal experts have reached has been proven to correlate with the evolution of the official legal position of the Chinese government. Institutional actors, such as SEPA, the UNEP's window agency in China, and the Fishery Administration of the Ministry of Agriculture, have been active in driving the development of some specific aspects of SCS policy practices. Therefore, examining the evolving dynamics at the domestic level will help locate the regime influence and increase the accuracy of predictions about the future trajectory of China's SCS policy.

The second realm of future investigation is the evolving US-China-ASEAN triangle and its impact on the management of the SCS dispute. This triangle is experiencing three new developments. First, China's fast-growing naval power and recent efforts to expand and diversify its presence along the nine-dash line have raised concerns among the ASEAN countries about the potential escalation of the dispute. Second, the active re-engagement of the

US with the ASEAN and the broader Asia-Pacific region gives rise to China's suspicion of a US encirclement plot. Although the Trump Administration introduced new dynamics into the SCS region, the general trend of the US deepening involvement in the Asia-Pacific region would certainly continue. Third, with the full implementation of the CAFTA in 2010, the withdrawal of the US from the Trans-Pacific Partnership (TPP) and the relatively progressive development of the Regional Comprehensive Economic Partnership (RCEP) negotiation, economic connections between China and ASEAN have become tighter than ever. In particular, the Philippines assumed the ASEAN presidency in 2017 with the determination to cool down regional tensions and promote closer cooperation between China and the ASEAN.

This research finds a mixed picture of the impact of these geopolitical dynamics on the SCS dispute. Some developments have helped bring forward the multilateral negotiation on the COC; others have contributed to regional tensions. Future research will focus on how these dynamics continue to develop and how they will affect the negotiation and the management of the SCS disputes. For China, will the cordial economic relationship with ASEAN be transferred into constructive political engagement on the SCS disputes? Will the United States remain objective and offer to facilitate negotiation through existing regional institutional architecture? Will American leaders take a confrontational approach to China and become more unequivocal in supporting their Asian allies at the expense of China's legitimate interests? For the ASEAN, will it remain unified and take the lead in the future SCS talks or will it begin to splinter due to varying views in terms of how the SCS dispute should be managed? These questions deserve further exploration.

A third area for future research is related to norm and policy innovation. The past two decades have witnessed the effectiveness of the norm of multilateralism in managing the SCS dispute. China's active participation in multilateral engagement is seen as a major progress towards solving the SCS dispute. Yet in this research, the examination of the SCS dispute in the context of the new maritime order points to the fact that multilateralism alone may be insufficient to bring forth the final resolution of the dispute. China's insistence on bilateral negotiation as the main approach to resolving the SCS dispute has been criticized as not conducive to agreement, but the fact that bilateral negotiation is not only feasible but an inevitable part of the complex negotiating processes on the SCS issue is often neglected. The successful conclusion of an equitable delimitation agreement between China and Vietnam is an example.

Forming a common ground for negotiation and the final resolution of the dispute requires continuous normative and policy innovations. In this sense, the urgent task before policy pundits is to devise more effective and suitable norms and policies to deal with the complexity of the SCS dispute. Moreover, as alluded to in previous chapters, China's deepening participation in the global maritime domain is transforming China's understanding of its maritime interests and marine governance from a local and regional perspective into a global perspective. Future research in this area needs to explore the following questions: Drawing from China's accumulating experience of global marine governance and practices in other regions, what are the possible norms and policy solutions suitable for the current situation of the SCS dispute? How can multilateral and bilateral approaches be combined in effective and flexible ways? How can these norms and policy innovations be promulgated and implemented? Can they be integrated into the existing regional institutional architecture or does the current architecture need to be reformed? The SCS disputes today are different from two decades ago when multilateralism was first promulgated in the region. Answers to these issues need to draw useful lessons from the past two decades of policy interaction and will help to push for progress in regional negotiations on the final resolution of the dispute.

Notes

1 "Page of South China Sea Arbitration Has Been Turned Over: Chinese FM," *Xinhua News*, July 26, 2016, available at: http://news.xinhuanet.com/english/2016-07/26/c_135541923.htm, accessed July 31, 2017.
2 Chinese Foreign Ministry, "Foreign Ministry Spokesperson Hua Chunying's Regular Press Conference on April 9, 2015," available at: http://www.fmprc.gov.cn/mfa_eng/xwfw_665399/s2510_665401/2511_665403/t1253488.shtml, accessed July 31, 2017.
3 Natalie Klein, *Dispute Settlement in the UN Convention on the Law of the Sea* (Cambridge: Cambridge University Press, 2005), 52.
4 The suggestion made here focuses on the leadership level rather than elaborating the legal technical issues of concrete cases of dispute.

Bibliography

Amer, R. and Zou, KY (eds.) 2011. *Conflict Management and Dispute Settlement in East Asia*, Ashgate, Farnham.

Klein, N. 2005. *Dispute Settlement in the UN Convention on the Law of the Sea*, Cambridge University Press, Cambridge, 52.

Wu, S.C. 2013. *Solving Disputes for Regional Cooperation and Development in the South China Sea: A Chinese Perspective*, Chandos Publishing, Oxford.

Appendix A: Declaration on the Territorial Sea

4 September 1958

The Government of the People's Republic of China declares:

1 The breadth of the territorial sea of the People's Republic of China shall be twelve nautical miles. This provision applies to all territories of the People's Republic of China, including the Chinese mainland and its coastal islands, as well as Taiwan and its surrounding islands, the Penghu islands, the Dongsha islands, the Xisha islands, the Zhongsha islands, the Nansha islands, and all other islands belonging to China which are separated from the mainland and its coastal islands by the high seas.

2 China's territorial sea along the mainland and its coastal islands takes as its baseline the line composed of the straight lines connecting base-points on the mainland coast and on the outermost of the coastal islands; the water area extending twelve nautical miles outwards from this baseline is China's territorial sea. The water areas inside the baseline, including Bohai Bay and the Qiongzhou Straits, are Chinese inland waters. The islands inside the baseline, including Dongyin Island, Gaoteng Island, the Mazu Islands, the Baichuan Islands, Wuqiu Island, the Greater and Lesser Jinmen Islands, Datan island, Ertan Island and Dongting Island, are islands of the Chinese inland waters.

3 No foreign vessels for military use and no foreign aircraft may enter China's territorial sea and the air space above it without the permission of the Government of the People's Republic of China.

While navigating Chinese territorial sea, ever foreign vessel must observe the relevant laws and regulations laid down by the Government of the People's Republic of China.

4 The principles provided in paragraphs (2) and (3) likewise apply to Taiwan and its surrounding islands, the Penghu Islands, the Dongsha Islands, the Xisha islands, the Zhongsha islands, the Nansha islands, and all other islands belonging to China.

The Taiwan and Penghu areas are still occupied by the United States armed force. This is an unlawful encroachment on the territorial integrity and sovereignty of the People's Republic of China. Taiwan, Penghu and such other areas are yet to be recovered, and the Government of the People's Republic of China has the right to recover these areas by all suitable means at a suitable time. This is China's internal affair, in which no foreign interference is tolerated.

Appendix B: The Law on the Territorial Sea and the Contiguous Zone of the People's Republic of China

The Law on the Territorial Sea and the Contiguous Zone of the People's Republic of China, adopted at the 24th meeting of the Standing Committee of the National People's Congress on 25 February 1992.

Article 1

This law is formulated in order to enable the People's Republic of China (PRC) to exercise its sovereignty over its territorial sea and its rights to exercise control over its contiguous zone, and to safeguard State security as well as its maritime rights and interests.

Article 2

The PRC's territorial sea refers to the waters adjacent to its territorial land.

The PRC's territorial land includes the mainland and its offshore islands, Taiwan and the various affiliated islands including Diaoyu Island, Penghu Islands, Dongsha Islands, Xisha Islands, Nansha (Spratly) Islands and other islands that belong to the People's Republic of China.

The PRC's internal waters refer to the waters along the baseline of the territorial sea facing the land.

Article 3

The extent of the PRC's territorial sea measures 12 nautical miles from the baseline of the territorial sea. The PRC's baseline of the territorial sea is designated with the method of straight baselines, formed by joining the various base points with straight lines.

The outer limit of the PRC's territorial sea refers to the line, every point of which is at a distance of 12 nautical miles from the nearest point of the baseline of the territorial sea.

Article 4

The PRC's contiguous zone refers to the waters that are outside of, but adjacent to, its territorial sea. The extent of the contiguous zone has a width of 12 nautical miles.

The outer limit of the PRC's contiguous zone is a line, every point of which has a nearest distance of 24 nautical miles from the baseline from which the territorial sea is measured.

Article 5

The People's Republic of China exercises sovereignty over its territorial sea and the airspace over the territorial sea, as well as its seabed and subsoil.

Article 6

Non-military foreign ships enjoy the right of innocent passage through the territorial sea of the People's Republic of China according to law.

To enter the territorial sea of the People's Republic of China, foreign military ships must obtain permission from the Government of the People's Republic of China.

Article 7

While passing through the territorial sea of the People's Republic of China, foreign submarines and other underwater vehicles shall navigate on the surface of the sea and show their flags.

Article 8

While passing through the territorial sea of the People's Republic of China, foreign ships shall abide by the laws and regulations of the People's Republic of China and shall not impair the peace, security and good order of the People's Republic of China.

Foreign nuclear-powered ships and other ships carrying nuclear, toxic or other dangerous substances must carry certain documents and observe special precautionary measures when they pass through the territorial sea of the People's Republic of China.

The Government of the People's Republic of China has the right to adopt all necessary measures to prevent and stop the passage of a ship which is not innocent through its territorial sea.

Foreign ships which violate the laws and regulations of the People's Republic of China shall be dealt with according to law by relevant departments of the People's Republic of China.

Article 9

To ensure the safety of navigation and satisfy other requirements, the Government of the People's Republic of China may require foreign ships passing through its territorial sea to use the designated sea lane or prescribed traffic separation scheme. Concrete methods should be issued by the Government of the People's Republic of China or its relevant responsible departments.

Article 10

The relevant responsible organs of the People's Republic of China shall have the right to order an immediate eviction of foreign military ships or ships owned by foreign Governments and operated for non-commercial purposes that violate the laws or regulations of the People's Republic of China while passing through the territorial sea of the People's Republic of China. Losses or damage caused shall be borne by the nations whose flag is being flown by the ship in question.

Article 11

Any international, foreign organization, or individual who intends to conduct activities connected with scientific research or marine survey shall first seek the consent of the People's Republic of China or its relevant responsible departments and abide by the laws and regulations of the People's Republic of China.

Whoever is found illegally entering the territorial sea of the People's Republic of China to conduct activities connected with scientific research or marine survey in violation of the preceding provisions shall be dealt with by the relevant organs of the People's Republic of China according to law.

Article 12

Foreign aircraft may not enter the air above the territorial sea of the People's Republic of China unless they do so in accordance with agreements or accords which the Governments of their countries have signed with the Government of the People's Republic of China, or they have been approved or accepted by the Government of the People's Republic of China or organs it has authorized.

Article 13

The People's Republic of China has the authority to exercise powers within its contiguous zone for the purpose of preventing or punishing infringement of its security, customs, fiscal sanitary laws and regulations or entry-exit control within its land territories, internal waters or territorial sea.

Article 14

When competent authorities of the People's Republic of China have good reasons to believe that a foreign ship has violated the laws and regulations of the People's Republic of China, they may exercise the right of hot pursuit.

The hot pursuit commences when the foreign ship, or one of its small boats, or other craft working as a team and using the ship pursued as a mother ship is within the limits of the internal waters, territorial sea or contiguous zone of the People's Republic of China.

If the foreign ships are in the contiguous zone of the People's Republic of China, the hot pursuit may proceed only when the rights of the relevant laws and regulations set forth in article 13 above have been violated.

As long as the hot pursuit is not interrupted, it may continue outside the territorial sea of the People's Republic of China or the contiguous zone. The hot pursuit ceases as soon as the ship pursued enters the territorial sea of its own country or of a third country.

The right of hot pursuit in this article is exercised by warships or military aircraft of the People's Republic of China, or by ships or aircraft authorized by the Government of the People's Republic of China to that effect.

Article 15

The baseline of the territorial sea of the People's Republic of China shall be established by the Government of the People's Republic of China.

Article 16

The Government of the People's Republic of China shall draw up relevant regulations in accordance with this law.

Article 17

This law becomes effective upon promulgation.

Appendix C: The Law on the Exclusive Economic Zone and Continental Shelf of the People's Republic of China

(Adopted at the third session of the Standing Committee of the Ninth National People's Congress, 26 June 1998)

Article 1

This Act is adopted with a view to safeguarding the sovereign rights and jurisdiction exercised by the People's Republic of China over the exclusive economic zone and the continental shelf and to protect China's maritime rights and interests.

Article 2

The exclusive economic zone of the People's Republic of China is an area beyond and adjacent to the territorial sea of the People's Republic of China extending to a distance of 200 nautical miles from the baselines from which the breadth of the territorial sea is measured.

The continental shelf of the People's Republic of China comprises the seabed and subsoil of the submarine areas that extend beyond its territorial sea throughout the natural prolongation of its land territory to the outer edge of the continental margin, or to a distance of 200 nautical miles from the baselines from which the breadth of the territorial sea is measured where the outer edge of the continental margin does not extend up to that distance.

Conflicting claims regarding the exclusive economic zone and the continental shelf by the People's Republic of China and States with opposite or adjacent coasts shall be settled, on the basis of international law and in accordance with the principle of equity, by an agreement delimiting the areas so claimed.

Article 3

In the exclusive economic zone the People's Republic of China shall exercise sovereign rights for the purpose of exploring and exploiting, conserving and managing the natural resources of the waters superjacent to the seabed and of the seabed and its subsoil, and with regard to other activities for the economic exploitation and exploration of the zone, such as the production of energy from the water, current and winds.

The People's Republic of China shall have jurisdiction in the exclusive economic zone with regard to the establishment and use of artificial islands, installations and structures; marine scientific research; and the protection and preservation of the marine environment.

The natural resources of the exclusive economic zone referred to in this Act include living and non-living resources.

Article 4

The People's Republic of China shall exercise sovereign rights over the continental shelf for the purpose of exploring it and exploiting its natural resources.

The People's Republic of China shall have jurisdiction over the continental shelf with regard to the establishment and use of artificial islands, installations and structures; marine scientific research; and the protection and preservation of the marine environment.

The People's Republic of China shall have the exclusive right to authorize and regulate drilling on the continental shelf for all purposes.

The natural resources of the continental shelf referred to in this Act consist of the mineral and other non-living resources of the seabed and subsoil together with living organisms belonging to sedentary species, that is to say, organisms which, at the harvestable stage, either are immobile on or under the seabed or are unable to move except in constant physical contact with the seabed or the subsoil.

Article 5

Any international organization, foreign organization or individual entering the exclusive economic zone of the People's Republic of China to engage in fishery activities must have the approval of the competent authorities of the People's Republic of China and comply with the laws and regulations of the People's Republic of China and any treaties or agreements concluded by the relevant States and the People's Republic of China.

The competent authorities of the People's Republic of China shall have the right to take any necessary conservation and management measures to ensure that the living resources of the exclusive economic zone are not endangered by over-exploitation.

Article 6

The competent authorities of the People's Republic of China shall have the right to conserve and manage the straddling fish stocks, highly migratory fish stocks and marine mammals of the exclusive economic zone, anadromous stocks originating in the rivers of the People's Republic of China and catadromous species that spend the greater part of their life cycle in the waters of the People's Republic of China.

The People's Republic of China shall have the primary interest in anadromous stocks originating in China's rivers.

Article 7

Any international organization, foreign organization or individual engaging in the exploration or exploitation of the natural resources of the exclusive economic zone or continental shelf of the People's Republic of China or to carry out drilling in the continental shelf of the People's Republic of China must have the approval of the competent authorities of the People's Republic of China and comply with the laws and regulations of the People's Republic of China.

Article 8

The People's Republic of China shall have exclusive rights in the exclusive economic zone and the continental shelf to establish and to authorize and regulate the establishment, operation and use of artificial islands, installations and structures.

The People's Republic of China shall have exclusive jurisdiction over the artificial islands, installations and structures in the exclusive economic zone and the continental shelf, including jurisdiction with regard to customs, fiscal, health, security and immigration laws and regulations.

The competent authorities of the People's Republic of China shall have the right to establish safety zones around the artificial islands, installations and structures in the exclusive economic zone and continental shelf in which they may take appropriate measures to ensure the safety both of navigation and of the artificial islands, installations and structures.

Article 9

Any international organization, foreign organization or individual engaging in marine scientific research in the exclusive economic zone and continental shelf of the People's Republic of China must have the approval of the competent authorities of the People's Republic of China and shall comply with the laws and regulations of the People's Republic of China.

Article 10

The competent authorities of the People's Republic of China shall have the right to take the necessary measures to prevent, reduce and control pollution of the marine environment and to protect and preserve the marine environment of the exclusive economic zone and the continental shelf.

Article 11

Any State, provided that it observes international law and the laws and regulations of the People's Republic of China, shall enjoy in the exclusive economic zone and the continental shelf of the People's Republic of China freedom of navigation and overflight and of laying submarine cables and pipelines, and shall enjoy other legal and practical marine benefits associated with these freedoms. The laying of submarine cables and pipelines must be authorized by the competent authorities of the People's Republic of China.

Article 12

The People's Republic of China may, in the exercise of its sovereign rights to explore, exploit, conserve and manage the living resources of the exclusive economic zone, take such measures, including boarding, inspection, arrest, detention and judicial proceedings, as may be necessary to ensure compliance with its laws and regulations.

In the event of a violation of the laws and regulations of the People's Republic of China in the exclusive economic zone or the continental shelf, the People's Republic of China shall have the right to take the necessary investigative measures in accordance with the law and may exercise the right of hot pursuit.

Article 13

Rights enjoyed by the People's Republic of China in the exclusive economic zone and the continental shelf that are not stipulated in this Act shall be exercised in accordance with international law and the laws and regulations of the People's Republic of China.

Article 14

The provisions of this Act shall not affect the historical rights of the People's Republic of China.

Article 15

The Government of the People's Republic of China may, in accordance with this Act, enact relevant regulations.

Article 16

This Act shall enter into force on the date of promulgation.

Appendix D: Summary of the Position Paper of the Government of the People's Republic of China on the Matter of Jurisdiction in the South China Sea Arbitration Initiated by the Republic of the Philippines

Editor's note: December 7, 2014

On 7 December, the Ministry of Foreign Affairs is authorized to release the Position Paper of the Government of the People's Republic of China on the Matter of Jurisdiction in the South China Sea Arbitration Initiated by the Republic of the Philippines. The full text of the Position Paper is available on the website of the Ministry, i.e., www.fmprc.gov.cn. The following is a summary of the Position Paper:

I.

On 22 January 2013, the Department of Foreign Affairs of the Republic of the Philippines presented a note verbale to the Embassy of the People's Republic of China in the Philippines, stating that the Philippines initiated compulsory arbitration proceedings with respect to the dispute with China over "maritime jurisdiction" in the South China Sea. On 19 February 2013, the Chinese Government rejected and returned the Philippines' note verbale together with the attached Notification and Statement of Claim. The Chinese Government has subsequently reiterated that it will neither accept nor participate in the arbitration thus initiated by the Philippines.

This Position Paper is intended to demonstrate that the arbitral tribunal established at the request of the Philippines for the present arbitration ("Arbitral Tribunal") does not have jurisdiction over this case. No acceptance by China is signified in this Position Paper of the views or claims advanced by the Philippines. Nor shall this Position Paper be regarded as China's acceptance of or participation in this arbitration.

II.

The essence of the subject-matter of the arbitration is the territorial sovereignty over several maritime features in the South China Sea, which does not concern the interpretation or application of the United Nations Convention on the Law of the Sea ("Convention").

China has indisputable sovereignty over the South China Sea Islands (the Dongsha Islands, the Xisha Islands, the Zhongsha Islands and the Nansha Islands) and the adjacent waters. Since the 1970s, the Philippines has illegally occupied or laid claims to some maritime features of China in the South China Sea. In addition, the Philippines has also illegally explored and exploited the resources on those maritime features and in the adjacent maritime areas. The Philippines' activities mentioned above have violated the Charter of the United Nations and international law, and seriously encroached upon China's territorial sovereignty and maritime rights and interests. The Chinese Government has always been firmly opposed to these actions of the Philippines, and consistently made solemn representations and protests to the Philippines.

The Philippines has summarized its claims for arbitration in three categories: First, China's assertion of the "historic rights" in the South China Sea is inconsistent with the Convention; Second, China's claim to entitlements, based on certain rocks, low-tide elevations and submerged features in the South China Sea, of 200 nautical miles and more, is inconsistent with the Convention. Third, China has unlawfully interfered with the Philippines' enjoyment and exercise of its rights under the Convention.

With regard to the first category of claims, it is obvious that the core of those claims is that China's maritime claims in the South China Sea have exceeded the extent allowed under the Convention. However, it is a general principle of international law that sovereignty over land territory is the basis for the determination of maritime rights. Only after the extent of China's territorial sovereignty in the South China Sea is determined can a decision be made on the extent of China's maritime claims in the South China Sea. As to the second category of claims, China believes that the nature and maritime entitlements of certain maritime features in the South China Sea cannot be considered in isolation from the issue of sovereignty. Regarding the third category of claims, China maintains that, based on its sovereignty over relevant maritime features and the maritime rights derived therefrom, China's relevant activities in the South China Sea are both lawful and justified. The Philippines claims that China's actions have encroached upon areas under its jurisdiction. Before this claim can be decided upon, sovereignty over the relevant maritime features must be ascertained and maritime delimitation completed.

By requesting the Arbitral Tribunal to apply the Convention to determine the extent of China's maritime rights in the South China Sea, without first having ascertained sovereignty over the relevant maritime features, and by formulating a series of claims for arbitration to that effect, the Philippines contravenes the general principles of international law and international jurisprudence on the settlement of international maritime disputes. To decide upon any of the Philippines' claims, the Arbitral Tribunal would inevitably have to determine, directly or indirectly, the issue of territorial sovereignty over both the maritime features in question and other maritime features in the South China Sea. Besides, such a decision would unavoidably produce, in practical terms, the effect of a maritime delimitation. The issue of territorial sovereignty falls beyond the purview of the Convention. China maintains that the Arbitral Tribunal manifestly has no jurisdiction over the present case.

III.

There exists an agreement between China and the Philippines to settle their disputes in the South China Sea through negotiation, and the Philippines is debarred from unilaterally initiating compulsory arbitration.

With regard to disputes concerning territorial sovereignty and maritime rights, China has always maintained that they should be peacefully resolved through negotiation between the countries directly concerned. In the present case, there has been a long-standing agreement between China and the Philippines on resolving their disputes in the South China Sea through friendly consultation and negotiation.

A series of bilateral instruments between China and the Philippines make it clear that both sides agree or undertake to resolve their disputes in the South China Sea by friendly consultation and negotiation. And the Declaration on the Conduct of Parties in the South China Sea ("DOC"), signed by both China and the Philippines, explicitly states that territorial and jurisdictional disputes shall be resolved peacefully by sovereign States directly concerned through friendly consultations and negotiations.

The relevant provisions in those bilateral instruments and the DOC are mutually reinforcing and form an agreement between China and the Philippines. On that basis, they have undertaken a mutual obligation to settle their relevant disputes through negotiations and have excluded any other means of settlement. In these circumstances, according to the provisions of Article 280, 281 and others of the Convention, the relevant disputes between the two States shall be resolved through negotiations and there shall be no recourse to arbitration or other compulsory procedures.

At present, in order to maintain stability in the region and create conditions for peaceful resolution of the disputes in the South China Sea, China and the ASEAN member States have established working mechanisms to effectively implement the DOC, and have been engaged in consultations regarding the "Code of Conduct in the South China Sea". By initiating compulsory arbitration at this moment, the Philippines is running counter to the common wish and joint efforts of China and the ASEAN member States. Its underlying goal is not, as the Philippines has proclaimed, to seek peaceful settlement of the South China Sea issue, but rather, by resorting to arbitration, to put political pressure on China, so as to deny China's lawful rights in the South China Sea through the so-called "interpretation or application" of the Convention, and to pursue a resolution of the South China Sea issue on its own terms. This is certainly unacceptable to China.

IV.

Even assuming, *arguendo*, that the subject-matter of the arbitration were concerned with the interpretation or application of the Convention, the subject-matter would still be an integral part of maritime delimitation and, having been excluded by the 2006 Declaration filed by China from the compulsory dispute settlement procedures, could not be submitted for arbitration.

On 25 August 2006, China deposited, pursuant to Article 298 of the Convention, with the Secretary-General of the United Nations a declaration stating that the Government of the People's Republic of China does not accept any of the compulsory settlement procedures provided for in the Convention with respect to disputes concerning maritime delimitation, among others.

Maritime delimitation is an integral, systematic process. The international law applicable to maritime delimitation includes both the Convention and general international law. Maritime delimitation involves a consideration of not only entitlements, effect of maritime features, and principles and methods of delimitation, but also all relevant factors that must be taken into account, in order to attain an equitable solution.

The subject-matter of the arbitration initiated by the Philippines constitutes an integral part of maritime delimitation between China and the Philippines, and, as such, can only be considered under the overarching framework of maritime delimitation between China and the Philippines, and in conjunction with all the relevant rights and interests the parties concerned enjoy in accordance with the convention, general international law, and historical or long-standing practice in the region for overall consideration.

Ostensibly, the Philippines is not seeking from the Arbitral Tribunal a ruling regarding maritime delimitation, but instead a decision, *inter alia*, that certain maritime features are part of the Philippines' EEZ and continental shelf, and that China has unlawfully interfered with the enjoyment and exercise by the Philippines of sovereign rights in its EEZ and continental shelf. The Philippines' claims have in effect covered the main aspects and steps in maritime delimitation. Should the Arbitral Tribunal address substantively the Philippines' claims, it would amount to a *de facto* maritime delimitation.

The exclusionary declarations filed by the States Parties to the Convention under Article 298 of the Convention must be respected. By initiating the present compulsory arbitration as an attempt to circumvent China's 2006 declaration, the Philippines is abusing the dispute settlement procedures under the Convention.

V.

China's right to freely choose the means of dispute settlement must be fully respected, and its rejection of and non-participation in the present arbitration are solidly grounded in international law.

Under international law, every State is free to choose the means of dispute settlement. In exercise of its power to decide on its jurisdiction, any judicial or arbitral body should respect the right of the States Parties to the Convention to freely choose the means of settlement.

While being fully aware that its claims essentially deal with territorial sovereignty, that China has never accepted the compulsory procedures in respect of those disputes, and that there has been an agreement existing between the two States to settle their relevant disputes by negotiation, the Philippines has nevertheless initiated, by unilateral action, compulsory procedures of arbitration. This surely contravenes the relevant provisions of the Convention, and undermines the peaceful process for the settlement of the disputes.

In view of what is stated above and in light of the manifest lack of jurisdiction on the part of the Arbitral Tribunal, the Chinese Government has decided not to accept or participate in the present arbitration, in order to preserve China's sovereign right to choose the means of peaceful settlement of its own free will and the effectiveness of its 2006 declaration, and to maintain the authority and solemnity of the international legal regime for the oceans.

VI.

The issue of the South China Sea involves a number of States, and is compounded by complex historical background and sensitive political factors. Its final resolution demands patience and political wisdom from all parties concerned. China always maintains that the parties concerned shall seek proper ways and means of settlement through consultation and negotiation on the basis of respect for history and international law. Pending its final settlement, all parties concerned should engage in dialogue and cooperation to preserve peace and stability of the South China Sea, enhance mutual trust, clear up doubts, and create conditions for the eventual resolution of the issue.

The unilateral initiation of the present arbitration by the Philippines will not change the history and fact of China's sovereignty over the South China Sea Islands and the adjacent waters; nor will it shake China's resolve and determination to safeguard its sovereignty and relevant maritime rights and interests; nor will it affect China's policy and position of resolving the disputes in the South China Sea by direct negotiation and working together with other States in the region to maintain peace and stability in the South China Sea.

Appendix E: Statement of the Ministry of Foreign Affairs of the People's Republic of China on the Award on Jurisdiction and Admissibility of the South China Sea Arbitration by the Arbitral Tribunal Established at the Request of the Republic of the Philippines

October 30, 2015

The award rendered on 29 October 2015 by the Arbitral Tribunal established at the request of the Republic of the Philippines (hereinafter referred to as the "Arbitral Tribunal") on jurisdiction and admissibility of the South China Sea arbitration is null and void, and has no binding effect on China.

(I) China has indisputable sovereignty over the South China Sea Islands and the adjacent waters. China's sovereignty and relevant rights in the South China Sea, formed in the long historical course, are upheld by successive Chinese governments, reaffirmed by China's domestic laws on many occasions, and protected under international law including the *United Nations Convention on the Law of the Sea* (UNCLOS). With regard to the issues of territorial sovereignty and maritime rights and interests, China will not accept any solution imposed on it or any unilateral resort to a third-party dispute settlement.

(II) The Philippines' unilateral initiation and obstinate pushing forward of the South China Sea arbitration by abusing the compulsory procedures for dispute settlement under the UNCLOS is a political provocation under the cloak of law. It is in essence not an effort to settle disputes but an attempt to negate China's territorial sovereignty and maritime rights and interests in the South China Sea. In the *Position Paper of the Government of the People's Republic of China on the Matter of Jurisdiction in the South China Sea Arbitration Initiated by the Republic of the Philippines*, which was released by the Chinese Ministry of Foreign Affairs on 7 December 2014 upon authorization, the Chinese government pointed out that the Arbitral Tribunal manifestly has no jurisdiction over the arbitration initiated by the Philippines, and elaborated on the legal grounds for China's non-acceptance of and non-participation in the arbitration. This position is clear and explicit, and will not change.

(III) As a sovereign state and a State Party to the UNCLOS, China is entitled to choose the means and procedures of dispute settlement of its own will. China has all along been committed to resolving disputes with its neighbors over territory and maritime jurisdiction through negotiations and consultations. Since the 1990s, China and the Philippines have repeatedly reaffirmed in bilateral documents that they shall resolve relevant disputes through negotiations and consultations. The *Declaration on the Conduct of Parties in the South China Sea* (DOC) explicitly states that the sovereign states directly concerned undertake to resolve their territorial and jurisdictional disputes by peaceful means through friendly consultations and negotiations. All these documents demonstrate that China and the Philippines have chosen, a long time ago, to settle their disputes in the South China Sea through negotiations and consultations. The breach of this consensus by the Philippines damages the basis of mutual trust between states.

(IV) Disregarding that the essence of this arbitration case is territorial sovereignty and maritime delimitation and related matters, maliciously evading the declaration on optional exceptions made by China in 2006 under Article 298 of the UNCLOS, and negating the consensus between China and the Philippines on resolving relevant disputes through negotiations and consultations, the Philippines and the Arbitral Tribunal have abused relevant procedures and obstinately forced ahead with the arbitration, and as a result, have severely violated the legitimate rights that China enjoys as a State Party to the UNCLOS, completely deviated from the purposes and objectives of the UNCLOS, and eroded the integrity and authority of the UNCLOS. As a State Party to the UNCLOS, China firmly opposes the acts of abusing the compulsory procedures for dispute settlement under the UNCLOS, and calls upon all parties concerned to work together to safeguard the integrity and authority of the UNCLOS.

(V) The Philippines' attempt to negate China's territorial sovereignty and maritime rights and interests in the South China Sea through arbitral proceeding will lead to nothing. China urges the Philippines to honor its own commitments, respect China's rights under international law, change its course and return to the right track of resolving relevant disputes in the South China Sea through negotiations and consultations.

Appendix F: Statement of the Ministry of Foreign Affairs of the People's Republic of China on the Award of 12 July 2016 of the Arbitral Tribunal in the South China Sea Arbitration Established at the Request of the Republic of the Philippines

July 12, 2016

With regard to the award rendered on 12 July 2016 by the Arbitral Tribunal in the South China Sea arbitration established at the unilateral request of the Republic of the Philippines (hereinafter referred to as the "Arbitral Tribunal"), the Ministry of Foreign Affairs of the People's Republic of China solemnly declares that the award is null and void and has no binding force. China neither accepts nor recognizes it.

1 On 22 January 2013, the then government of the Republic of the Philippines unilaterally initiated arbitration on the relevant disputes in the South China Sea between China and the Philippines. On 19 February 2013, the Chinese government solemnly declared that it neither accepts nor participates in that arbitration and has since repeatedly reiterated that position. On 7 December 2014, the Chinese government released the *Position Paper of the Government of the People's Republic of China on the Matter of Jurisdiction in the South China Sea Arbitration Initiated by the Republic of the Philippines*, pointing out that the Philippines' initiation of arbitration breaches the agreement between the two states, violates the *United Nations Convention on the Law of the Sea* (UNCLOS), and goes against the general practice of international arbitration, and that the Arbitral Tribunal has no jurisdiction. On 29 October 2015, the Arbitral Tribunal rendered an award on jurisdiction and admissibility. The Chinese government immediately stated that the award is null and void and has no binding force. China's positions are clear and consistent.

2 The unilateral initiation of arbitration by the Philippines is out of bad faith. It aims not to resolve the relevant disputes between China and the Philippines, or to maintain peace and stability in the South China Sea, but to deny China's territorial sovereignty and maritime rights and interests in the South China Sea. The initiation of this arbitration violates international law. First, the subject-matter of the arbitration initiated by the Philippines is in essence an issue of territorial sovereignty over some

islands and reefs of Nansha Qundao (the Nansha Islands), and inevitably concerns and cannot be separated from maritime delimitation between China and the Philippines. Fully aware that territorial issues are not subject to UNCLOS, and that maritime delimitation disputes have been excluded from the UNCLOS compulsory dispute settlement procedures by China's 2006 declaration, the Philippines deliberately packaged the relevant disputes as mere issues concerning the interpretation or application of UNCLOS. Second, the Philippines' unilateral initiation of arbitration infringes upon China's right as a state party to UNCLOS to choose on its own will the procedures and means for dispute settlement. As early as in 2006, pursuant to Article 298 of UNCLOS, China excluded from the compulsory dispute settlement procedures of UNCLOS disputes concerning, among others, maritime delimitation, historic bays or titles, military and law enforcement activities. Third, the Philippines' unilateral initiation of arbitration violates the bilateral agreement reached between China and the Philippines, and repeatedly reaffirmed over the years, to resolve relevant disputes in the South China Sea through negotiations. Fourth, the Philippines' unilateral initiation of arbitration violates the commitment made by China and the ASEAN Member States, including the Philippines, in the 2002 *Declaration on the Conduct of Parties in the South China Sea* (DOC) to resolve the relevant disputes through negotiations by states directly concerned. By unilaterally initiating the arbitration, the Philippines violates UNCLOS and its provisions on the application of dispute settlement procedures, the principle of "*pacta sunt servanda*" and other rules and principles of international law.

3 The Arbitral Tribunal disregards the fact that the essence of the subject-matter of the arbitration initiated by the Philippines is issues of territorial sovereignty and maritime delimitation, erroneously interprets the common choice of means of dispute settlement already made jointly by China and the Philippines, erroneously construes the legal effect of the relevant commitment in the DOC, deliberately circumvents the optional exceptions declaration made by China under Article 298 of UNCLOS, selectively takes relevant islands and reefs out of the macro-geographical framework of Nanhai Zhudao (the South China Sea Islands), subjectively and speculatively interprets and applies UNCLOS, and obviously errs in ascertaining facts and applying the law. The conduct of the Arbitral Tribunal and its awards seriously contravene the general practice of international arbitration, completely deviate from the object and purpose of UNCLOS to promote peaceful settlement of disputes, substantially impair the integrity and authority of UNCLOS, gravely infringe upon China's legitimate rights as a sovereign state and state party to UNCLOS, and are unjust and unlawful.

4 China's territorial sovereignty and maritime rights and interests in the South China Sea shall under no circumstances be affected by those awards. China opposes and will never accept any claim or action based on those awards.

5 The Chinese government reiterates that, regarding territorial issues and maritime delimitation disputes, China does not accept any means of third party dispute settlement or any solution imposed on China. The Chinese government will continue to abide by international law and basic norms governing international relations as enshrined in the *Charter of the United Nations*, including the principles of respecting state sovereignty and territorial integrity and peaceful settlement of disputes, and continue to work with states directly concerned to resolve the relevant disputes in the South China Sea through negotiations and consultations on the basis of respecting historical facts and in accordance with international law, so as to maintain peace and stability in the South China Sea.

Appendix G: Statement of the Government of the People's Republic of China on China's Territorial Sovereignty and Maritime Rights and Interests in the South China Sea

July 12, 2016

To reaffirm China's territorial sovereignty and maritime rights and interests in the South China Sea, enhance cooperation in the South China Sea with other countries, and uphold peace and stability in the South China Sea, the Government of the People's Republic of China hereby states as follows:

(I) China's Nanhai Zhudao (the South China Sea Islands) consist of Dongsha Qundao (the Dongsha Islands), Xisha Qundao (the Xisha Islands), Zhongsha Qundao (the Zhongsha Islands) and Nansha Qundao (the Nansha Islands). The activities of the Chinese people in the South China Sea date back to over 2,000 years ago. China is the first to have discovered, named, and explored and exploited Nanhai Zhudao and relevant waters, and the first to have exercised sovereignty and jurisdiction over them continuously, peacefully and effectively, thus establishing territorial sovereignty and relevant rights and interests in the South China Sea.

(II) Following the end of the Second World War, China recovered and resumed the exercise of sovereignty over Nanhai Zhudao which had been illegally occupied by Japan during its war of aggression against China. To strengthen the administration over Nanhai Zhudao, the Chinese government in 1947 reviewed and updated the geographical names of Nanhai Zhudao, compiled *Nan Hai Zhu Dao Di Li Zhi Lüe* (A Brief Account of the Geography of the South China Sea Islands), and drew *Nan Hai Zhu Dao Wei Zhi Tu* (Location Map of the South China Sea Islands) on which the dotted line is marked. This map was officially published and made known to the world by the Chinese government in February 1948.

(III) Since its founding on 1 October 1949, the People's Republic of China has been firm in upholding China's territorial sovereignty and maritime rights and interests in the South China Sea. A series of legal instruments, such as the 1958 *Declaration of the Government of the People's Republic of China on China's Territorial Sea*, the 1992 *Law of the*

People's Republic of China on the Territorial Sea and the Contiguous Zone, the 1998 *Law of the People's Republic of China on the Exclusive Economic Zone and the Continental Shelf* and the 1996 *Decision of the Standing Committee of the National People's Congress of the People's Republic of China on the Ratification of the United Nations Convention on the Law of the Sea*, have further reaffirmed China's territorial sovereignty and maritime rights and interests in the South China Sea.

(IV) Based on the practice of the Chinese people and the Chinese government in the long course of history and the position consistently upheld by successive Chinese governments, and in accordance with national law and international law, including the *United Nations Convention on the Law of the Sea*, China has territorial sovereignty and maritime rights and interests in the South China Sea, including, inter alia:

- i China has sovereignty over Nanhai Zhudao, consisting of Dongsha Qundao, Xisha Qundao, Zhongsha Qundao and Nansha Qundao;
- ii China has internal waters, territorial sea and contiguous zone, based on Nanhai Zhudao;
- iii China has exclusive economic zone and continental shelf, based on Nanhai Zhudao;
- iv China has historic rights in the South China Sea.

(V) The above positions are consistent with relevant international law and practice.

(VI) China is always firmly opposed to the invasion and illegal occupation by certain states of some islands and reefs of China's Nansha Qundao, and activities infringing upon China's rights and interests in relevant maritime areas under China's jurisdiction. China stands ready to continue to resolve the relevant disputes peacefully through negotiation and consultation with the states directly concerned on the basis of respecting historical facts and in accordance with international law. Pending final settlement, China is also ready to make every effort with the states directly concerned to enter into provisional arrangements of a practical nature, including joint development in relevant maritime areas, in order to achieve win-win results and jointly maintain peace and stability in the South China Sea.

(VII) China respects and upholds the freedom of navigation and overflight enjoyed by all states under international law in the South China Sea, and stays ready to work with other coastal states and the international community to ensure the safety of and the unimpeded access to the international shipping lanes in the South China Sea.

Index

For Product Safety Concerns and Information please contact our EU representative GPSR@taylorandfrancis.com
Taylor & Francis Verlag GmbH, Kaufingerstraße 24, 80331 München, Germany

www.ingramcontent.com/pod-product-compliance
Ingram Content Group UK Ltd.
Pitfield, Milton Keynes, MK11 3LW, UK
UKHW020146200926
475702UK00021B/1836
* 9 7 8 0 3 6 7 8 8 8 9 8 5 *